Grand Blue Dreaming 10

PRESENTED BY KENJI INOUE & KIMITAKE YOSHIOKA

THE STORY SO FAR

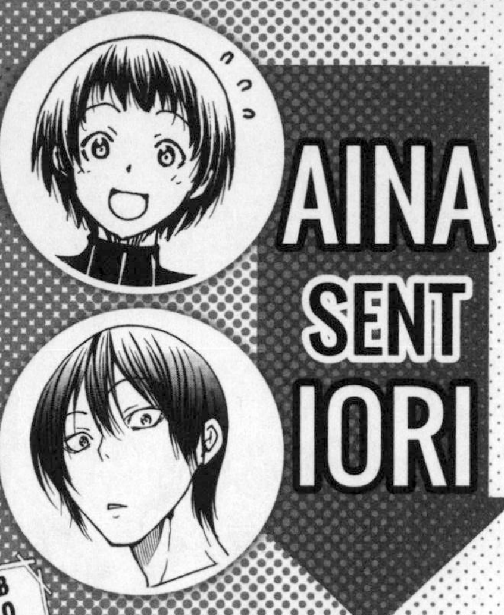

AINA SENT IORI

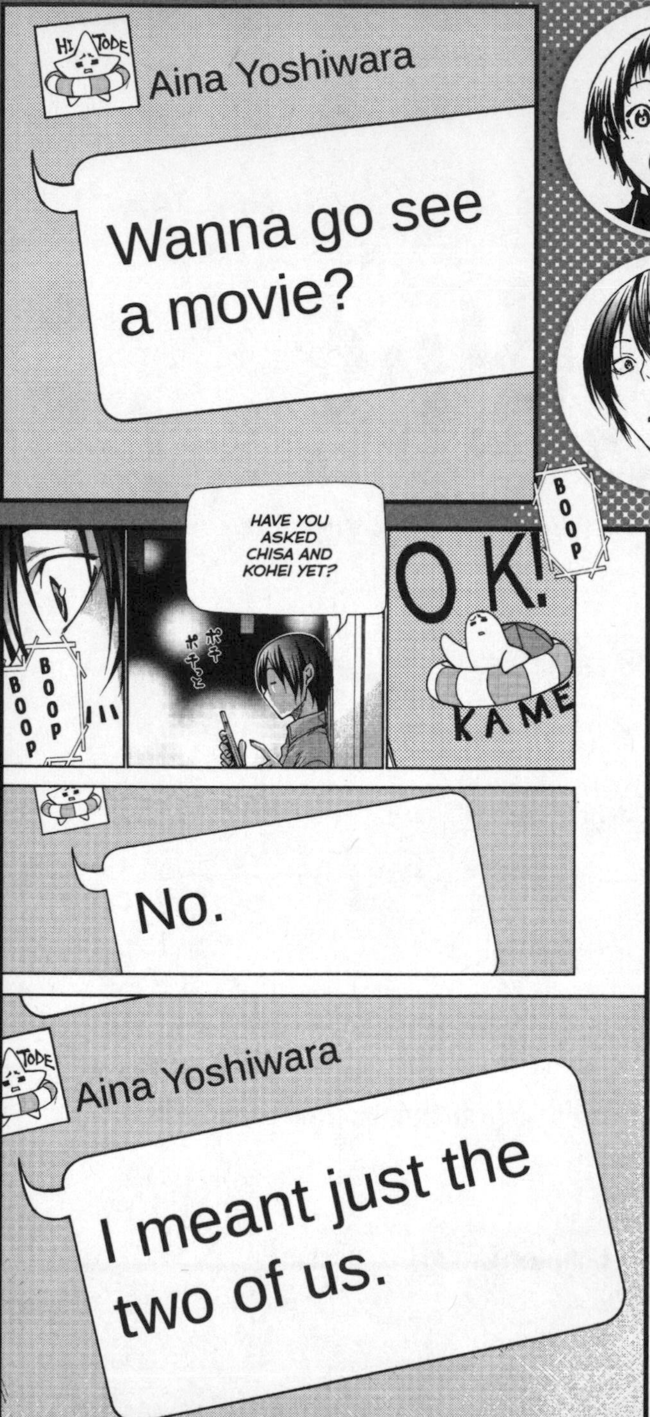
HI TODE
Aina Yoshiwara
Wanna go see a movie?
BOOP
OK!
KAME
HAVE YOU ASKED CHISA AND KOHEI YET?
BOOP BOOP BOOP
No.
TODE
Aina Yoshiwara
I meant just the two of us.

A DECISIVE INVITATION THAT SHE CAN'T TAKE BACK!!

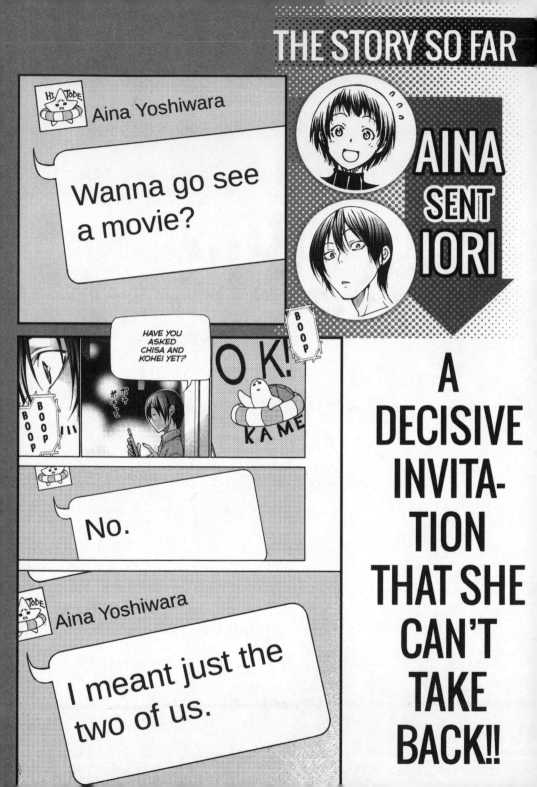

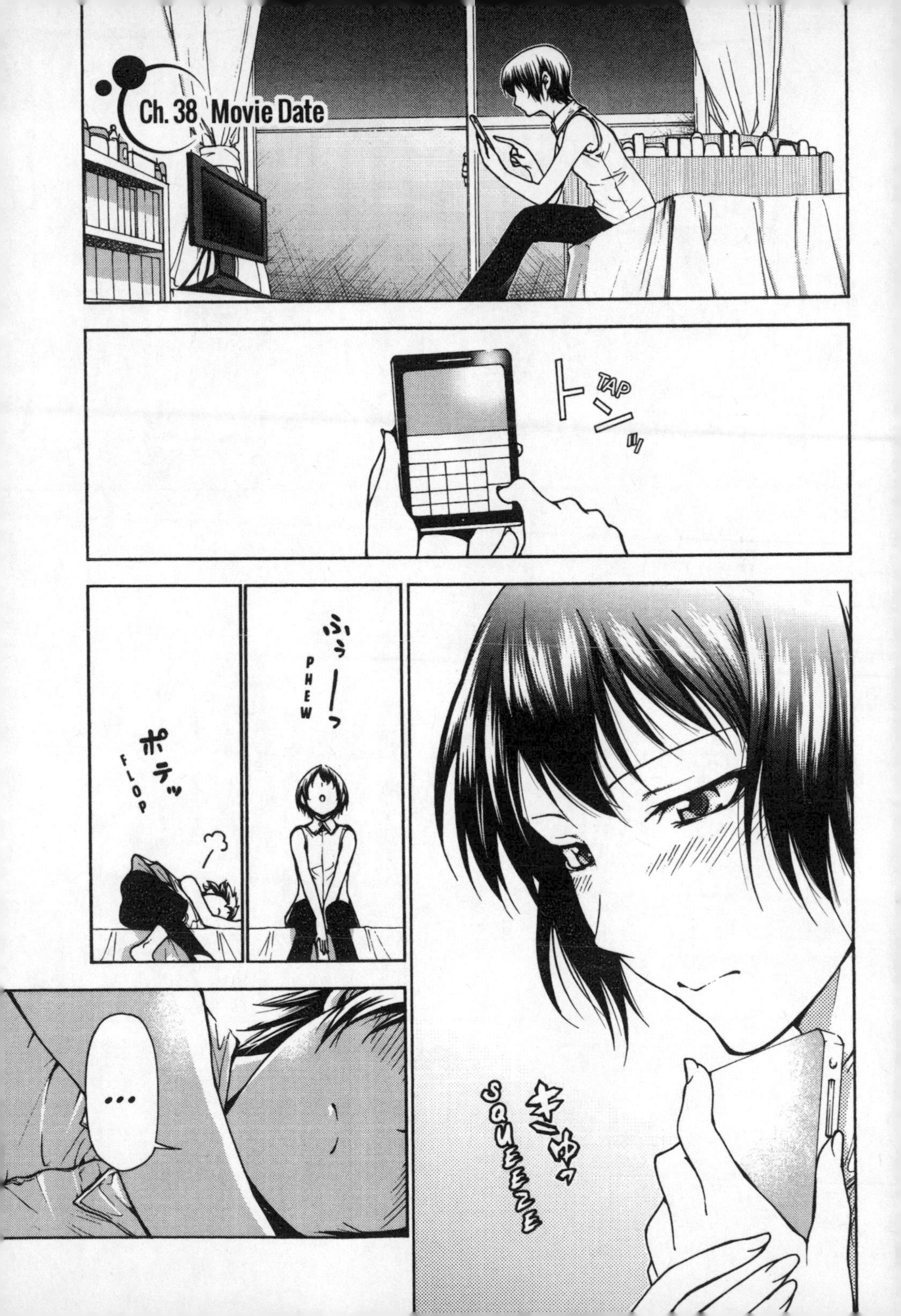
Ch. 38 Movie Date
トンッ
TAP
SQUEEZE
ふぅーっ
PHEW
ポテッ
FLOP
...

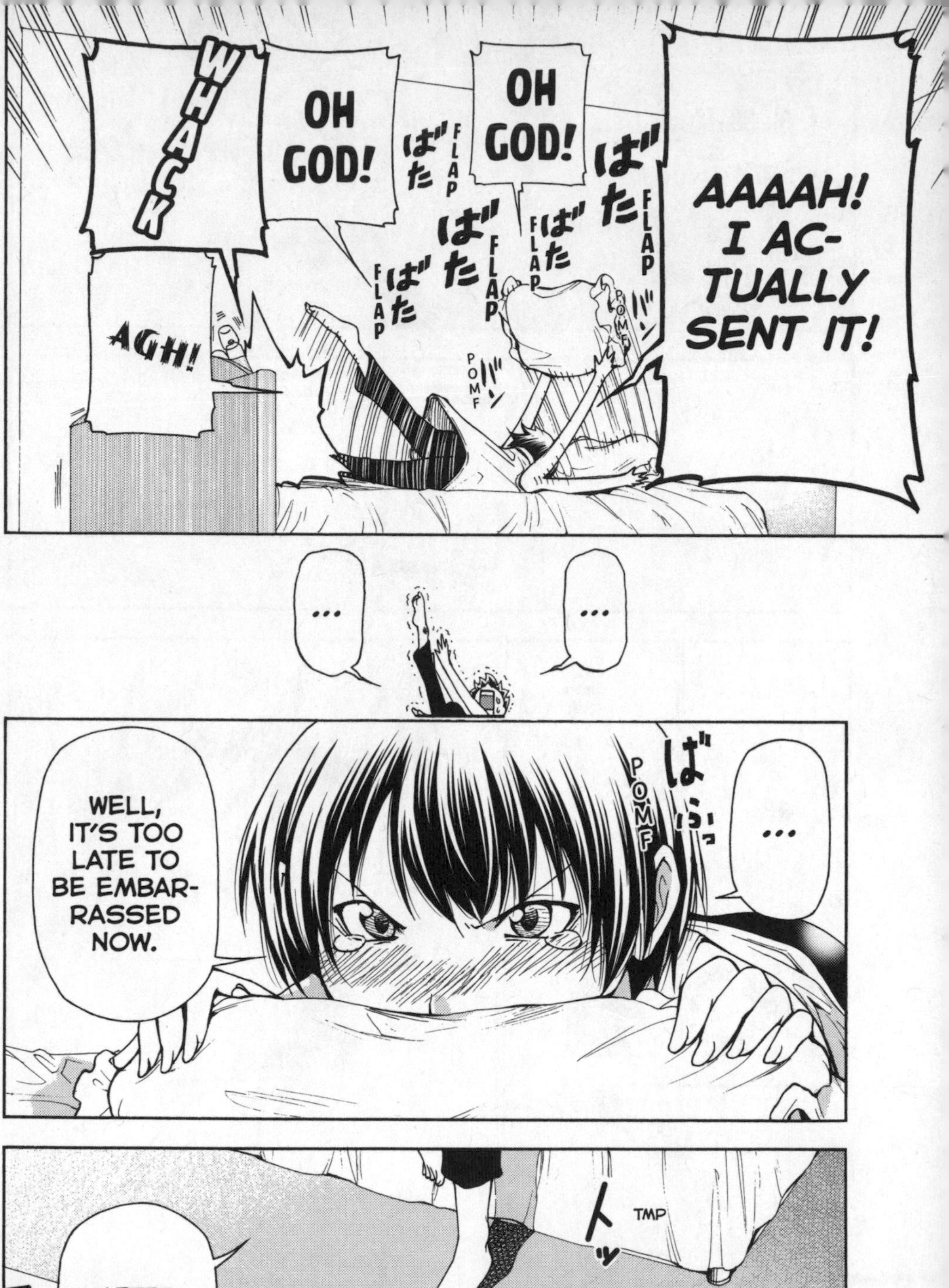
AAAAH! I AC-TUALLY SENT IT!
バン POMF
ばた FLAP
ばた FLAP
OH GOD!
ばた FLAP
ばた FLAP
バン POMF
OH GOD!
WHACK
AGH!
...
...
...
ばふっ POMF
WELL, IT'S TOO LATE TO BE EMBAR-RASSED NOW.
トッ TMP
AFTER ALL...

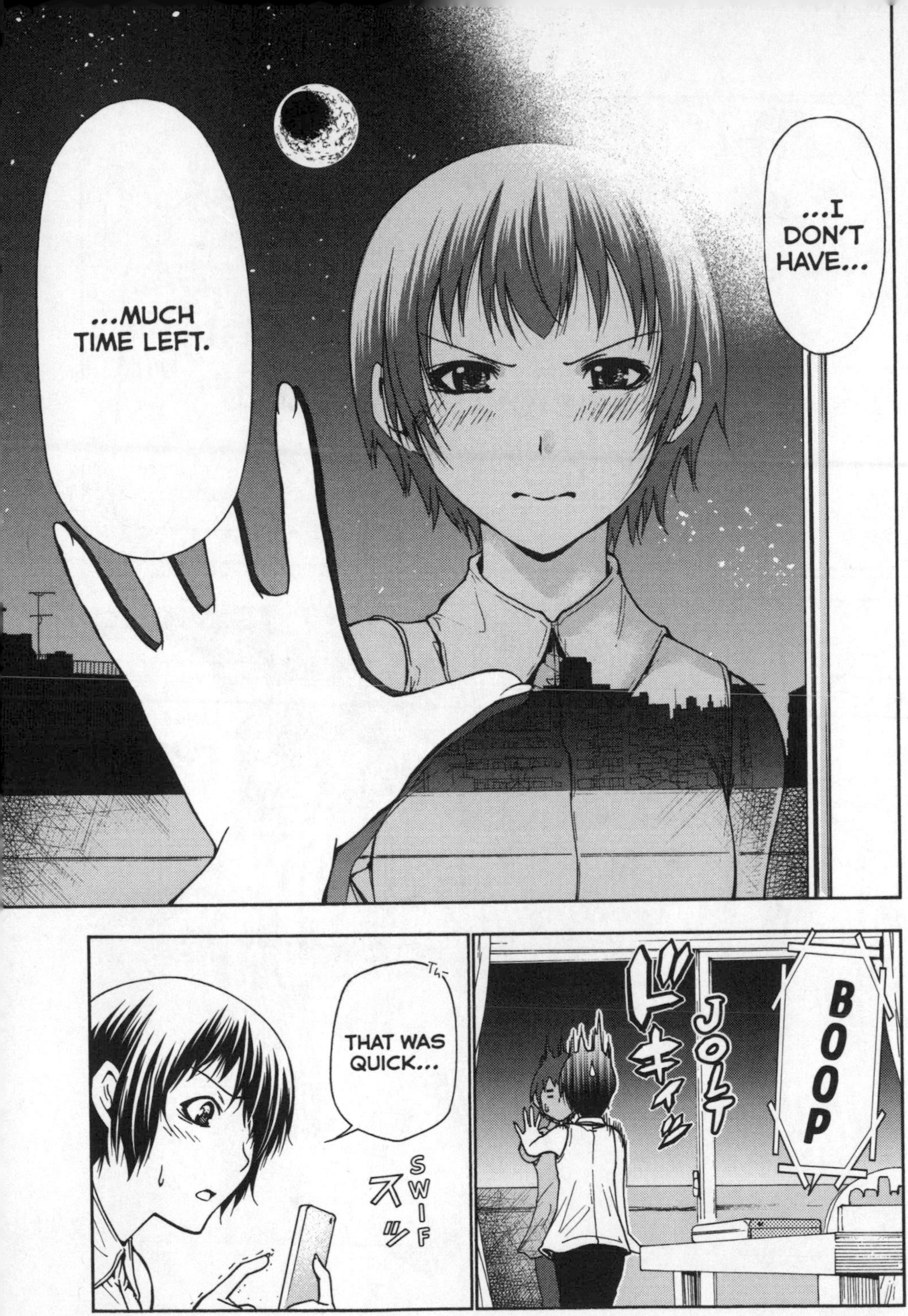
...I DON'T HAVE...
...MUCH TIME LEFT.
BOOP
JOLT
ドキィッ
THAT WAS QUICK...
SWIF
スッ

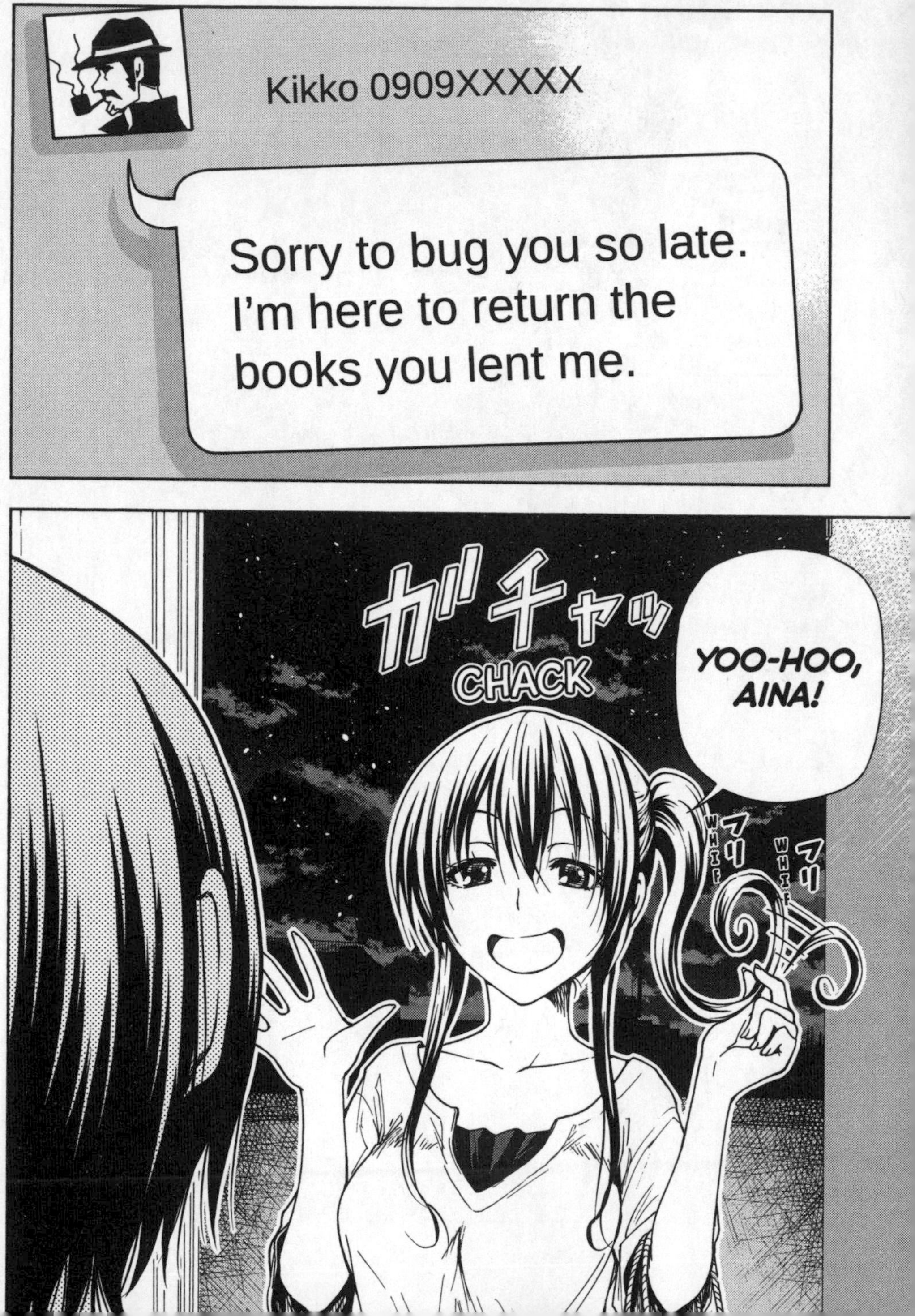
Kikko 0909XXXXX
Sorry to bug you so late. I'm here to return the books you lent me.
YOO-HOO, AINA!
ガチャッ
CHACK
フリ
WHIF
フリ
WHIF

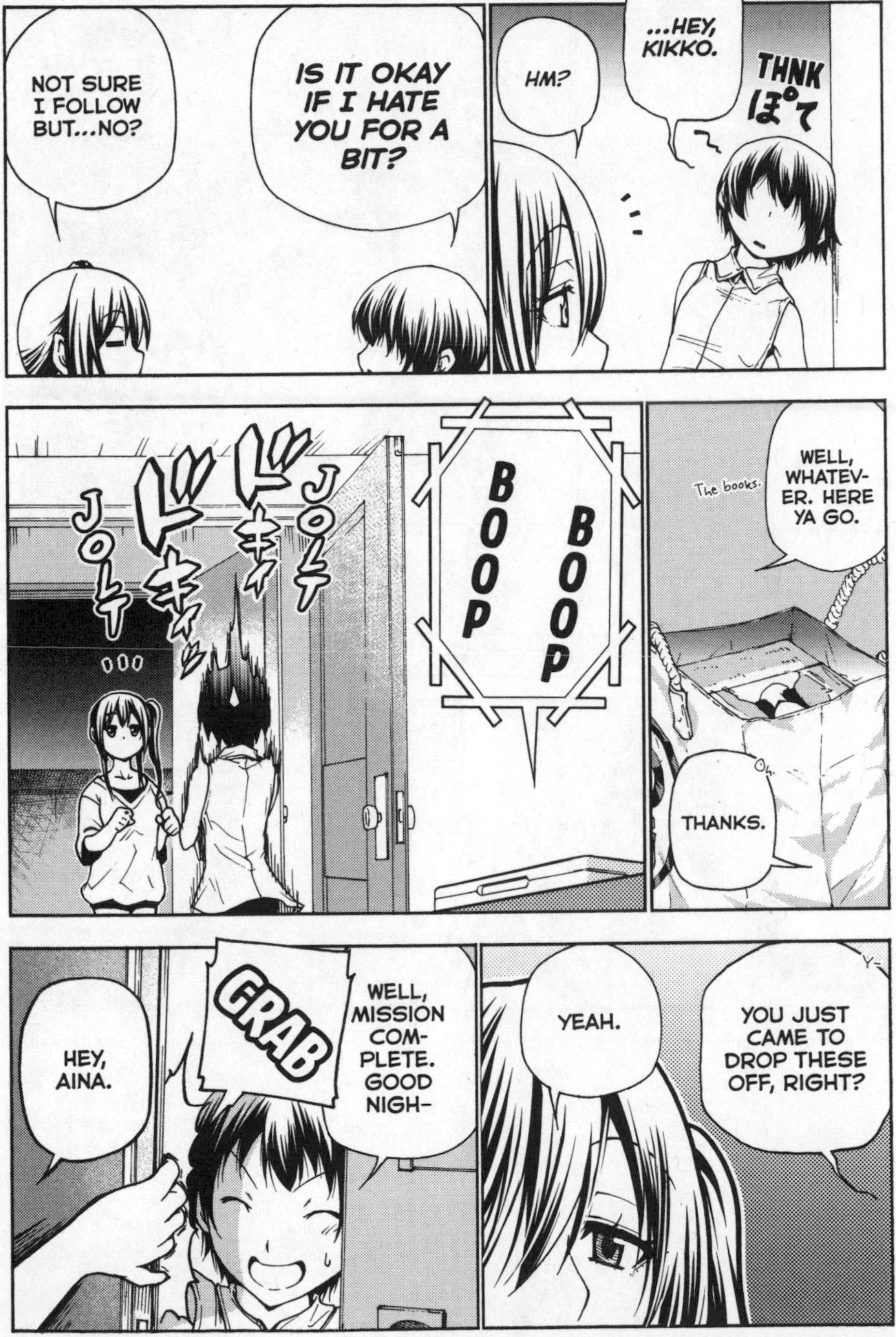
...HEY, KIKKO.
THNK
ぽて
HM?
IS IT OKAY IF I HATE YOU FOR A BIT?
NOT SURE I FOLLOW BUT...NO?
The books.
WELL, WHATEVER. HERE YA GO.
Oh.
THANKS.
BOOP BOOP
JOLT
ドキィ
JOLT
ドキィ
YOU JUST CAME TO DROP THESE OFF, RIGHT?
Y-
YEAH.
WELL, MISSION COMPLETE. GOOD NIGH-
GRAB
HEY, AINA.

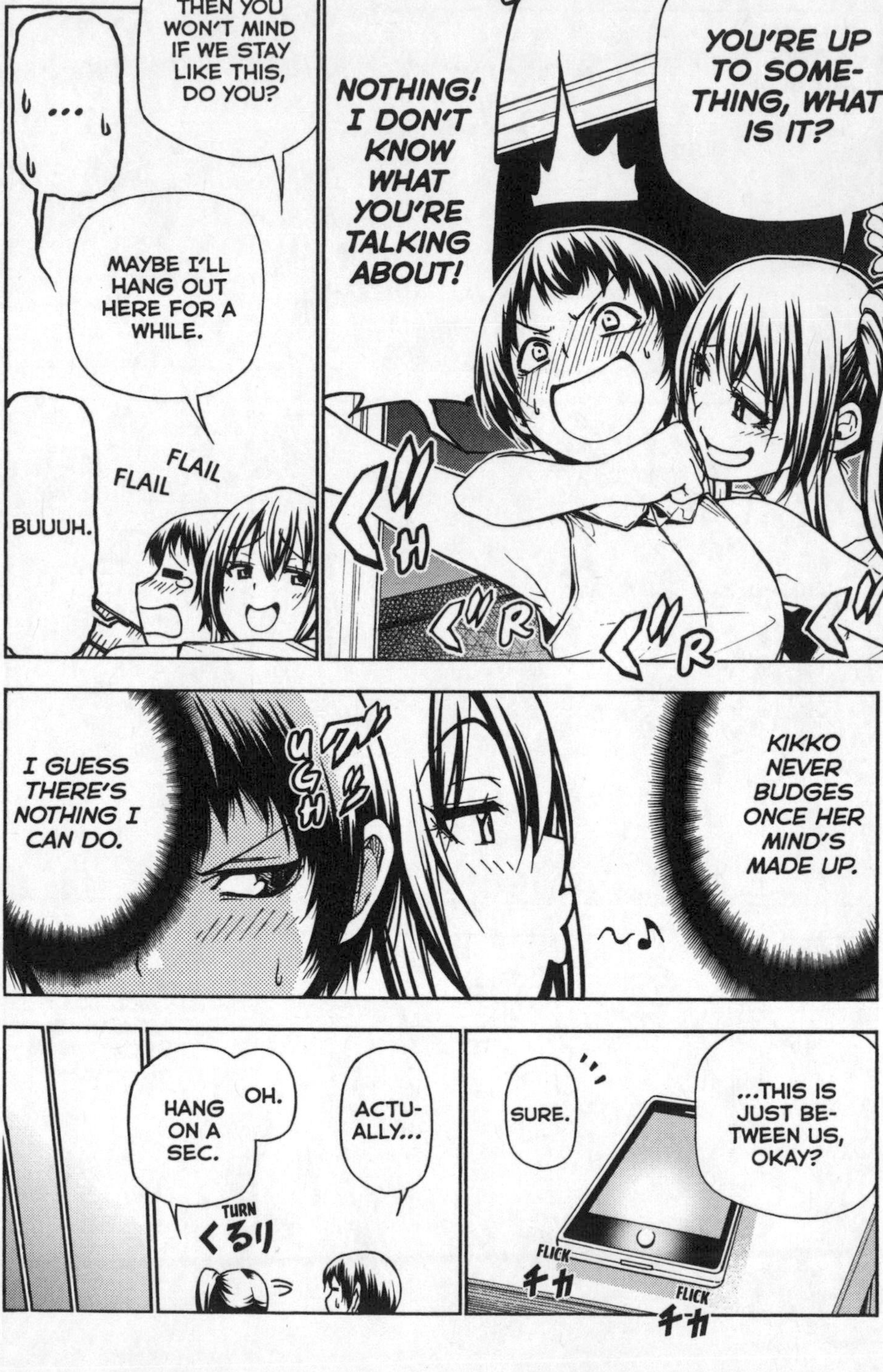
YOU'RE UP TO SOME-THING, WHAT IS IT?
NOTHING! I DON'T KNOW WHAT YOU'RE TALKING ABOUT!
THEN YOU WON'T MIND IF WE STAY LIKE THIS, DO YOU?
...
MAYBE I'LL HANG OUT HERE FOR A WHILE.
FLAIL
FLAIL
BUUUH.
KIKKO NEVER BUDGES ONCE HER MIND'S MADE UP.
UGH
I GUESS THERE'S NOTHING I CAN DO.
...THIS IS JUST BE-TWEEN US, OKAY?
SURE.
FLICK
FLICK
ACTU-ALLY...
OH.
HANG ON A SEC.
TURN

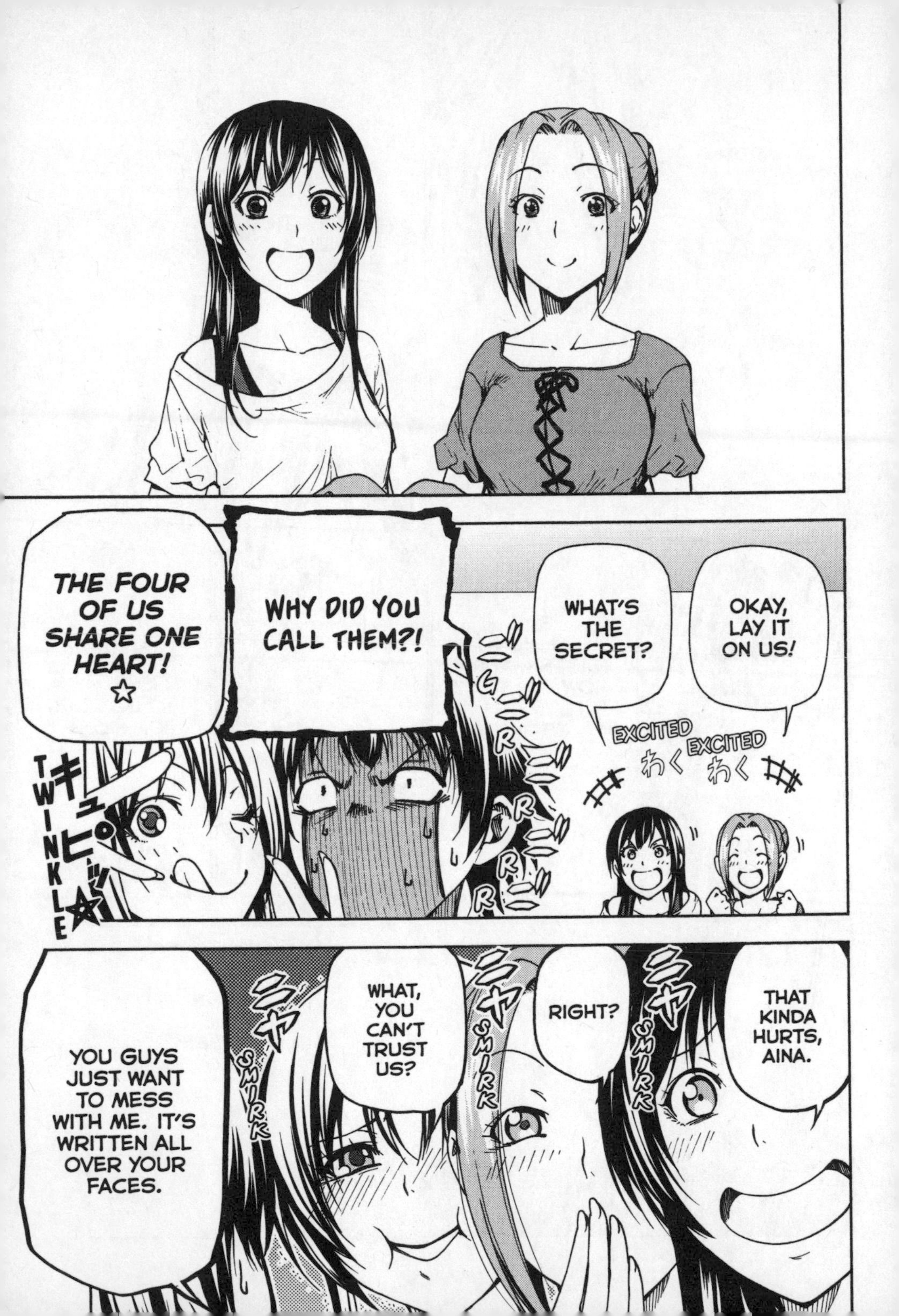
OKAY, LAY IT ON US!
WHAT'S THE SECRET?
EXCITED わく EXCITED わく
WHY DID YOU CALL THEM?!
GRRRRR
THE FOUR OF US SHARE ONE HEART! ☆
TWINKLE☆
THAT KINDA HURTS, AINA.
ニヤ SMIRK
RIGHT?
ニヤ SMIRK
WHAT, YOU CAN'T TRUST US?
ニヤ SMIRK
YOU GUYS JUST WANT TO MESS WITH ME. IT'S WRITTEN ALL OVER YOUR FACES.

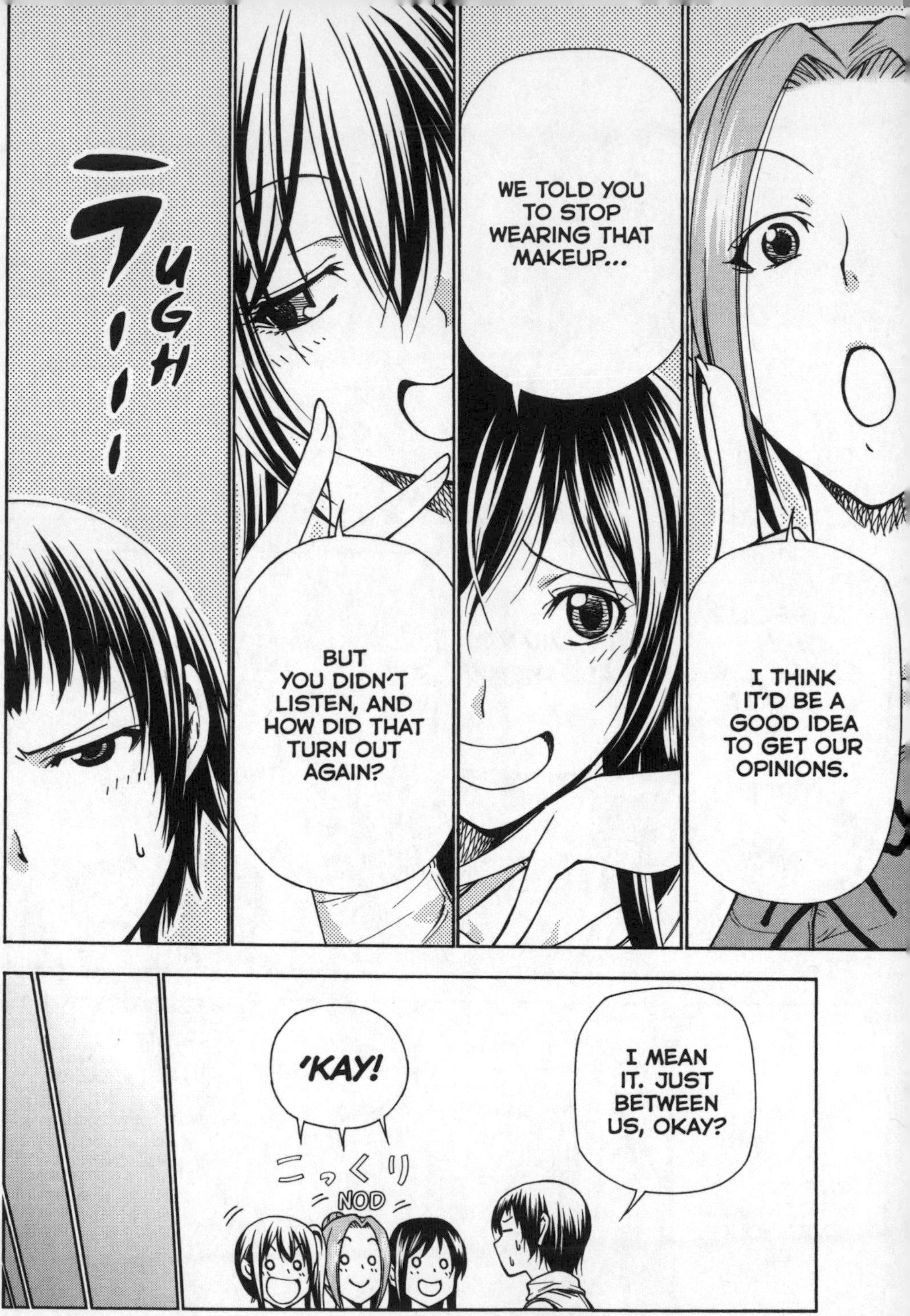
I THINK IT'D BE A GOOD IDEA TO GET OUR OPINIONS.
WE TOLD YOU TO STOP WEARING THAT MAKEUP...
BUT YOU DIDN'T LISTEN, AND HOW DID THAT TURN OUT AGAIN?
UGH
I MEAN IT. JUST BETWEEN US, OKAY?
'KAY!
こっくり
NOD

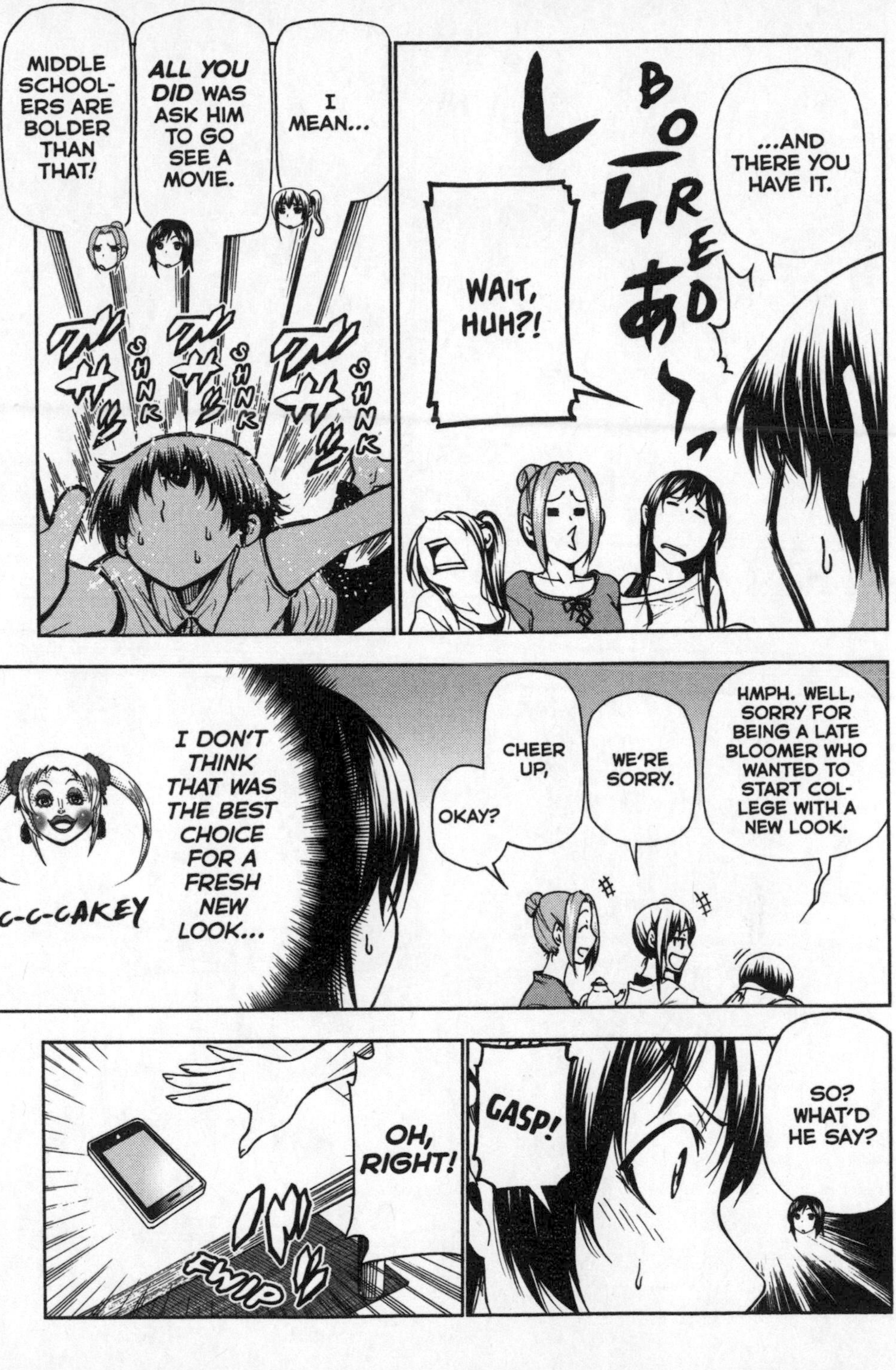
...AND THERE YOU HAVE IT.
BORED
WAIT, HUH?!
I MEAN...
ALL YOU DID WAS ASK HIM TO GO SEE A MOVIE.
MIDDLE SCHOOLERS ARE BOLDER THAN THAT!
SHNK
SHNK
SHNK
HMPH. WELL, SORRY FOR BEING A LATE BLOOMER WHO WANTED TO START COLLEGE WITH A NEW LOOK.
WE'RE SORRY.
CHEER UP, OKAY?
I DON'T THINK THAT WAS THE BEST CHOICE FOR A FRESH NEW LOOK...
C-C-CAKEY
SO? WHAT'D HE SAY?
GASP!
OH, RIGHT!
FWIP

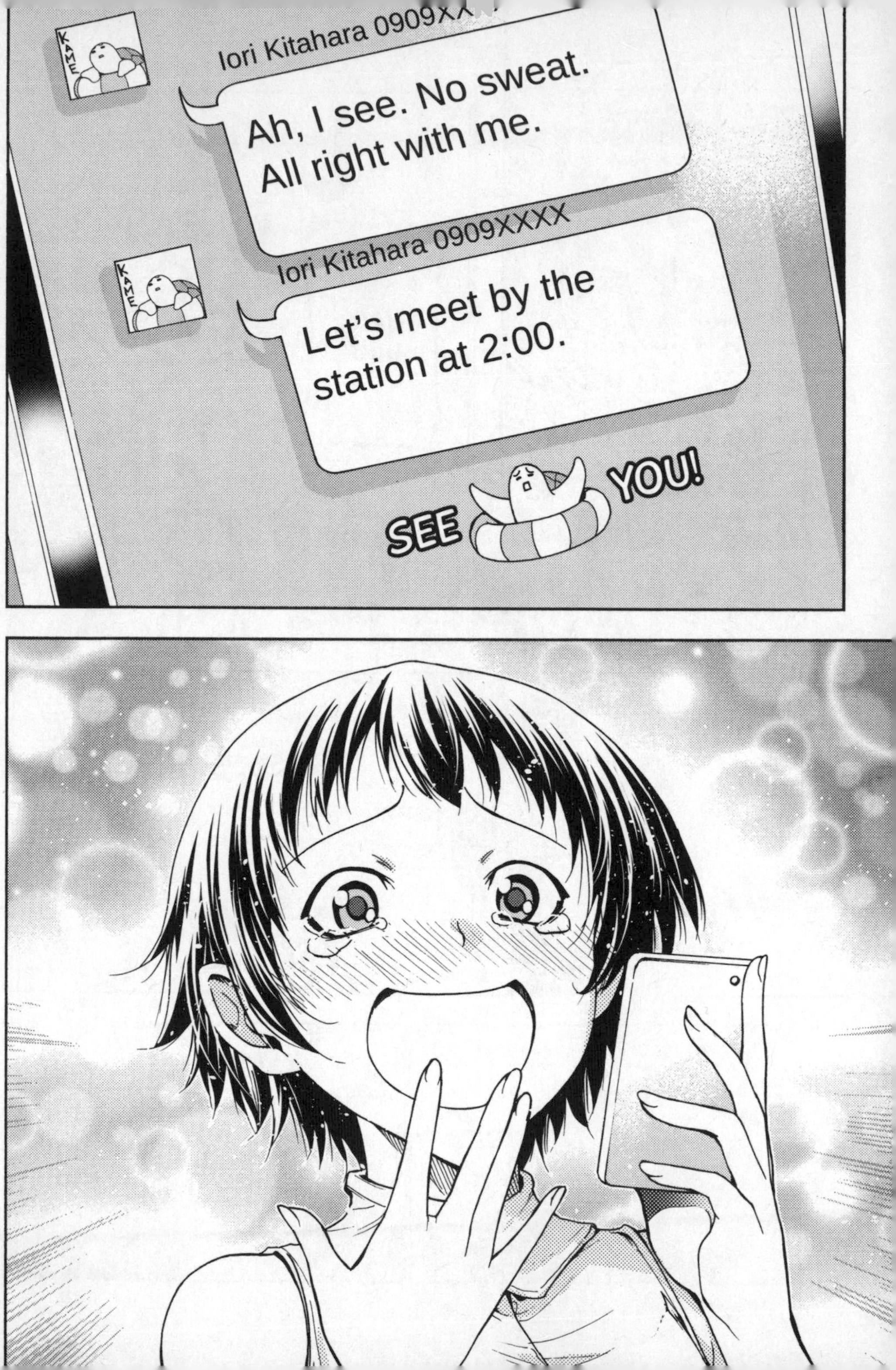
Iori Kitahara 0909XX
Ah, I see. No sweat. All right with me.
Iori Kitahara 0909XXXX
Let's meet by the station at 2:00.
SEE YOU!

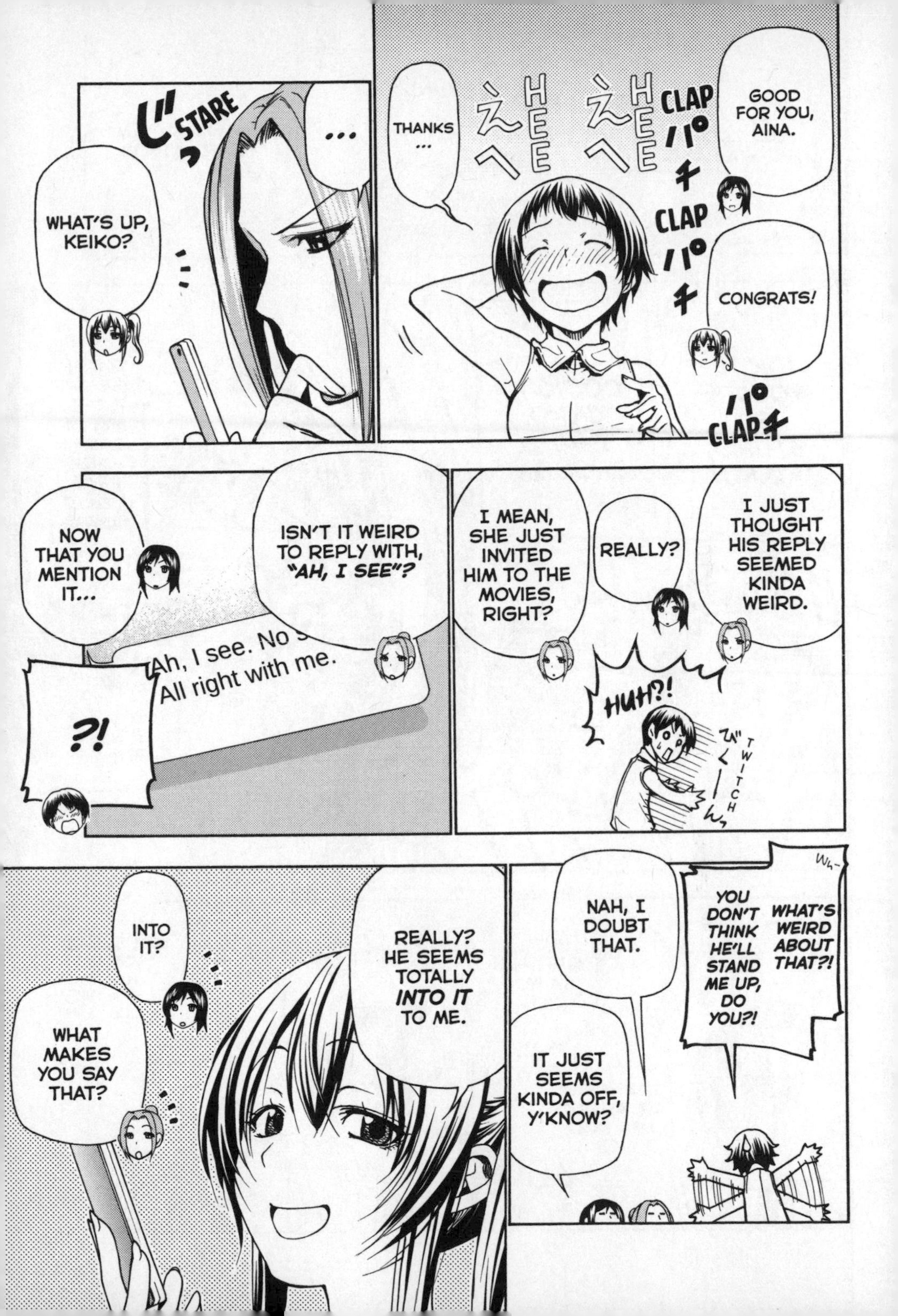
GOOD FOR YOU, AINA.
CLAP パチ
CLAP パチ
HEHE えへへ
HEHE えへへ
THANKS...
CONGRATS!
CLAP パチ
...
じっ STARE
WHAT'S UP, KEIKO?
I JUST THOUGHT HIS REPLY SEEMED KINDA WEIRD.
REALLY?
I MEAN, SHE JUST INVITED HIM TO THE MOVIES, RIGHT?
HUH?!
びくーん TWITCH
ISN'T IT WEIRD TO REPLY WITH, "AH, I SEE"?
NOW THAT YOU MENTION IT...
Ah, I see. No
All right with me.
?!
Wh-
WHAT'S WEIRD ABOUT THAT?!
YOU DON'T THINK HE'LL STAND ME UP, DO YOU?!
NAH, I DOUBT THAT.
IT JUST SEEMS KINDA OFF, Y'KNOW?
REALLY? HE SEEMS TOTALLY INTO IT TO ME.
INTO IT?
WHAT MAKES YOU SAY THAT?

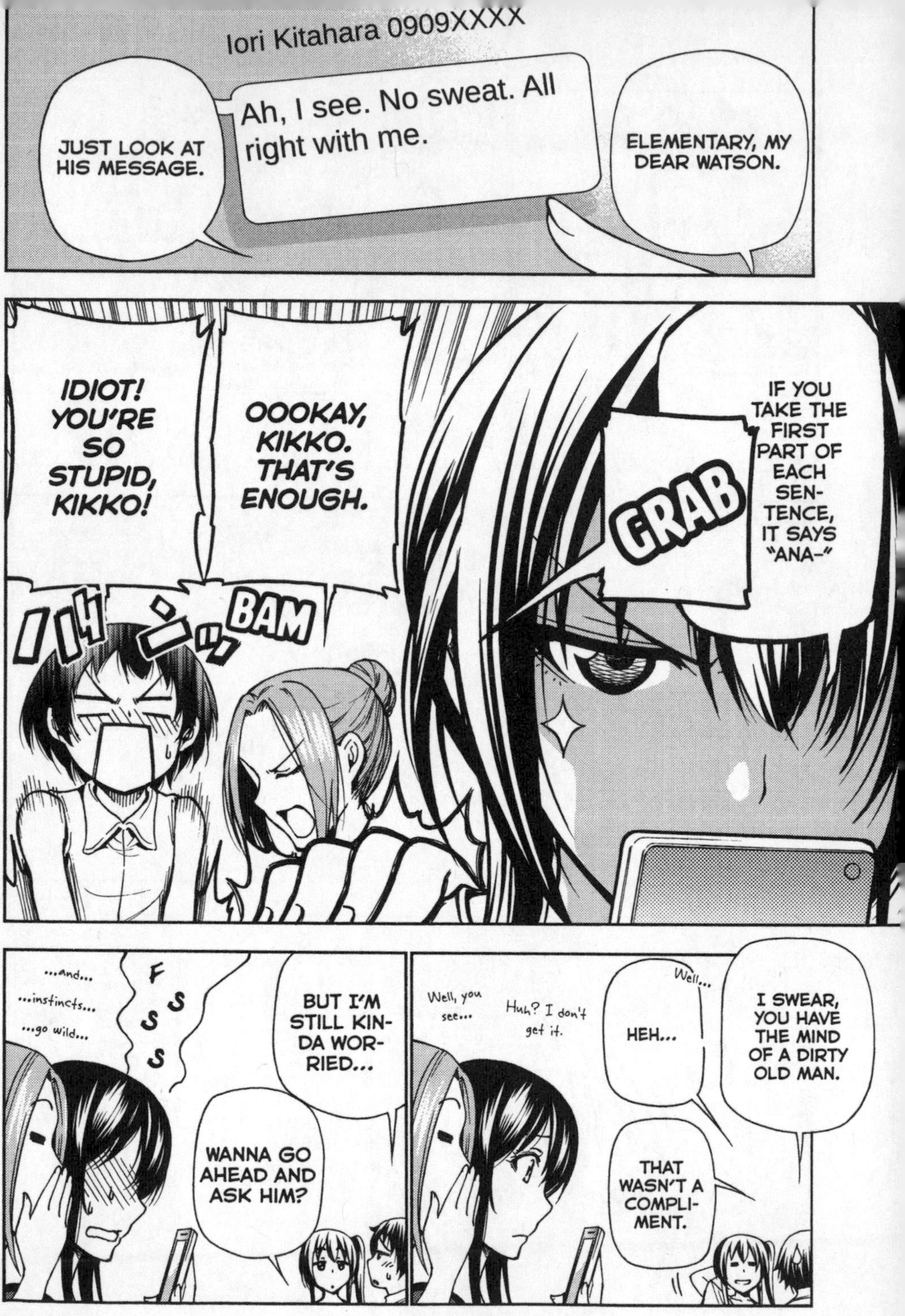
ELEMENTARY, MY DEAR WATSON.
Iori Kitahara 0909XXXX
Ah, I see. No sweat. All right with me.
JUST LOOK AT HIS MESSAGE.
IF YOU TAKE THE FIRST PART OF EACH SEN-TENCE, IT SAYS "ANA-"
GRAB
OOOKAY, KIKKO. THAT'S ENOUGH.
IDIOT! YOU'RE SO STUPID, KIKKO!
BAM
I SWEAR, YOU HAVE THE MIND OF A DIRTY OLD MAN.
Well...
HEH...
THAT WASN'T A COMPLI-MENT.
Huh? I don't get it.
Well, you see...
BUT I'M STILL KIN-DA WOR-RIED...
WANNA GO AHEAD AND ASK HIM?
FSSS
...and...
...instincts...
...go wild...

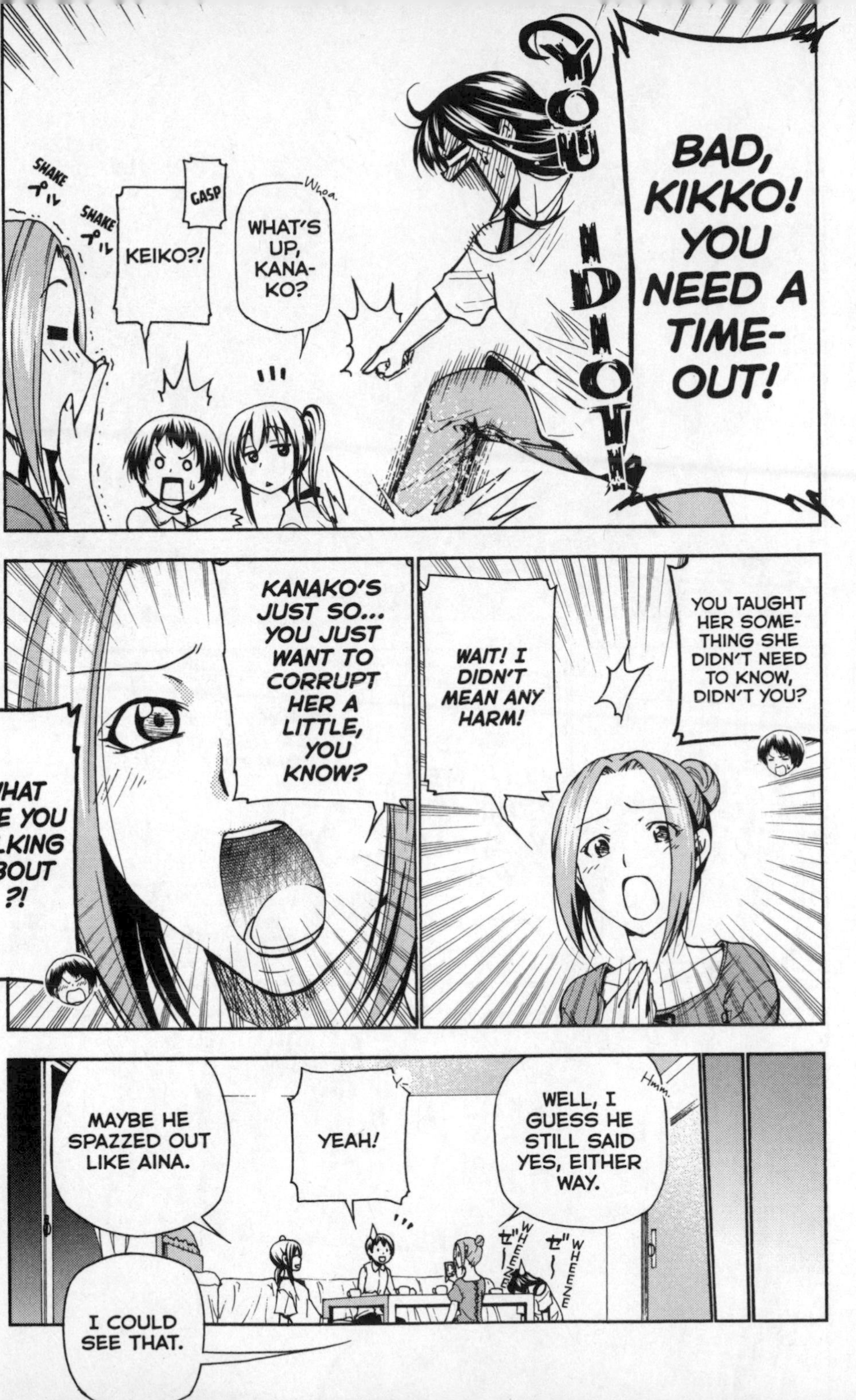
BAD, KIKKO! YOU NEED A TIME-OUT!
IDIOT!
Whoa.
WHAT'S UP, KANA-KO?
GASP
KEIKO?!
SHAKE
SHAKE
YOU TAUGHT HER SOME-THING SHE DIDN'T NEED TO KNOW, DIDN'T YOU?
WAIT! I DIDN'T MEAN ANY HARM!
KANAKO'S JUST SO... YOU JUST WANT TO CORRUPT HER A LITTLE, YOU KNOW?
WHAT ARE YOU TALKING ABOUT?!
Hmm.
WELL, I GUESS HE STILL SAID YES, EITHER WAY.
Y-
YEAH!
MAYBE HE SPAZZED OUT LIKE AINA.
WHEEZE
WHEEZE
I COULD SEE THAT.

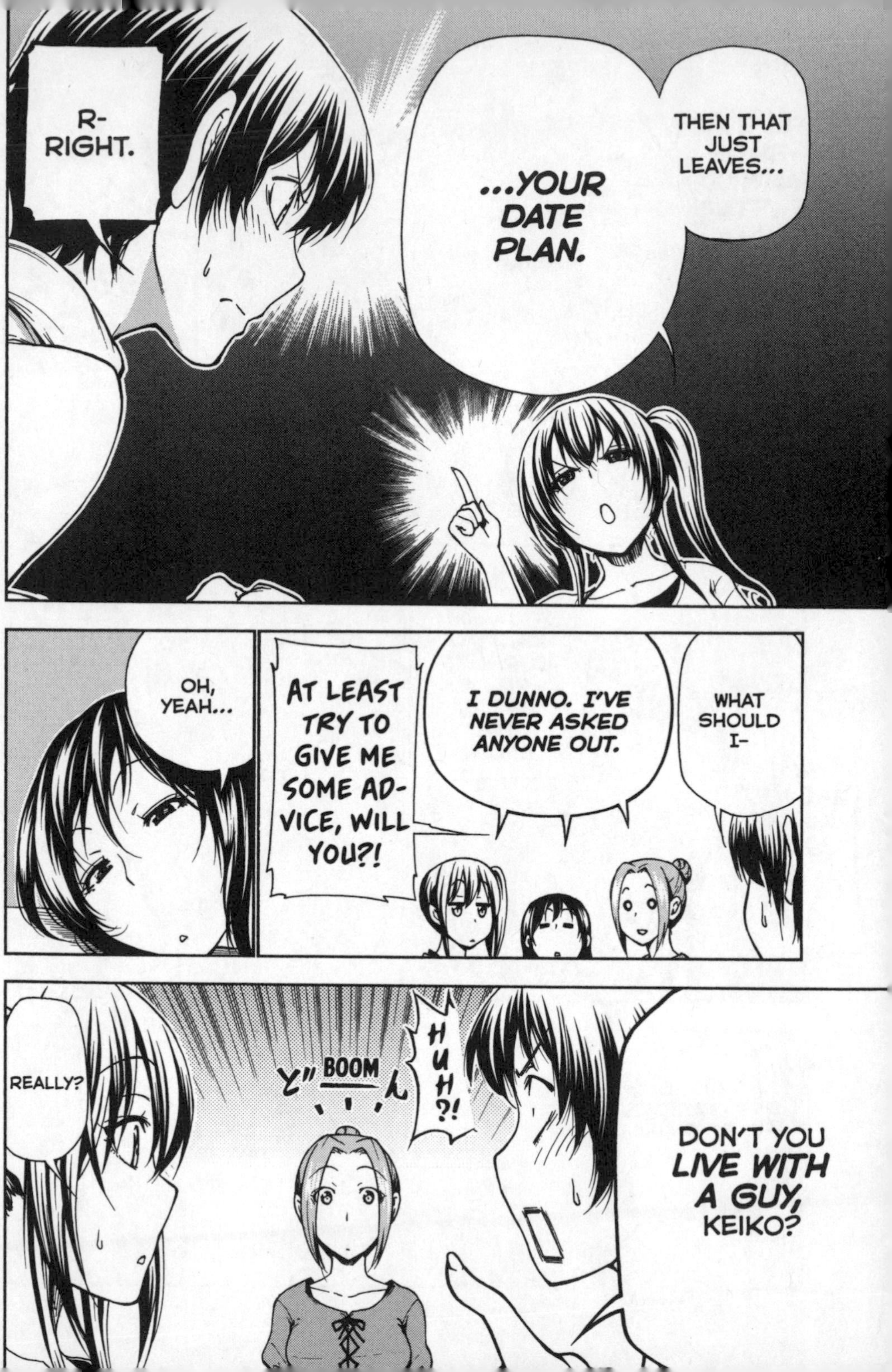
THEN THAT JUST LEAVES...
...YOUR DATE PLAN.
R- RIGHT.
WHAT SHOULD I-
I DUNNO. I'VE NEVER ASKED ANYONE OUT.
AT LEAST TRY TO GIVE ME SOME AD-VICE, WILL YOU?!
OH, YEAH...
DON'T YOU LIVE WITH A GUY, KEIKO?
HUH?!
ど" BOOM ん
REALLY?

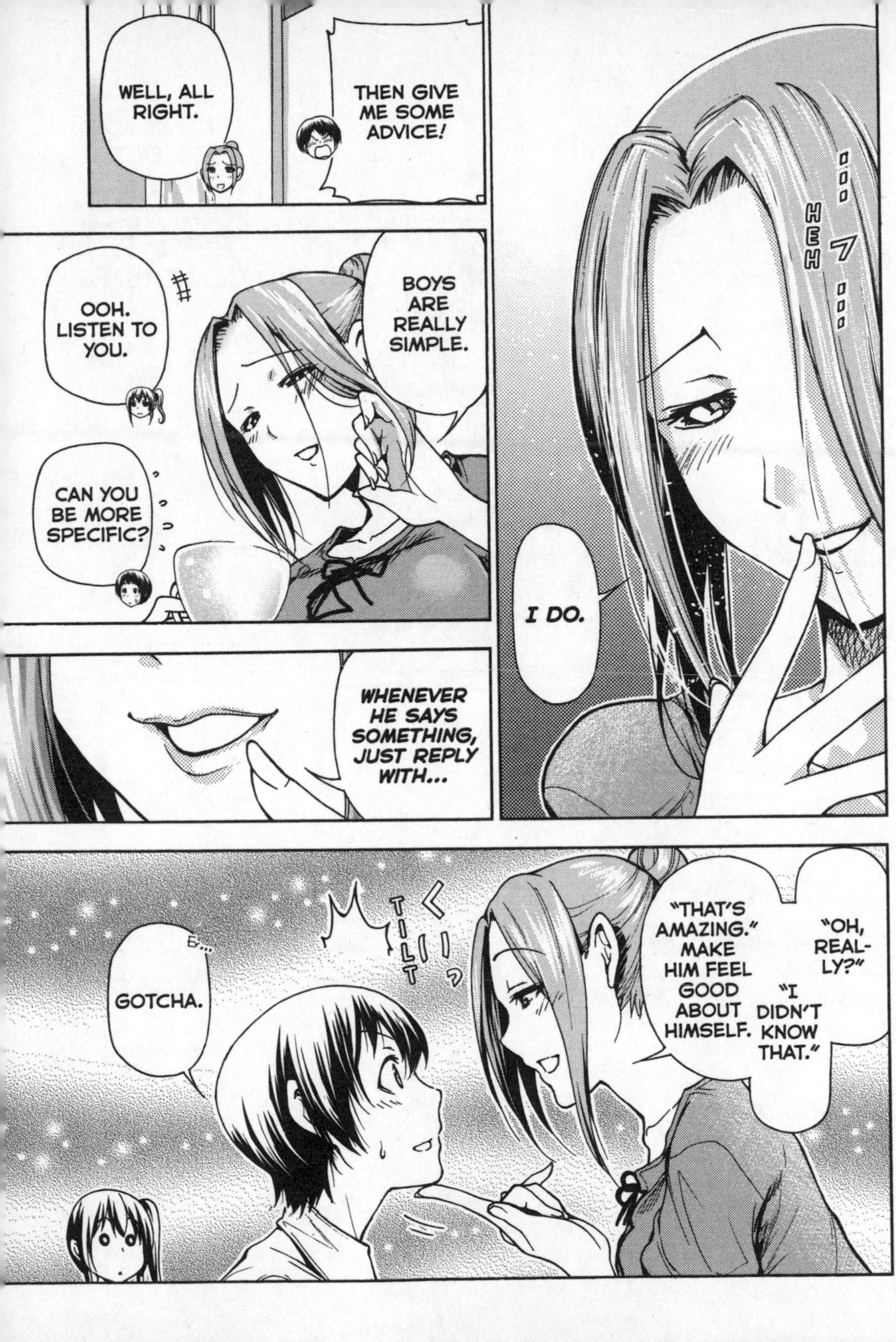
...HEH...
I DO.
THEN GIVE ME SOME ADVICE!
WELL, ALL RIGHT.
BOYS ARE REALLY SIMPLE.
OOH. LISTEN TO YOU.
CAN YOU BE MORE SPECIFIC?
WHENEVER HE SAYS SOMETHING, JUST REPLY WITH...
"OH, REALLY?"
"I DIDN'T KNOW THAT."
"THAT'S AMAZING." MAKE HIM FEEL GOOD ABOUT HIMSELF.
TILT
GOTCHA.

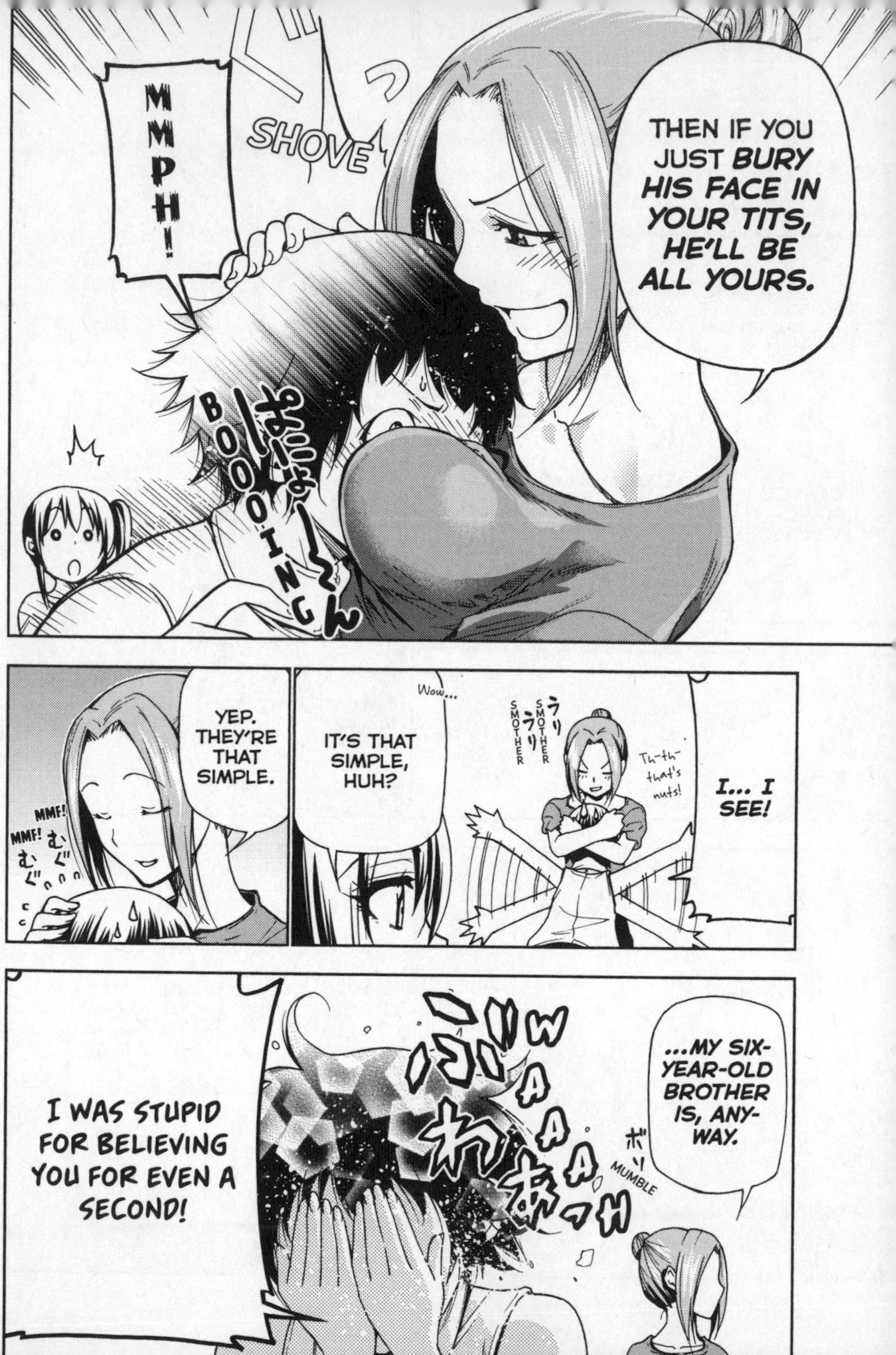
THEN IF YOU JUST BURY HIS FACE IN YOUR TITS, HE'LL BE ALL YOURS.
SHOVE
MMPH!
BOOOOING
I... I SEE!
SMOTHER
SMOTHER
Th-th-that's nuts!
Wow...
IT'S THAT SIMPLE, HUH?
YEP. THEY'RE THAT SIMPLE.
MMF!
MMF!
...MY SIX-YEAR-OLD BROTHER IS, ANYWAY.
MUMBLE
WAAAH
I WAS STUPID FOR BELIEVING YOU FOR EVEN A SECOND!

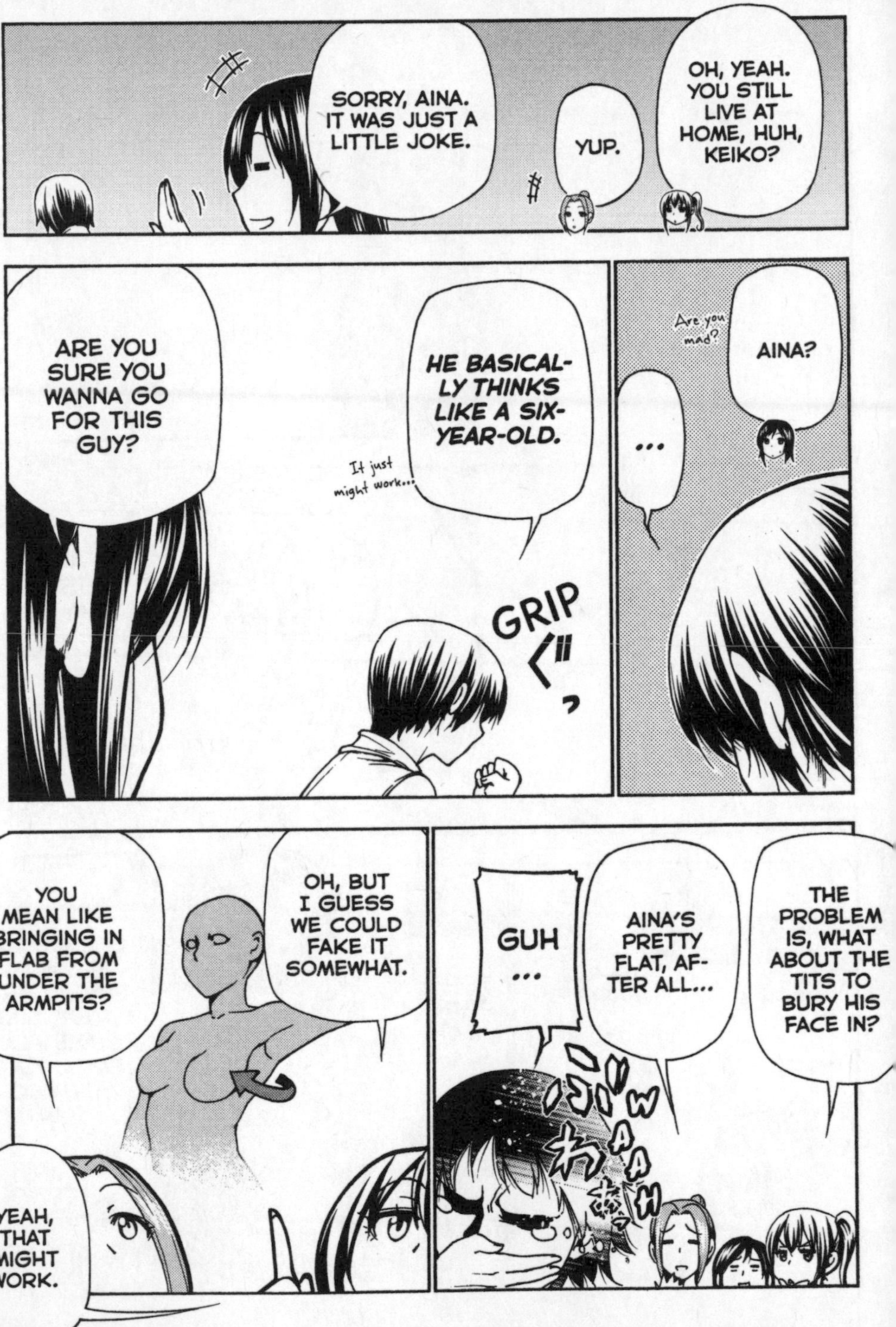

OH, YEAH. YOU STILL LIVE AT HOME, HUH, KEIKO?
YUP.
SORRY, AINA. IT WAS JUST A LITTLE JOKE.
AINA?
Are you mad?
...
HE BASICALLY THINKS LIKE A SIX-YEAR-OLD.
It just might work...
ARE YOU SURE YOU WANNA GO FOR THIS GUY?
GRIP
THE PROBLEM IS, WHAT ABOUT THE TITS TO BURY HIS FACE IN?
AINA'S PRETTY FLAT, AFTER ALL...
GUH ...
WAAAH
OH, BUT I GUESS WE COULD FAKE IT SOMEWHAT.
YOU MEAN LIKE BRINGING IN FLAB FROM UNDER THE ARMPITS?
YEAH, THAT MIGHT WORK.

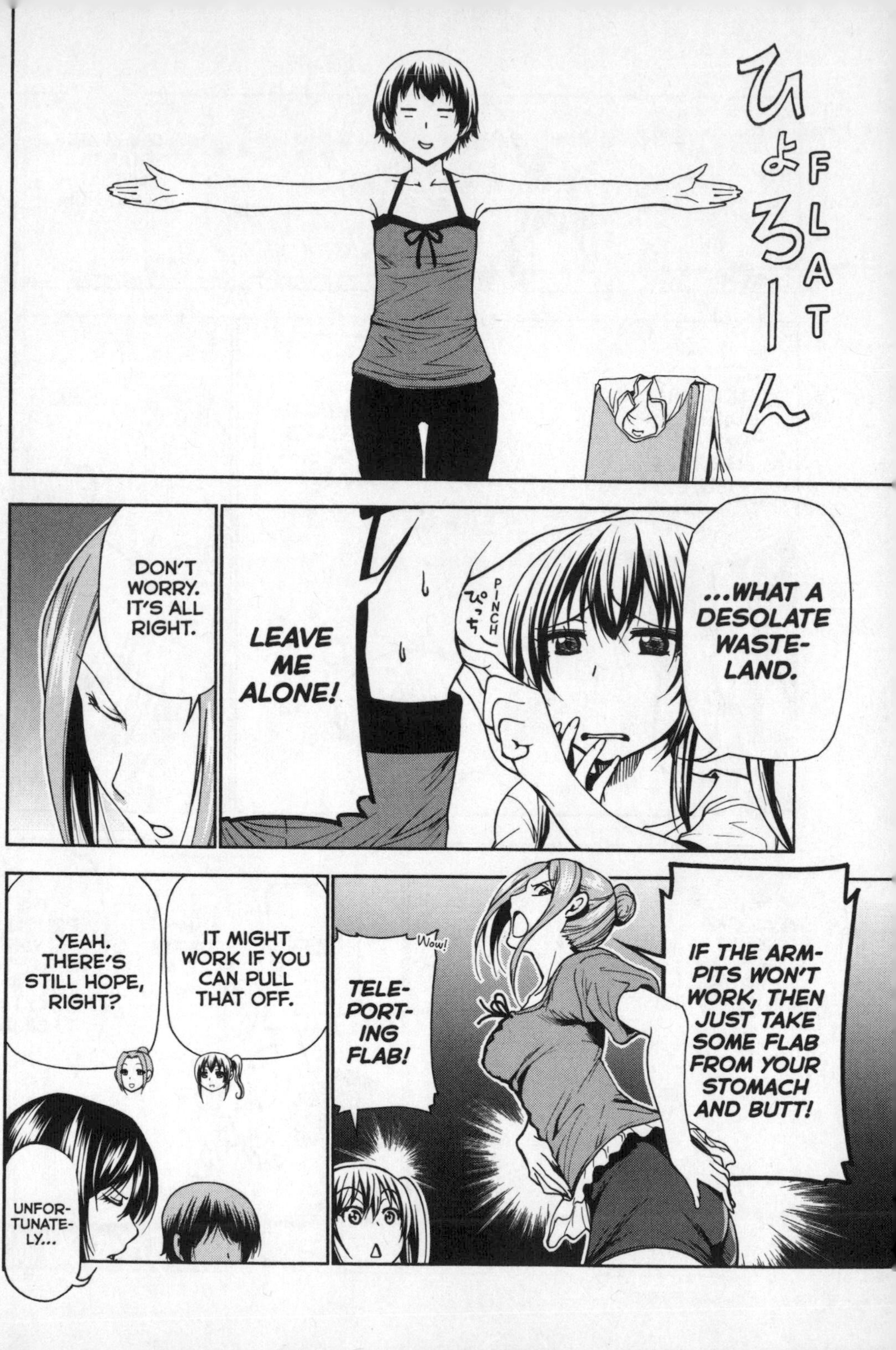
ひょろーん
FLAT
ぴっち
PINCH
...WHAT A DESOLATE WASTE-LAND.
LEAVE ME ALONE!
DON'T WORRY. IT'S ALL RIGHT.
IF THE ARM-PITS WON'T WORK, THEN JUST TAKE SOME FLAB FROM YOUR STOMACH AND BUTT!
Wow!
TELE-PORT-ING FLAB!
IT MIGHT WORK IF YOU CAN PULL THAT OFF.
YEAH. THERE'S STILL HOPE, RIGHT?
UNFOR-TUNATE-LY...

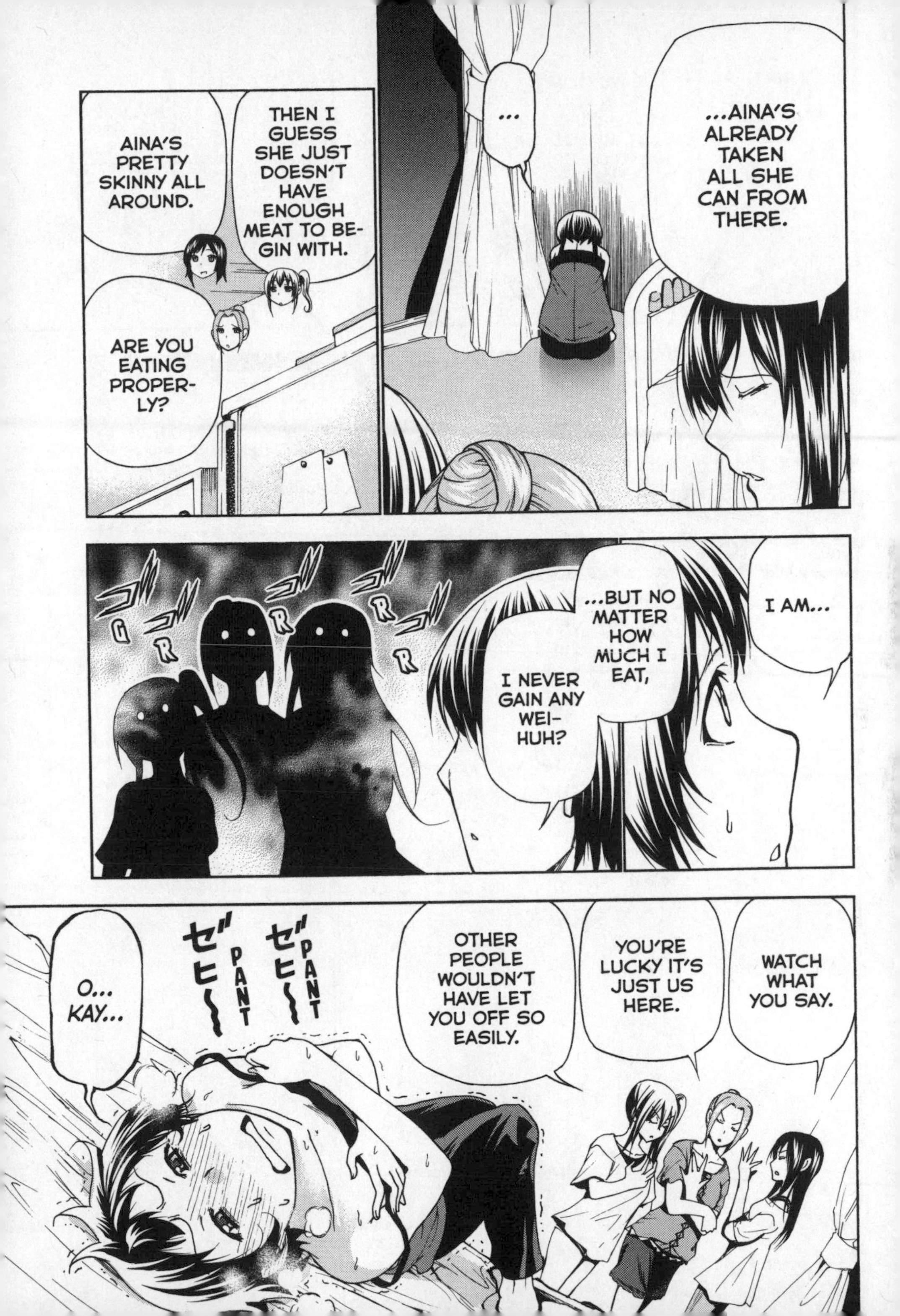
...AINA'S ALREADY TAKEN ALL SHE CAN FROM THERE.
...
THEN I GUESS SHE JUST DOESN'T HAVE ENOUGH MEAT TO BE-GIN WITH.
AINA'S PRETTY SKINNY ALL AROUND.
ARE YOU EATING PROPER-LY?
I AM...
...BUT NO MATTER HOW MUCH I EAT,
I NEVER GAIN ANY WEI- HUH?
G R R R R R
WATCH WHAT YOU SAY.
YOU'RE LUCKY IT'S JUST US HERE.
OTHER PEOPLE WOULDN'T HAVE LET YOU OFF SO EASILY.
ゼヒ~ PANT
ゼヒ~ PANT
O... KAY...

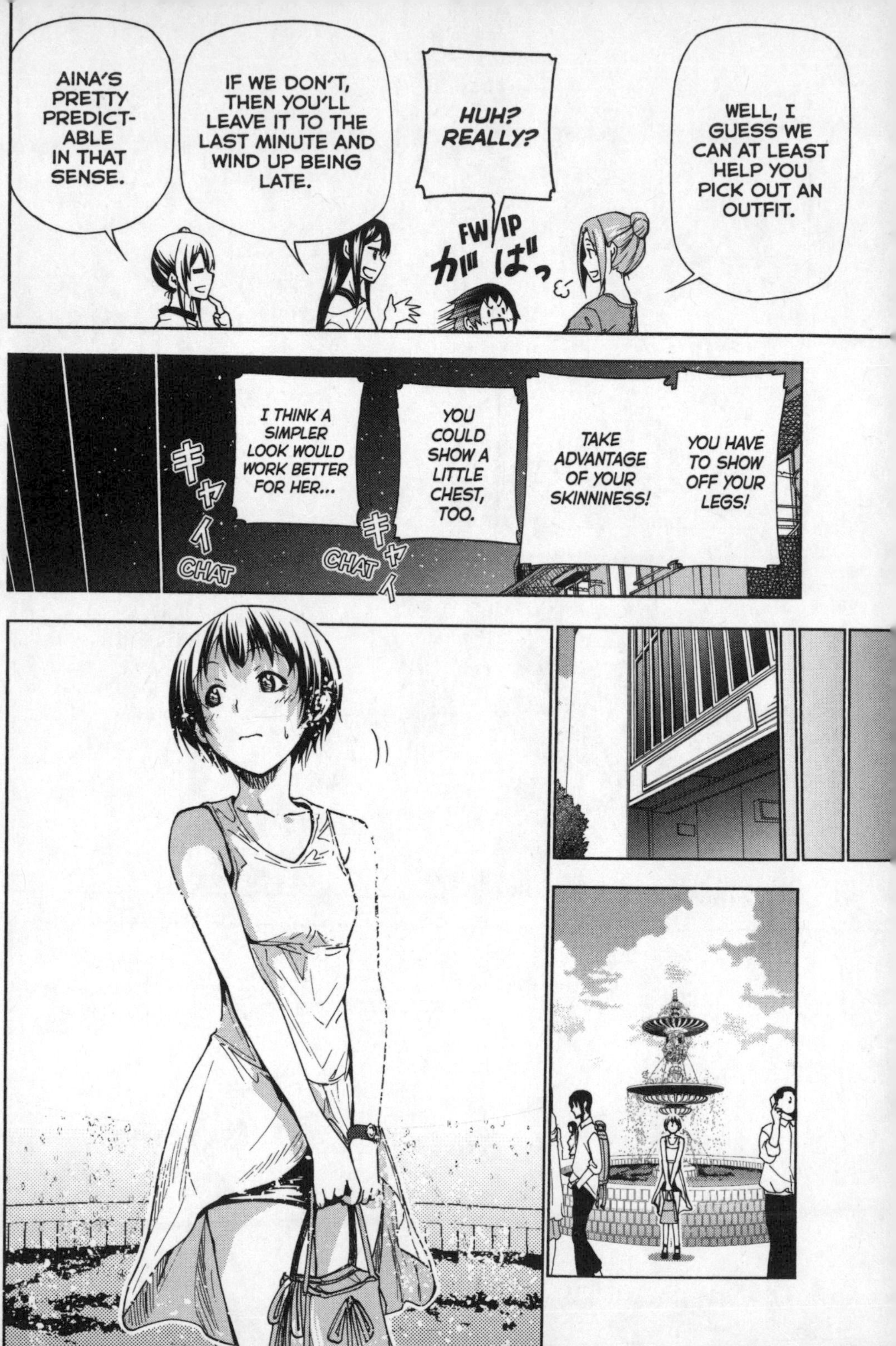
WELL, I GUESS WE CAN AT LEAST HELP YOU PICK OUT AN OUTFIT.
HUH? REALLY?
FWIP
ガばっ
IF WE DON'T, THEN YOU'LL LEAVE IT TO THE LAST MINUTE AND WIND UP BEING LATE.
AINA'S PRETTY PREDICT-ABLE IN THAT SENSE.
YOU HAVE TO SHOW OFF YOUR LEGS!
TAKE ADVANTAGE OF YOUR SKINNINESS!
YOU COULD SHOW A LITTLE CHEST, TOO.
キャイ
CHAT
I THINK A SIMPLER LOOK WOULD WORK BETTER FOR HER...
キャイ
CHAT

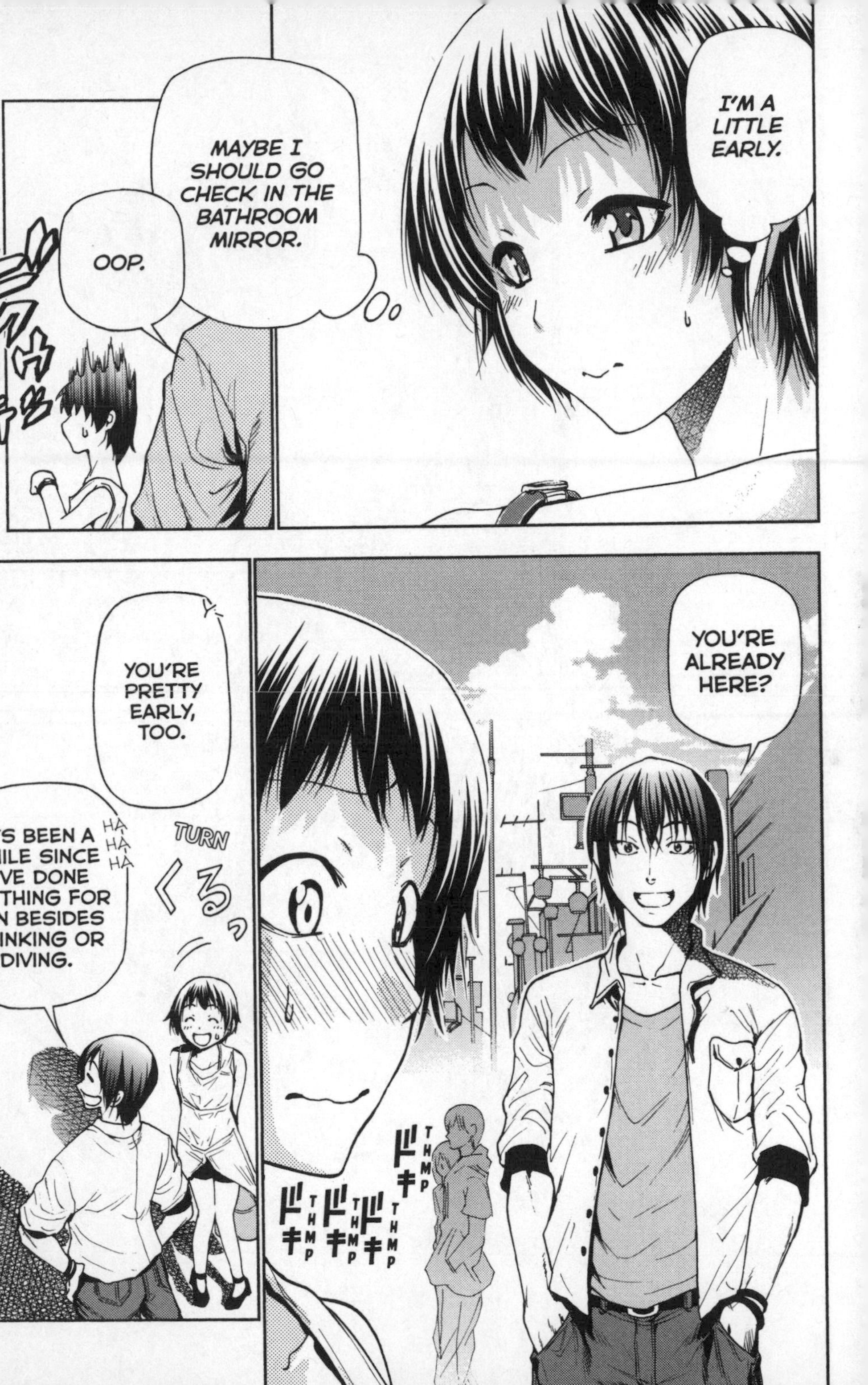
I'M A LITTLE EARLY.
MAYBE I SHOULD GO CHECK IN THE BATHROOM MIRROR.
OOP.
ビクッ
JOLT
YOU'RE ALREADY HERE?
ドキ
THMP
ドキ
THMP
ドキ
THMP
ドキ
THMP
YOU'RE PRETTY EARLY, TOO.
TURN
くるっ
HA HA HA
IT'S BEEN A WHILE SINCE I'VE DONE ANYTHING FOR FUN BESIDES DRINKING OR DIVING.

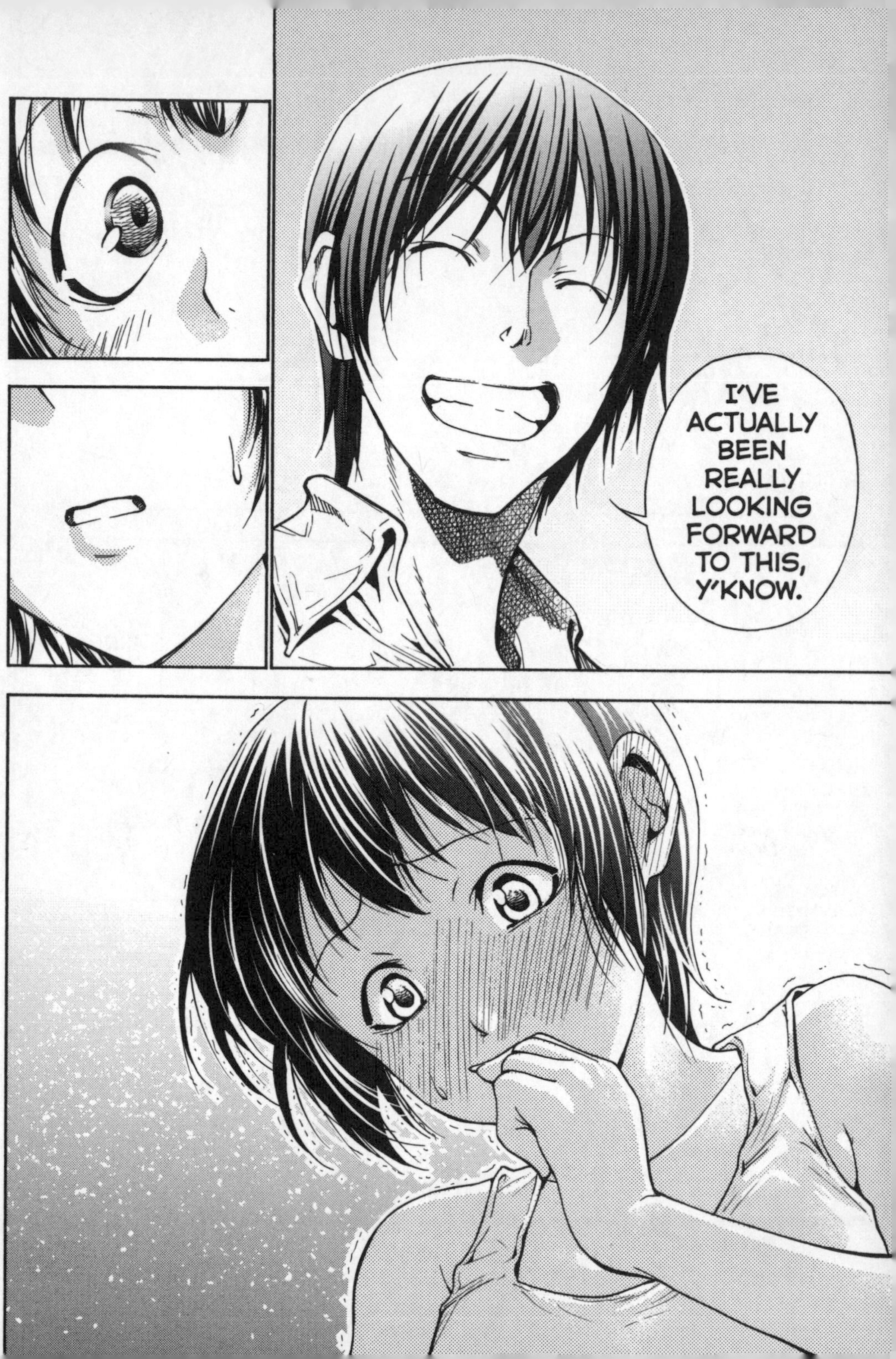
I'VE ACTUALLY BEEN REALLY LOOKING FORWARD TO THIS, Y'KNOW.

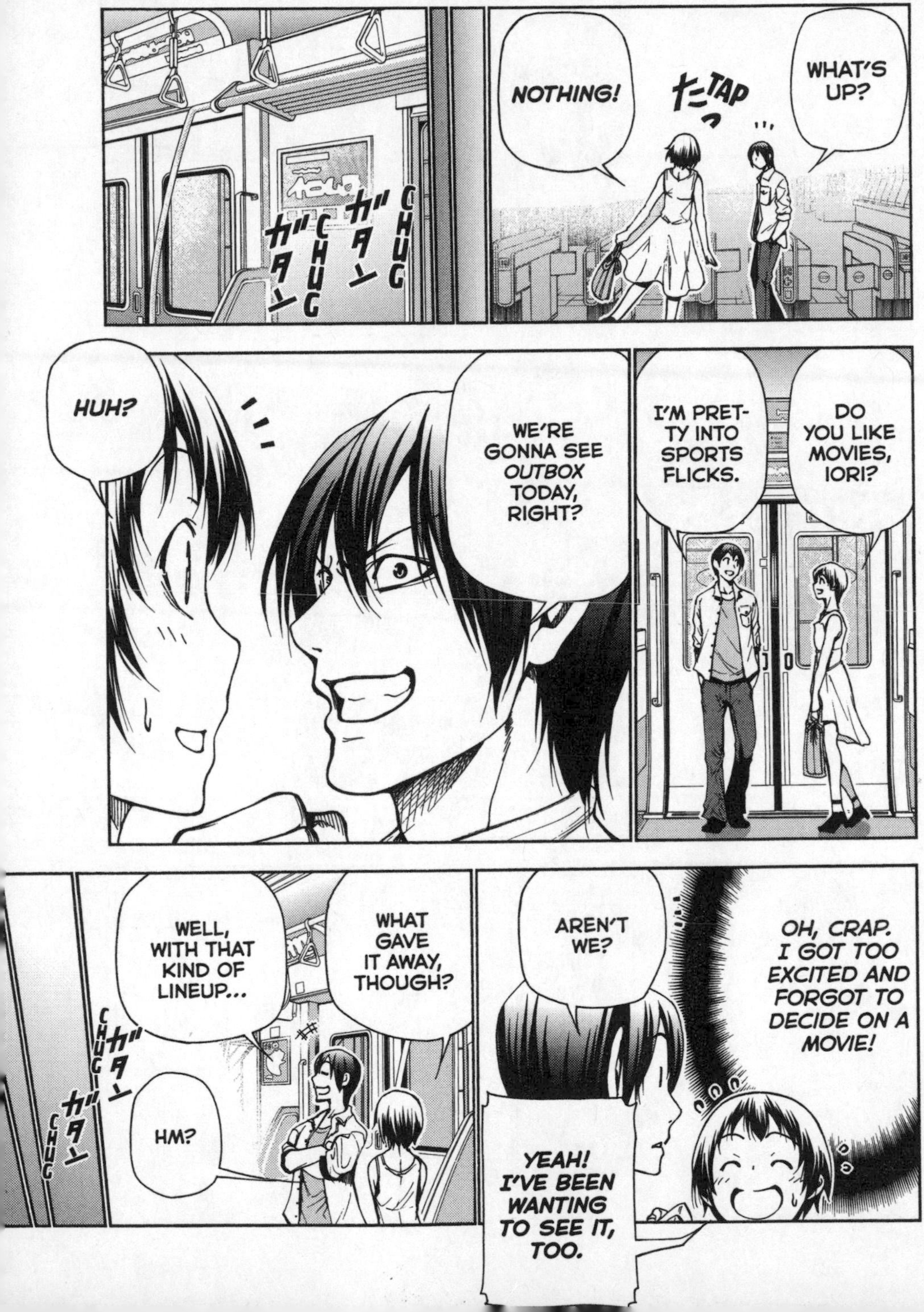
WHAT'S UP?
たっ TAP
NOTHING!
ガタン CHUG
ガタン CHUG
DO YOU LIKE MOVIES, IORI?
I'M PRET-TY INTO SPORTS FLICKS.
WE'RE GONNA SEE *OUTBOX* TODAY, RIGHT?
HUH?
OH, CRAP. I GOT TOO EXCITED AND FORGOT TO DECIDE ON A MOVIE!
AREN'T WE?
YEAH! I'VE BEEN WANTING TO SEE IT, TOO.
WHAT GAVE IT AWAY, THOUGH?
WELL, WITH THAT KIND OF LINEUP...
HM?
ガタン CHUG
ガタン CHUG

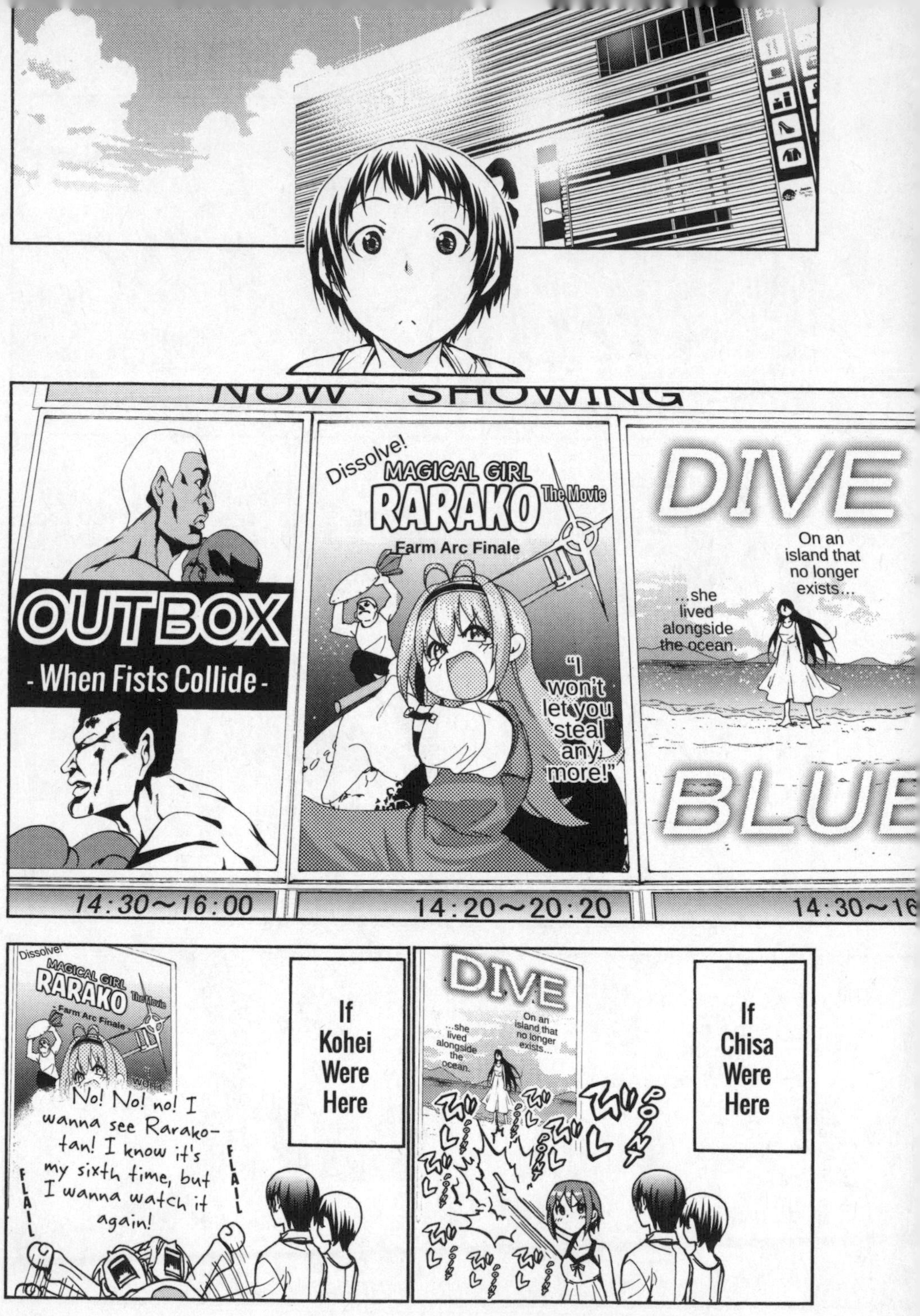
NOW SHOWING
DIVE
On an island that no longer exists...
...she lived alongside the ocean.
BLUE
14:30~16
Dissolve!
MAGICAL GIRL RARAKO The Movie
Farm Arc Finale
"I won't let you steal any more!"
14:20~20:20
OUTBOX
- When Fists Collide -
14:30~16:00
If Chisa Were Here
DIVE
On an island that no longer exists...
...she lived alongside the ocean.
If Kohei Were Here
Dissolve!
MAGICAL GIRL RARAKO The Movie
Farm Arc Finale
No! No! no! I wanna see Rarako-tan! I know it's my sixth time, but I wanna watch it again!
FLAIL
FLAIL

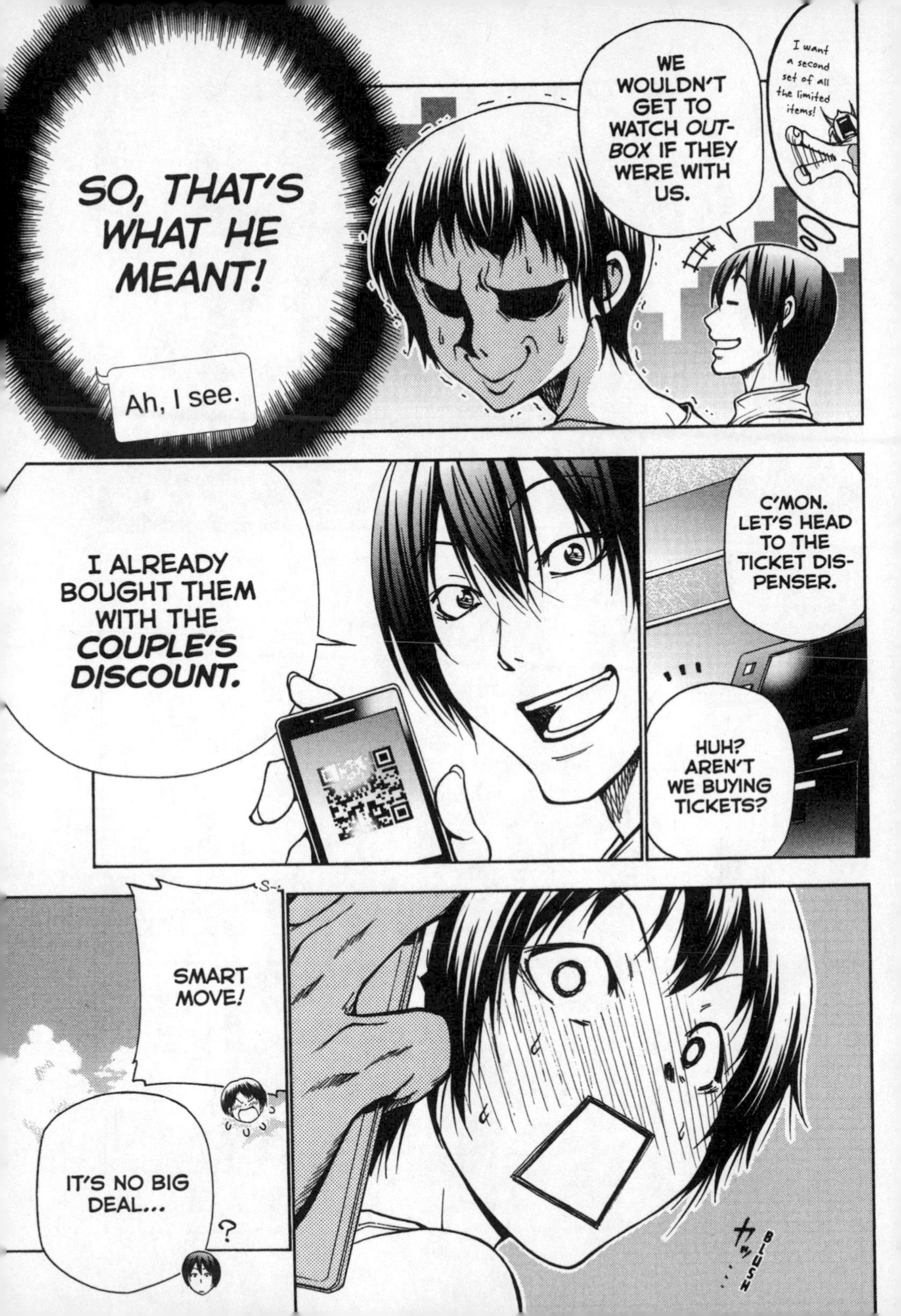
I want a second set of all the limited items!
WE WOULDN'T GET TO WATCH *OUT-BOX* IF THEY WERE WITH US.
SO, THAT'S WHAT HE MEANT!
Ah, I see.
C'MON. LET'S HEAD TO THE TICKET DIS-PENSER.
...
HUH? AREN'T WE BUYING TICKETS?
I ALREADY BOUGHT THEM WITH THE *COUPLE'S DISCOUNT.*
カッ BLUSH
...
S-
SMART MOVE!
IT'S NO BIG DEAL...
?

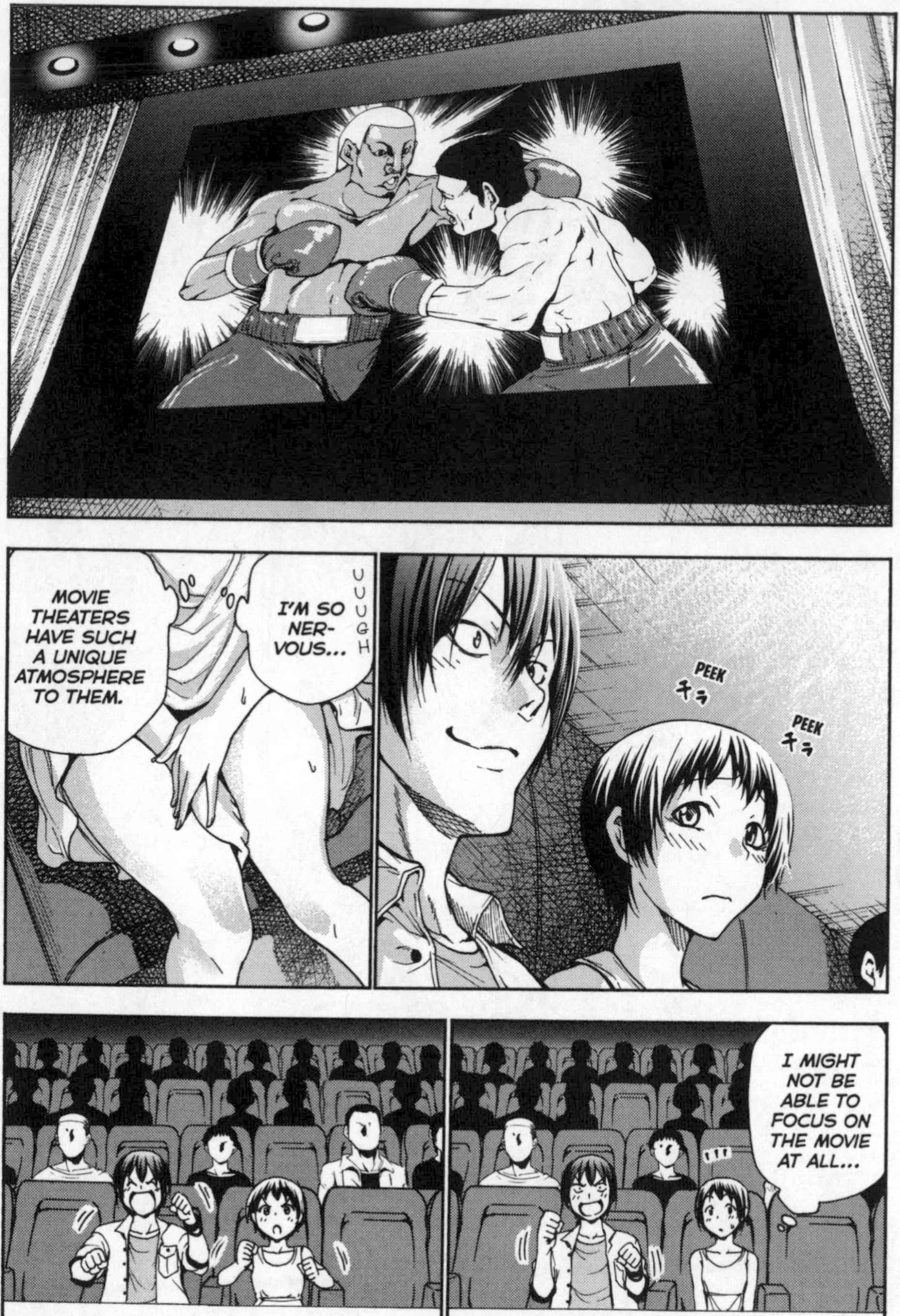
PEEK
チラ
PEEK
チラ
UUUGH
I'M SO NERVOUS...
MOVIE THEATERS HAVE SUCH A UNIQUE ATMOSPHERE TO THEM.
I MIGHT NOT BE ABLE TO FOCUS ON THE MOVIE AT ALL...

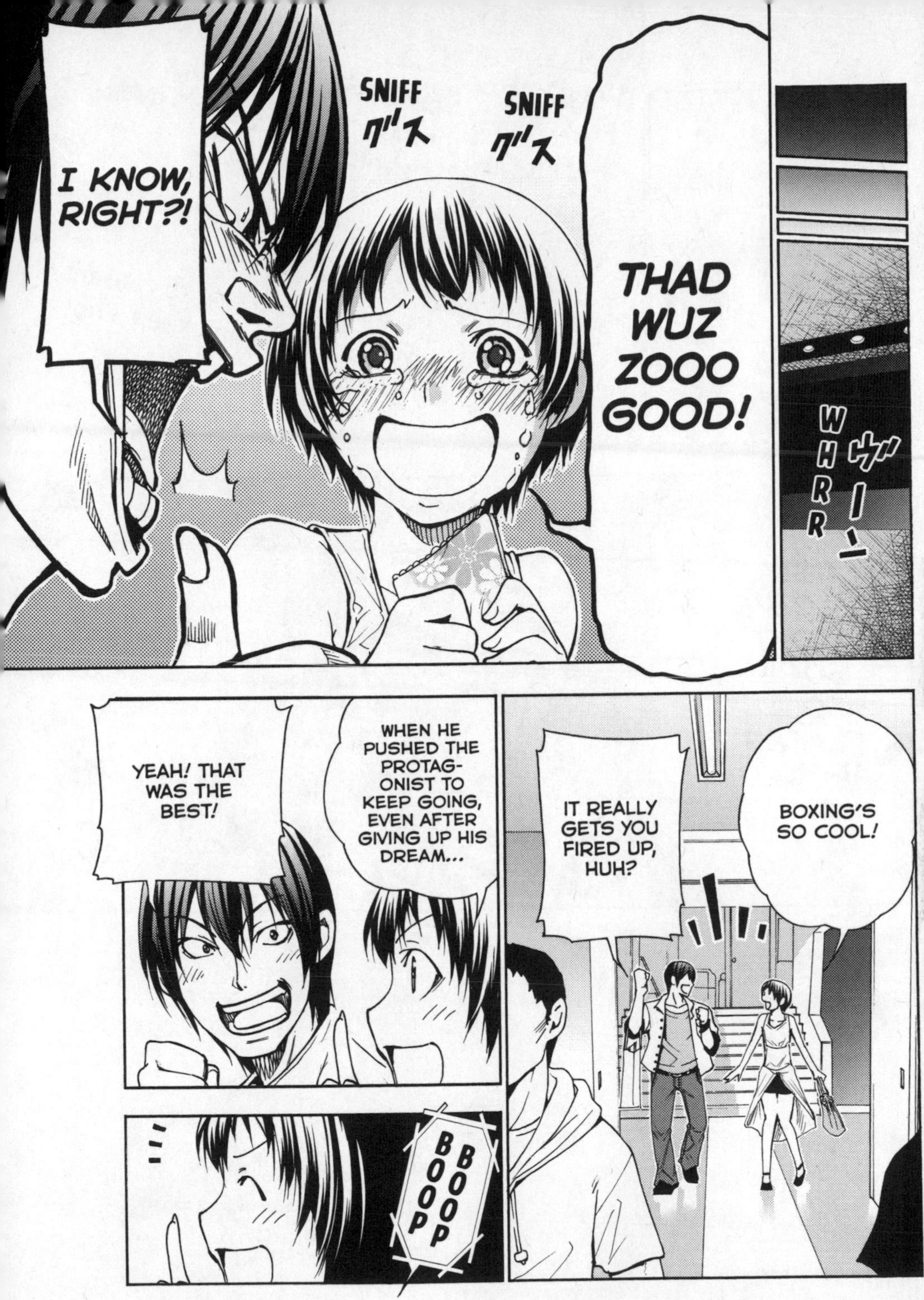
WHRR
ヴィー
THAD WUZ ZOOO GOOD!
SNIFF グス
SNIFF グス
I KNOW, RIGHT?!
BOXING'S SO COOL!
IT REALLY GETS YOU FIRED UP, HUH?
WHEN HE PUSHED THE PROTAG-ONIST TO KEEP GOING, EVEN AFTER GIVING UP HIS DREAM...
YEAH! THAT WAS THE BEST!
BOOP BOOP

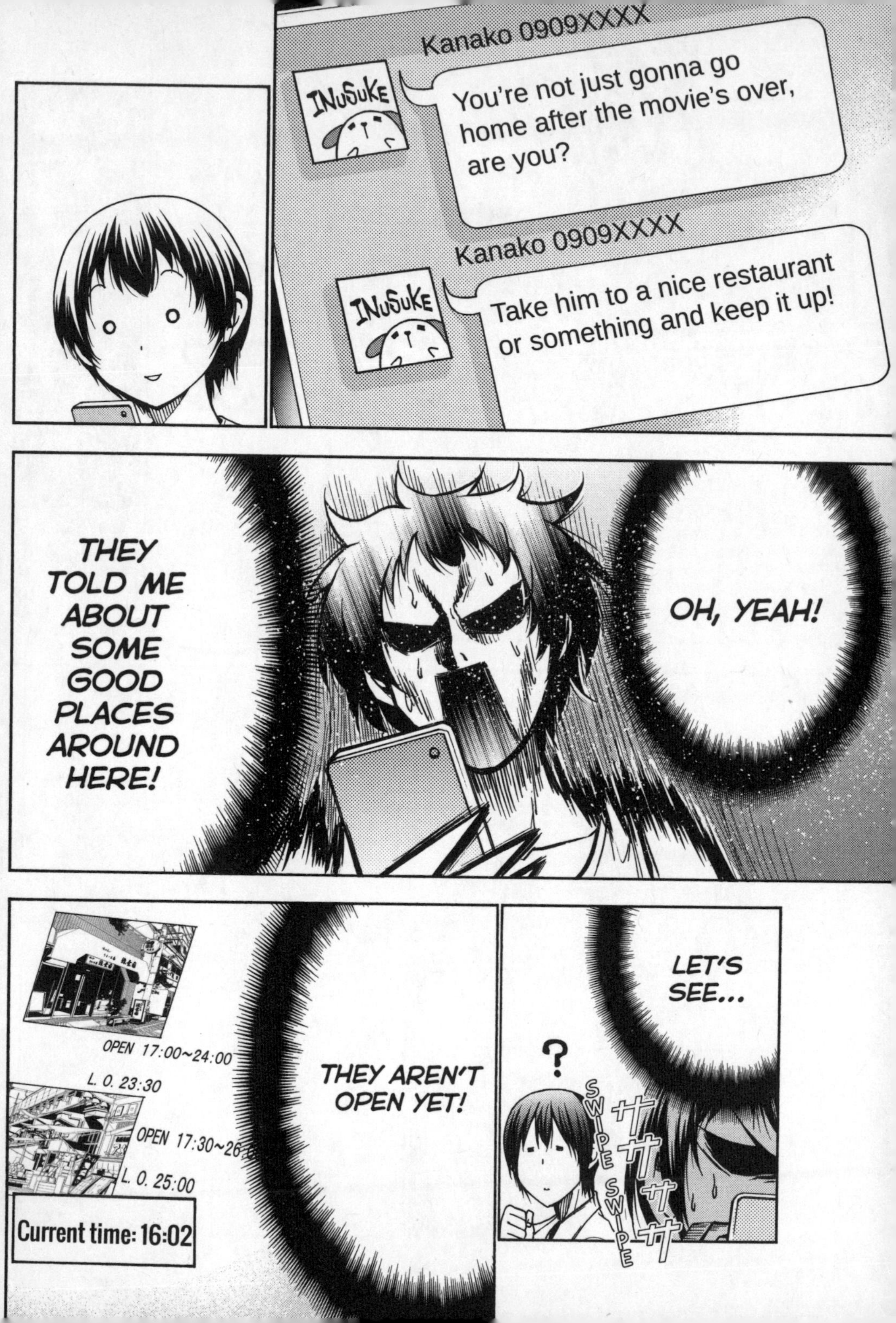
Kanako 0909XXXX
INUSUKE
You're not just gonna go home after the movie's over, are you?
Kanako 0909XXXX
INUSUKE
Take him to a nice restaurant or something and keep it up!
OH, YEAH!
THEY TOLD ME ABOUT SOME GOOD PLACES AROUND HERE!
LET'S SEE...
?
SWIPE
SWIPE
THEY AREN'T OPEN YET!
OPEN 17:00~24:00
L. O. 23:30
OPEN 17:30~26:00
L. O. 25:00
Current time: 16:02

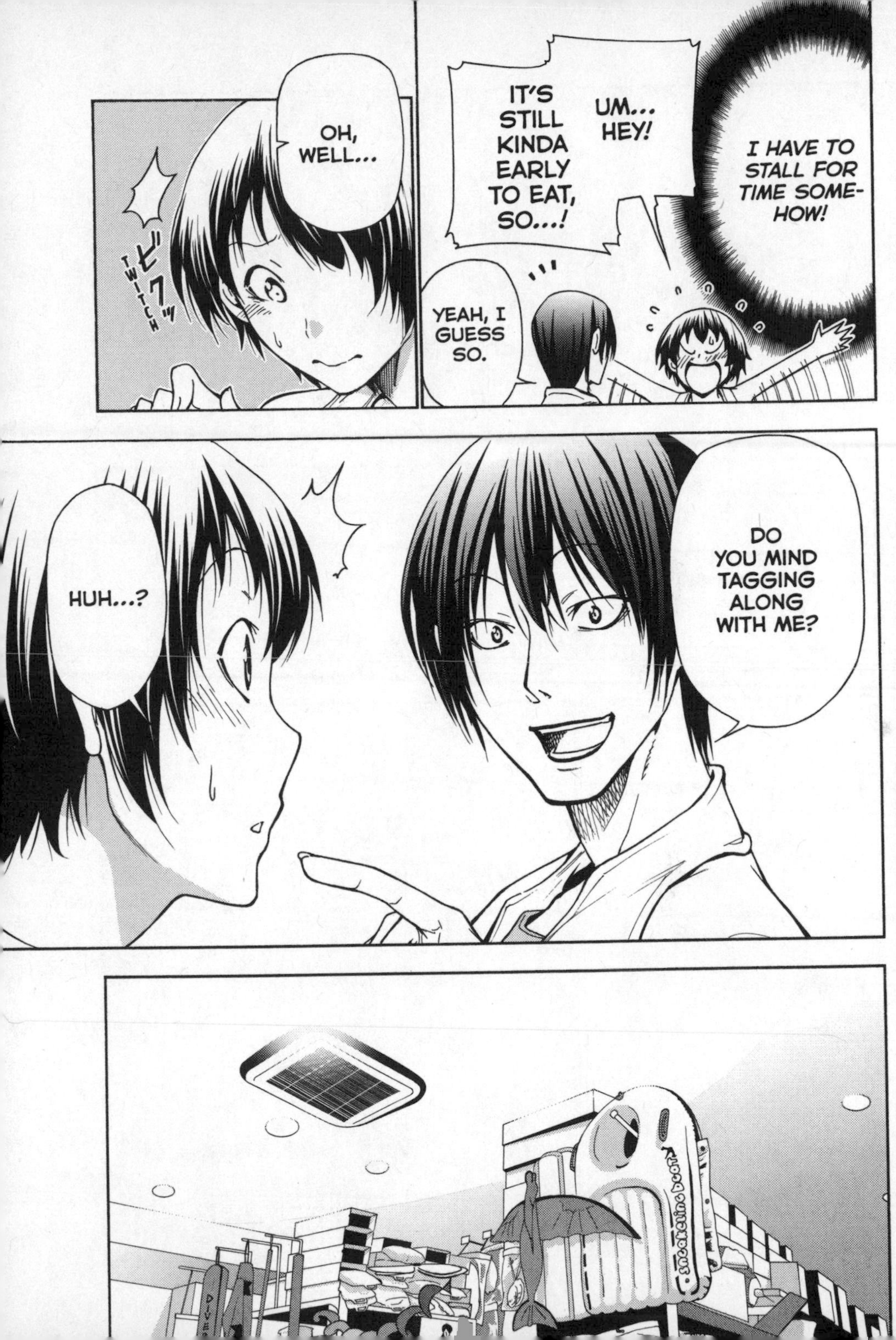
I HAVE TO STALL FOR TIME SOMEHOW!
UM... HEY!
IT'S STILL KINDA EARLY TO EAT, SO...!
YEAH, I GUESS SO.
OH, WELL...
TWITCH
DO YOU MIND TAGGING ALONG WITH ME?
HUH...?

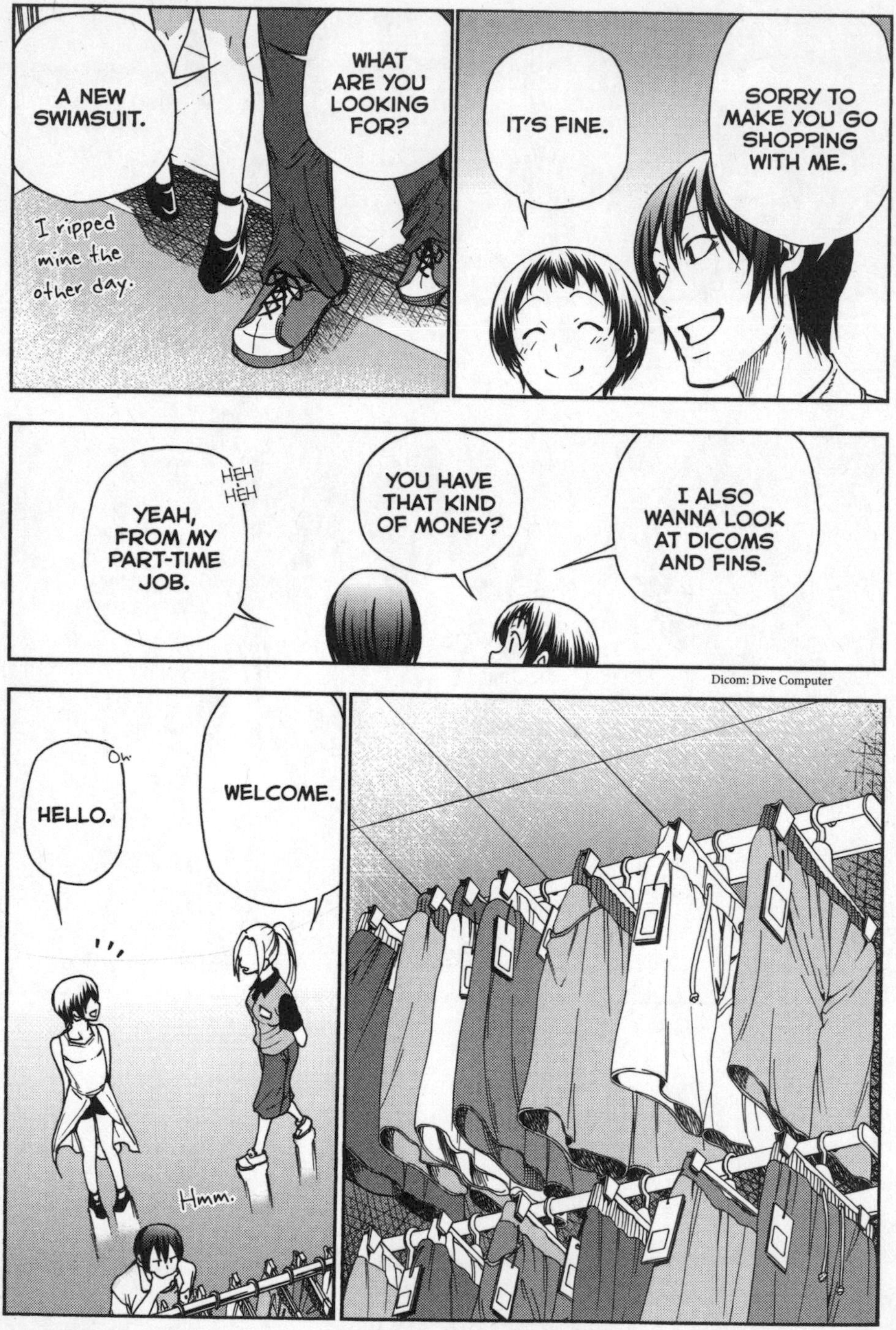
SORRY TO MAKE YOU GO SHOPPING WITH ME.
IT'S FINE.
WHAT ARE YOU LOOKING FOR?
A NEW SWIMSUIT.
I ripped mine the other day.
I ALSO WANNA LOOK AT DICOMS AND FINS.
YOU HAVE THAT KIND OF MONEY?
HEH HEH
YEAH, FROM MY PART-TIME JOB.
WELCOME.
Oh
HELLO.
Hmm.
Dicom: Dive Computer

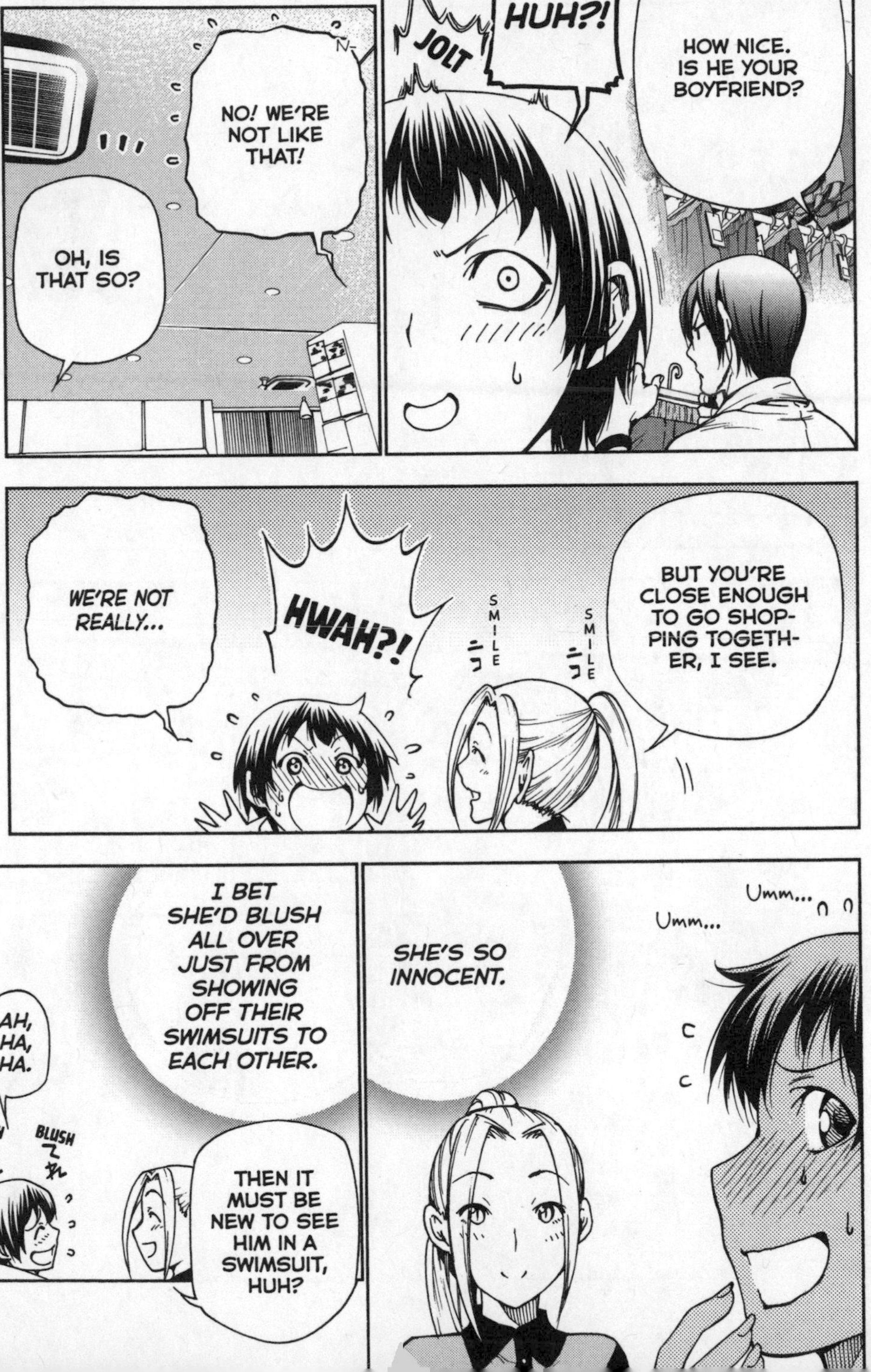
HOW NICE. IS HE YOUR BOYFRIEND?
JOLT
HUH?!
N-
NO! WE'RE NOT LIKE THAT!
OH, IS THAT SO?
BUT YOU'RE CLOSE ENOUGH TO GO SHOP-PING TOGETH-ER, I SEE.
SMILE
SMILE
HWAH?!
WE'RE NOT REALLY...
Umm...
Umm...
SHE'S SO INNOCENT.
I BET SHE'D BLUSH ALL OVER JUST FROM SHOWING OFF THEIR SWIMSUITS TO EACH OTHER.
THEN IT MUST BE NEW TO SEE HIM IN A SWIMSUIT, HUH?
BLUSH
BLUSH
AH, HA, HA.

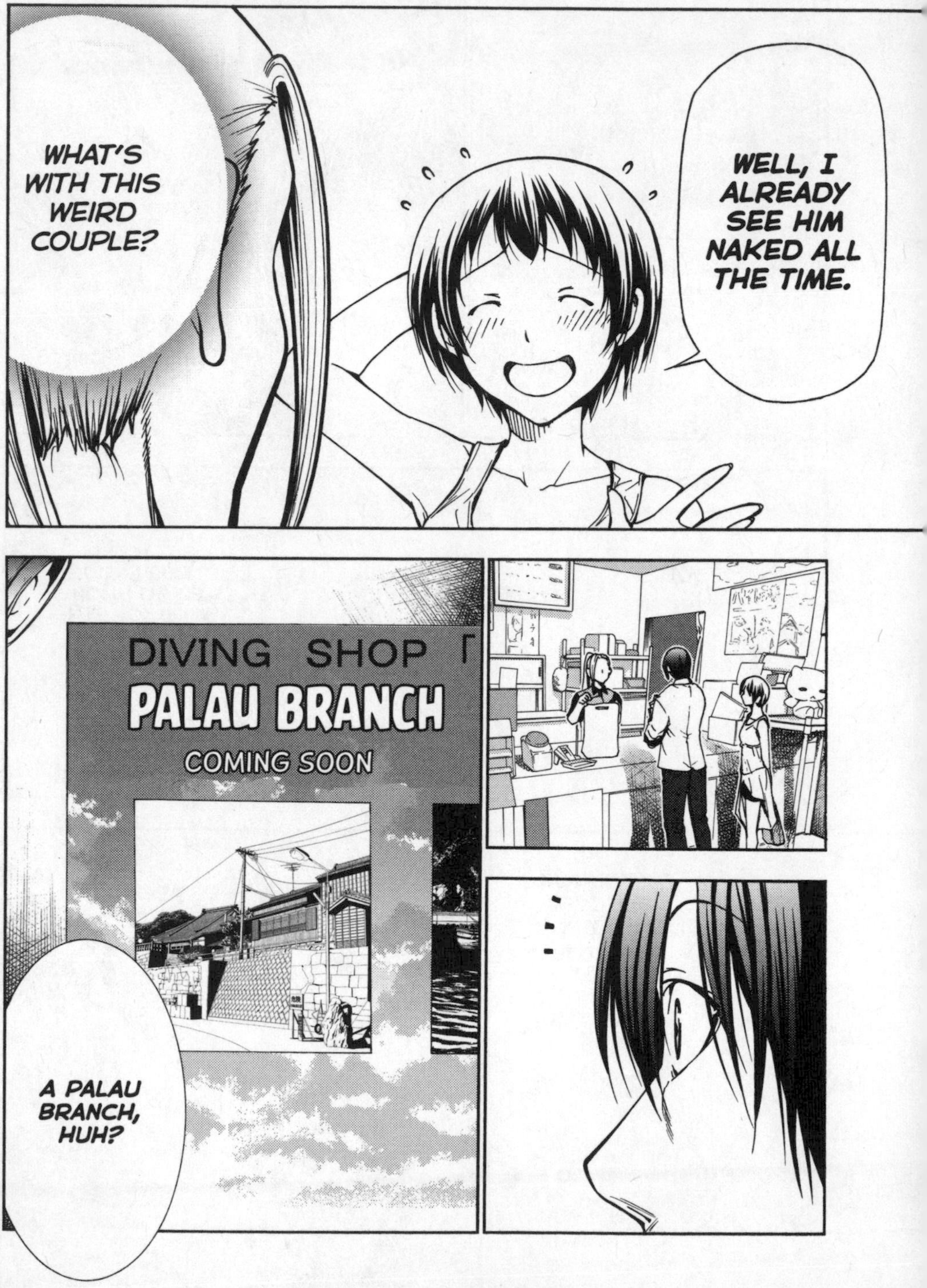
WELL, I ALREADY SEE HIM NAKED ALL THE TIME.
WHAT'S WITH THIS WEIRD COUPLE?
...
DIVING SHOP「
PALAU BRANCH
COMING SOON
A PALAU BRANCH, HUH?

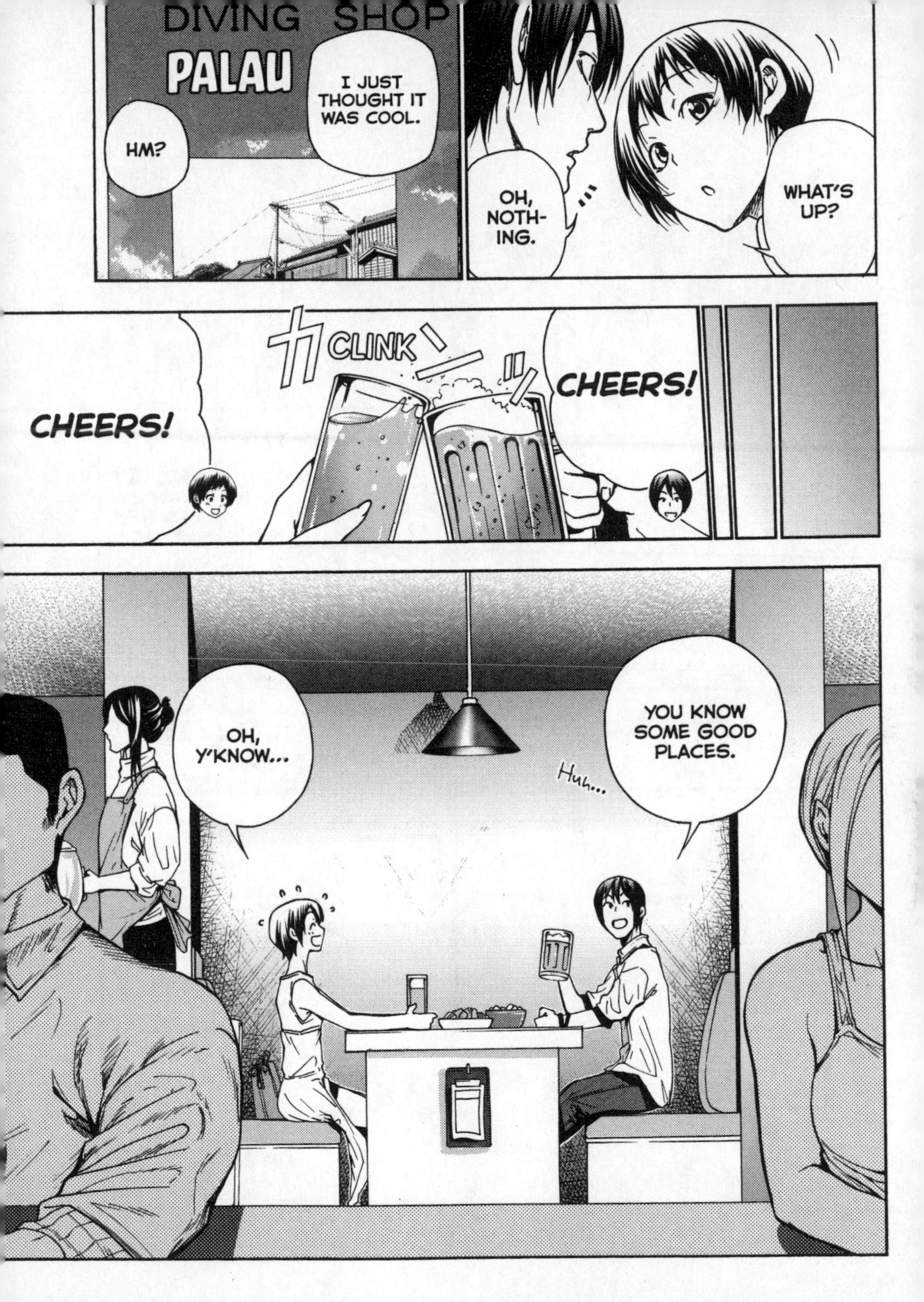
WHAT'S UP?
...
OH, NOTH-ING.
DIVING SHOP
PALAU
I JUST THOUGHT IT WAS COOL.
HM?
CHEERS!
CLINK
CHEERS!
YOU KNOW SOME GOOD PLACES.
Huh...
OH, Y'KNOW...

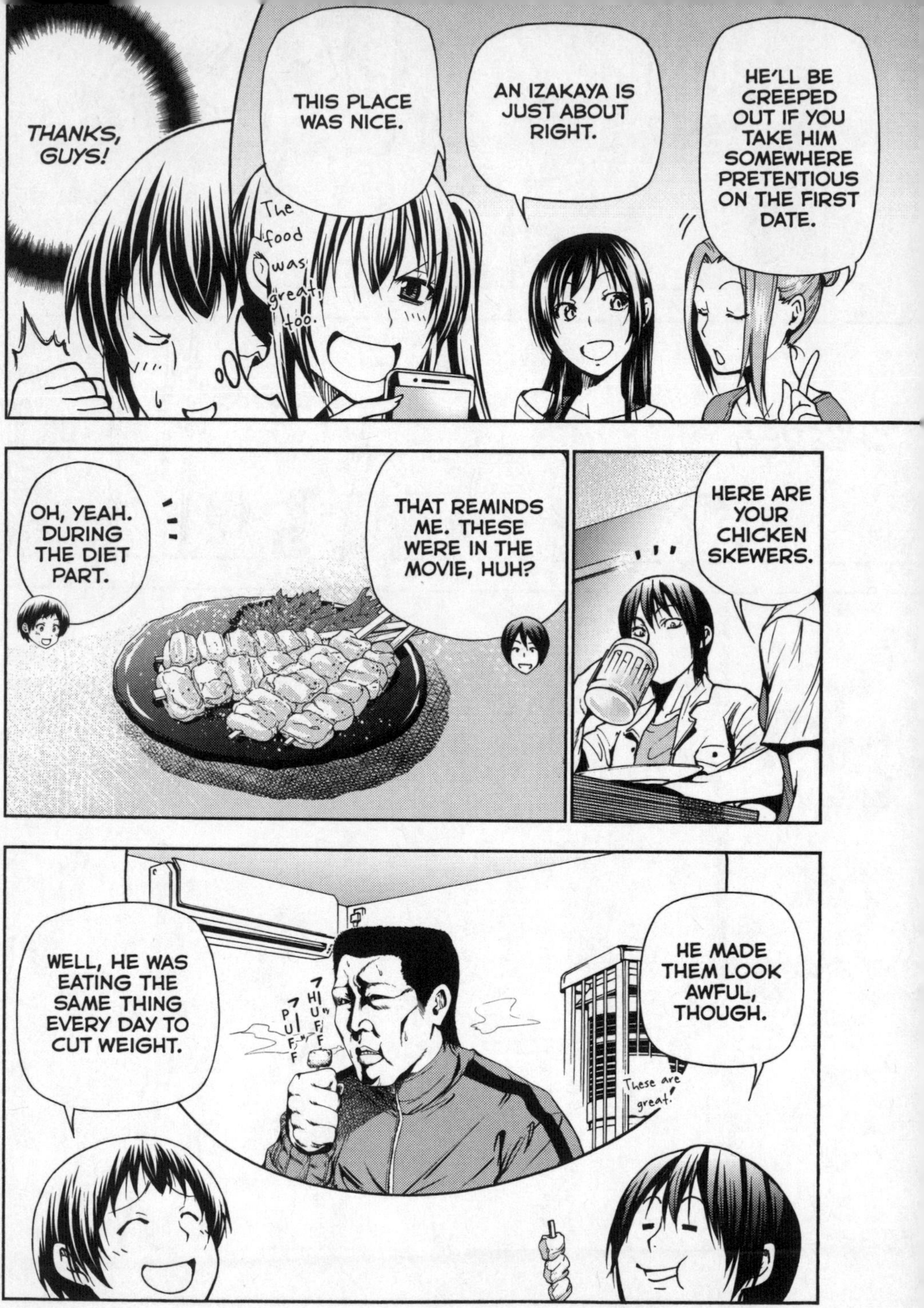
HE'LL BE CREEPED OUT IF YOU TAKE HIM SOMEWHERE PRETENTIOUS ON THE FIRST DATE.
AN IZAKAYA IS JUST ABOUT RIGHT.
THIS PLACE WAS NICE.
The food was great, too.
THANKS, GUYS!
HERE ARE YOUR CHICKEN SKEWERS.
THAT REMINDS ME. THESE WERE IN THE MOVIE, HUH?
OH, YEAH. DURING THE DIET PART.
HE MADE THEM LOOK AWFUL, THOUGH.
These are great!
HUFF
PUFF
WELL, HE WAS EATING THE SAME THING EVERY DAY TO CUT WEIGHT.

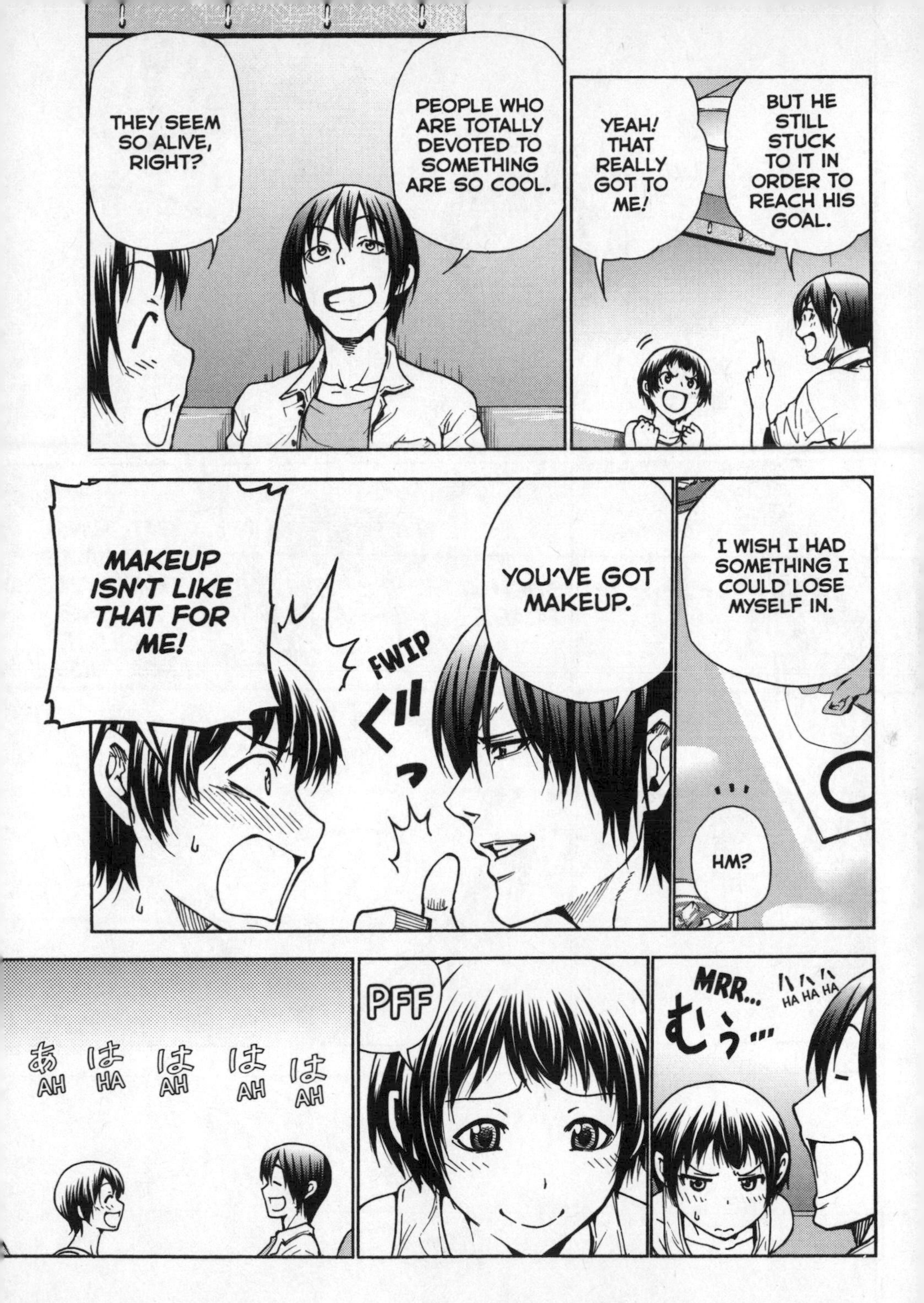
BUT HE STILL STUCK TO IT IN ORDER TO REACH HIS GOAL.
YEAH! THAT REALLY GOT TO ME!
PEOPLE WHO ARE TOTALLY DEVOTED TO SOMETHING ARE SO COOL.
THEY SEEM SO ALIVE, RIGHT?
I WISH I HAD SOMETHING I COULD LOSE MYSELF IN.
...
HM?
YOU'VE GOT MAKEUP.
FWIP
ぐッ
MAKEUP ISN'T LIKE THAT FOR ME!
ハハハ
HA HA HA
MRR...
むぅ…
PFF
あははははは
AH HA AH AH AH

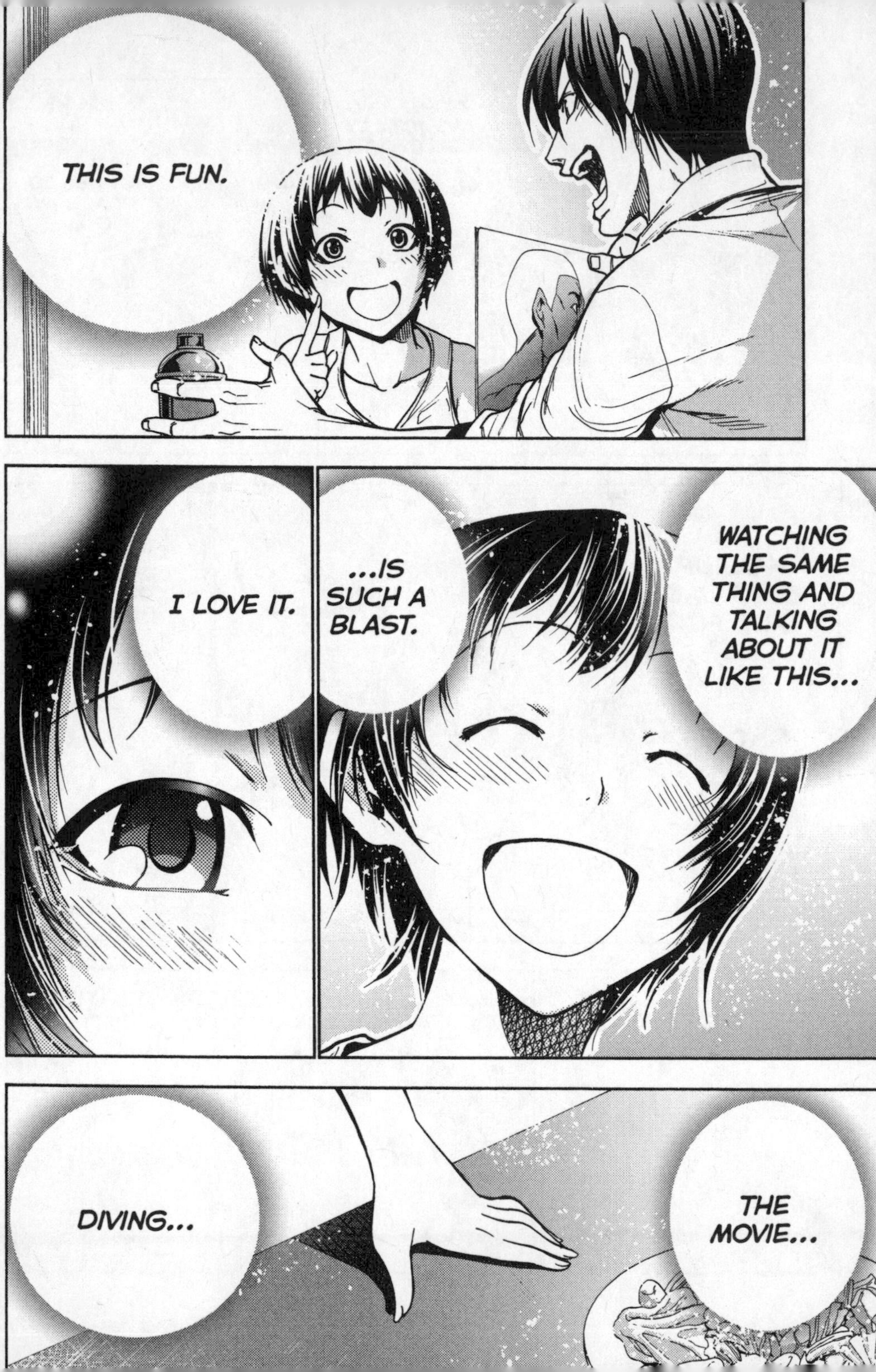
THIS IS FUN.
WATCHING THE SAME THING AND TALKING ABOUT IT LIKE THIS...
...IS SUCH A BLAST.
I LOVE IT.
THE MOVIE...
DIVING...

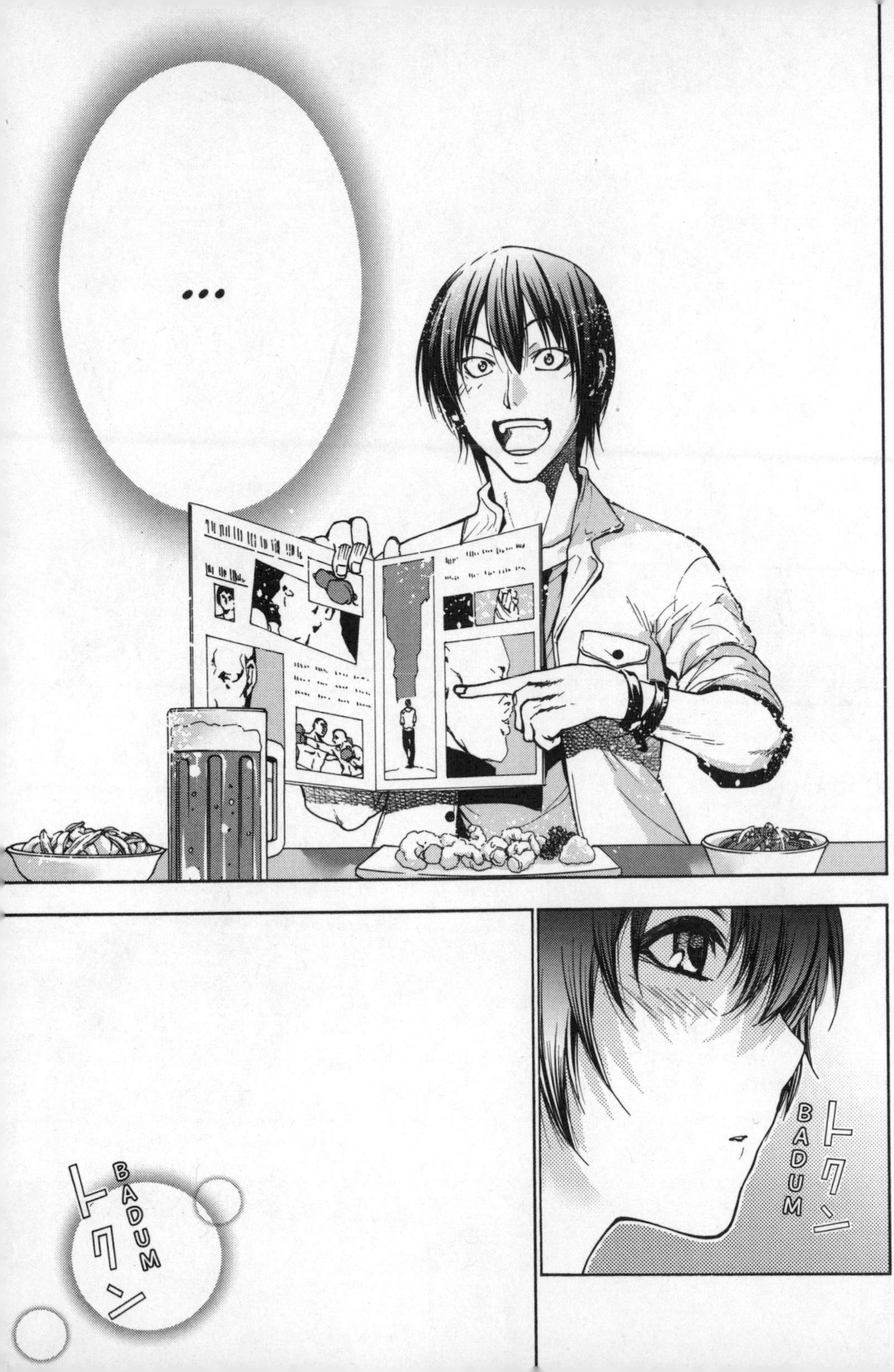
...
トクン
BADUM
トクン
BADUM

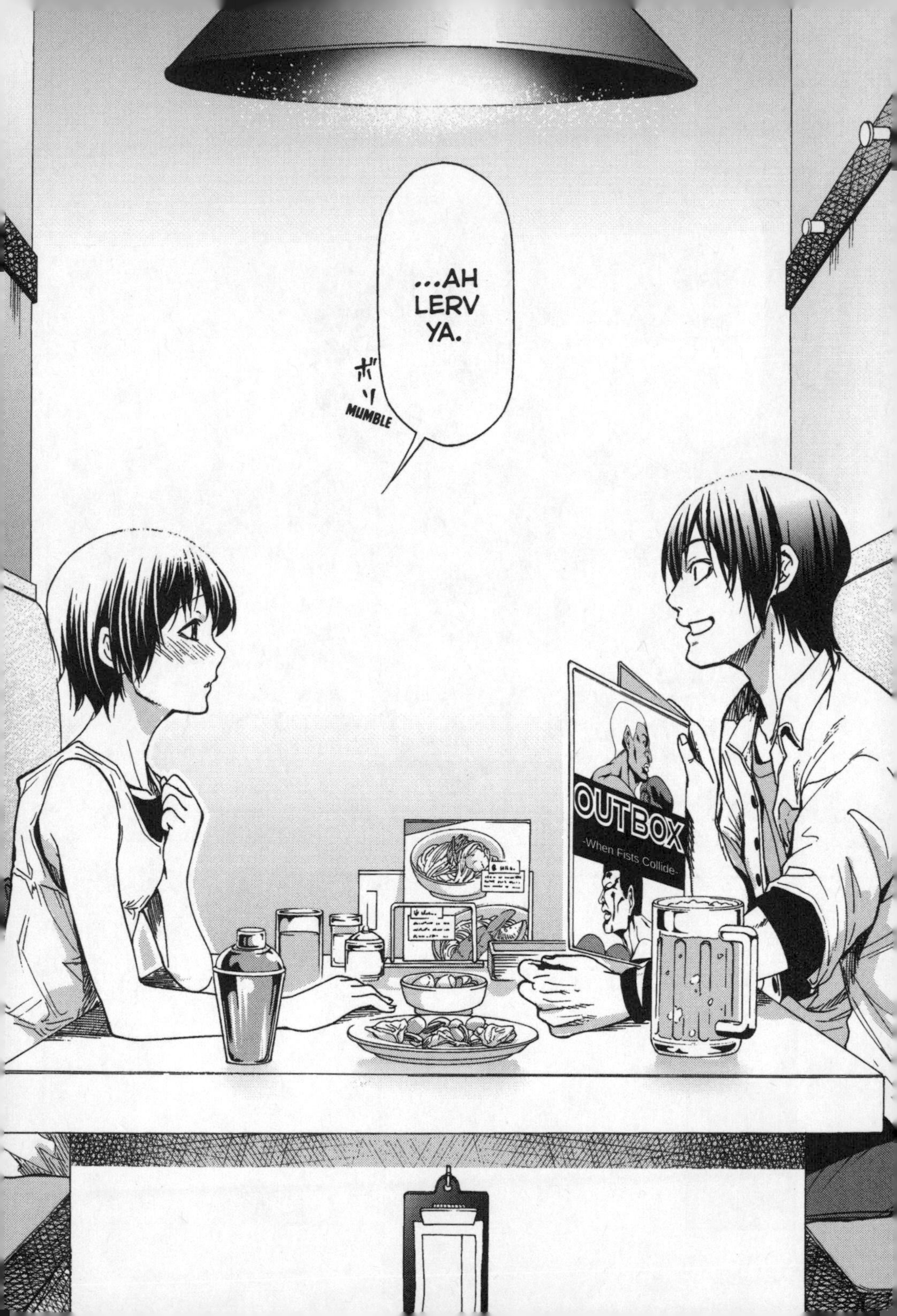
...AH LERV YA.
ボソ
MUMBLE
OUTBOX
-When Fists Collide-

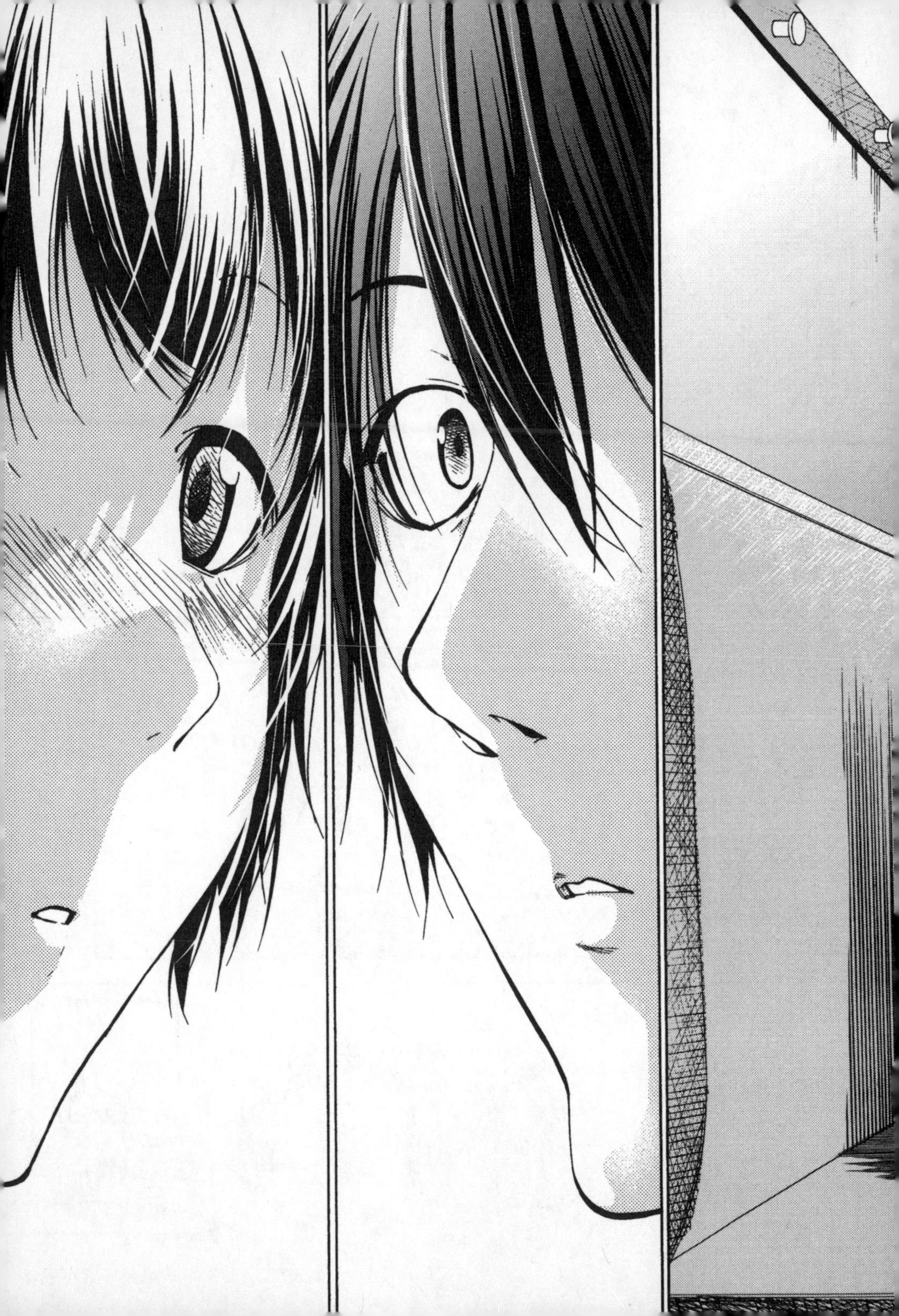

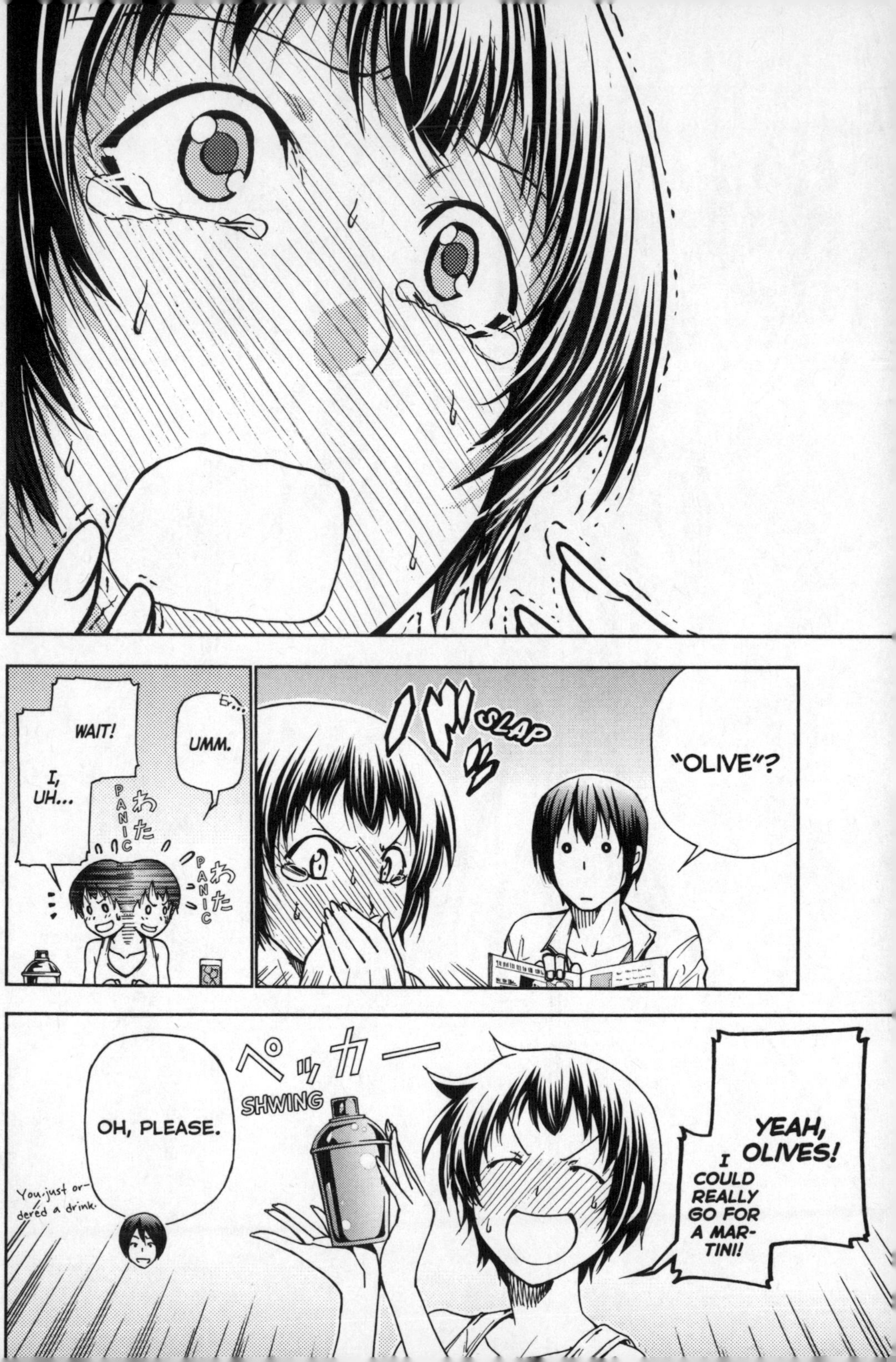
"OLIVE"?
SLAP
Er...
UMM.
WAIT!
I, UH...
PANIC わた
PANIC わた
YEAH, OLIVES! I COULD REALLY GO FOR A MARTINI!
ペッカー
SHWING
OH, PLEASE.
You just ordered a drink.

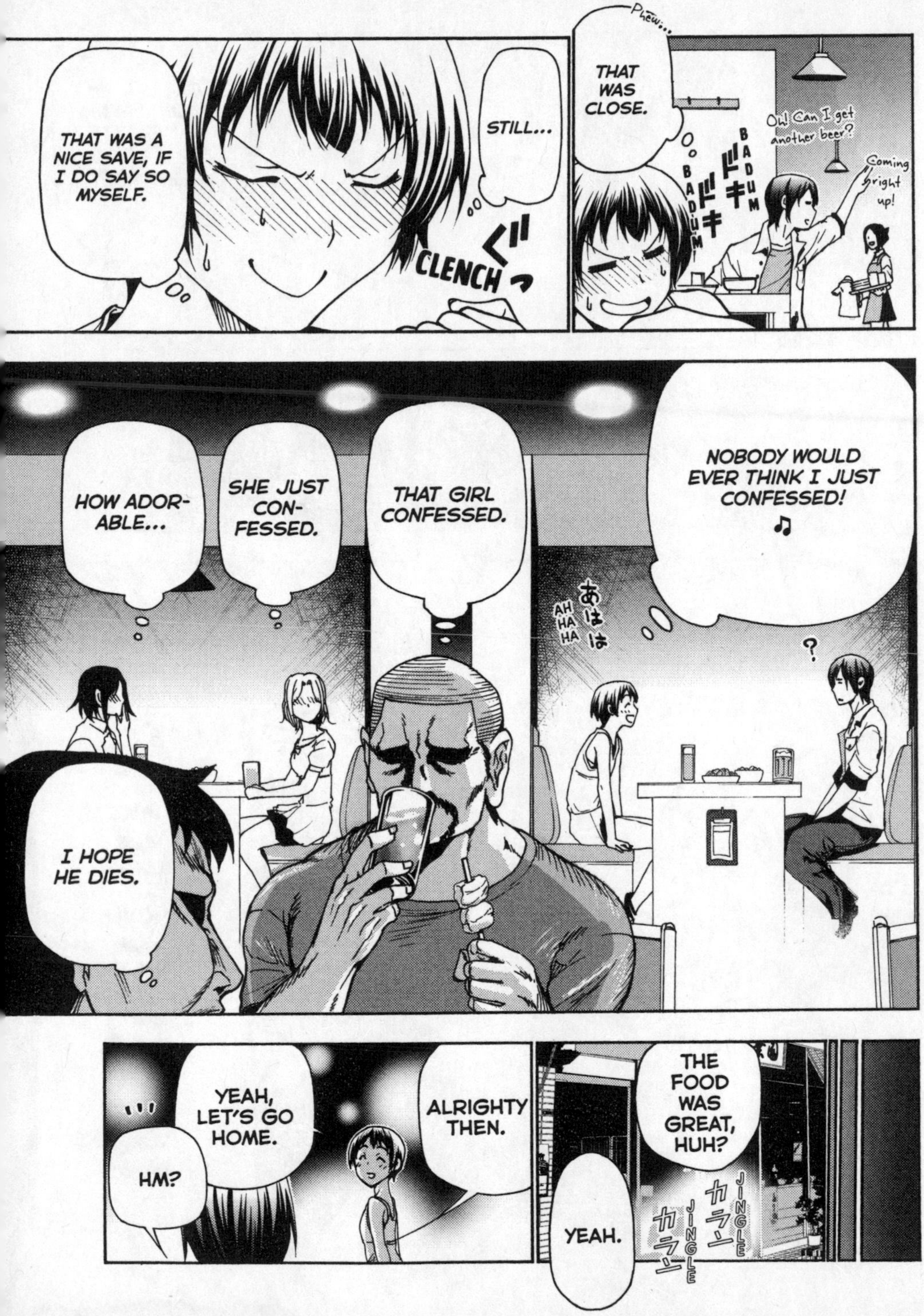
Phew...
THAT WAS CLOSE.
ドキドキ BADUM BADUM
Oh! Can I get another beer?
Coming right up!
STILL...
ぐっ CLENCH
THAT WAS A NICE SAVE, IF I DO SAY SO MYSELF.
NOBODY WOULD EVER THINK I JUST CONFESSED! ♫
あはは AH HA HA
?
THAT GIRL CONFESSED.
SHE JUST CON-FESSED.
HOW ADOR-ABLE...
I HOPE HE DIES.
THE FOOD WAS GREAT, HUH?
カランカラン JINGLE JINGLE
YEAH.
ALRIGHTY THEN.
YEAH, LET'S GO HOME.
...
HM?

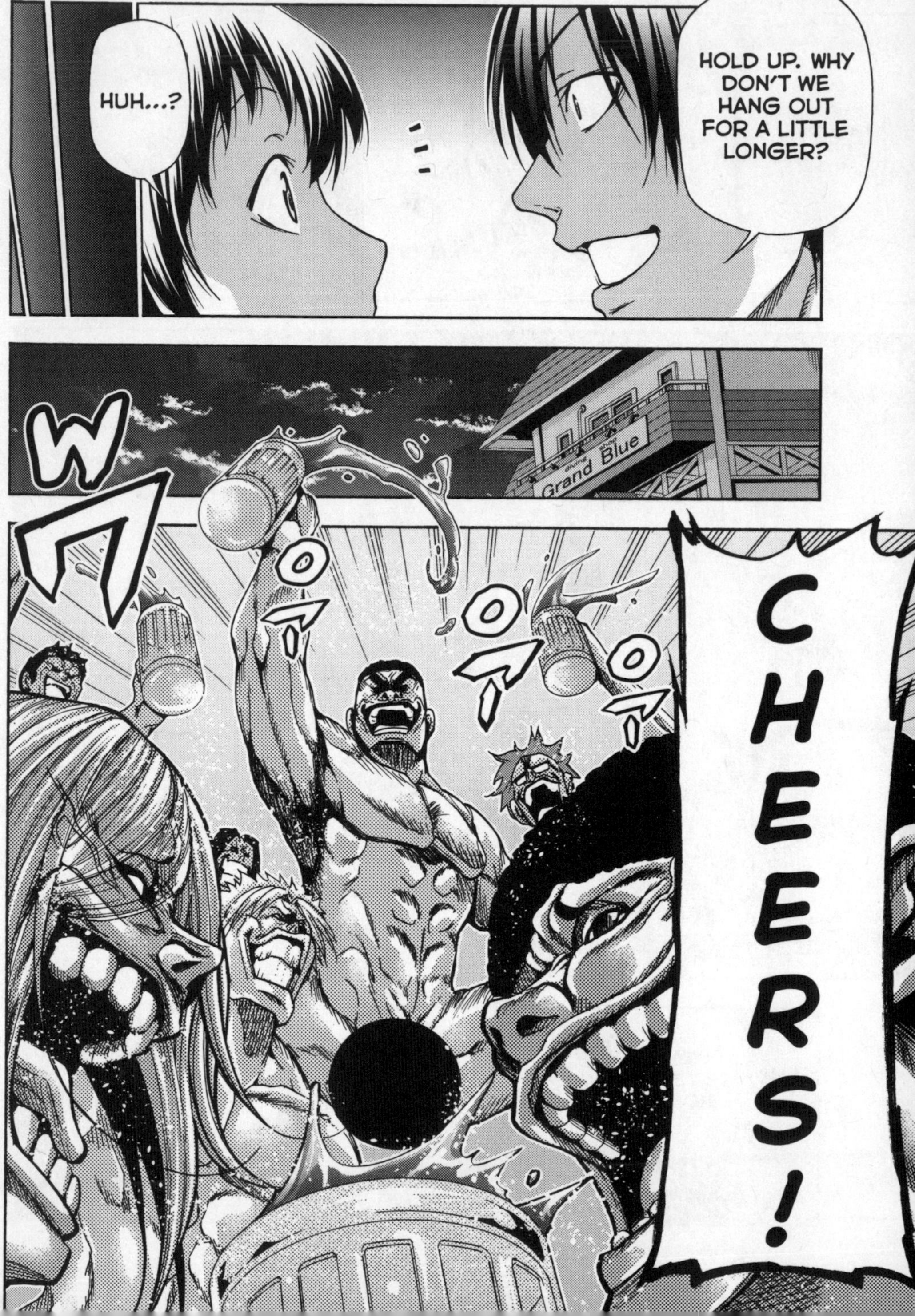
HOLD UP. WHY DON'T WE HANG OUT FOR A LITTLE LONGER?
HUH...?
Grand Blue
WOOO
CHERS!

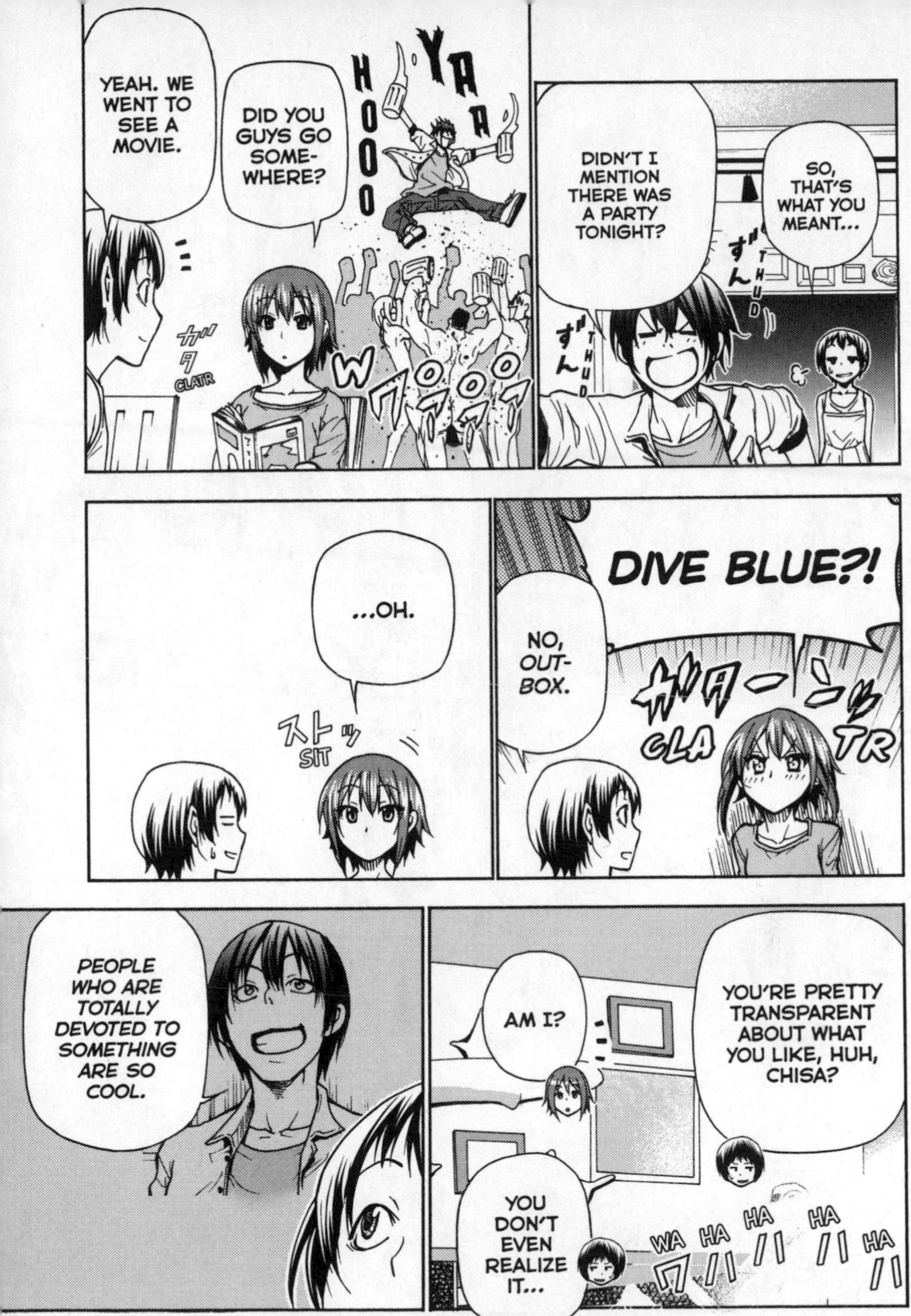
DIDN'T I MENTION THERE WAS A PARTY TONIGHT?
SO, THAT'S WHAT YOU MEANT...
ずん THUD
ずん THUD
HOOO
YAA
DID YOU GUYS GO SOME-WHERE?
YEAH. WE WENT TO SEE A MOVIE.
W
カタ CLATR
DIVE BLUE?!
NO, OUT-BOX.
ガタ-ン CLA TR
...OH.
ストッ SIT
YOU'RE PRETTY TRANSPARENT ABOUT WHAT YOU LIKE, HUH, CHISA?
AM I?
YOU DON'T EVEN REALIZE IT...
WA HA HA HA HA
PEOPLE WHO ARE TOTALLY DEVOTED TO SOMETHING ARE SO COOL.

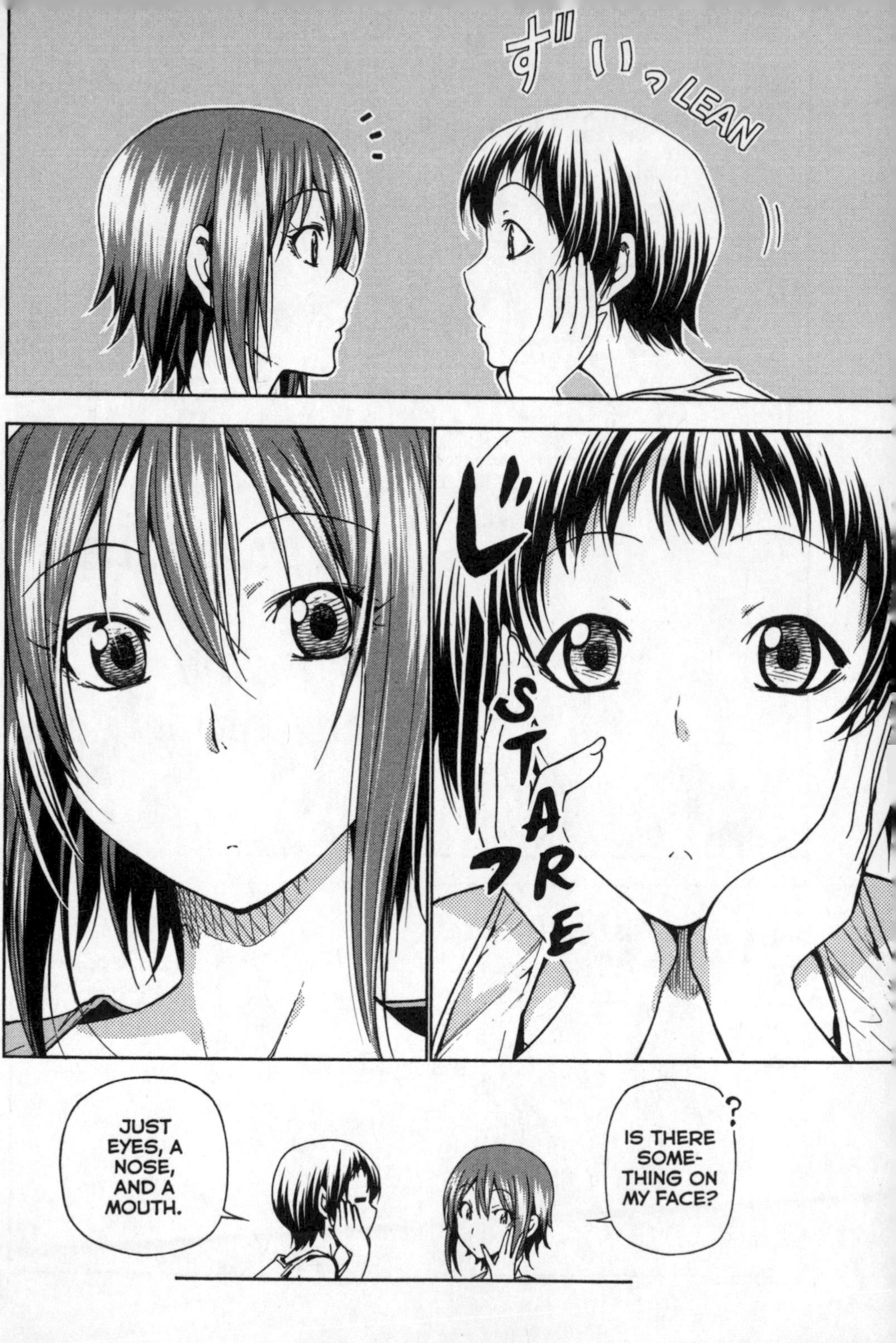
ずいっ
LEAN
じーっ
STARE
?
IS THERE SOME-THING ON MY FACE?
JUST EYES, A NOSE, AND A MOUTH.

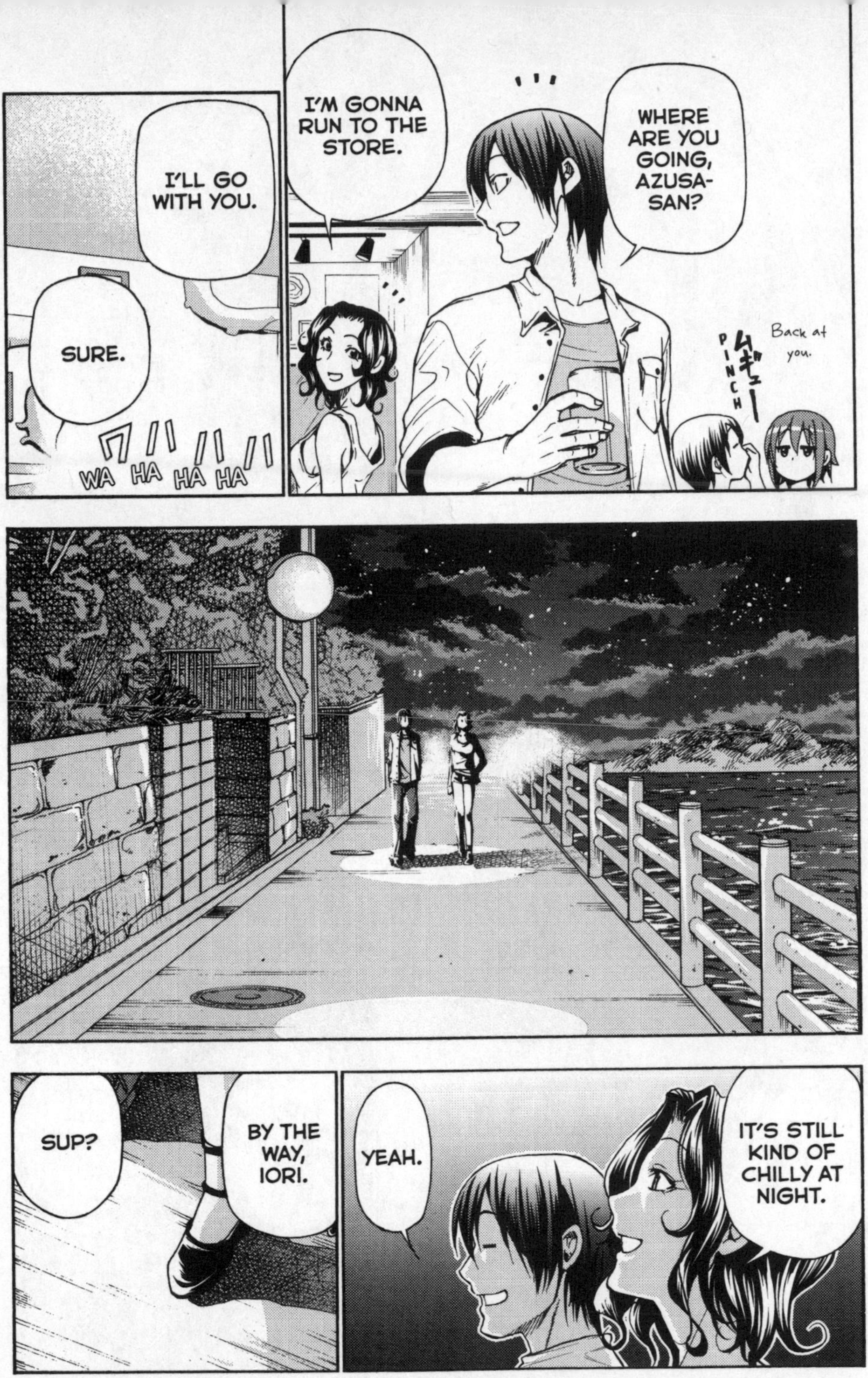
WHERE ARE YOU GOING, AZUSA-SAN?
I'M GONNA RUN TO THE STORE.
ムギュー
PINCH
Back at you.
I'LL GO WITH YOU.
SURE.
ワハハハ
WA HA HA HA
IT'S STILL KIND OF CHILLY AT NIGHT.
YEAH.
BY THE WAY, IORI.
SUP?

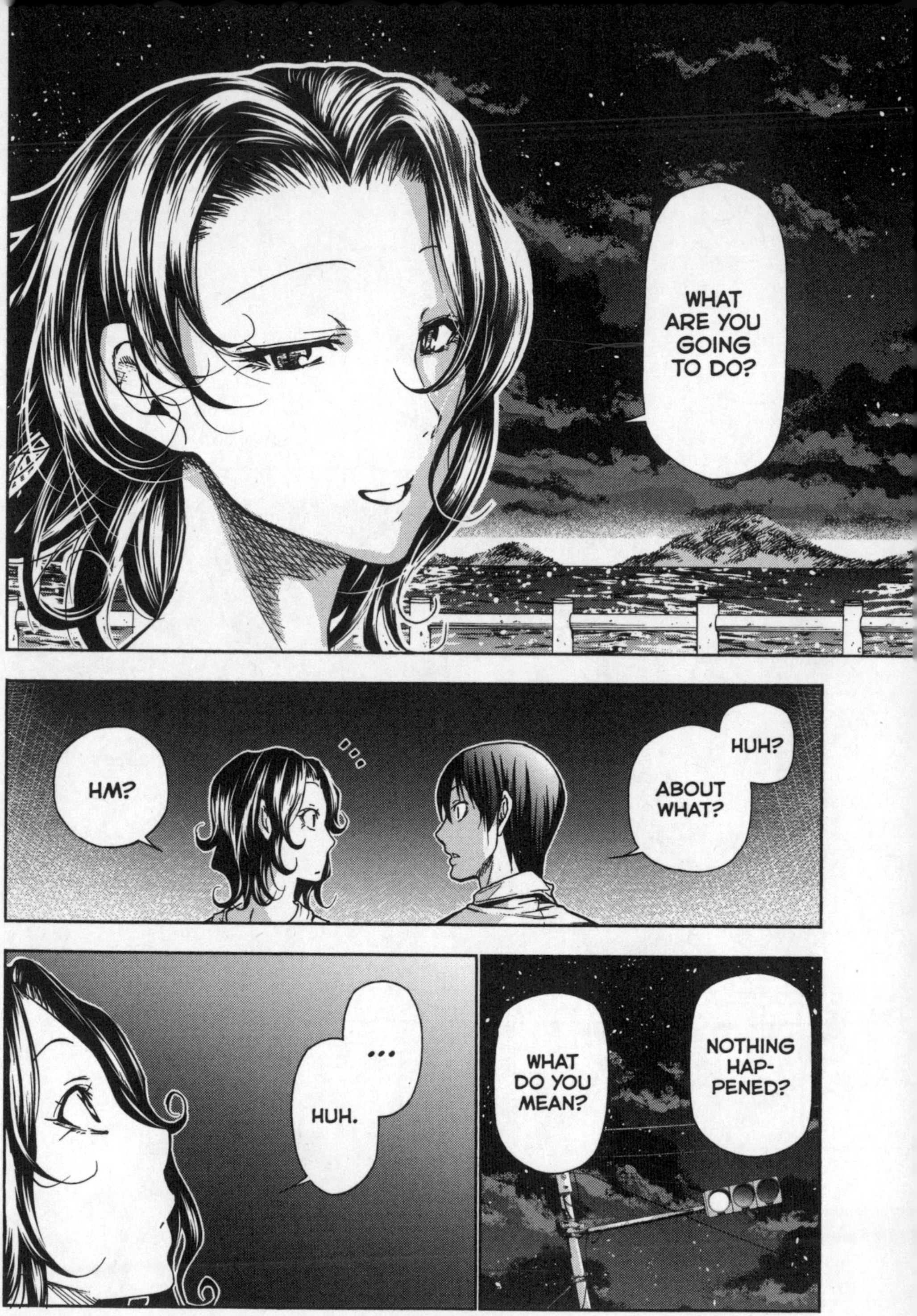
WHAT ARE YOU GOING TO DO?
HUH? ABOUT WHAT?
HM?
NOTHING HAP-PENED?
WHAT DO YOU MEAN?
... HUH.

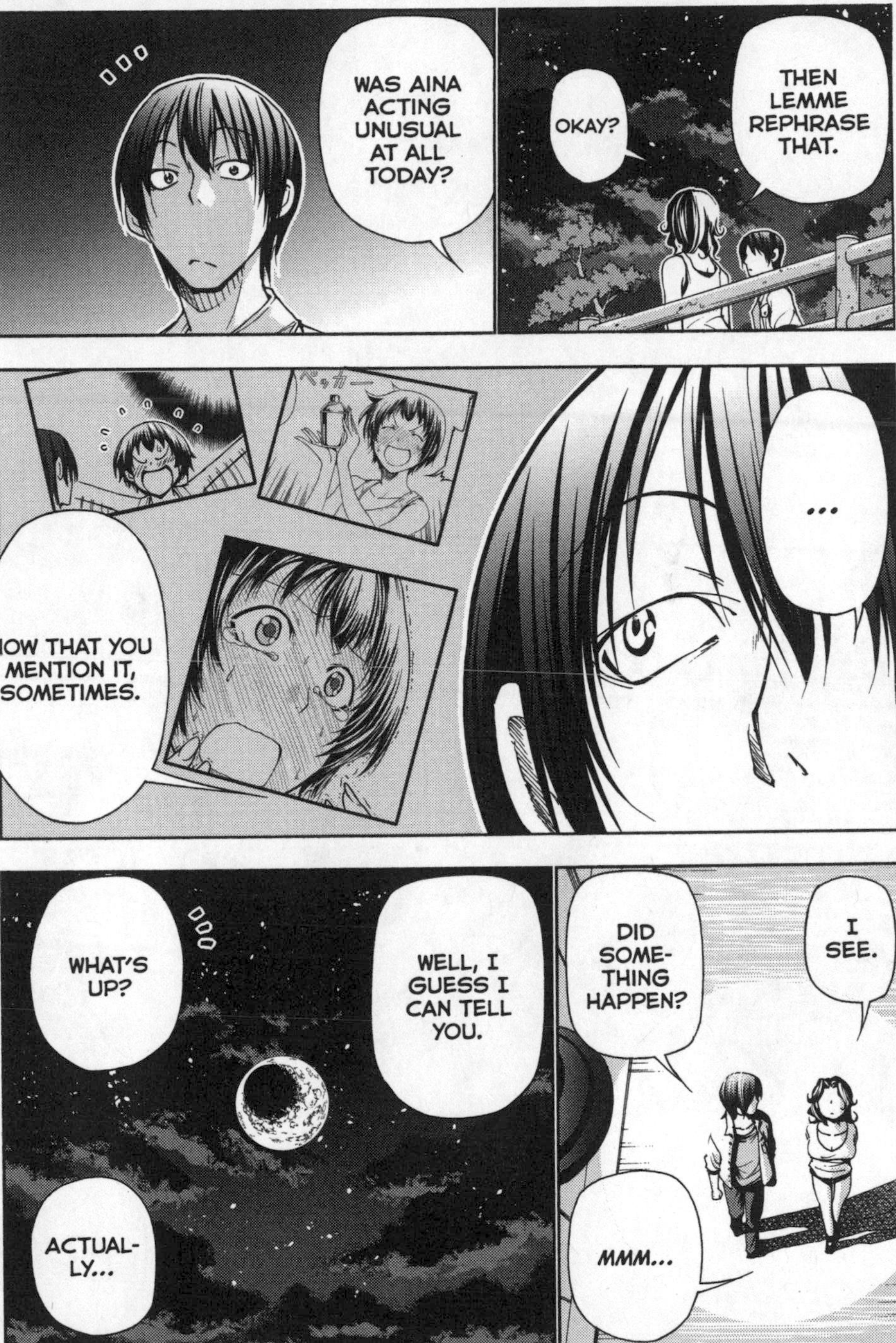
THEN LEMME REPHRASE THAT.
OKAY?
WAS AINA ACTING UNUSUAL AT ALL TODAY?
...
NOW THAT YOU MENTION IT, SOMETIMES.
I SEE.
DID SOME-THING HAPPEN?
MMM...
WELL, I GUESS I CAN TELL YOU.
WHAT'S UP?
ACTUAL-LY...

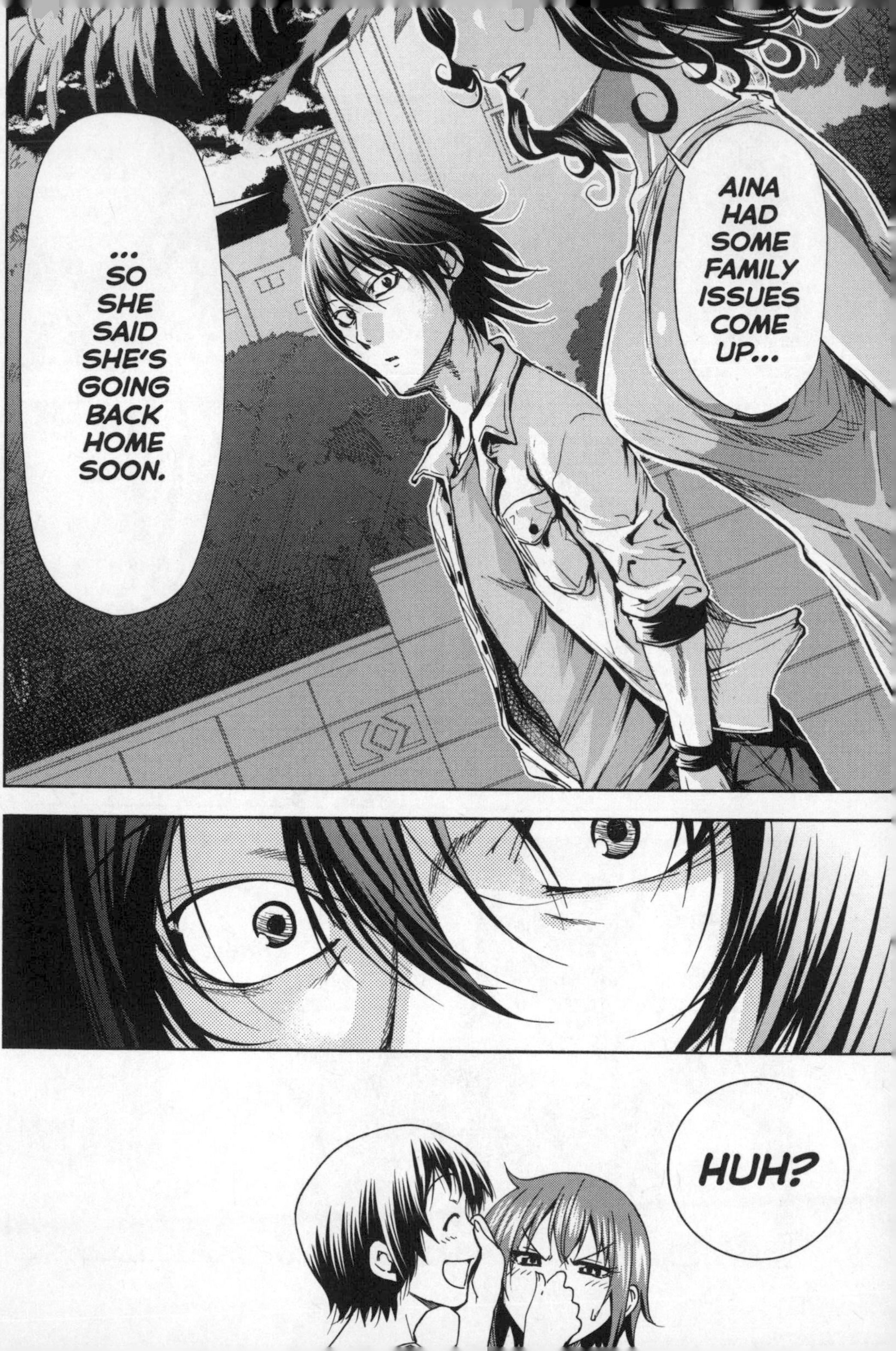
AINA HAD SOME FAMILY ISSUES COME UP...
... SO SHE SAID SHE'S GOING BACK HOME SOON.
HUH?

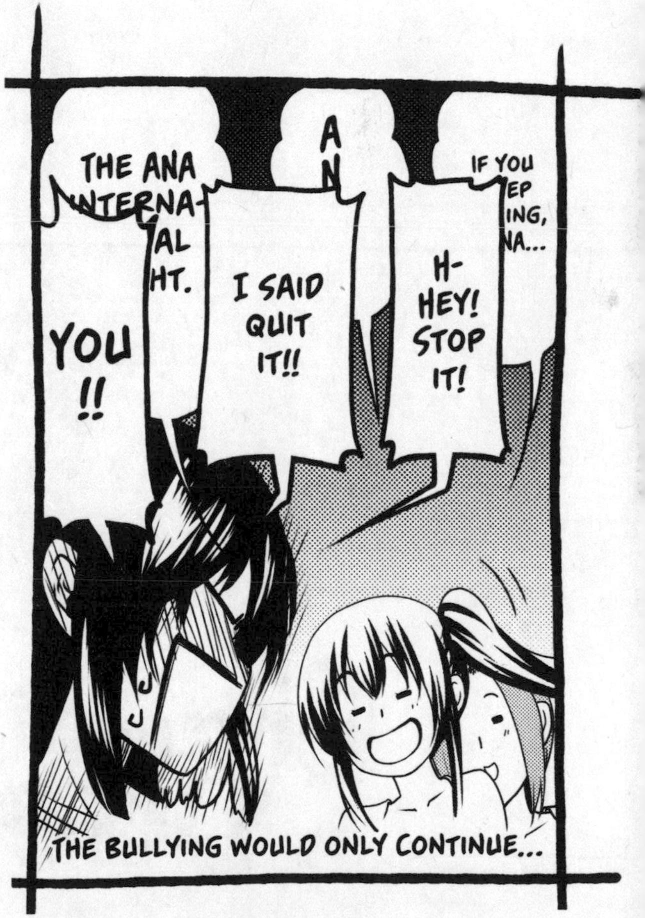
IF YOU
H-HEY! STOP IT!
I SAID QUIT IT!!
THE ANA
YOU!!
THE BULLYING WOULD ONLY CONTINUE...

Grand Blue Dreaming

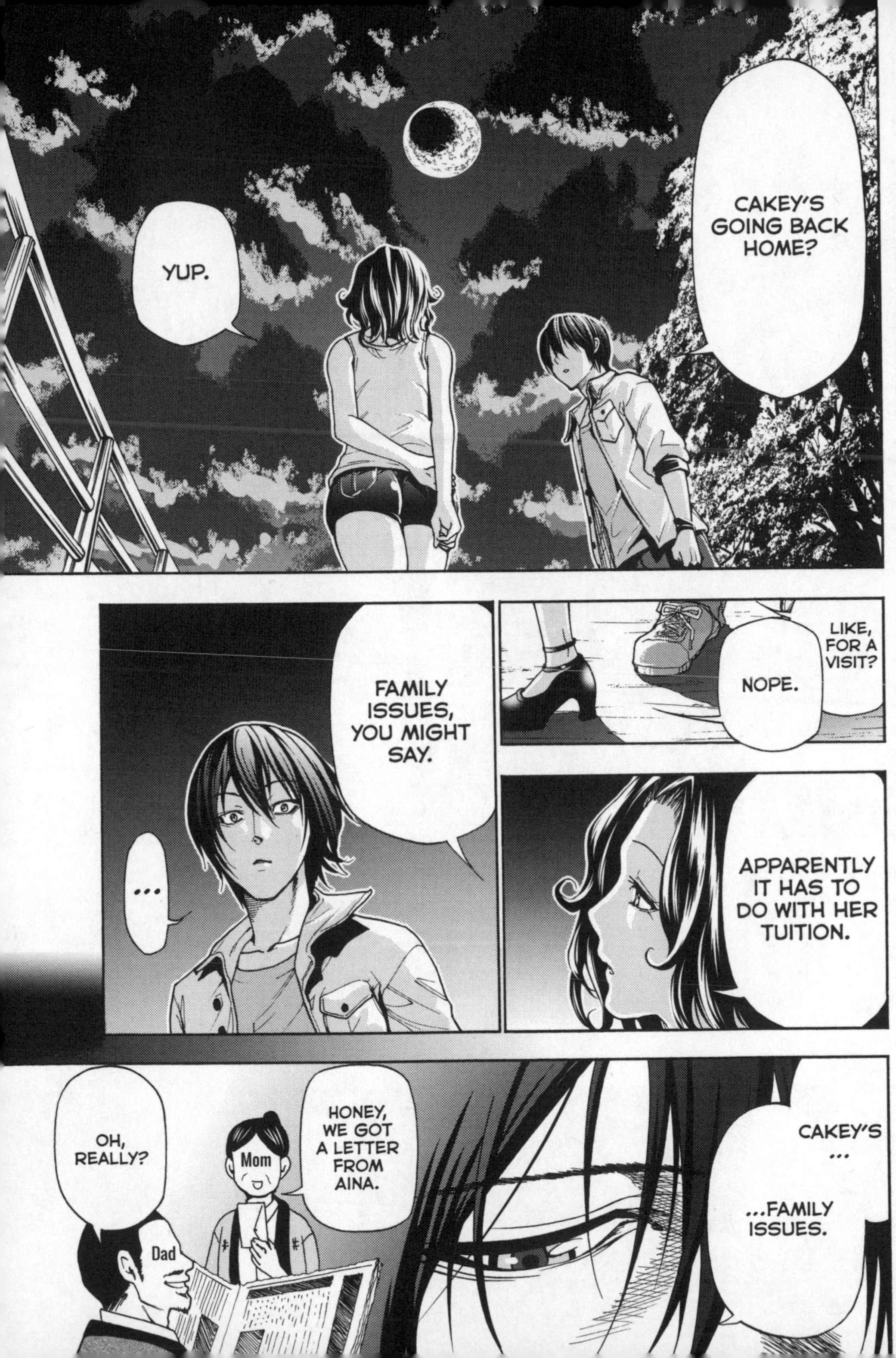
CAKEY'S GOING BACK HOME?
YUP.
LIKE, FOR A VISIT?
NOPE.
APPARENTLY IT HAS TO DO WITH HER TUITION.
FAMILY ISSUES, YOU MIGHT SAY.
...
CAKEY'S ...
...FAMILY ISSUES.
HONEY, WE GOT A LETTER FROM AINA.
Mom
OH, REALLY?
Dad

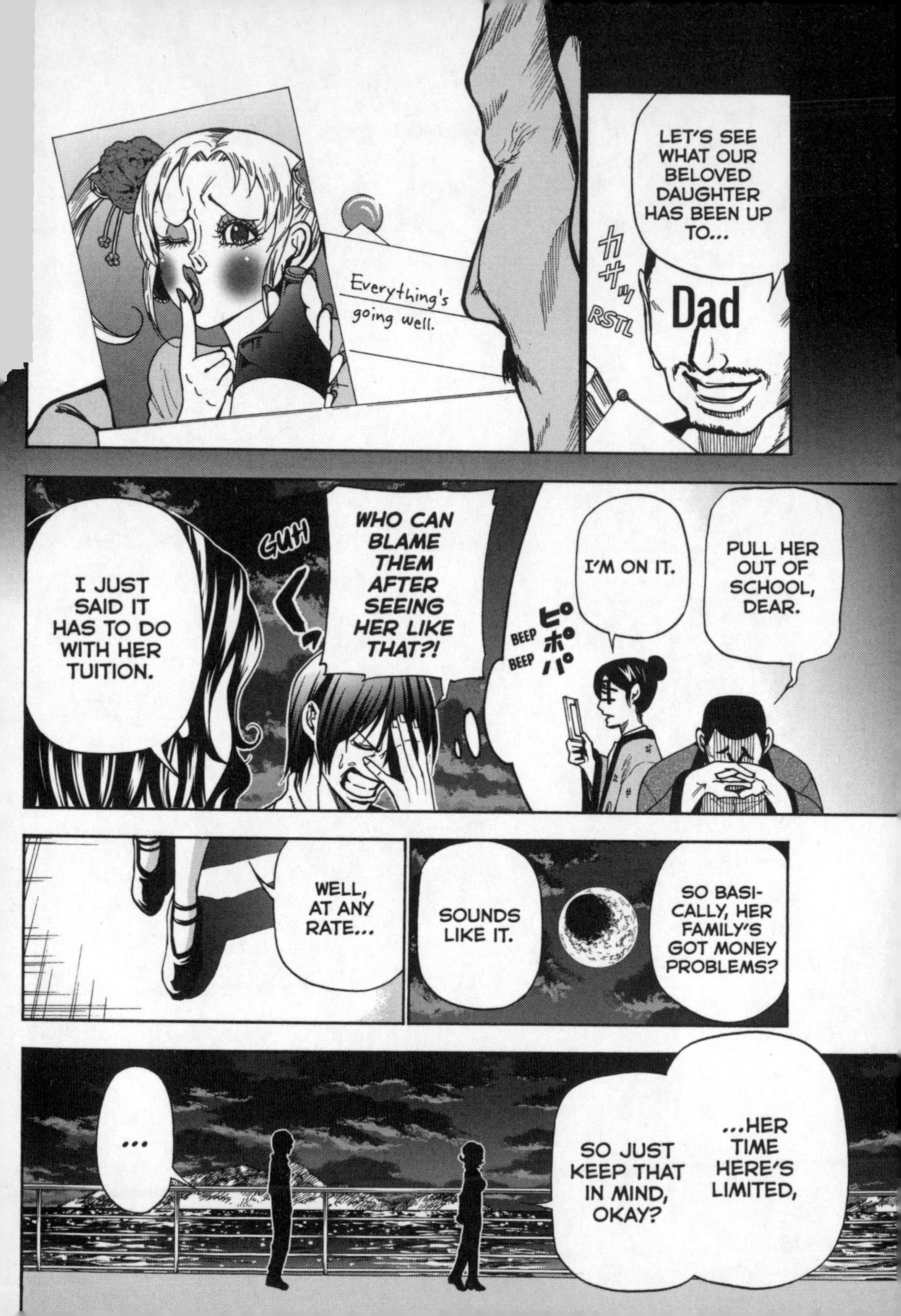
LET'S SEE WHAT OUR BELOVED DAUGHTER HAS BEEN UP TO...
カサッ
RSTL
Dad
Everything's going well.
PULL HER OUT OF SCHOOL, DEAR.
I'M ON IT.
ピポパ
BEEP BEEP
WHO CAN BLAME THEM AFTER SEEING HER LIKE THAT?!
GUH
I JUST SAID IT HAS TO DO WITH HER TUITION.
SO BASI-CALLY, HER FAMILY'S GOT MONEY PROBLEMS?
SOUNDS LIKE IT.
WELL, AT ANY RATE...
...HER TIME HERE'S LIMITED,
SO JUST KEEP THAT IN MIND, OKAY?
...

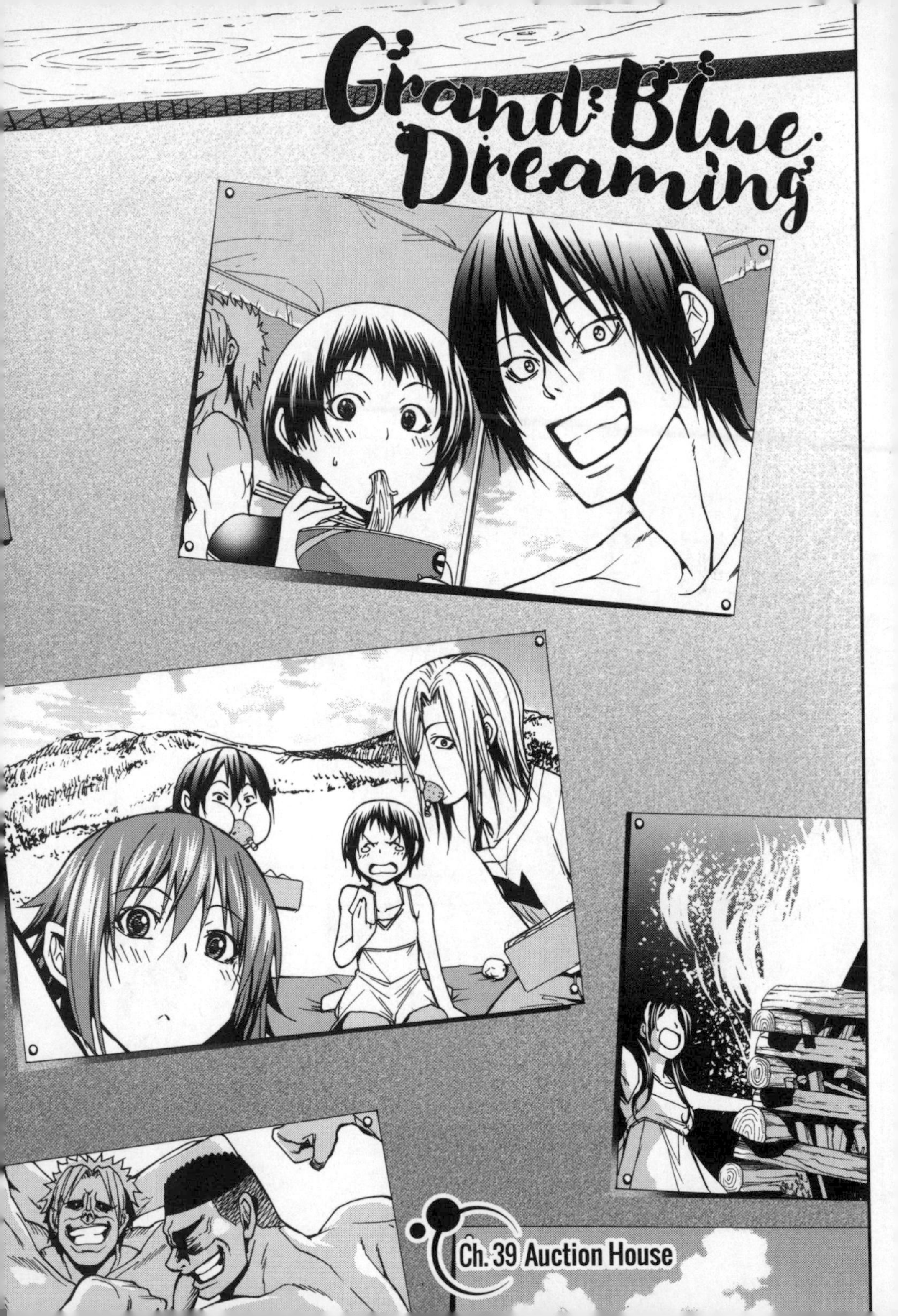
Grand Blue Dreaming
Ch. 39 Auction House

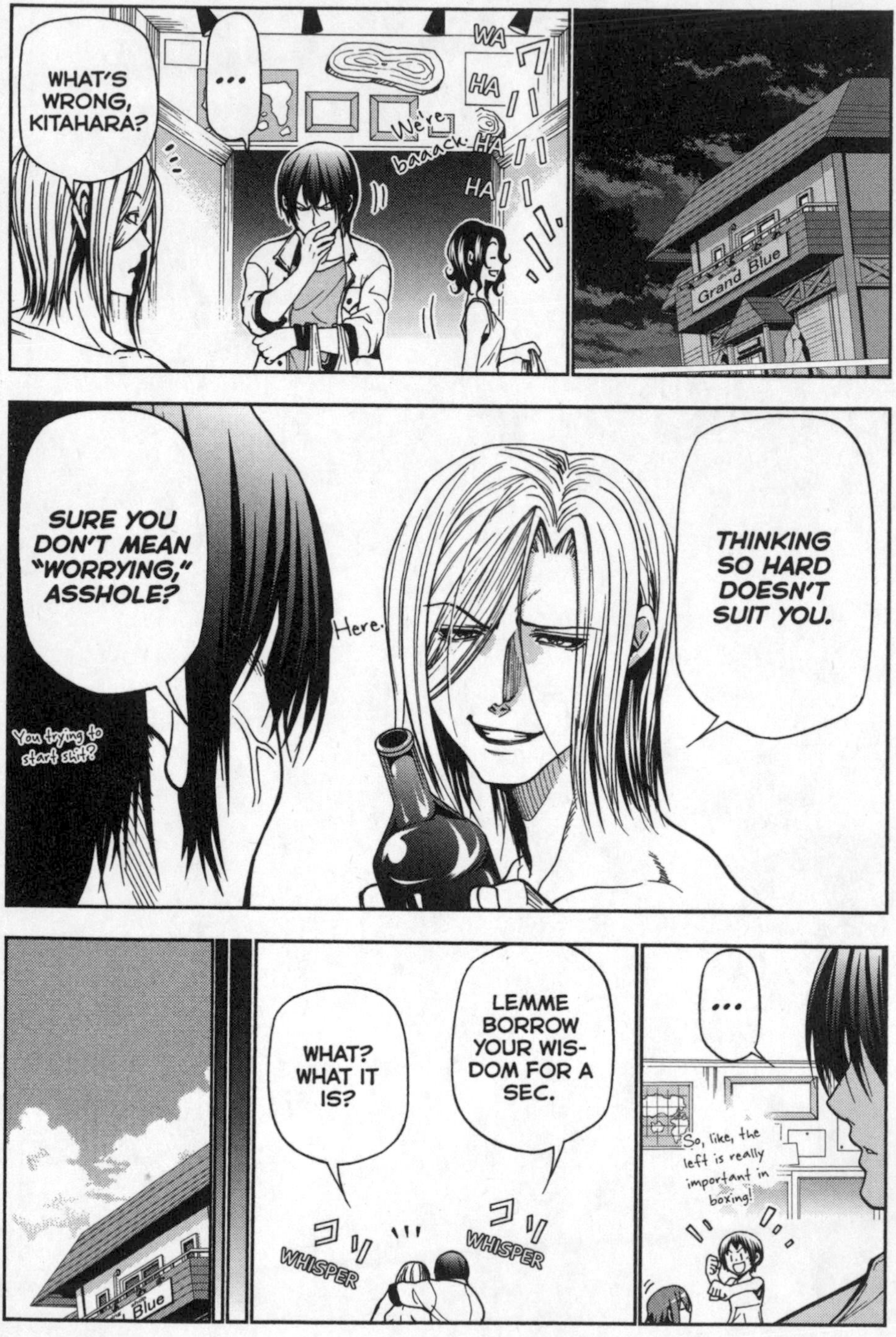
Grand Blue
WA
HA
HA
HA
...
We're baaack.
WHAT'S WRONG, KITAHARA?
THINKING SO HARD DOESN'T SUIT YOU.
Here.
SURE YOU DON'T MEAN "WORRYING," ASSHOLE?
You trying to start shit?
...
So, like, the left is really important in boxing!
LEMME BORROW YOUR WISDOM FOR A SEC.
WHISPER
WHAT? WHAT IT IS?
WHISPER
Blue

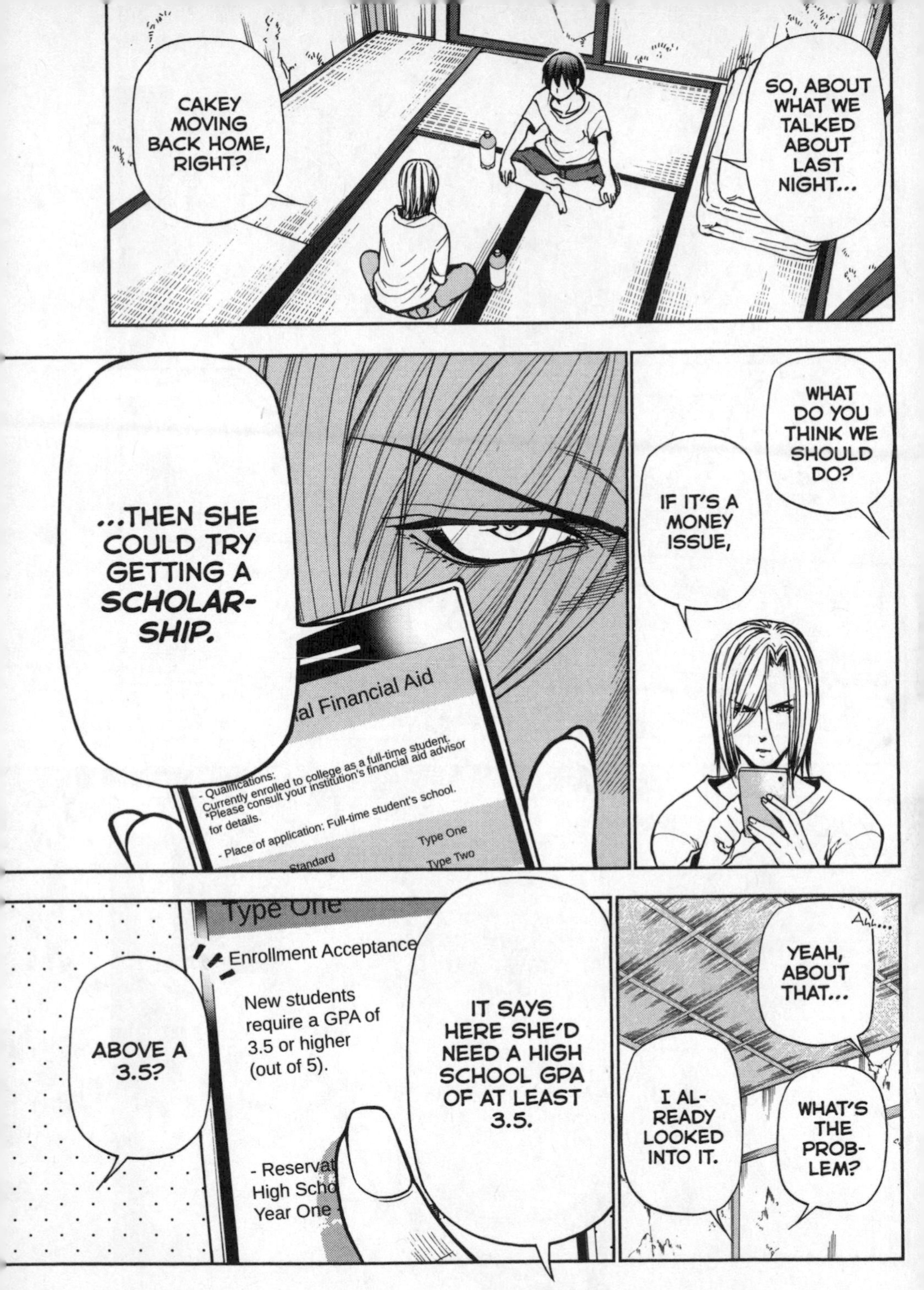
SO, ABOUT WHAT WE TALKED ABOUT LAST NIGHT...
CAKEY MOVING BACK HOME, RIGHT?
WHAT DO YOU THINK WE SHOULD DO?
IF IT'S A MONEY ISSUE,
...THEN SHE COULD TRY GETTING A *SCHOLARSHIP.*
Financial Aid
- Qualifications:
Currently enrolled to college as a full-time student.
*Please consult your institution's financial aid advisor for details.
- Place of application: Full-time student's school.
Type One
Type Two
Ahh...
YEAH, ABOUT THAT...
WHAT'S THE PROBLEM?
I ALREADY LOOKED INTO IT.
IT SAYS HERE SHE'D NEED A HIGH SCHOOL GPA OF AT LEAST 3.5.
Type One
Enrollment Acceptance
New students require a GPA of 3.5 or higher (out of 5).
ABOVE A 3.5?

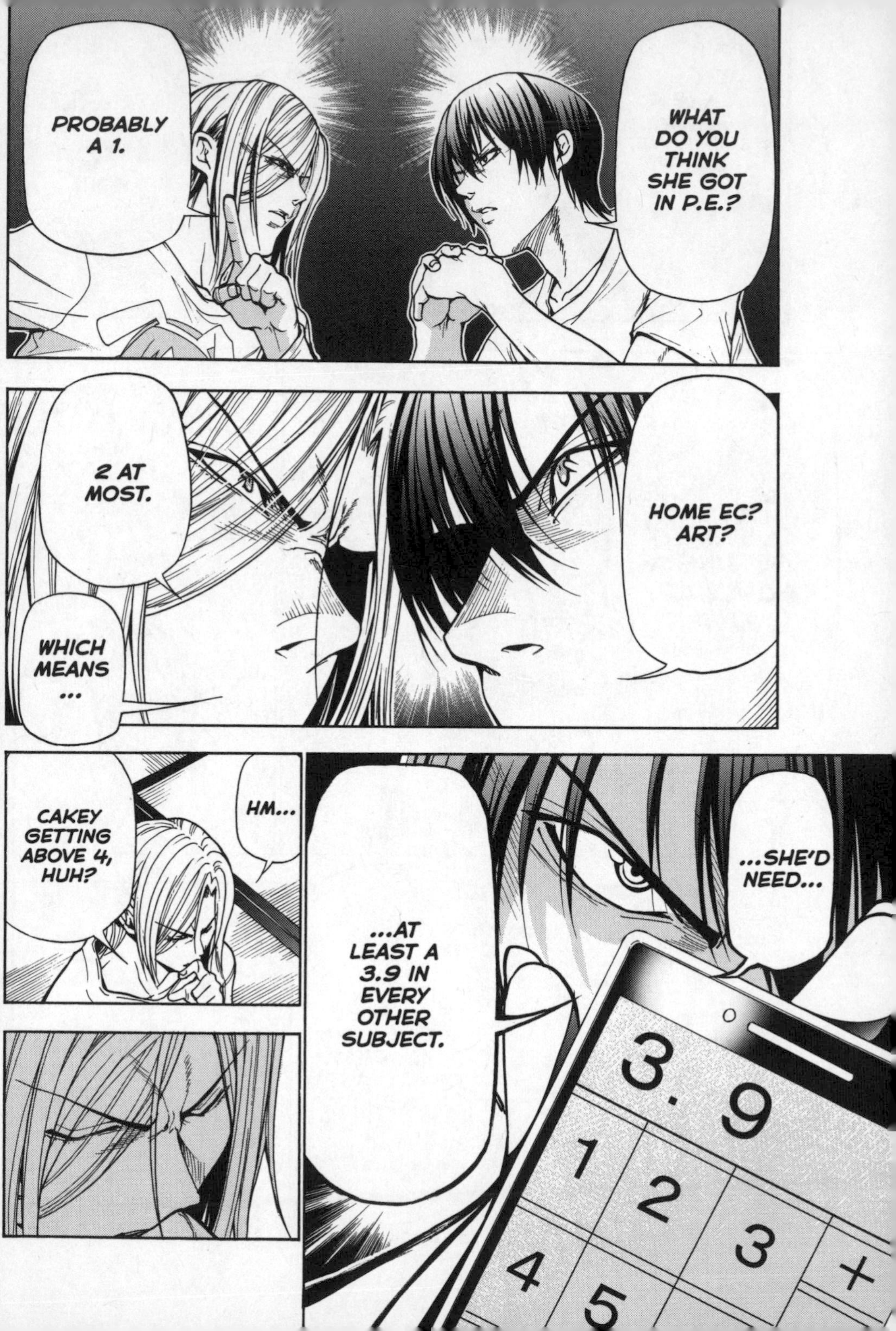
WHAT DO YOU THINK SHE GOT IN P.E.?
PROBABLY A 1.
HOME EC? ART?
2 AT MOST.
WHICH MEANS ...
...SHE'D NEED...
...AT LEAST A 3.9 IN EVERY OTHER SUBJECT.
3.9
HM...
CAKEY GETTING ABOVE 4, HUH?

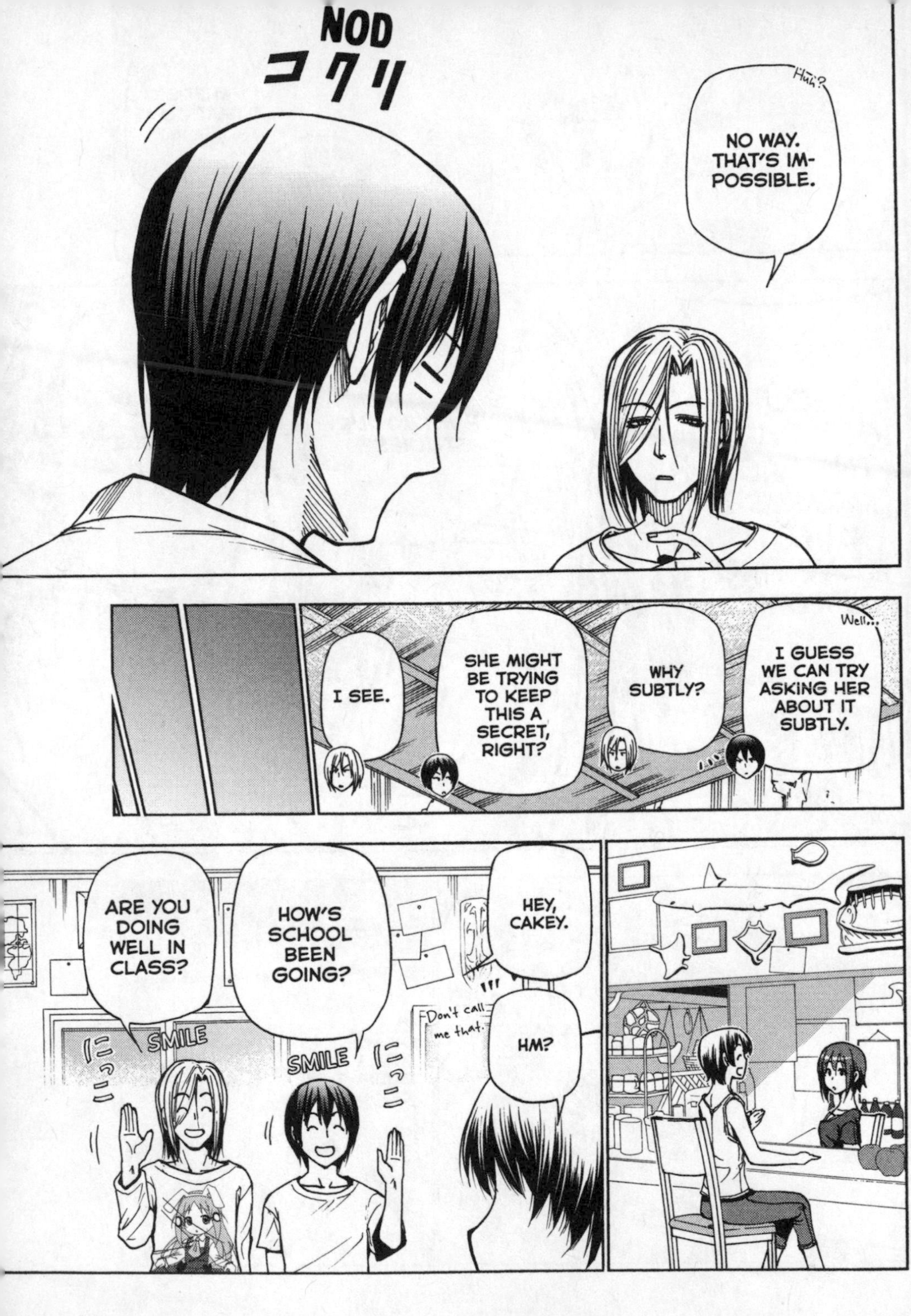
Huh?
NO WAY. THAT'S IM-POSSIBLE.
NOD
コクリ
Well...
I GUESS WE CAN TRY ASKING HER ABOUT IT SUBTLY.
WHY SUBTLY?
SHE MIGHT BE TRYING TO KEEP THIS A SECRET, RIGHT?
I SEE.
HEY, CAKEY.
HM?
Don't call me that.
HOW'S SCHOOL BEEN GOING?
SMILE
にっこ
ARE YOU DOING WELL IN CLASS?
SMILE
にっこ

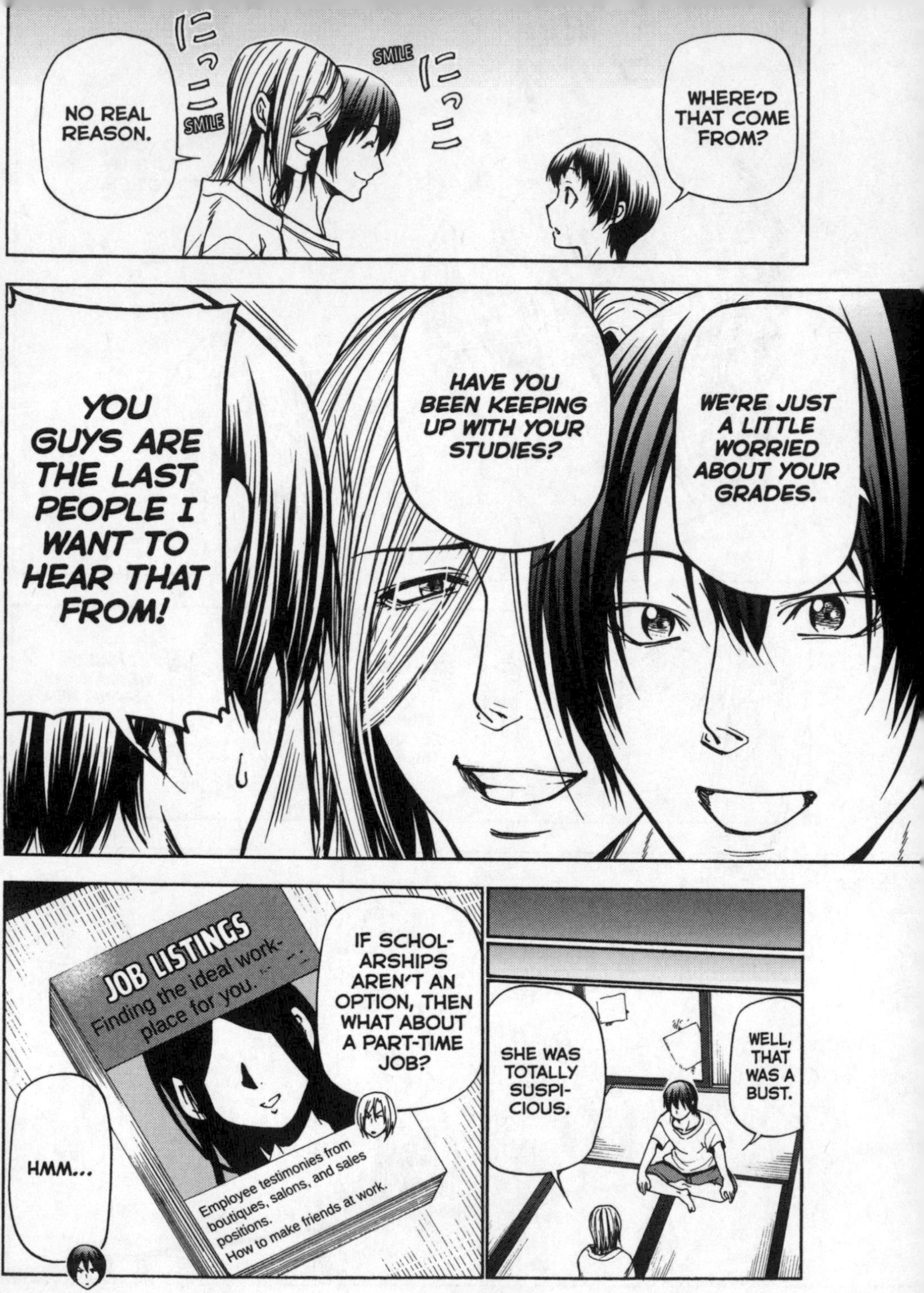
WHERE'D THAT COME FROM?
SMILE
SMILE
NO REAL REASON.
WE'RE JUST A LITTLE WORRIED ABOUT YOUR GRADES.
HAVE YOU BEEN KEEPING UP WITH YOUR STUDIES?
YOU GUYS ARE THE LAST PEOPLE I WANT TO HEAR THAT FROM!
WELL, THAT WAS A BUST.
SHE WAS TOTALLY SUSPICIOUS.
IF SCHOLARSHIPS AREN'T AN OPTION, THEN WHAT ABOUT A PART-TIME JOB?
JOB LISTINGS
Finding the ideal workplace for you.
Employee testimonies from boutiques, salons, and sales positions.
How to make friends at work.
HMM...

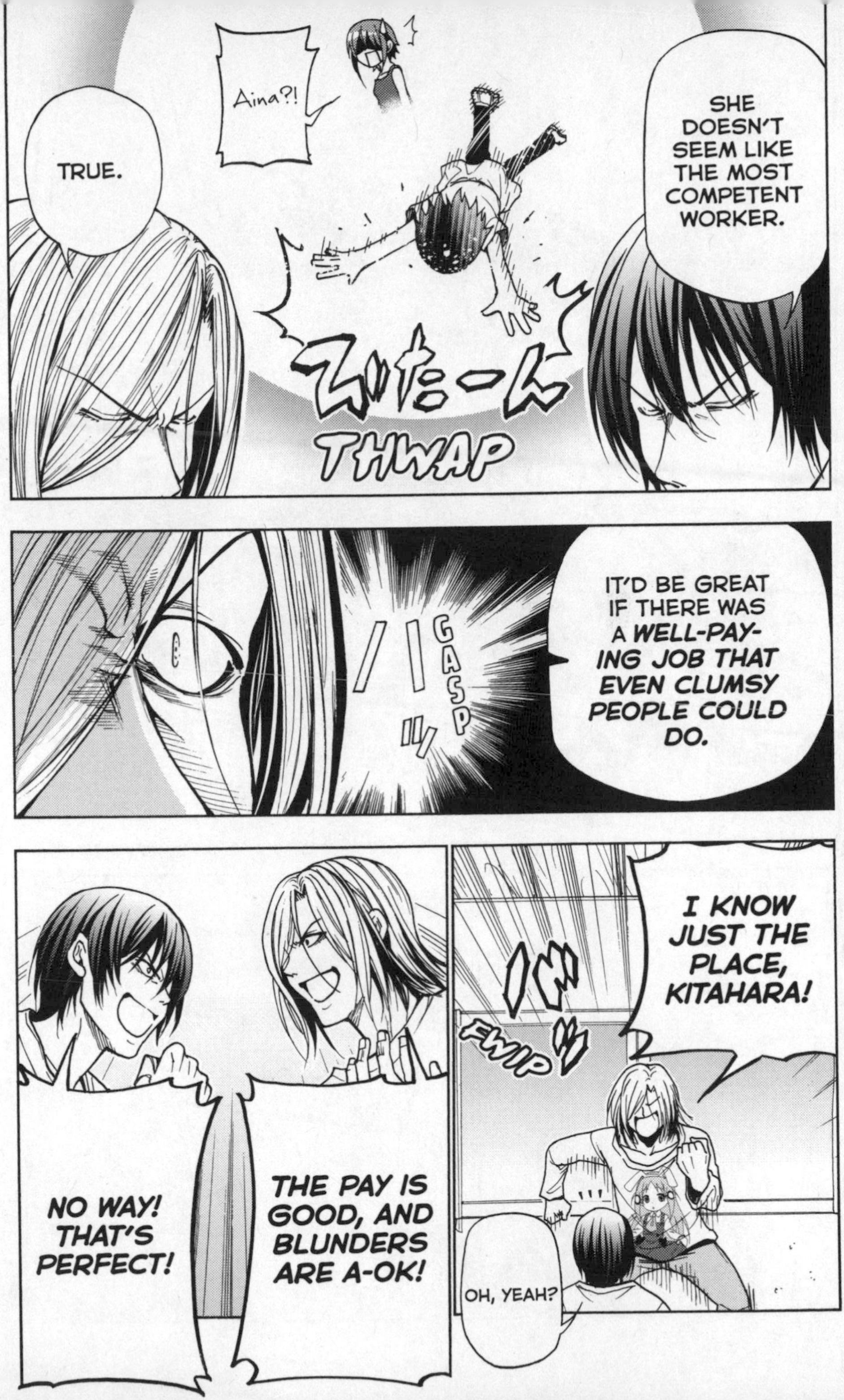
SHE DOESN'T SEEM LIKE THE MOST COMPETENT WORKER.
Aina?!
TRUE.
THWAP
IT'D BE GREAT IF THERE WAS A WELL-PAYING JOB THAT EVEN CLUMSY PEOPLE COULD DO.
GASP
I KNOW JUST THE PLACE, KITAHARA!
FWIP
OH, YEAH?
THE PAY IS GOOD, AND BLUNDERS ARE A-OK!
NO WAY! THAT'S PERFECT!

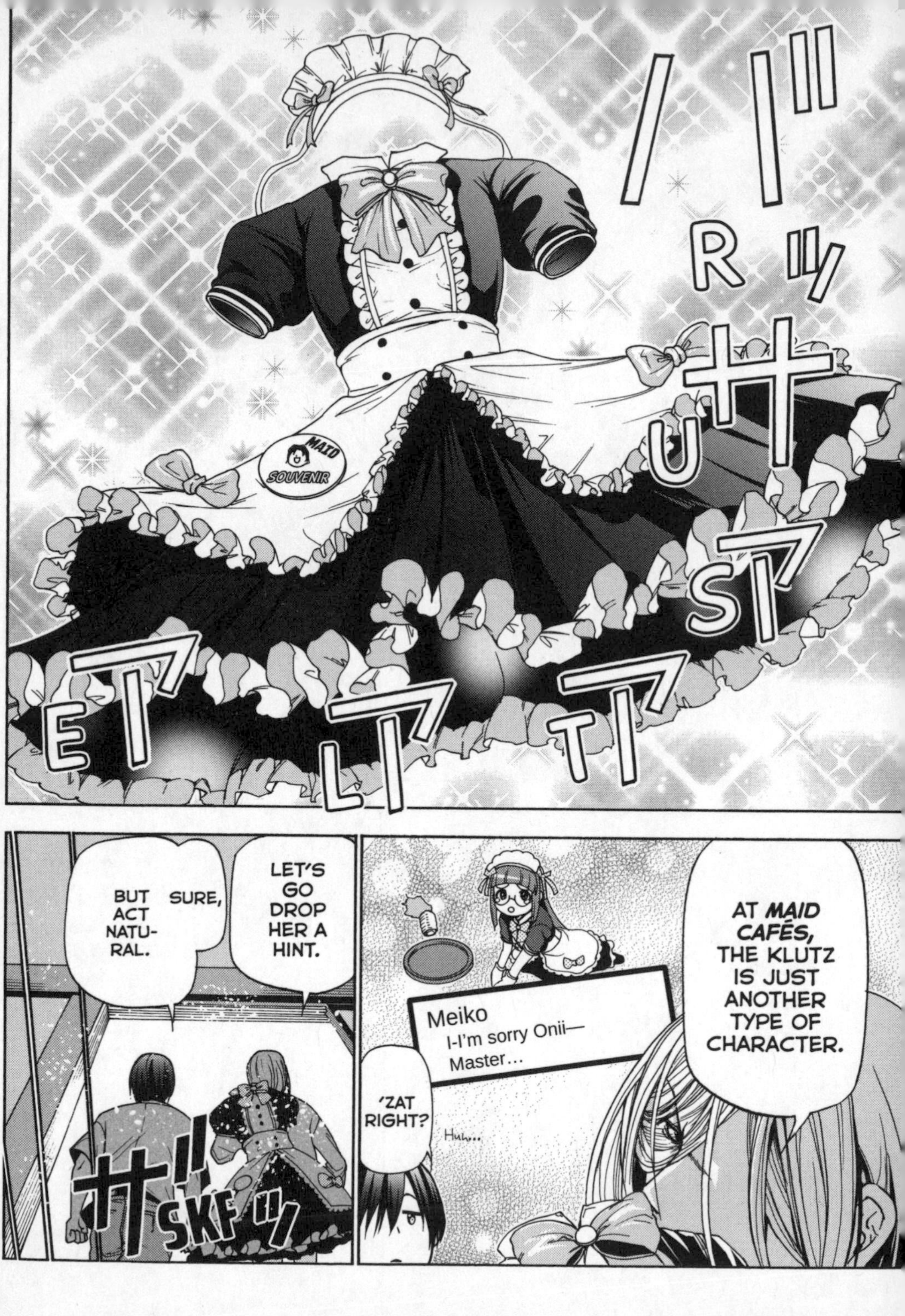
RUSTLE
MAID
SOUVENIR
AT MAID CAFÉS, THE KLUTZ IS JUST ANOTHER TYPE OF CHARACTER.
Meiko
I-I'm sorry Onii—Master…
'ZAT RIGHT?
Huh...
LET'S GO DROP HER A HINT.
SURE, BUT ACT NATURAL.
SKF

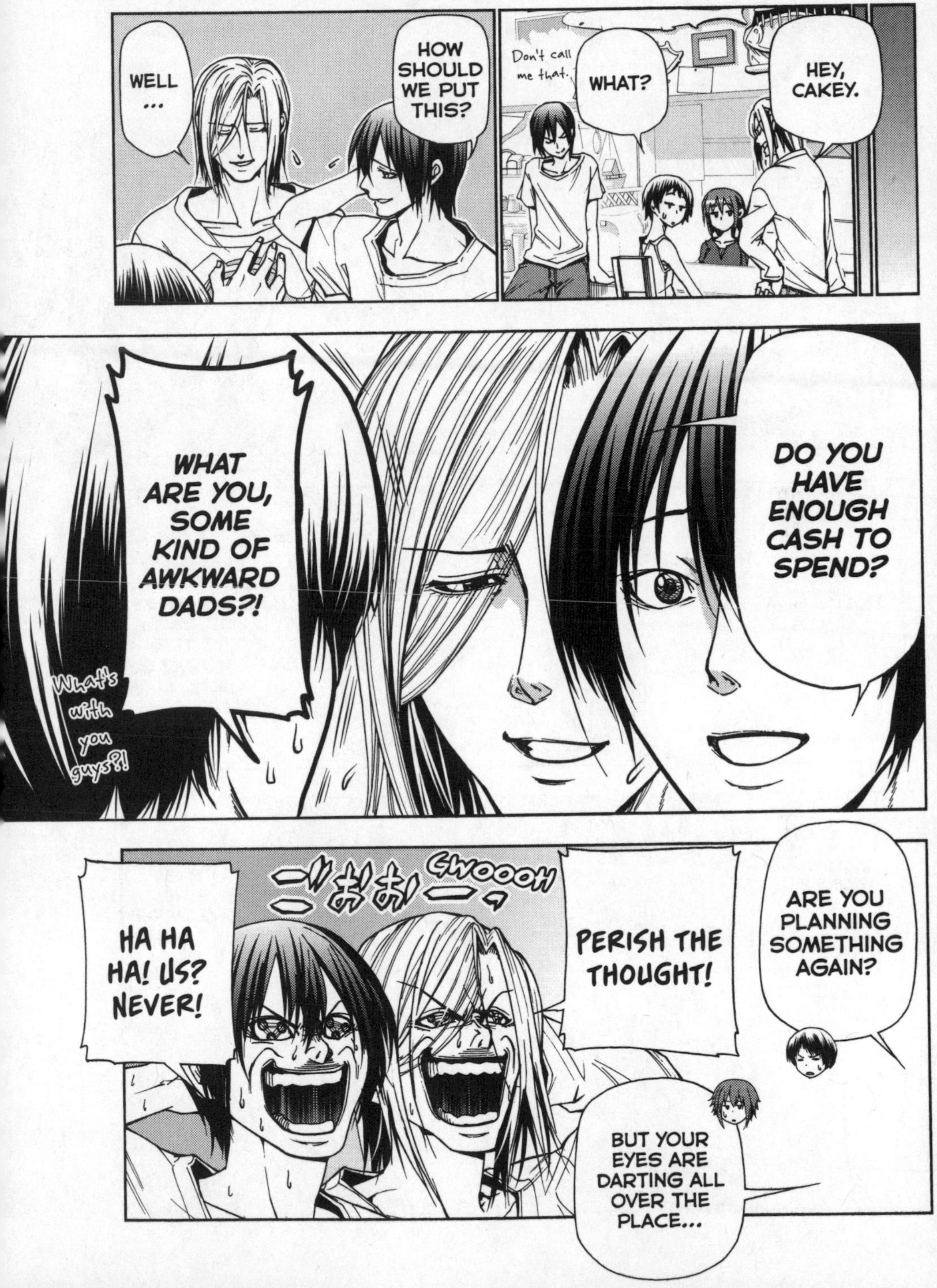
HEY, CAKEY.
WHAT?
Don't call me that.
HOW SHOULD WE PUT THIS?
WELL ...
DO YOU HAVE ENOUGH CASH TO SPEND?
WHAT ARE YOU, SOME KIND OF AWKWARD DADS?!
What's with you guys?!
ARE YOU PLANNING SOMETHING AGAIN?
PERISH THE THOUGHT!
GWOOOOH
HA HA HA! US? NEVER!
BUT YOUR EYES ARE DARTING ALL OVER THE PLACE...

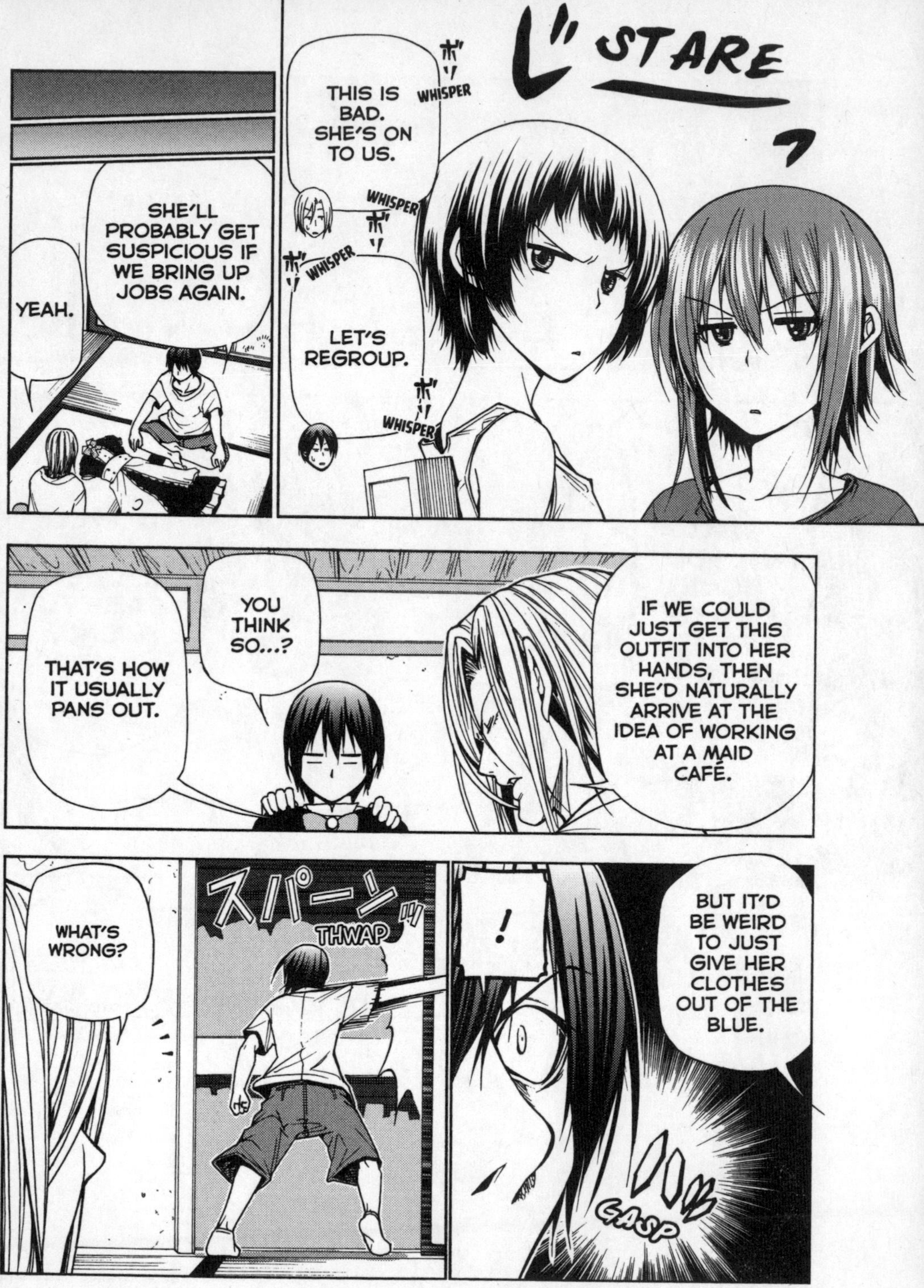
ジ
STARE
THIS IS BAD. SHE'S ON TO US.
WHISPER
WHISPER
WHISPER
LET'S REGROUP.
WHISPER
SHE'LL PROBABLY GET SUSPICIOUS IF WE BRING UP JOBS AGAIN.
YEAH.
IF WE COULD JUST GET THIS OUTFIT INTO HER HANDS, THEN SHE'D NATURALLY ARRIVE AT THE IDEA OF WORKING AT A MAID CAFÉ.
YOU THINK SO...?
THAT'S HOW IT USUALLY PANS OUT.
BUT IT'D BE WEIRD TO JUST GIVE HER CLOTHES OUT OF THE BLUE.
!
GASP
スパーン
THWAP
WHAT'S WRONG?

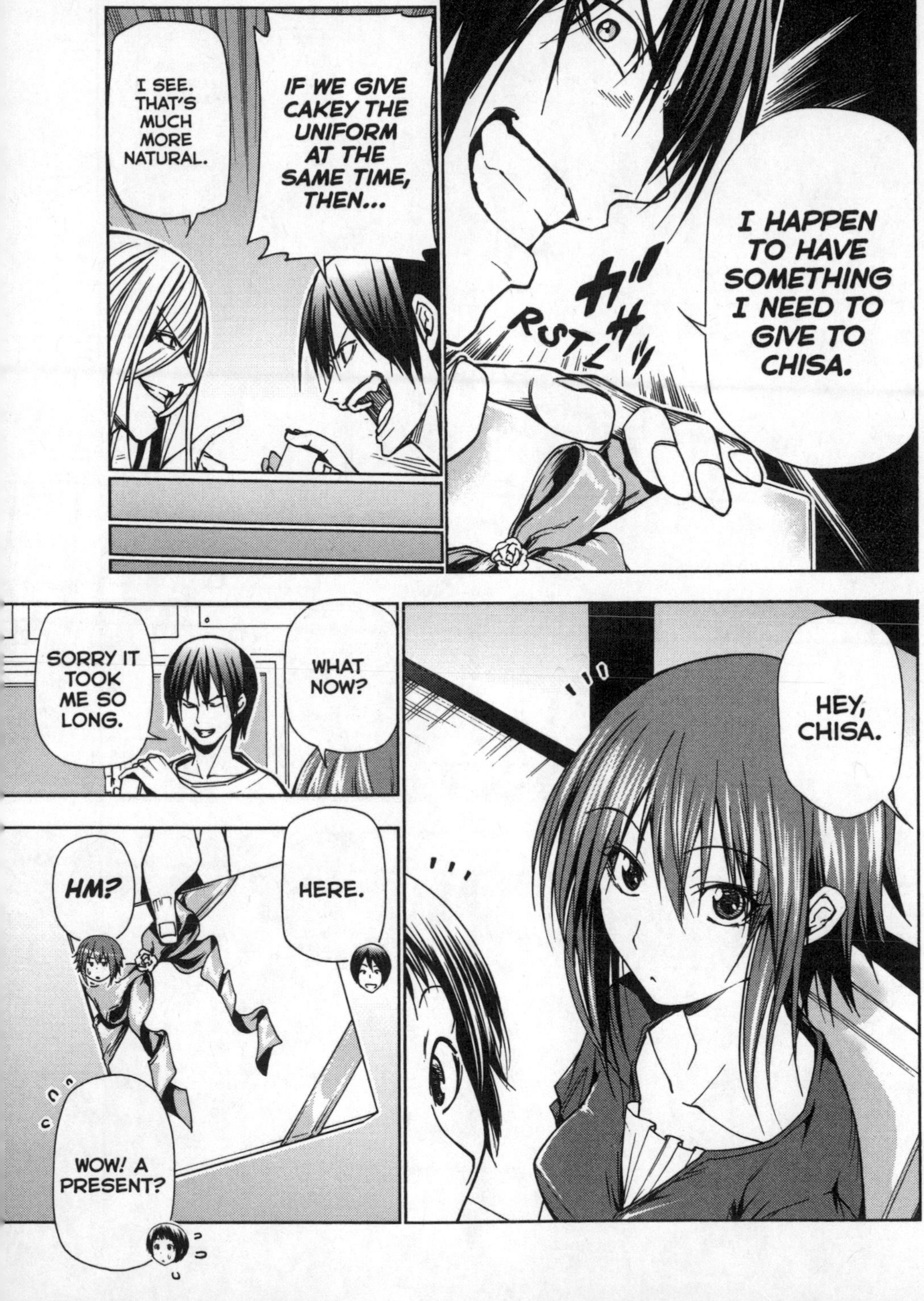
I HAPPEN TO HAVE SOMETHING I NEED TO GIVE TO CHISA.
RSTL
IF WE GIVE CAKEY THE UNIFORM AT THE SAME TIME, THEN...
I SEE. THAT'S MUCH MORE NATURAL.
HEY, CHISA.
WHAT NOW?
SORRY IT TOOK ME SO LONG.
HERE.
HM?
WOW! A PRESENT?

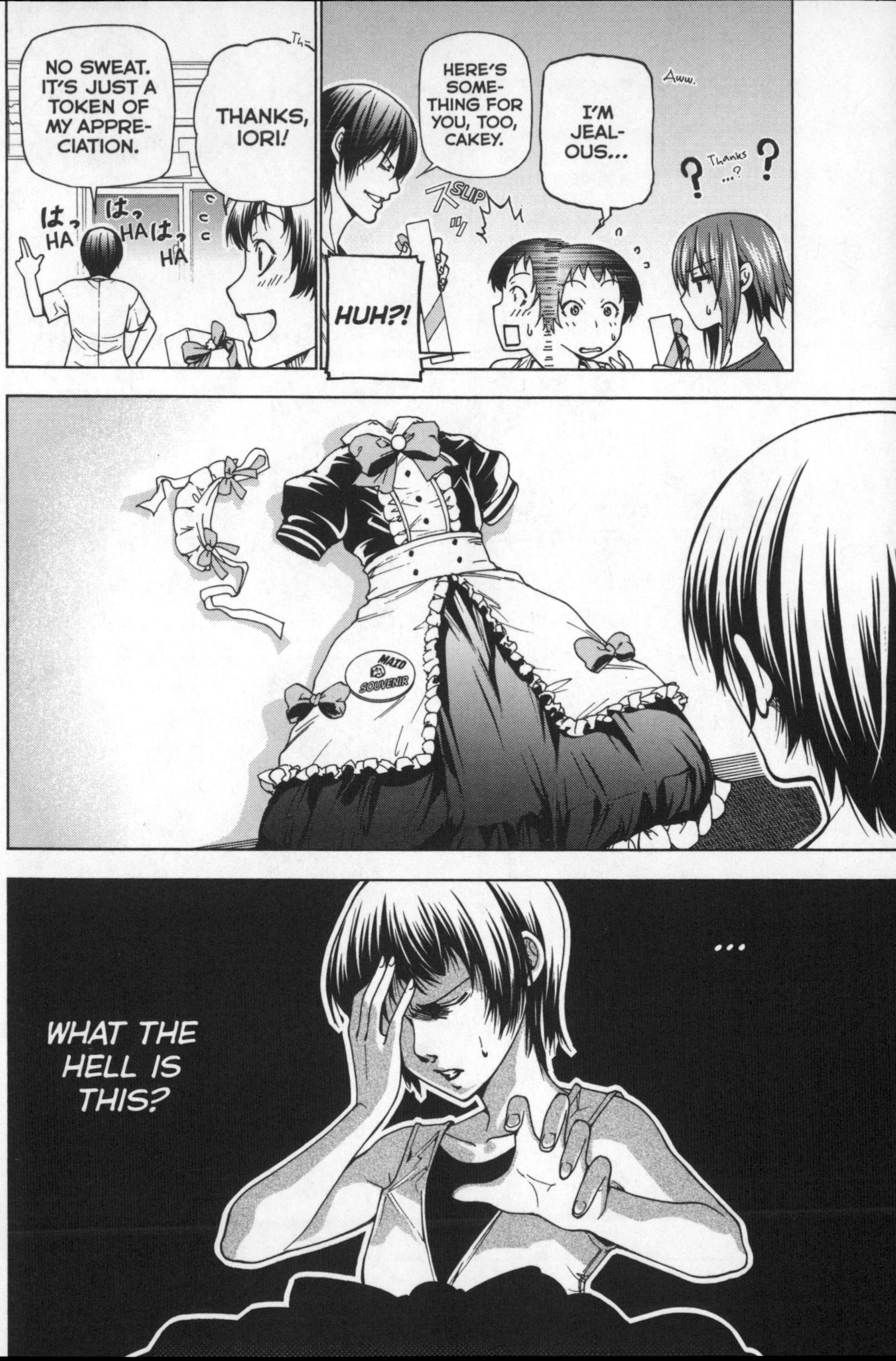
Aww.
I'M JEALOUS...
HERE'S SOMETHING FOR YOU, TOO, CAKEY.
Thanks ...?
SLIP
HUH?!
THANKS, IORI!
NO SWEAT. IT'S JUST A TOKEN OF MY APPRECIATION.
はっ HA はっ HA はっ HA
MAID SOUVENIR
...
WHAT THE HELL IS THIS?

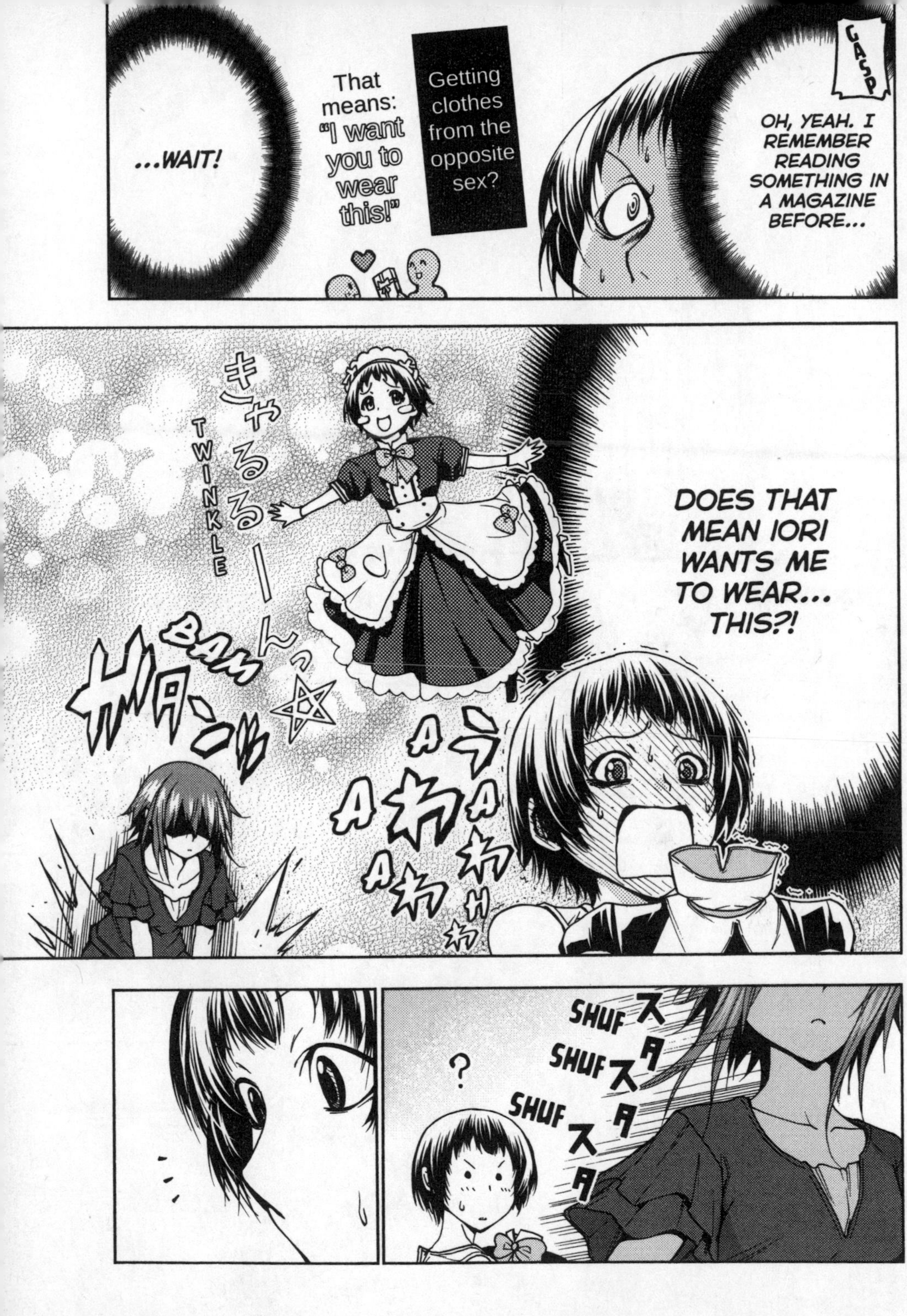
GASP
OH, YEAH. I REMEMBER READING SOMETHING IN A MAGAZINE BEFORE...
Getting clothes from the opposite sex?
That means: "I want you to wear this!"
...WAIT!
DOES THAT MEAN IORI WANTS ME TO WEAR... THIS?!
きゃるーんっ☆
TWINKLE
BAM
ガタンッ
AAAAAH
SHUF スタ
SHUF スタ
SHUF スタ
?
...

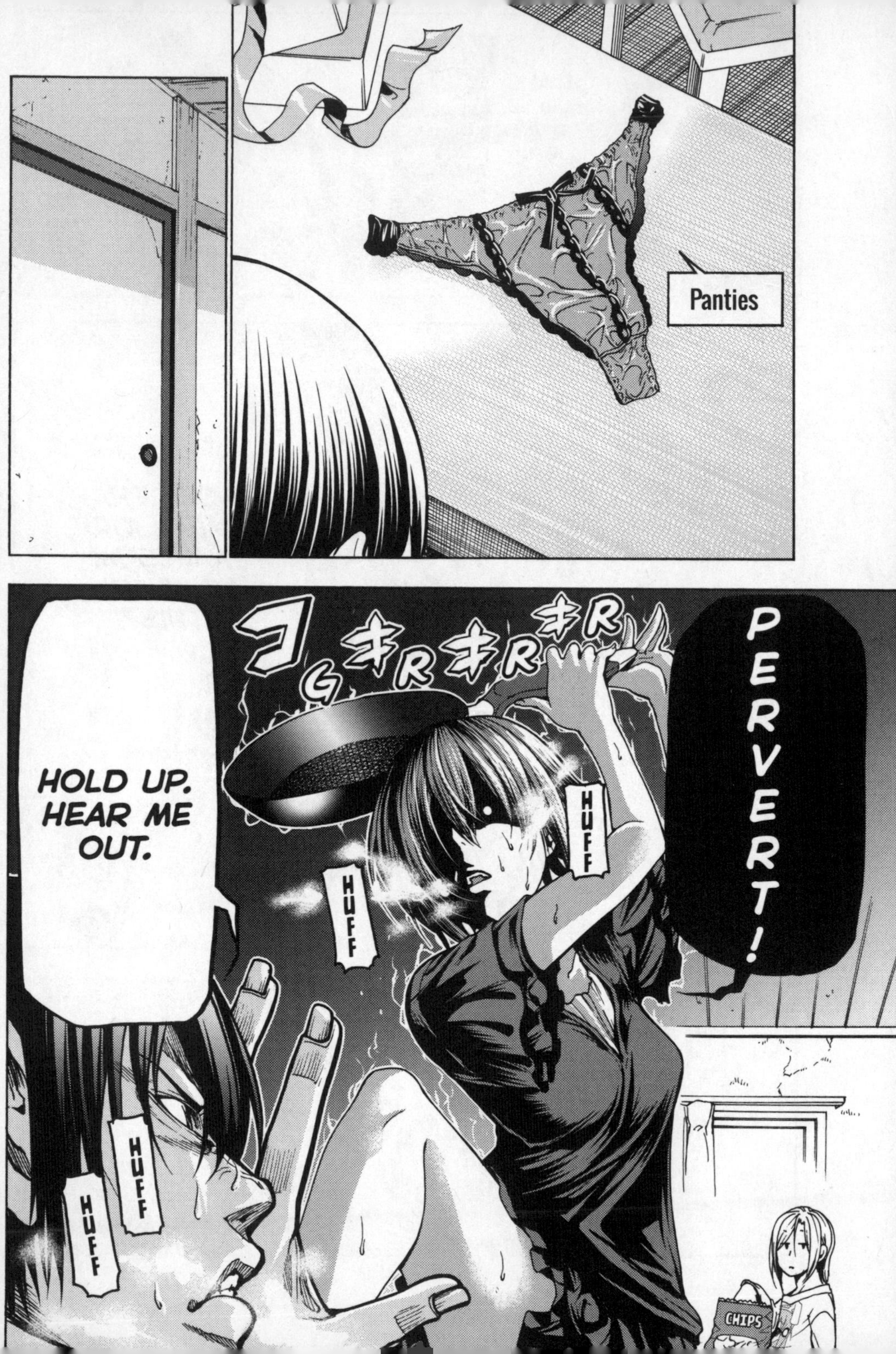
Panties
PERVERT!
GRRR
HUFF
HUFF
HOLD UP. HEAR ME OUT.
HUFF
HUFF
CHIPS

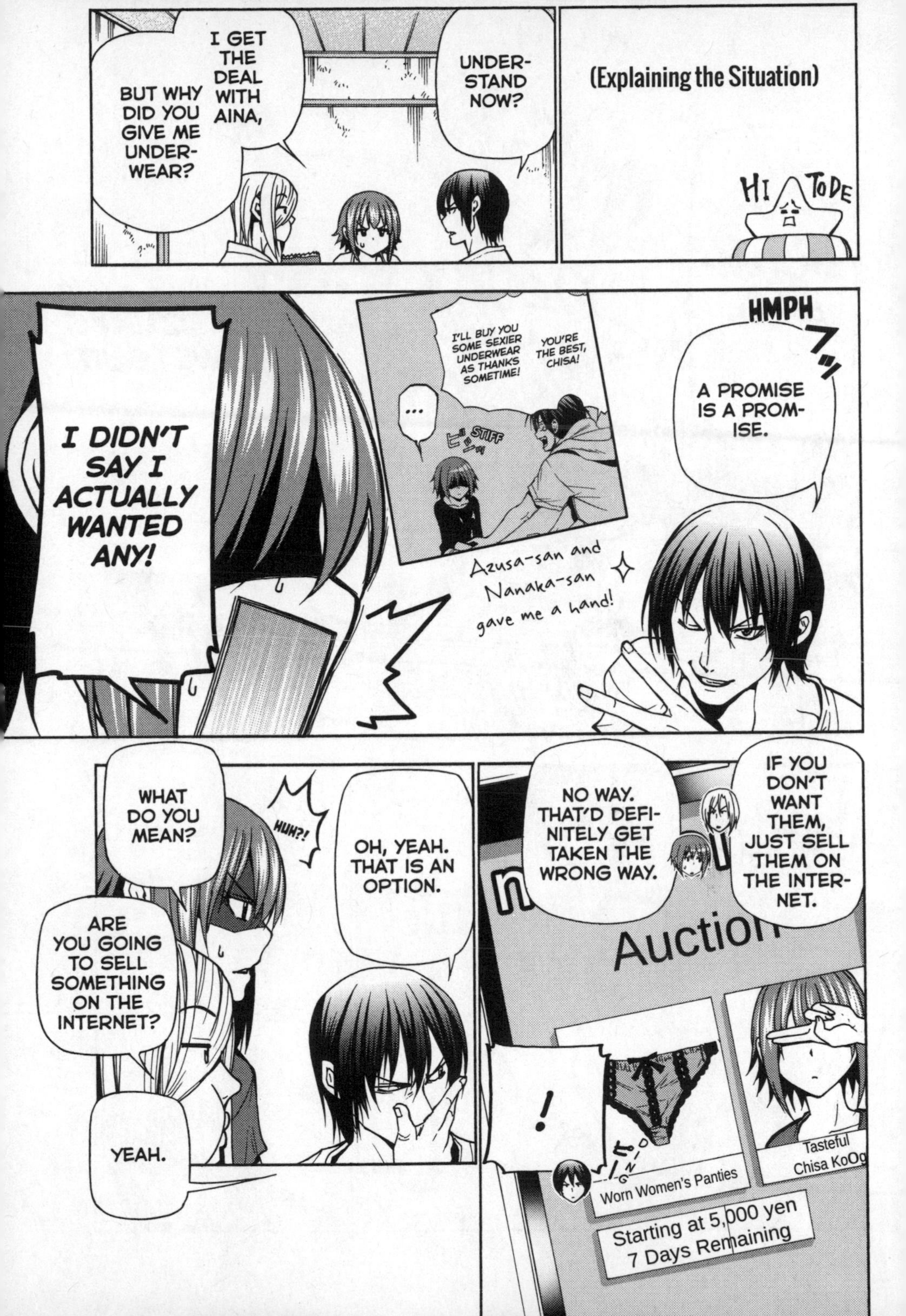
(Explaining the Situation)
HI TODE
UNDERSTAND NOW?
I GET THE DEAL WITH AINA,
BUT WHY DID YOU GIVE ME UNDERWEAR?
HMPH
A PROMISE IS A PROMISE.
YOU'RE THE BEST, CHISA!
I'LL BUY YOU SOME SEXIER UNDERWEAR AS THANKS SOMETIME!
...
STIFF
Azusa-san and Nanaka-san gave me a hand!
I DIDN'T SAY I ACTUALLY WANTED ANY!
IF YOU DON'T WANT THEM, JUST SELL THEM ON THE INTERNET.
NO WAY. THAT'D DEFINITELY GET TAKEN THE WRONG WAY.
Auction
Tasteful Chisa KoOg
Worn Women's Panties
Starting at 5,000 yen
7 Days Remaining
DING
!
OH, YEAH. THAT IS AN OPTION.
HUH?!
WHAT DO YOU MEAN?
ARE YOU GOING TO SELL SOMETHING ON THE INTERNET?
YEAH.

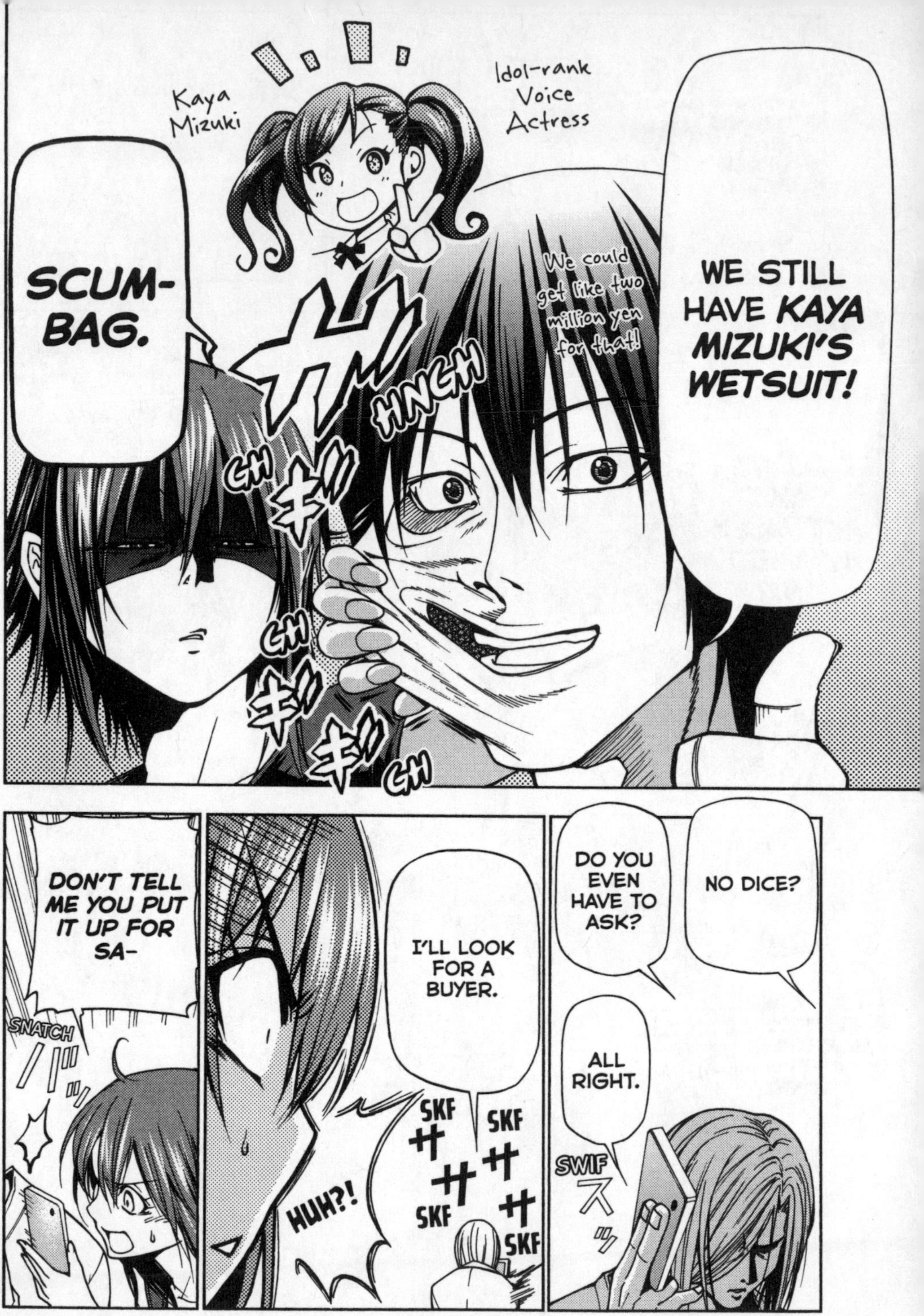
WE STILL HAVE KAYA MIZUKI'S WETSUIT!
Idol-rank Voice Actress
Kaya Mizuki
We could get like two million yen for that!
HNCH
GH
GH
GH
SCUM-BAG.
NO DICE?
DO YOU EVEN HAVE TO ASK?
ALL RIGHT.
SWIF
I'LL LOOK FOR A BUYER.
SKF
SKF
SKF
SKF
HUH?!
DON'T TELL ME YOU PUT IT UP FOR SA-
SNATCH

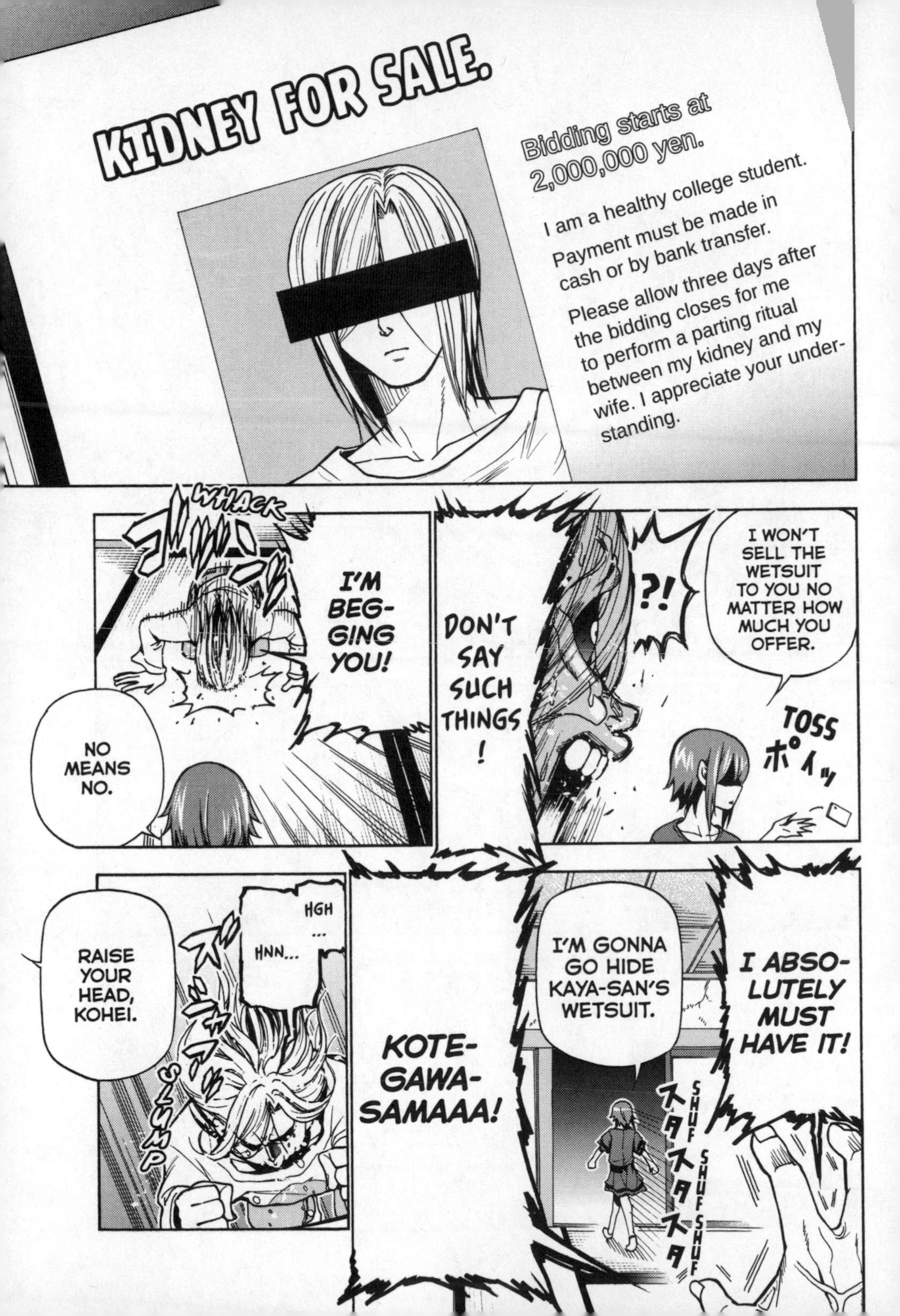
KIDNEY FOR SALE.
Bidding starts at 2,000,000 yen.
I am a healthy college student.
Payment must be made in cash or by bank transfer.
Please allow three days after the bidding closes for me to perform a parting ritual between my kidney and my wife. I appreciate your understanding.
I WON'T SELL THE WETSUIT TO YOU NO MATTER HOW MUCH YOU OFFER.
?!
TOSS
ポイッ
DON'T SAY SUCH THINGS!
WHACK
I'M BEGGING YOU!
NO MEANS NO.
I ABSOLUTELY MUST HAVE IT!
I'M GONNA GO HIDE KAYA-SAN'S WETSUIT.
SHUF SHUF SHUF SHUF
スタスタスタ
KOTEGAWA-SAMAAA!
HGH...
HNN...
RAISE YOUR HEAD, KOHEI.
SLUMP

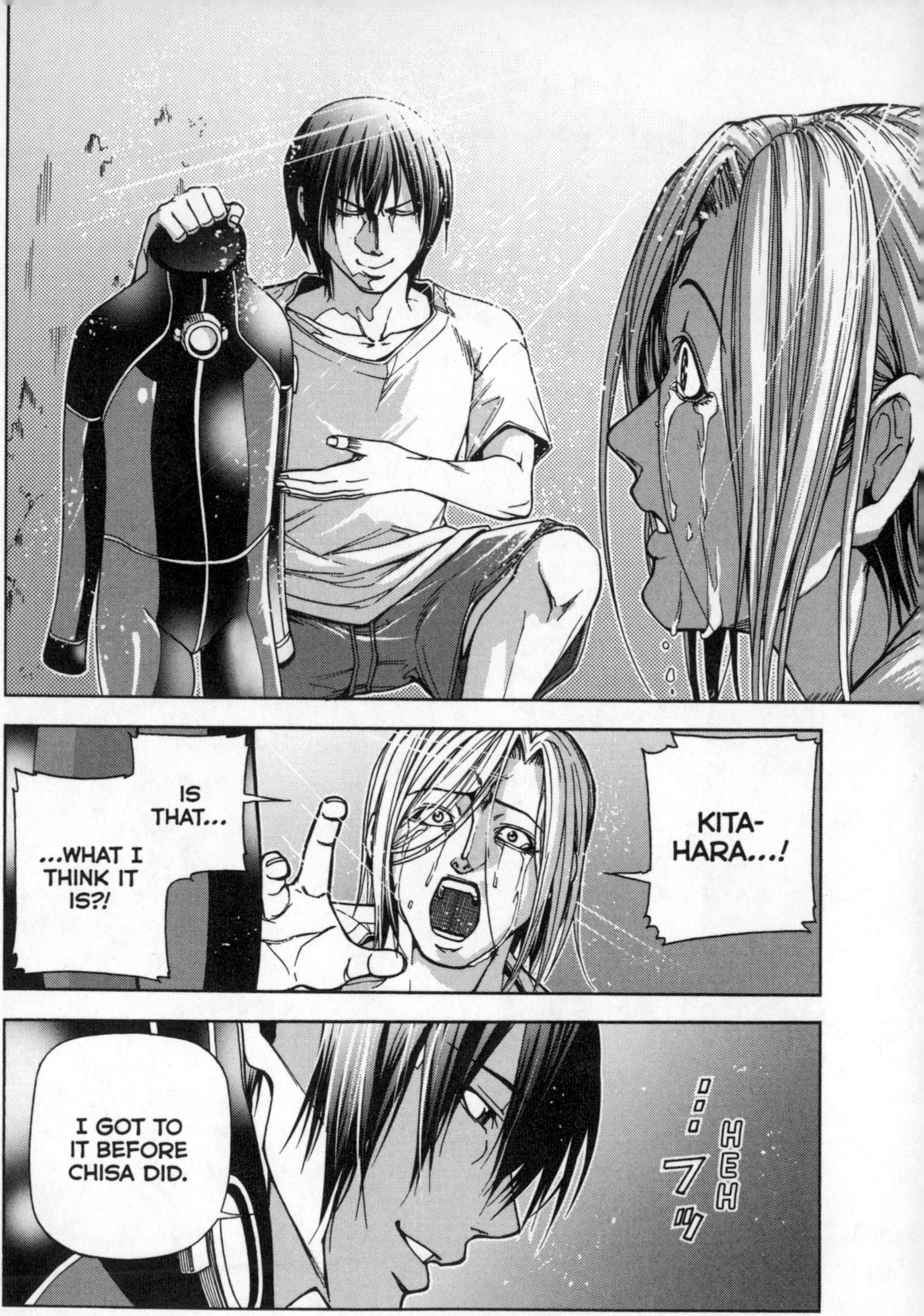
KITA-HARA...!
IS THAT...
...WHAT I THINK IT IS?!
HEH
フッ
I GOT TO IT BEFORE CHISA DID.

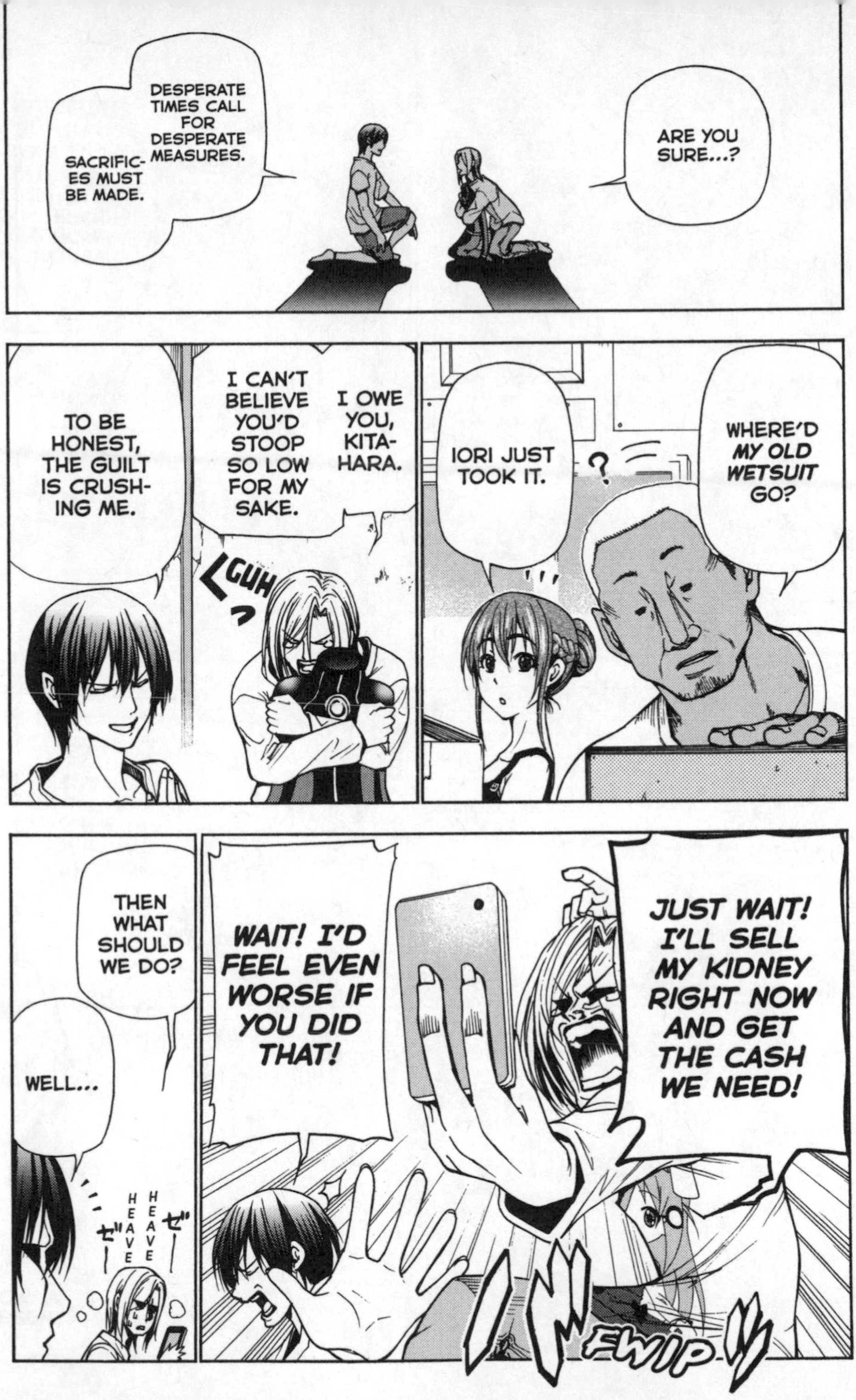
ARE YOU SURE...?
DESPERATE TIMES CALL FOR DESPERATE MEASURES.
SACRIFIC-ES MUST BE MADE.
WHERE'D MY OLD WETSUIT GO?
?
IORI JUST TOOK IT.
I OWE YOU, KITA-HARA.
I CAN'T BELIEVE YOU'D STOOP SO LOW FOR MY SAKE.
GUH
TO BE HONEST, THE GUILT IS CRUSHING ME.
JUST WAIT! I'LL SELL MY KIDNEY RIGHT NOW AND GET THE CASH WE NEED!
WAIT! I'D FEEL EVEN WORSE IF YOU DID THAT!
FWIP
THEN WHAT SHOULD WE DO?
WELL...
HEAVE
HEAVE

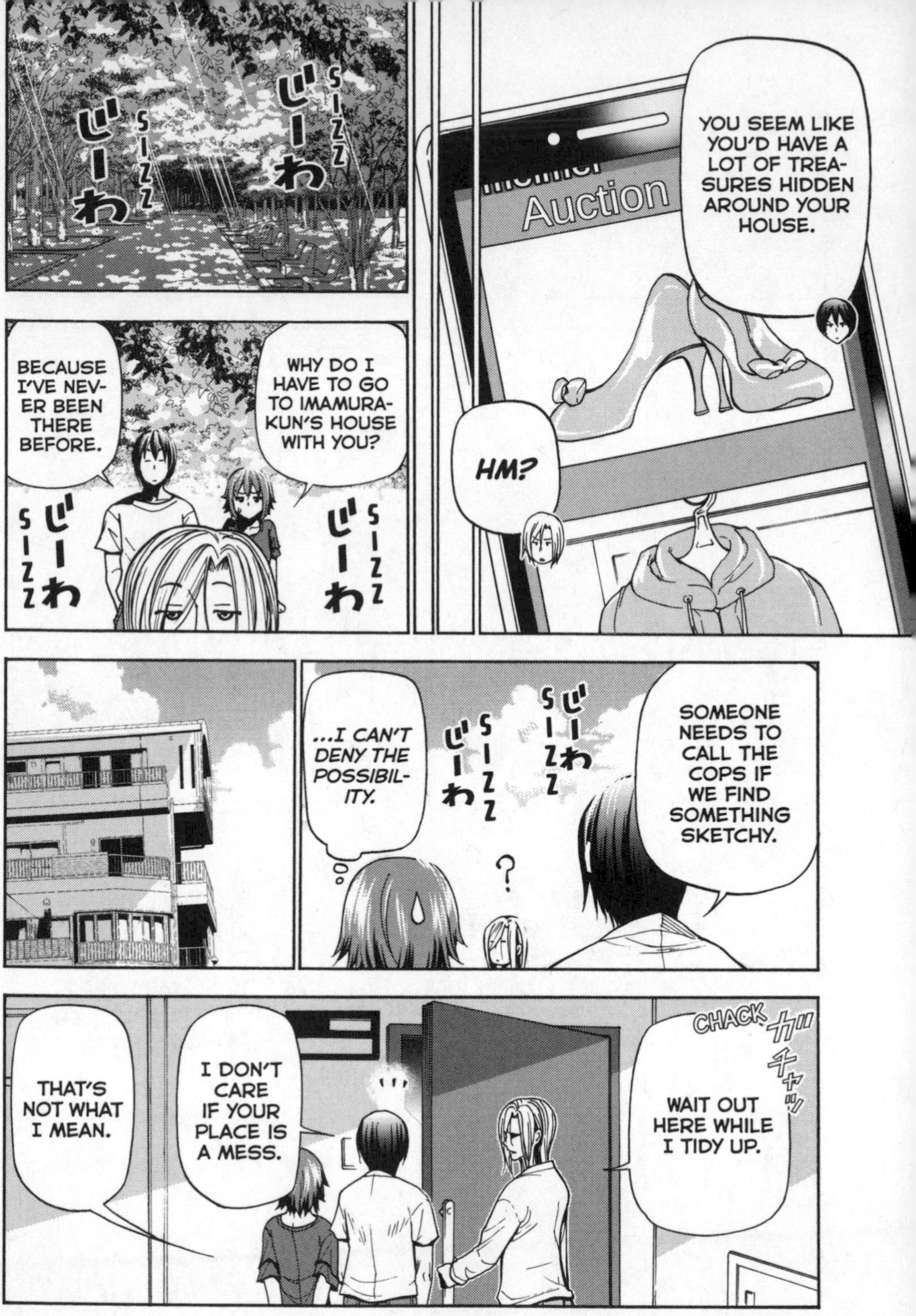
Auction
YOU SEEM LIKE YOU'D HAVE A LOT OF TREASURES HIDDEN AROUND YOUR HOUSE.
HM?
じーわ SIZZ
じーわ SIZZ
WHY DO I HAVE TO GO TO IMAMURA-KUN'S HOUSE WITH YOU?
BECAUSE I'VE NEVER BEEN THERE BEFORE.
じーわ SIZZ
じーわ SIZZ
SOMEONE NEEDS TO CALL THE COPS IF WE FIND SOMETHING SKETCHY.
じーわ SIZZ
じーわ SIZZ
...I CAN'T DENY THE POSSIBILITY.
?
CHACK ガチャッ
WAIT OUT HERE WHILE I TIDY UP.
I DON'T CARE IF YOUR PLACE IS A MESS.
THAT'S NOT WHAT I MEAN.

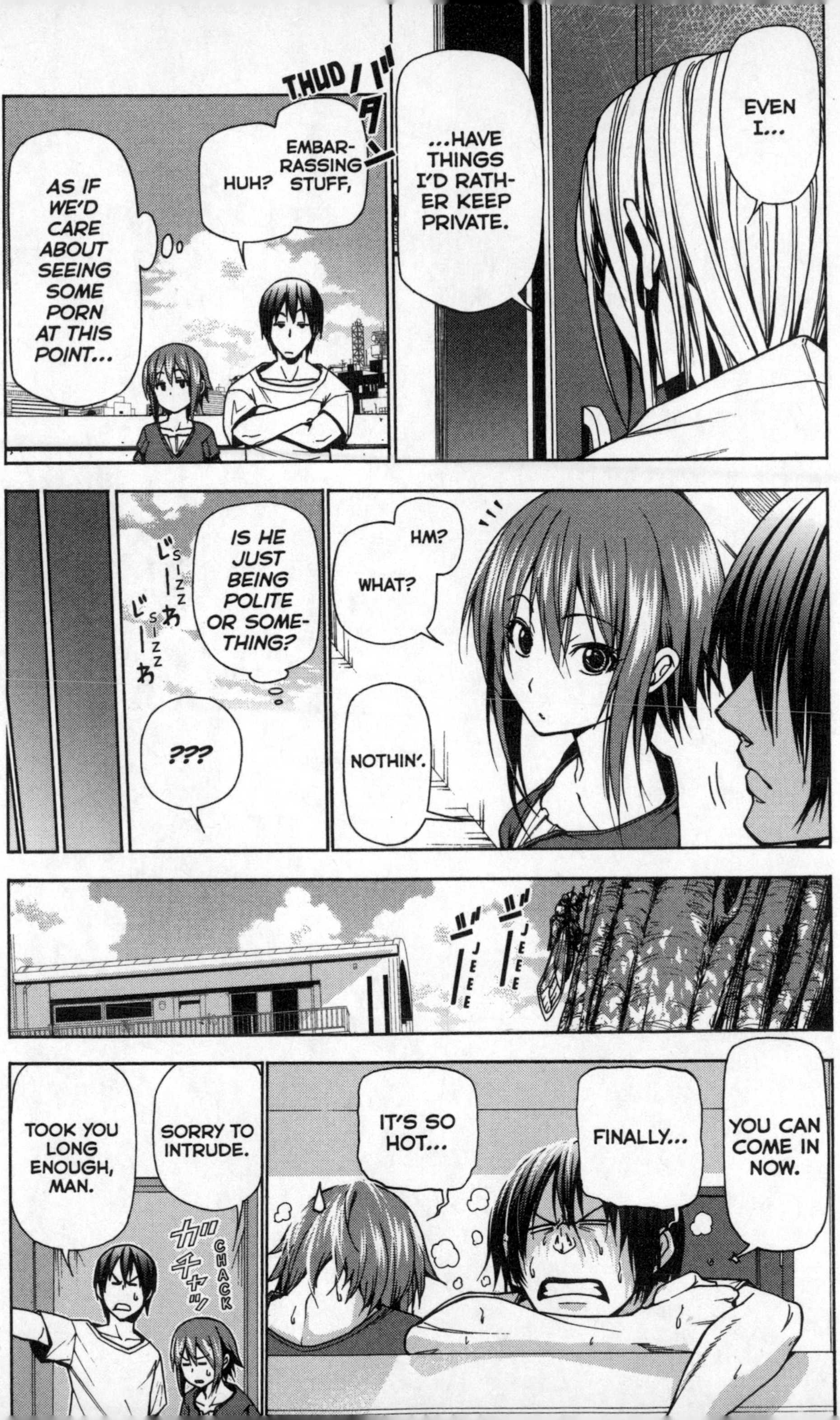
EVEN I...
...HAVE THINGS I'D RATHER KEEP PRIVATE.
THUD
EMBARRASSING STUFF, HUH?
AS IF WE'D CARE ABOUT SEEING SOME PORN AT THIS POINT...
HM? WHAT?
NOTHIN'.
IS HE JUST BEING POLITE OR SOMETHING?
SIZZ
SIZZ
???
JEEE
JEEE
YOU CAN COME IN NOW.
FINALLY...
IT'S SO HOT...
SORRY TO INTRUDE.
TOOK YOU LONG ENOUGH, MAN.
CHACK

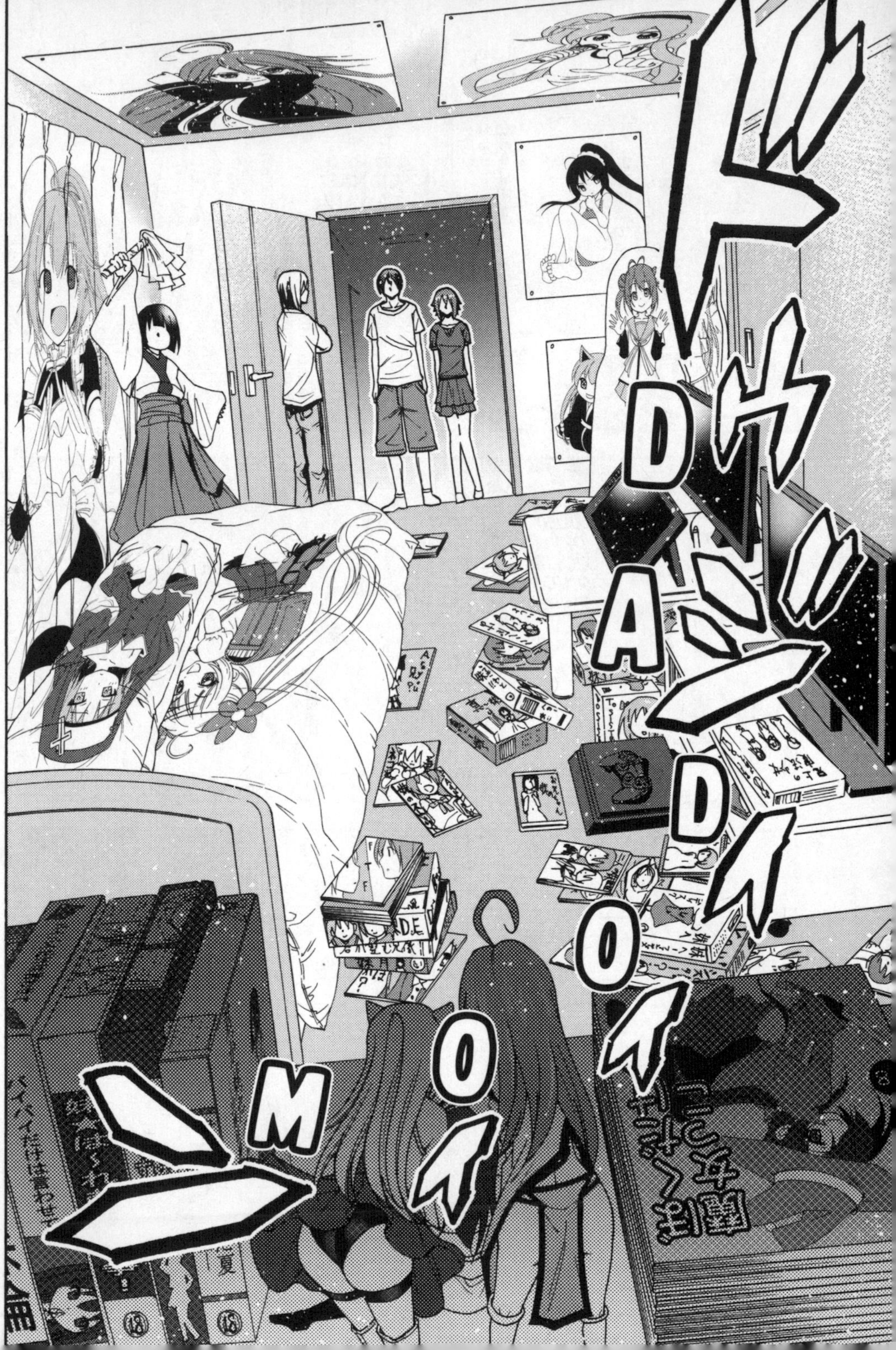
DADOOM
バイバイだけは言わせて

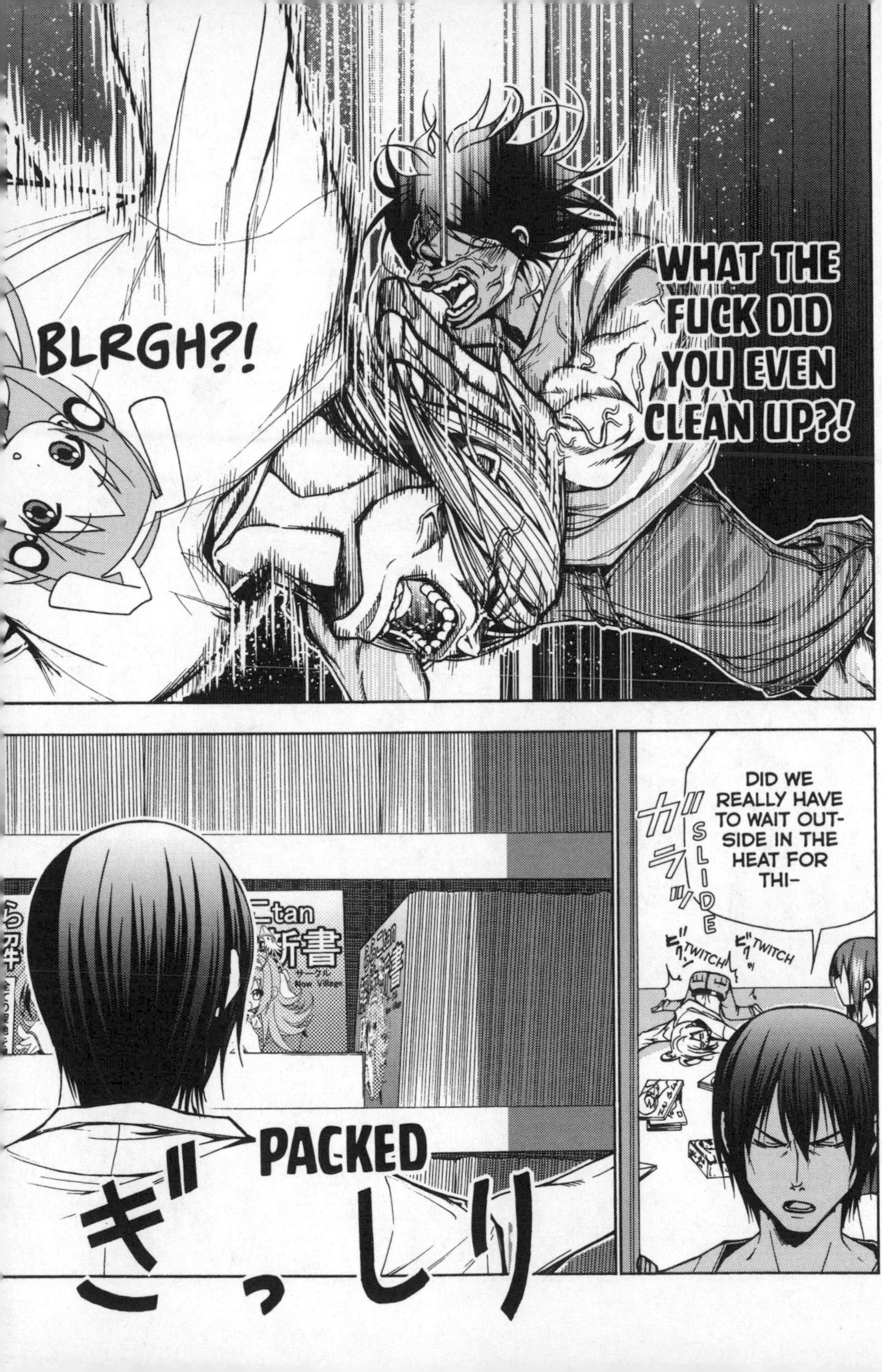
WHAT THE FUCK DID YOU EVEN CLEAN UP?!
BLRGH?!
ガラッ
SLIDE
DID WE REALLY HAVE TO WAIT OUT-SIDE IN THE HEAT FOR THI-
ビクッ TWITCH
ビクッ TWITCH
PACKED
ぎっしり

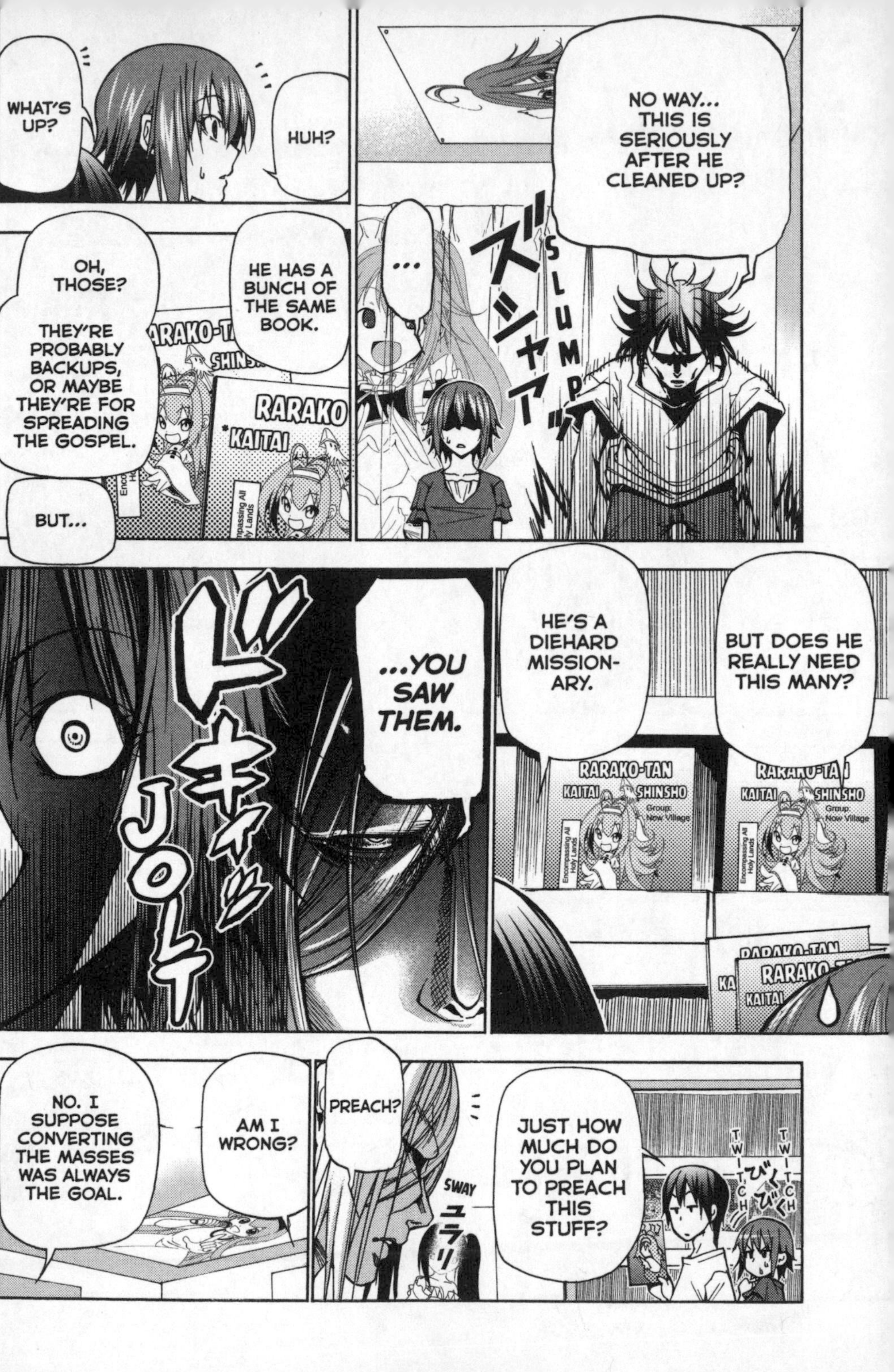
NO WAY... THIS IS SERIOUSLY AFTER HE CLEANED UP?
HUH?
WHAT'S UP?
...
SLUMP
HE HAS A BUNCH OF THE SAME BOOK.
OH, THOSE? THEY'RE PROBABLY BACKUPS, OR MAYBE THEY'RE FOR SPREADING THE GOSPEL.
RARAKO-TAN
SHINSHO
RARAKO
*KAITAI
Encompassing All Holy Lands
BUT...
BUT DOES HE REALLY NEED THIS MANY?
HE'S A DIEHARD MISSIONARY.
RARAKO-TAN
KAITAI
SHINSHO
Group: Now Village
Encompassing All Holy Lands
RARAKO-TAN
KAITAI
SHINSHO
Group: Now Village
Encompassing All Holy Lands
...YOU SAW THEM.
JOLT
JUST HOW MUCH DO YOU PLAN TO PREACH THIS STUFF?
TWITCH
TWITCH
PREACH?
SWAY
AM I WRONG?
NO. I SUPPOSE CONVERTING THE MASSES WAS ALWAYS THE GOAL.

*Kaitai Shinsho: A medical text translated into Japanese in the Edo period.

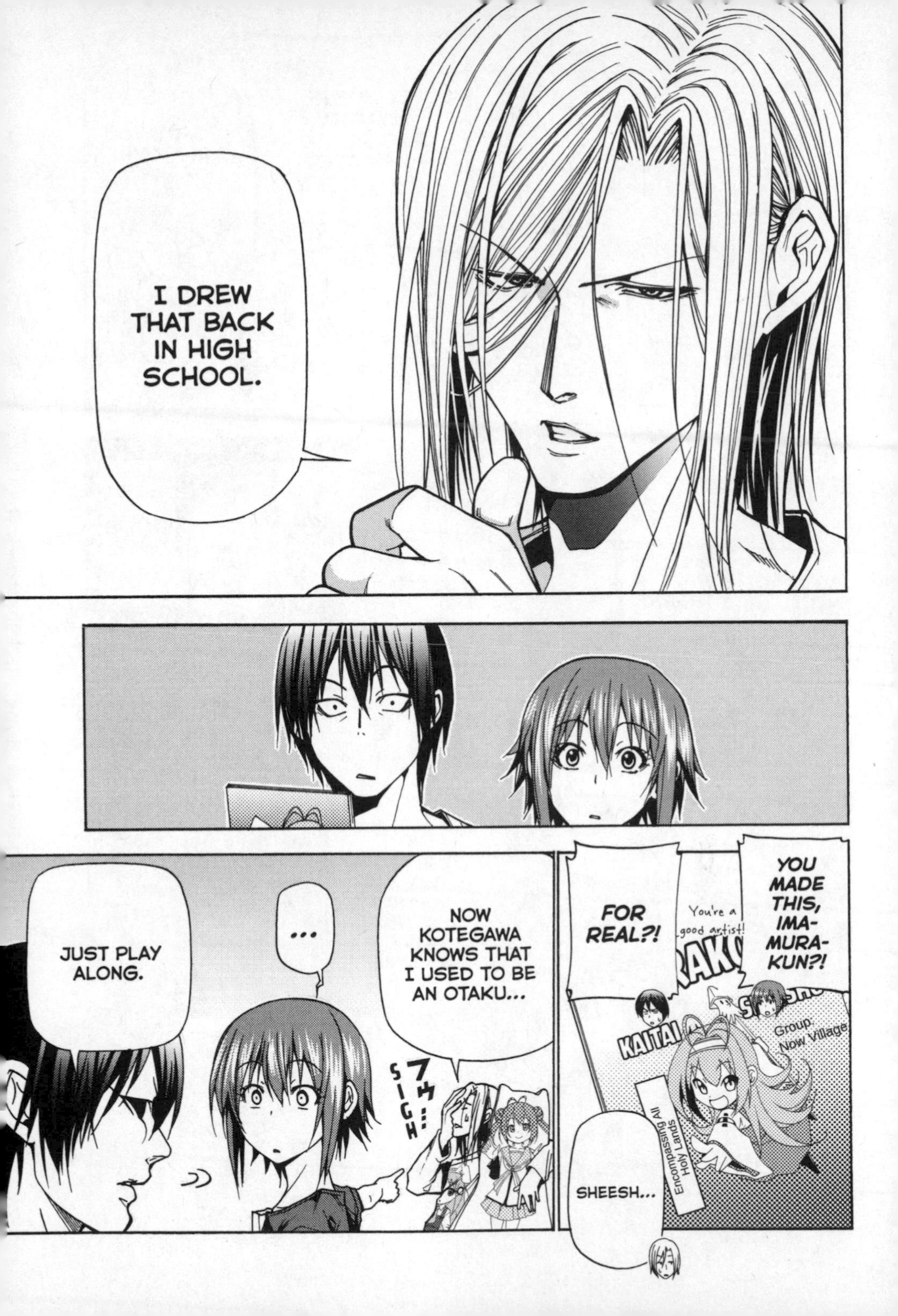
I DREW THAT BACK IN HIGH SCHOOL.
YOU MADE THIS, IMA-MURA-KUN?!
FOR REAL?!
You're a good artist!
KAITAI
Group: Now Village
Encompassing All Holy Lands
SHEESH...
NOW KOTEGAWA KNOWS THAT I USED TO BE AN OTAKU...
SIGH
...
JUST PLAY ALONG.

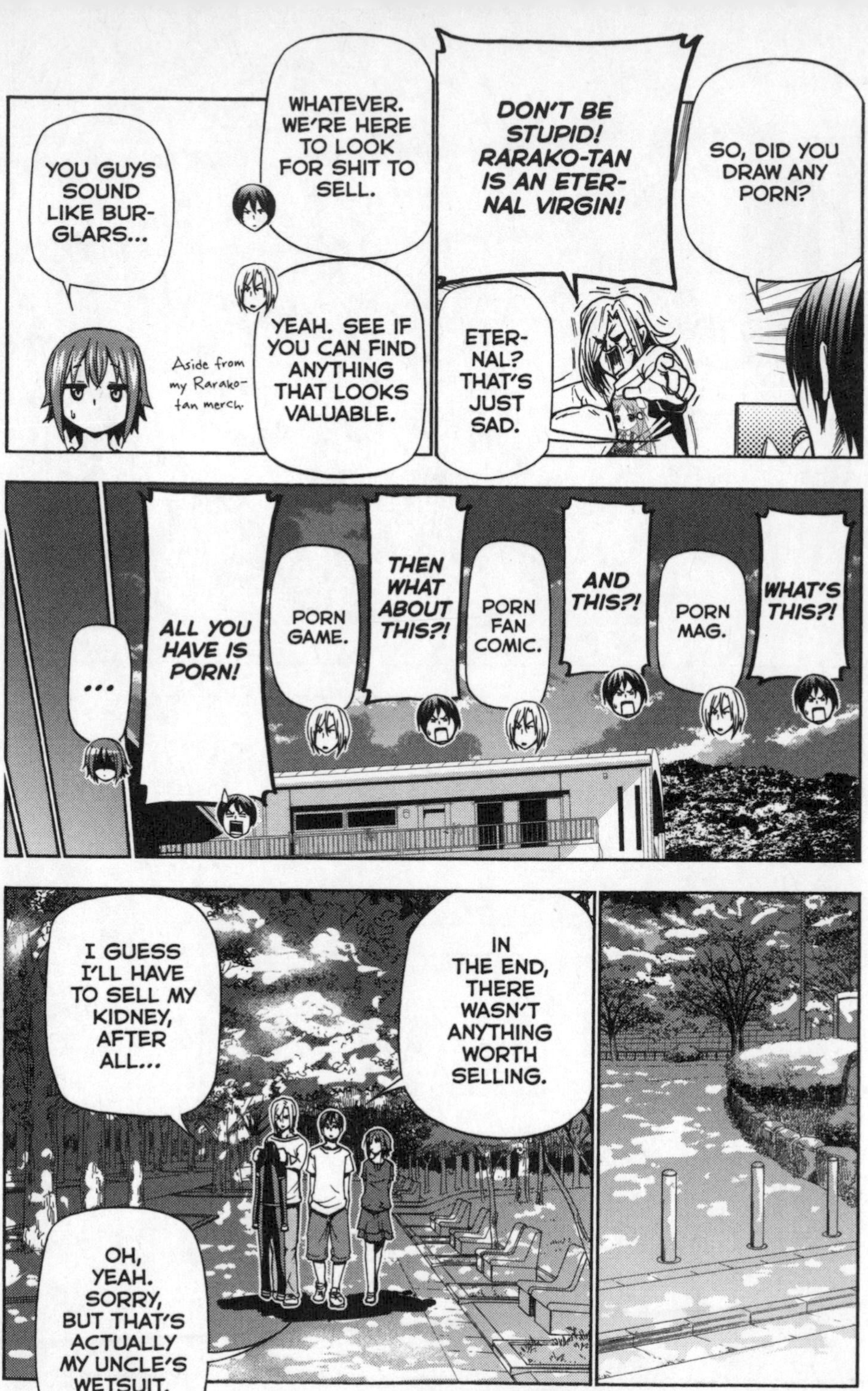
SO, DID YOU DRAW ANY PORN?
DON'T BE STUPID! RARAKO-TAN IS AN ETERNAL VIRGIN!
ETERNAL? THAT'S JUST SAD.
WHATEVER. WE'RE HERE TO LOOK FOR SHIT TO SELL.
YEAH. SEE IF YOU CAN FIND ANYTHING THAT LOOKS VALUABLE.
YOU GUYS SOUND LIKE BURGLARS...
Aside from my Rarako-tan merch.
WHAT'S THIS?!
PORN MAG.
AND THIS?!
PORN FAN COMIC.
THEN WHAT ABOUT THIS?!
PORN GAME.
ALL YOU HAVE IS PORN!
...
IN THE END, THERE WASN'T ANYTHING WORTH SELLING.
I GUESS I'LL HAVE TO SELL MY KIDNEY, AFTER ALL...
OH, YEAH. SORRY, BUT THAT'S ACTUALLY MY UNCLE'S WETSUIT.

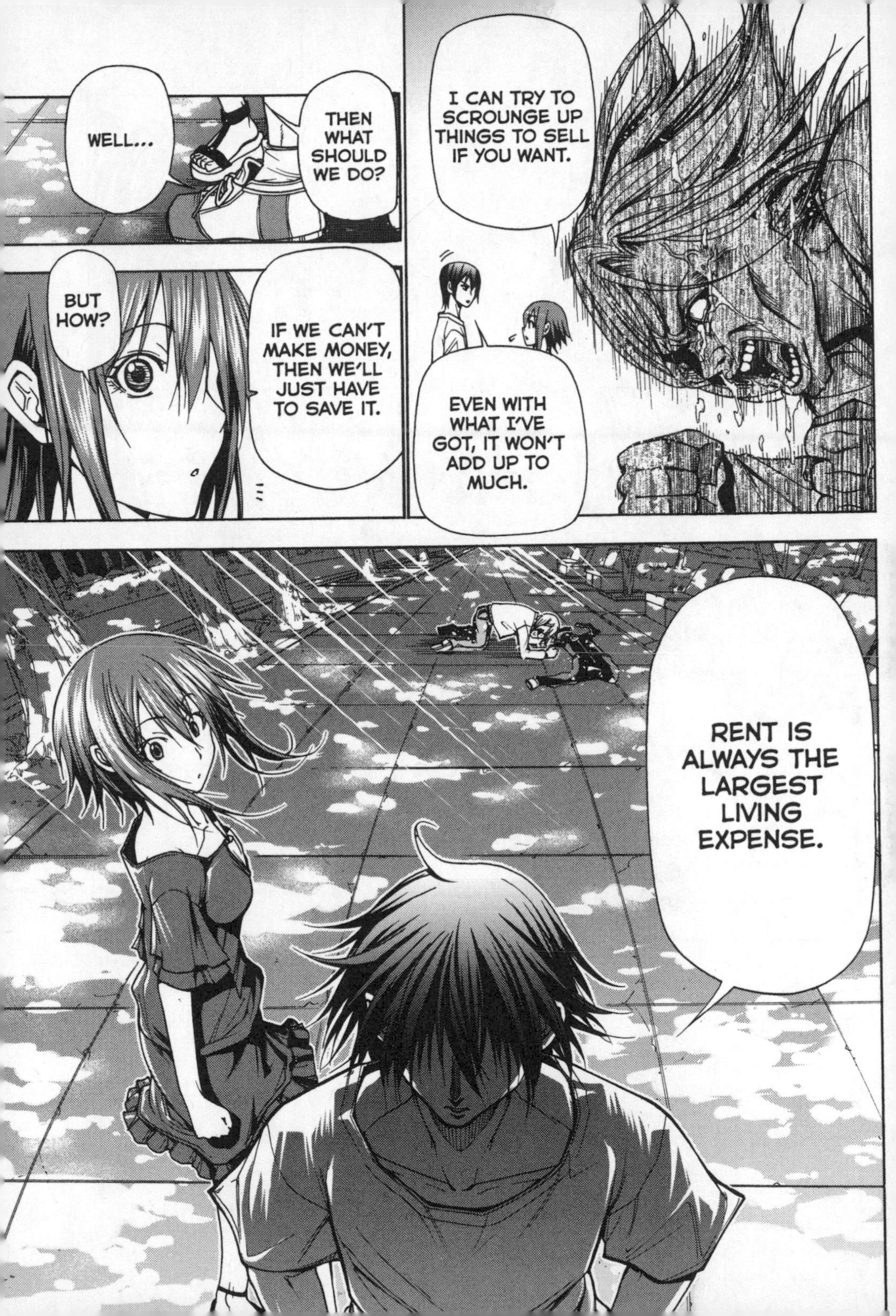
I CAN TRY TO SCROUNGE UP THINGS TO SELL IF YOU WANT.
EVEN WITH WHAT I'VE GOT, IT WON'T ADD UP TO MUCH.
THEN WHAT SHOULD WE DO?
WELL...
IF WE CAN'T MAKE MONEY, THEN WE'LL JUST HAVE TO SAVE IT.
BUT HOW?
RENT IS ALWAYS THE LARGEST LIVING EXPENSE.

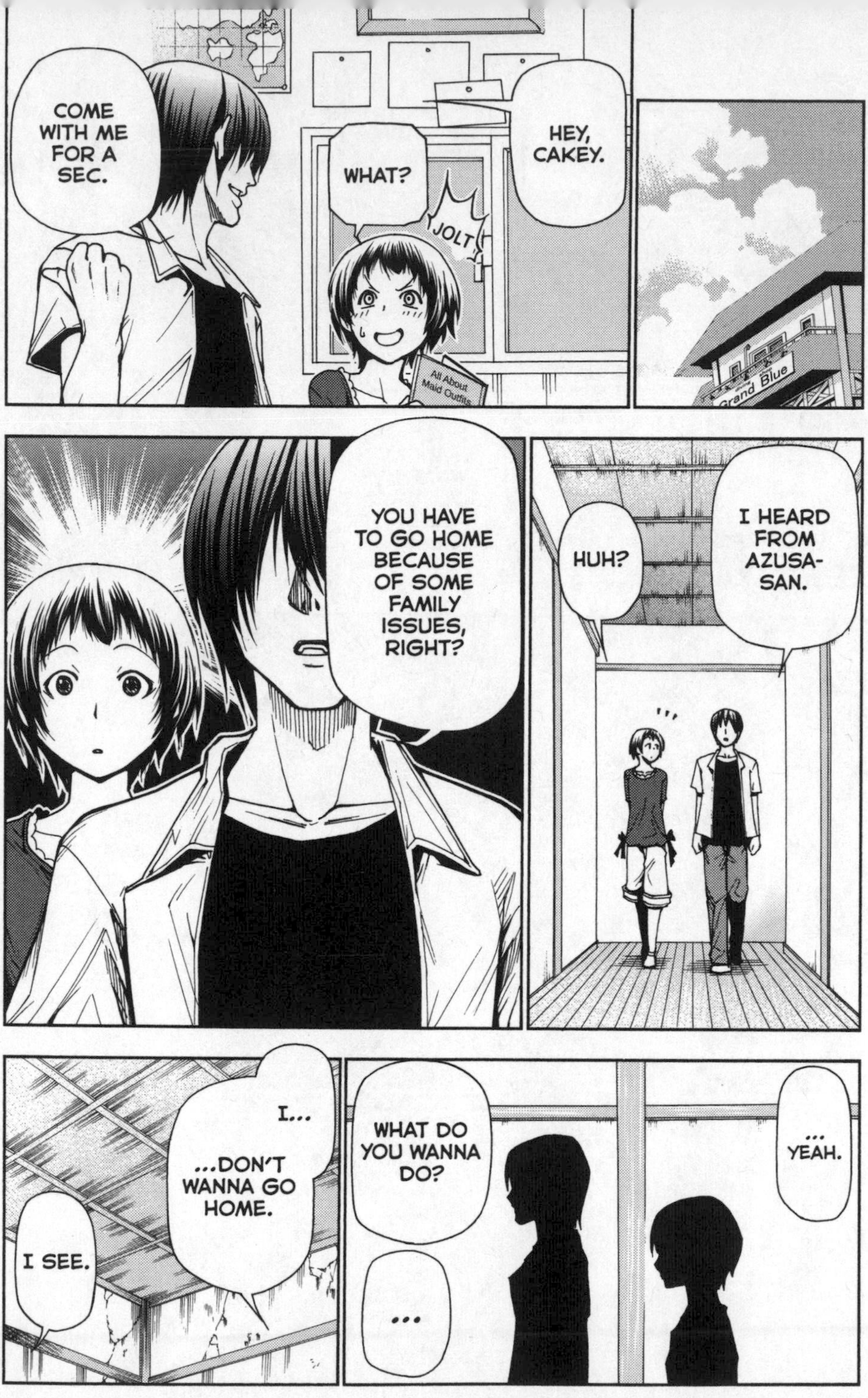
Grand Blue
HEY, CAKEY.
WHAT?
JOLT
All About Maid Outfits
COME WITH ME FOR A SEC.
I HEARD FROM AZUSA-SAN.
HUH?
YOU HAVE TO GO HOME BECAUSE OF SOME FAMILY ISSUES, RIGHT?
...YEAH.
WHAT DO YOU WANNA DO?
...
I...
...DON'T WANNA GO HOME.
I SEE.

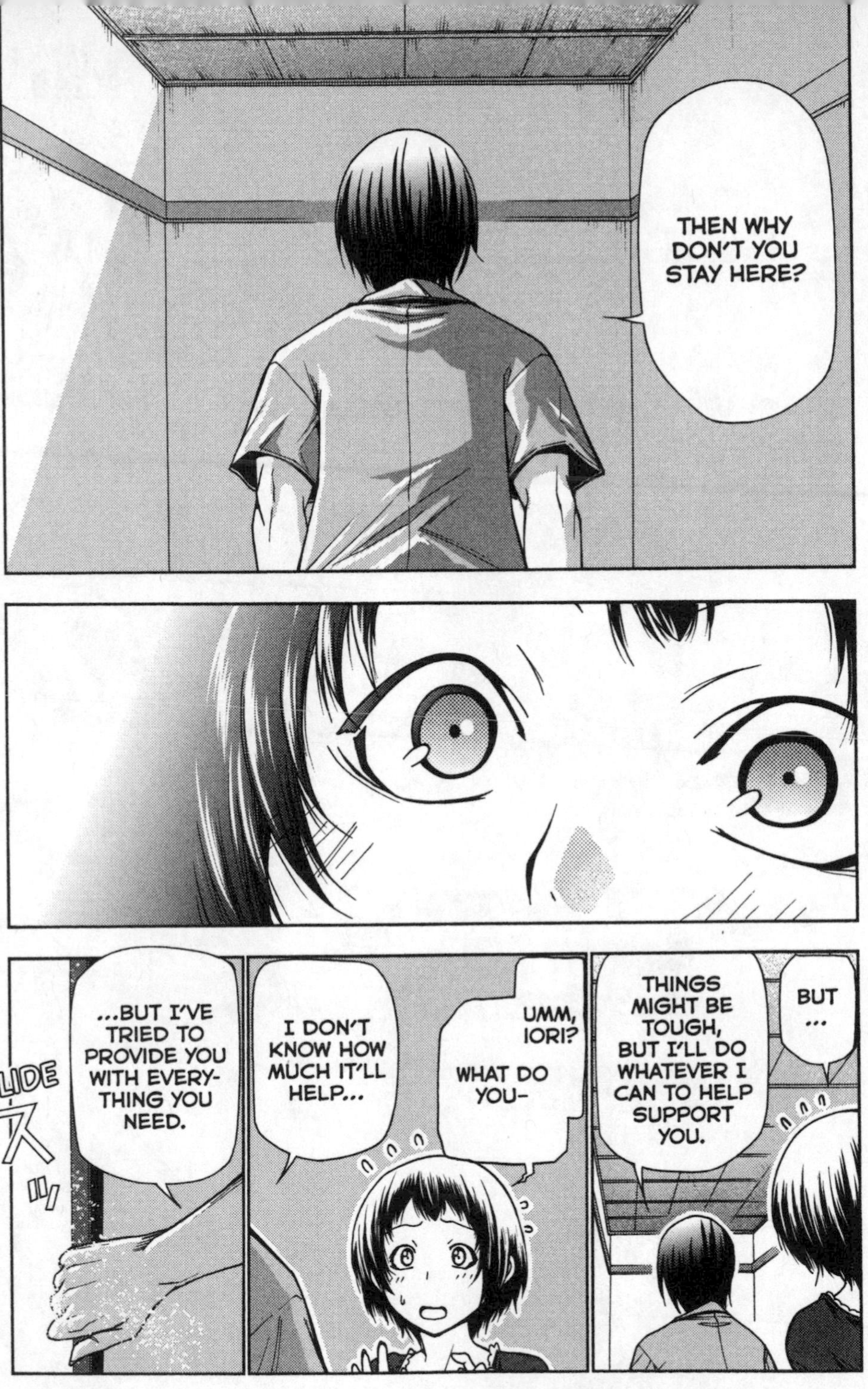
THEN WHY DON'T YOU STAY HERE?
BUT ...
THINGS MIGHT BE TOUGH, BUT I'LL DO WHATEVER I CAN TO HELP SUPPORT YOU.
UMM, IORI?
WHAT DO YOU-
I DON'T KNOW HOW MUCH IT'LL HELP...
...BUT I'VE TRIED TO PROVIDE YOU WITH EVERY-THING YOU NEED.
SLIDE
スッ

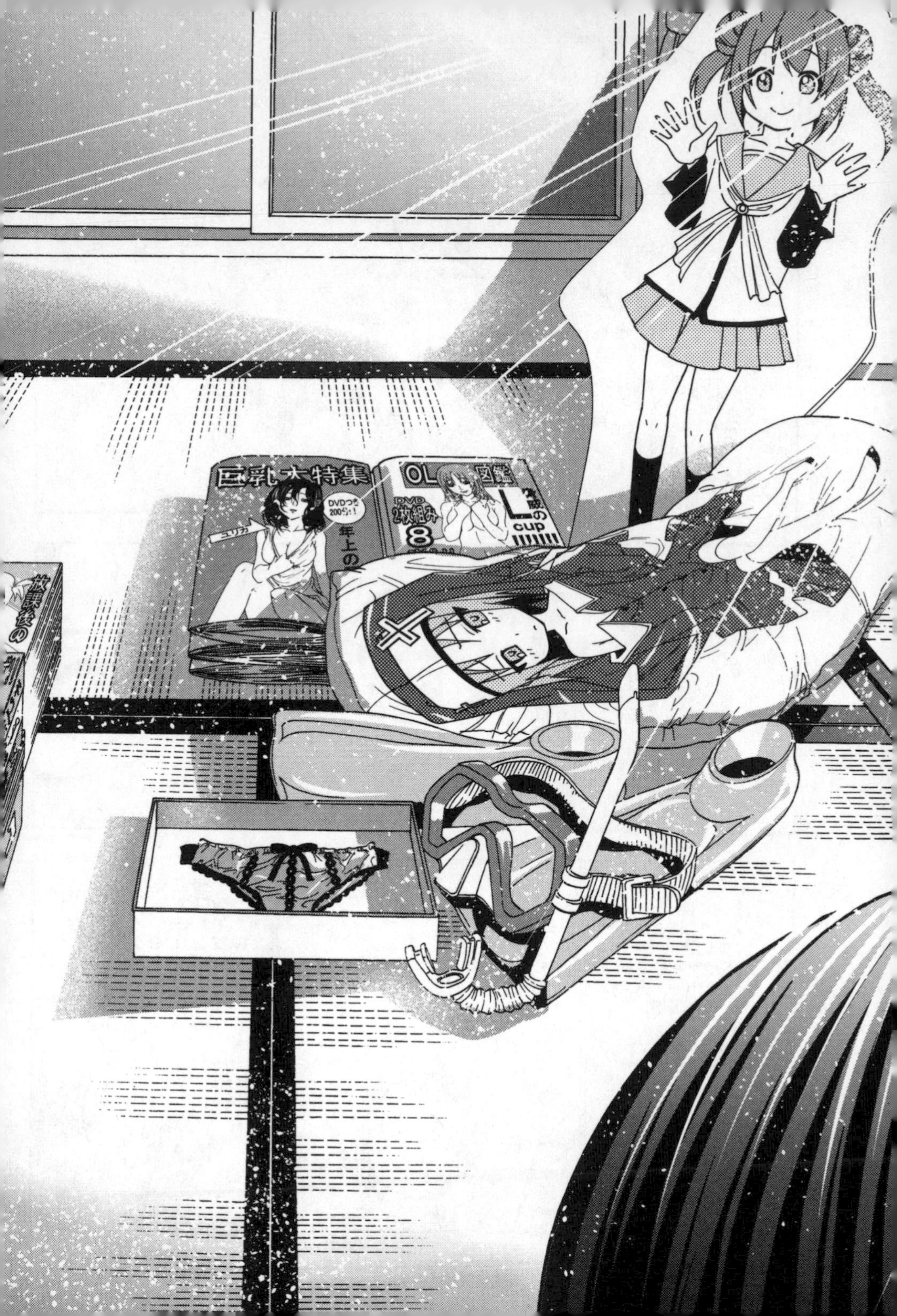
巨乳大特集
DVDつき200分!!
ユリカ
年上の
OL図鑑
DVD 2枚組み
8
Lのcup
放課後の

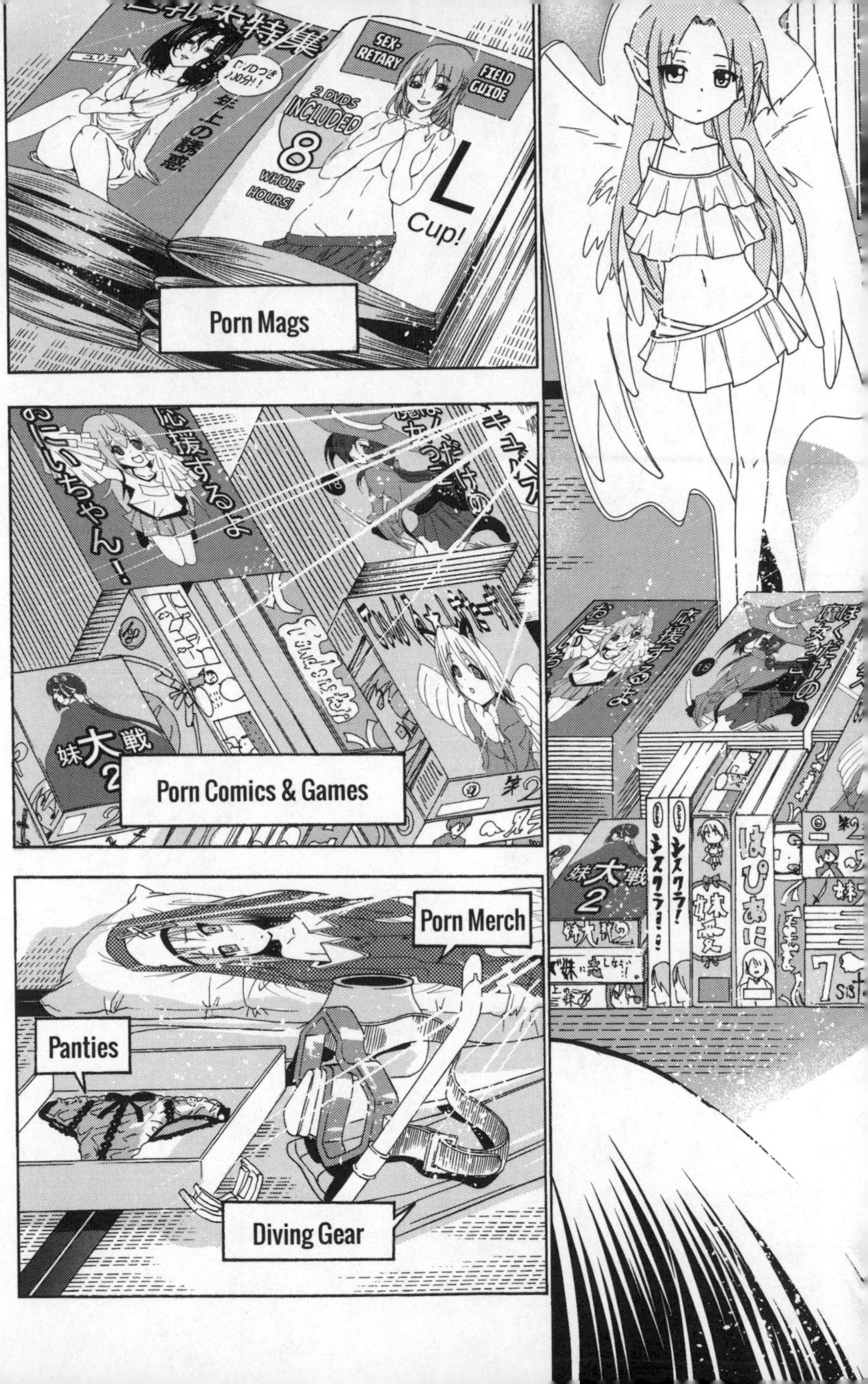
妹大戦
2
はぴあに
妹愛
SEX-
RETARY
FIELD
GUIDE
2 DVDS
INCLUDED
8
WHOLE
HOURS!
L
Cup!
ユリカ
Porn Mags
応援するよ
妹大戦
2
Porn Comics & Games
Porn Merch
Panties
Diving Gear

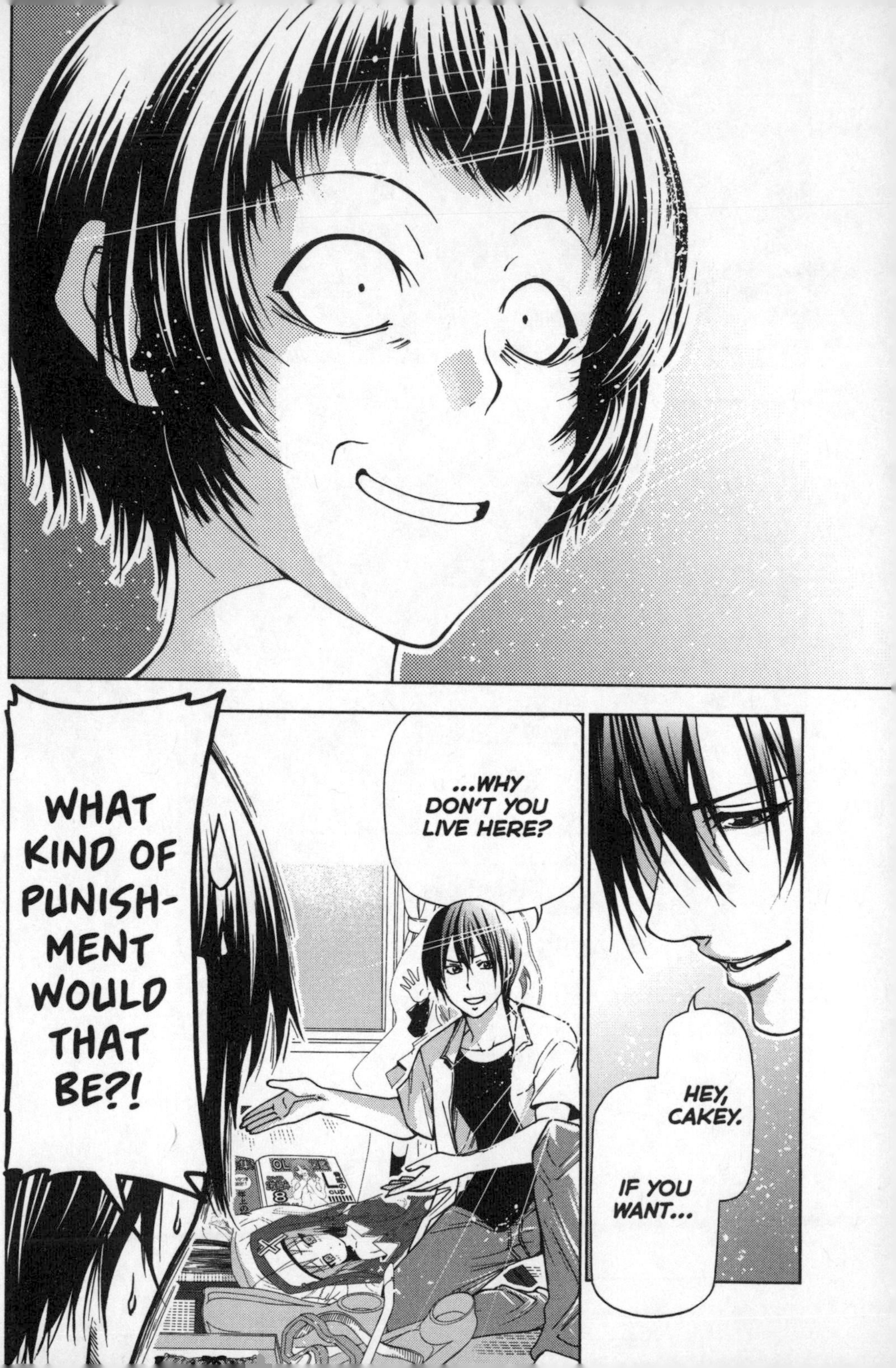
HEY, CAKEY.
IF YOU WANT...
...WHY DON'T YOU LIVE HERE?
WHAT KIND OF PUNISHMENT WOULD THAT BE?!

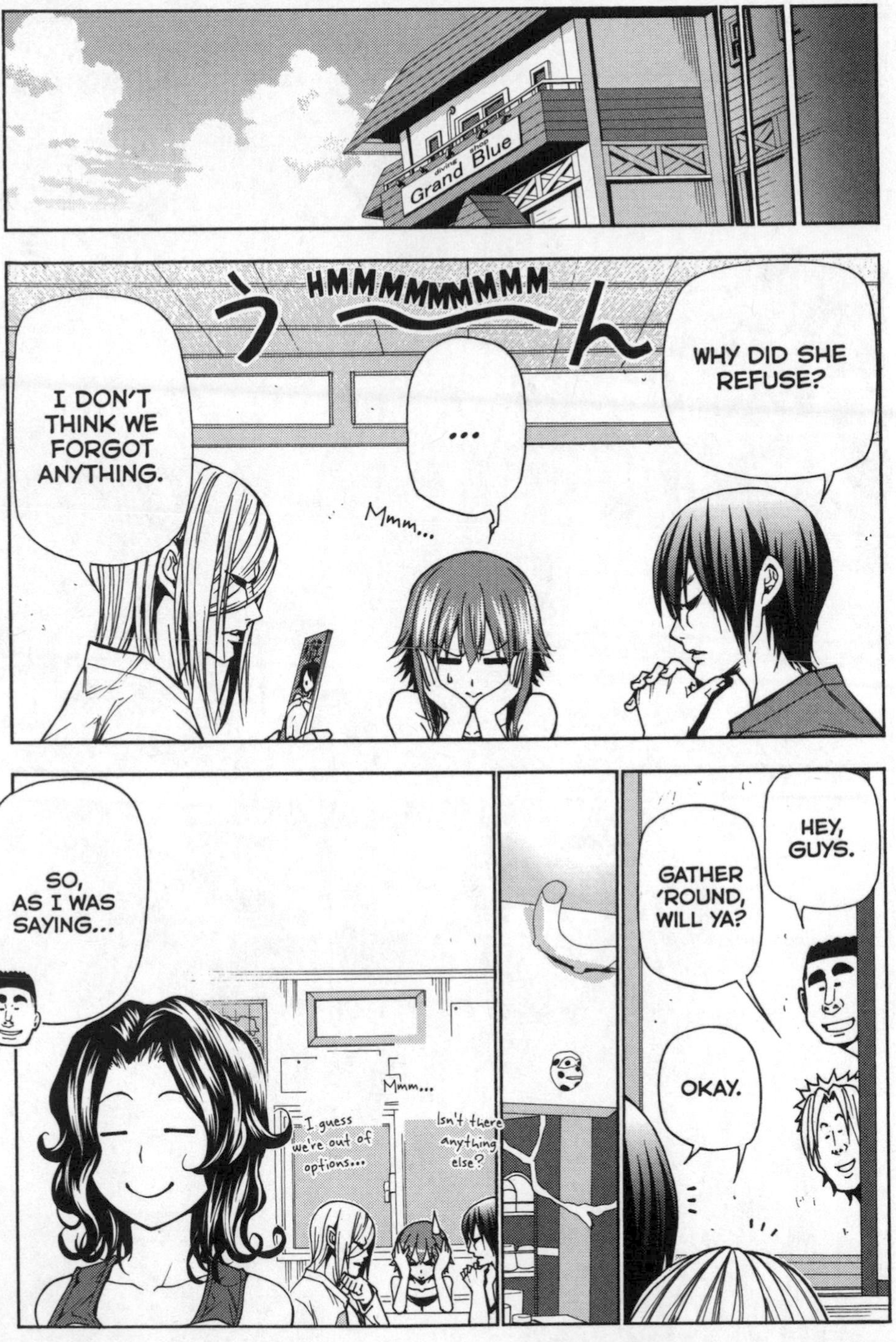
diving shop
Grand Blue
WHY DID SHE REFUSE?
うーん
HMMMMMMMM
...
Mmm...
I DON'T THINK WE FORGOT ANYTHING.
HEY, GUYS.
GATHER 'ROUND, WILL YA?
OKAY.
SO, AS I WAS SAYING...
Mmm...
Isn't there anything else?
I guess we're out of options...

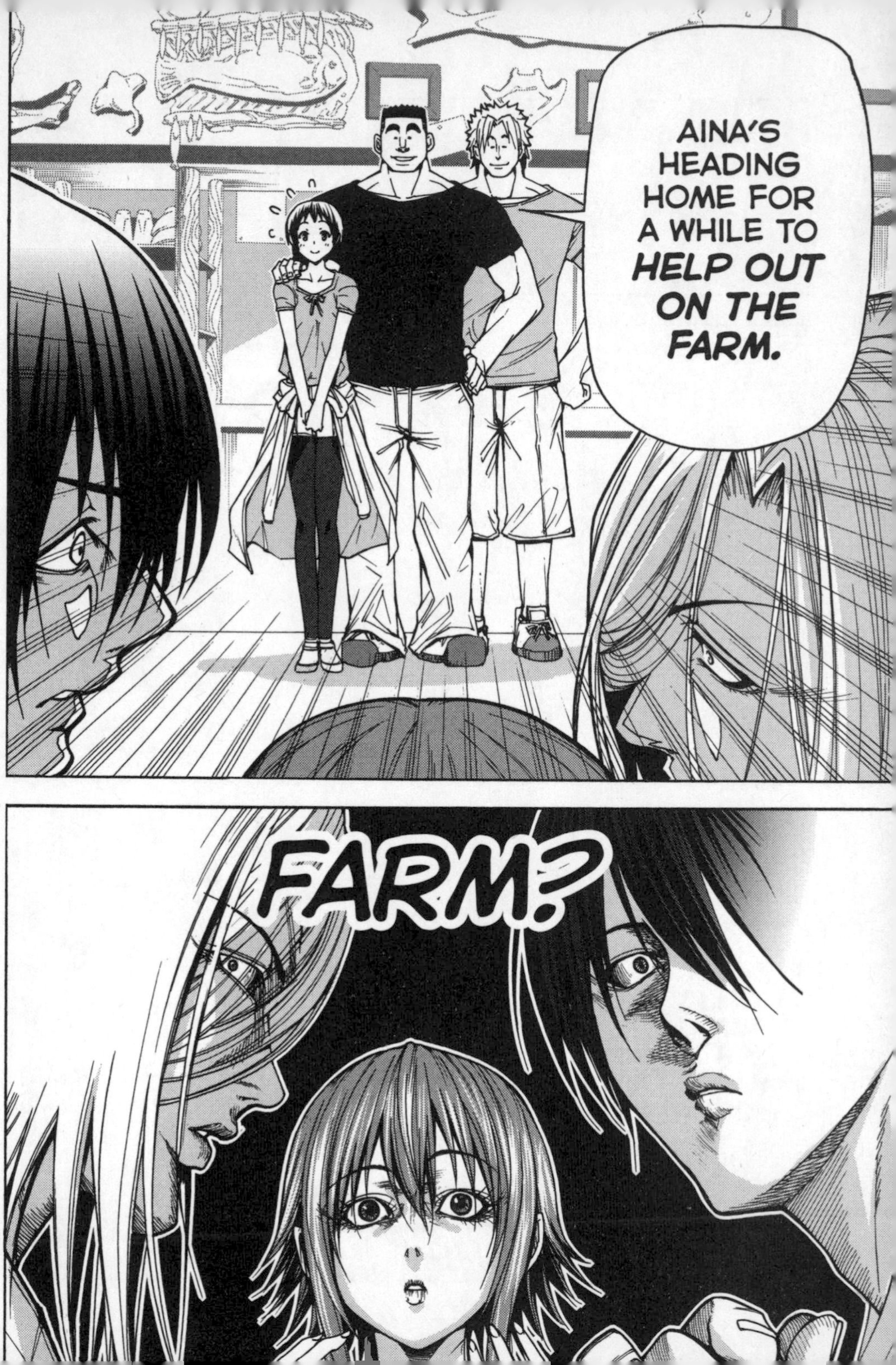
AINA'S HEADING HOME FOR A WHILE TO HELP OUT ON THE FARM.
FARM?

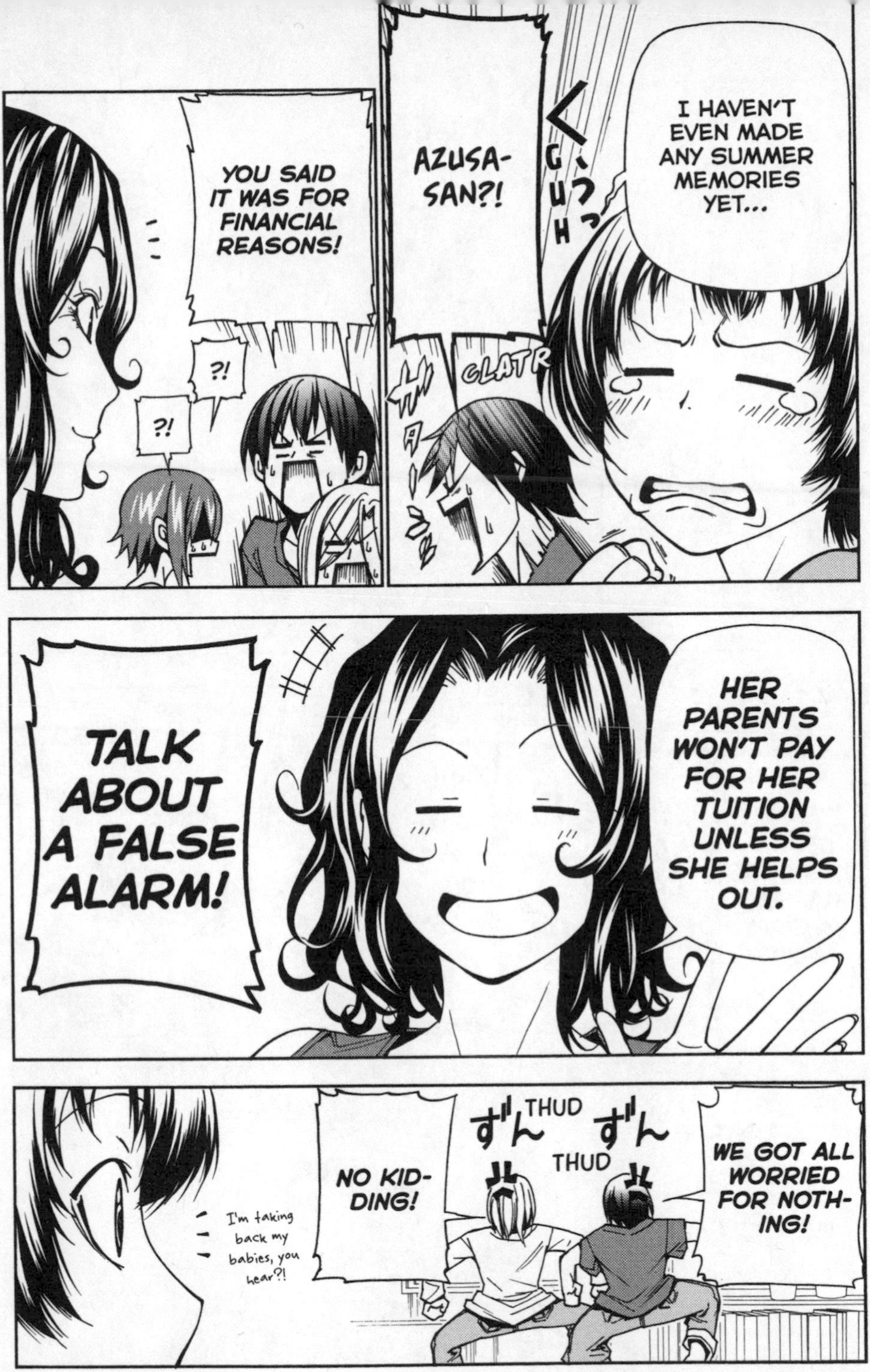
I HAVEN'T EVEN MADE ANY SUMMER MEMORIES YET...
GUH
AZUSA-SAN?!
CLATR
YOU SAID IT WAS FOR FINANCIAL REASONS!
?!
?!
HER PARENTS WON'T PAY FOR HER TUITION UNLESS SHE HELPS OUT.
TALK ABOUT A FALSE ALARM!
WE GOT ALL WORRIED FOR NOTH-ING!
ずん THUD
ずん THUD
NO KID-DING!
I'm taking back my babies, you hear?!

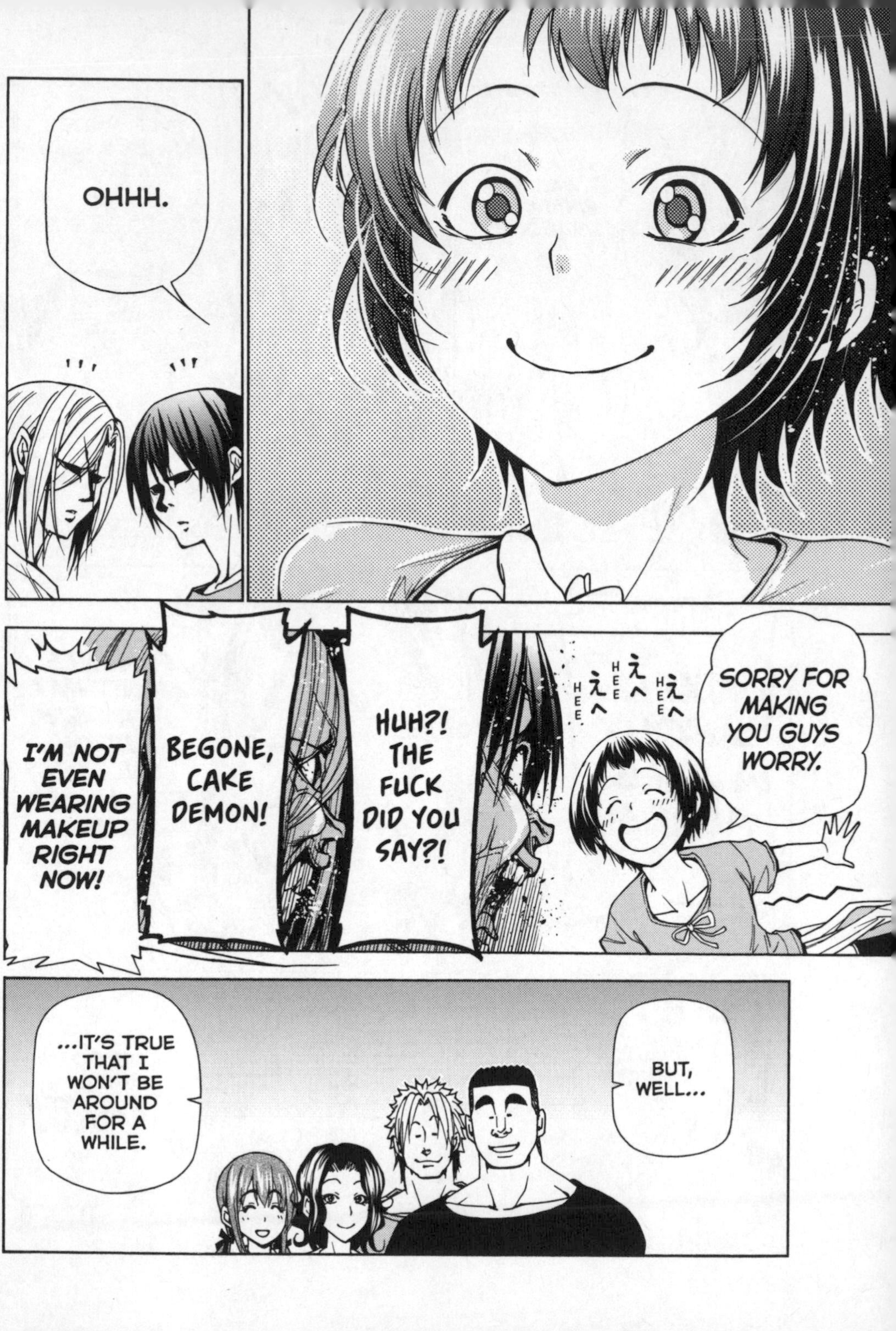
OHHH.
えへ HEE えへ HEE えへ HEE
SORRY FOR MAKING YOU GUYS WORRY.
HUH?! THE FUCK DID YOU SAY?!
BEGONE, CAKE DEMON!
I'M NOT EVEN WEARING MAKEUP RIGHT NOW!
BUT, WELL...
...IT'S TRUE THAT I WON'T BE AROUND FOR A WHILE.

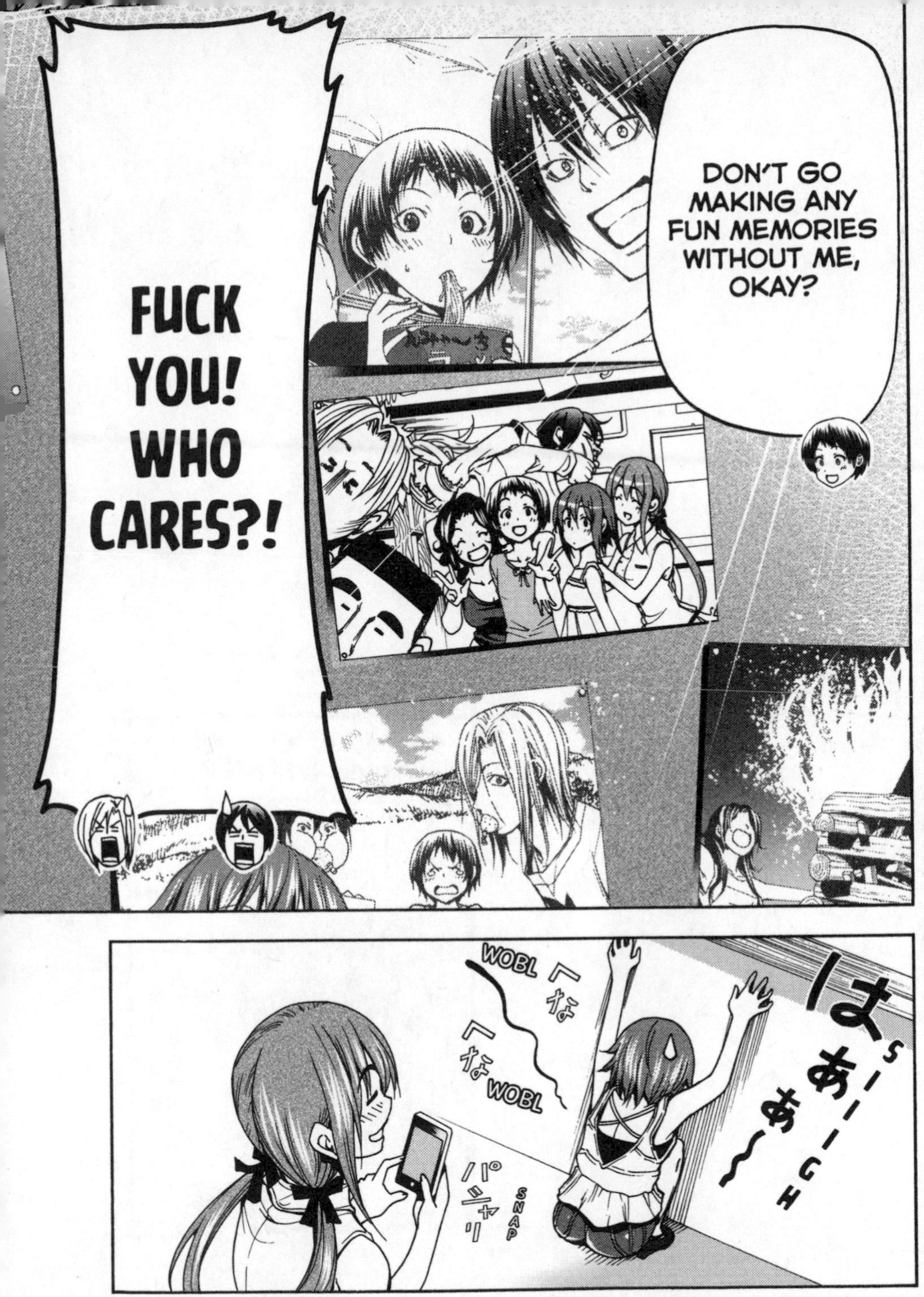
DON'T GO MAKING ANY FUN MEMORIES WITHOUT ME, OKAY?
FUCK YOU! WHO CARES?!
はぁ～ S--I--GH
へなへな WOBL WOBL
パシャリ SNAP

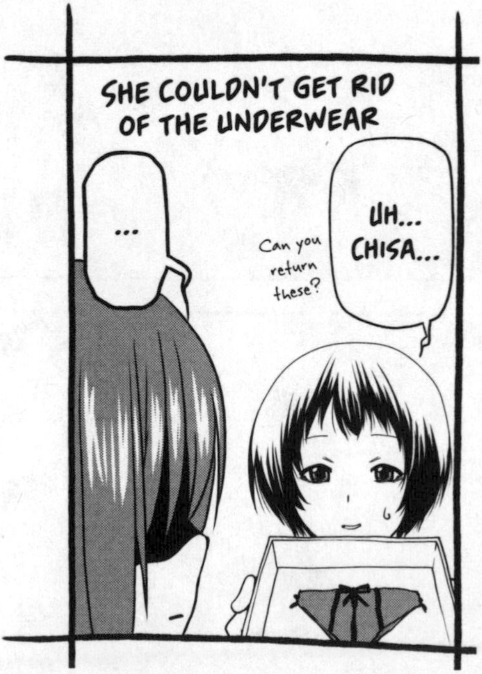
SHE COULDN'T GET RID OF THE UNDERWEAR
UH... CHISA...
Can you return these?
...

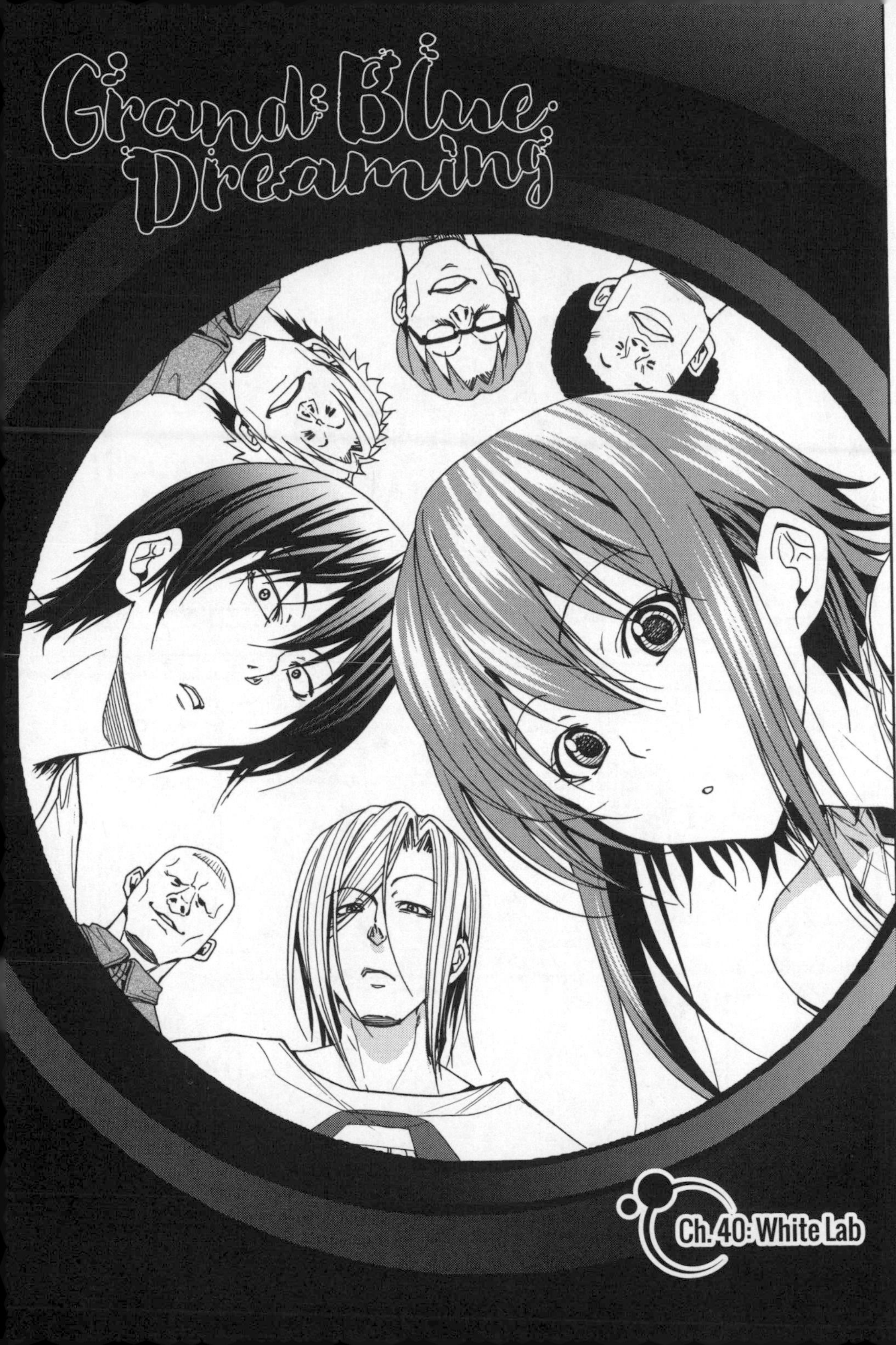
Grand Blue Dreaming
Ch. 40: White Lab

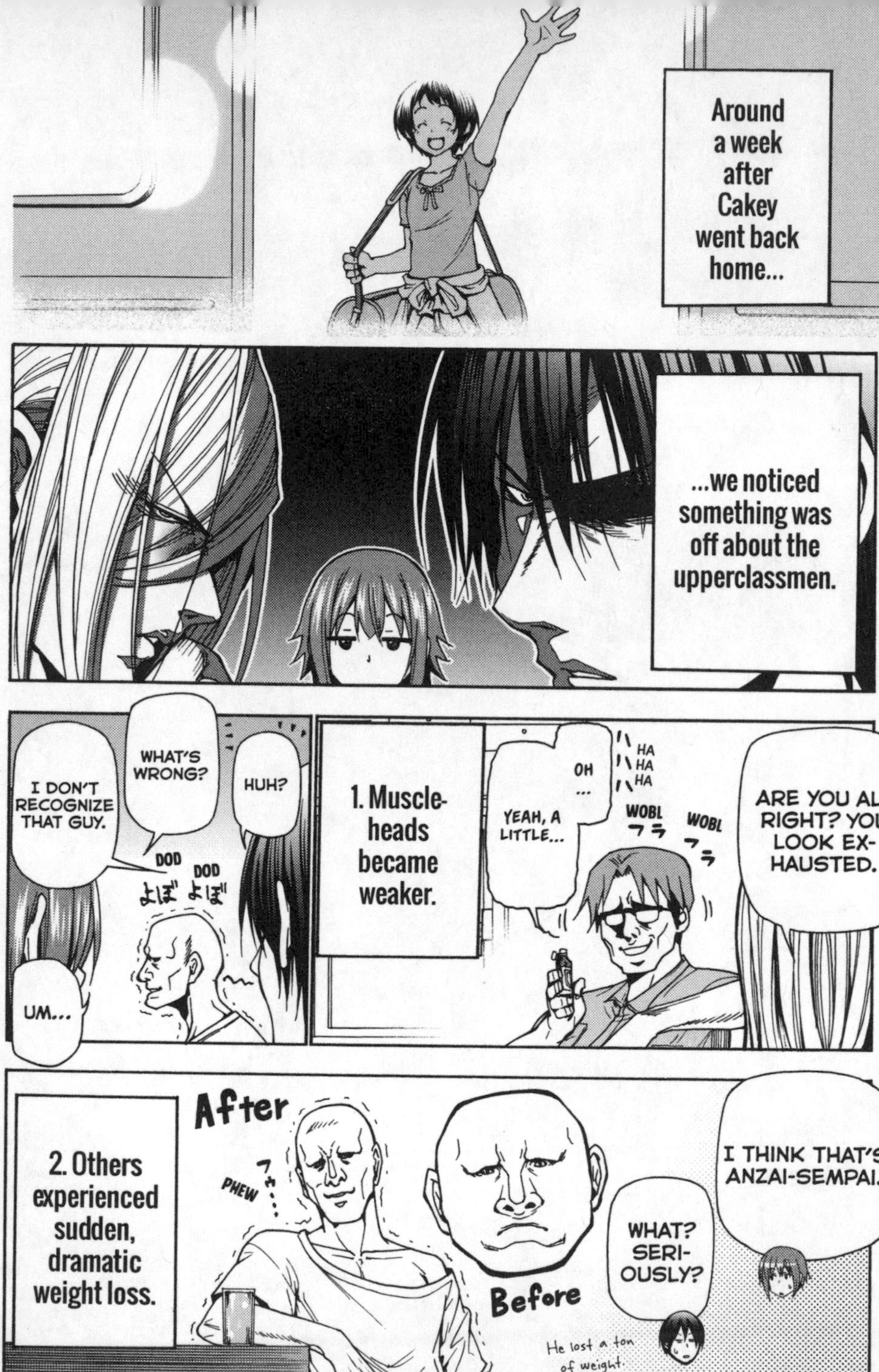
Around a week after Cakey went back home...
...we noticed something was off about the upperclassmen.
ARE YOU ALL RIGHT? YOU LOOK EX-HAUSTED.
HA HA HA
OH ...
YEAH, A LITTLE...
WOBL WOBL
1. Muscle-heads became weaker.
HUH?
WHAT'S WRONG?
I DON'T RECOGNIZE THAT GUY.
DOD DOD
よぼ よぼ
UM...
I THINK THAT'S ANZAI-SEMPAI.
WHAT? SERI-OUSLY?
He lost a ton of weight.
Before
After
PHEW
2. Others experienced sudden, dramatic weight loss.

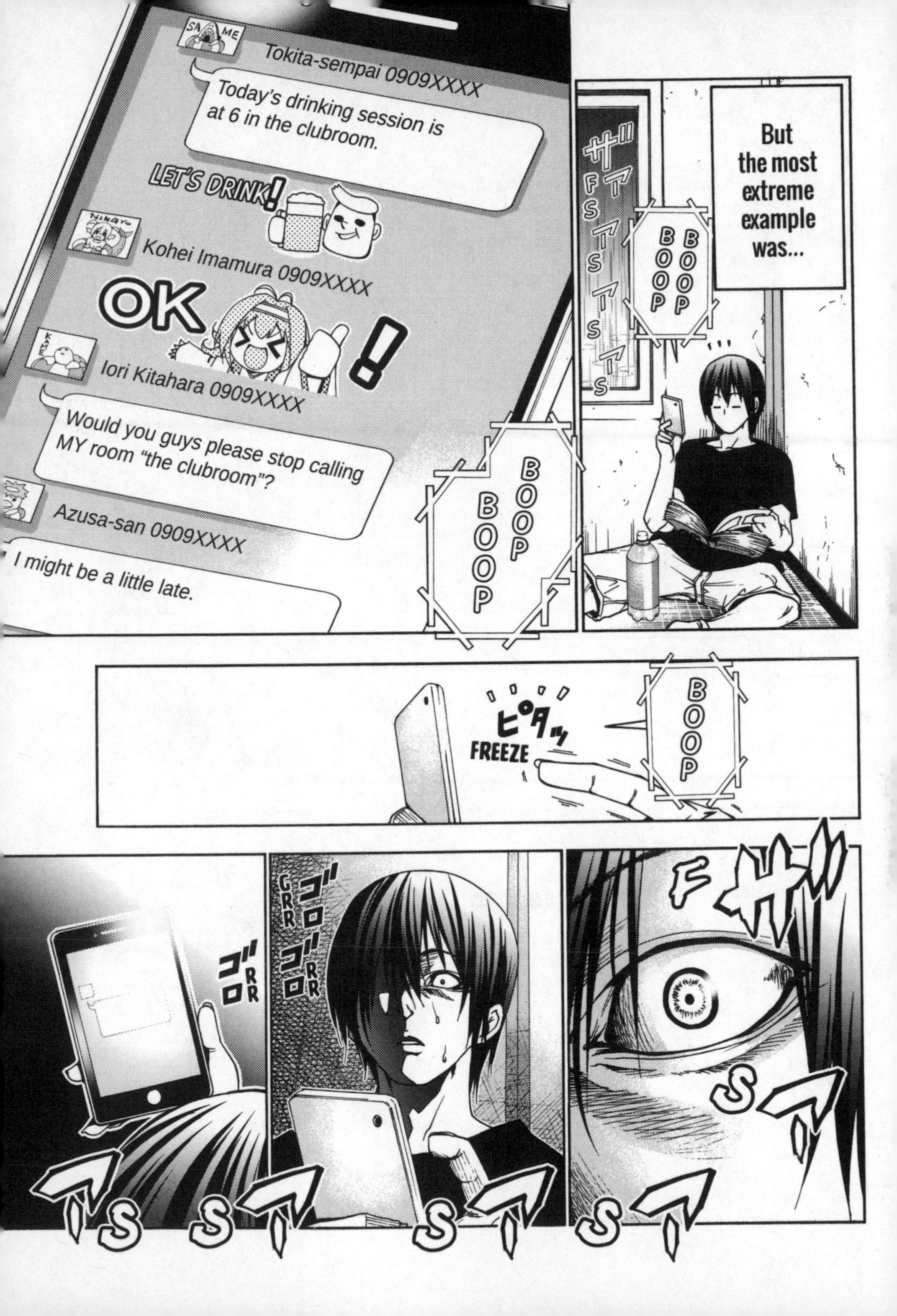

But the most extreme example was...
FSSSS
BOOP BOOP
BOOP BOOP
Tokita-sempai 0909XXXX
Today's drinking session is at 6 in the clubroom.
LET'S DRINK!
Kohei Imamura 0909XXXX
OK!
Iori Kitahara 0909XXXX
Would you guys please stop calling MY room "the clubroom"?
Azusa-san 0909XXXX
I might be a little late.
BOOP
FREEZE
FH!!
S
GRR
RR
S S S S

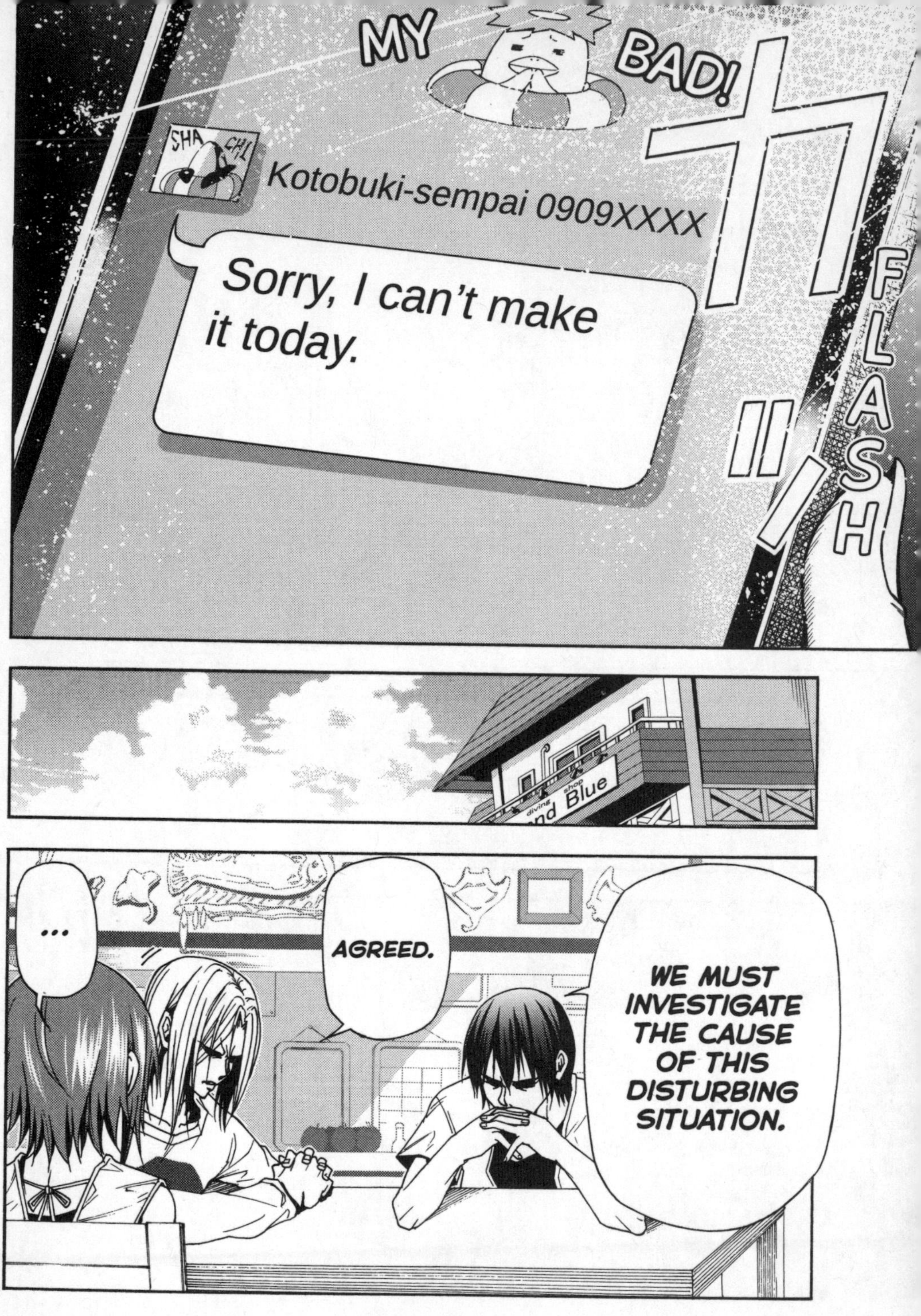
MY BAD!
SHA CHI
Kotobuki-sempai 0909XXXX
Sorry, I can't make it today.
FLASH
diving shop
WE MUST INVESTIGATE THE CAUSE OF THIS DISTURBING SITUATION.
AGREED.
...

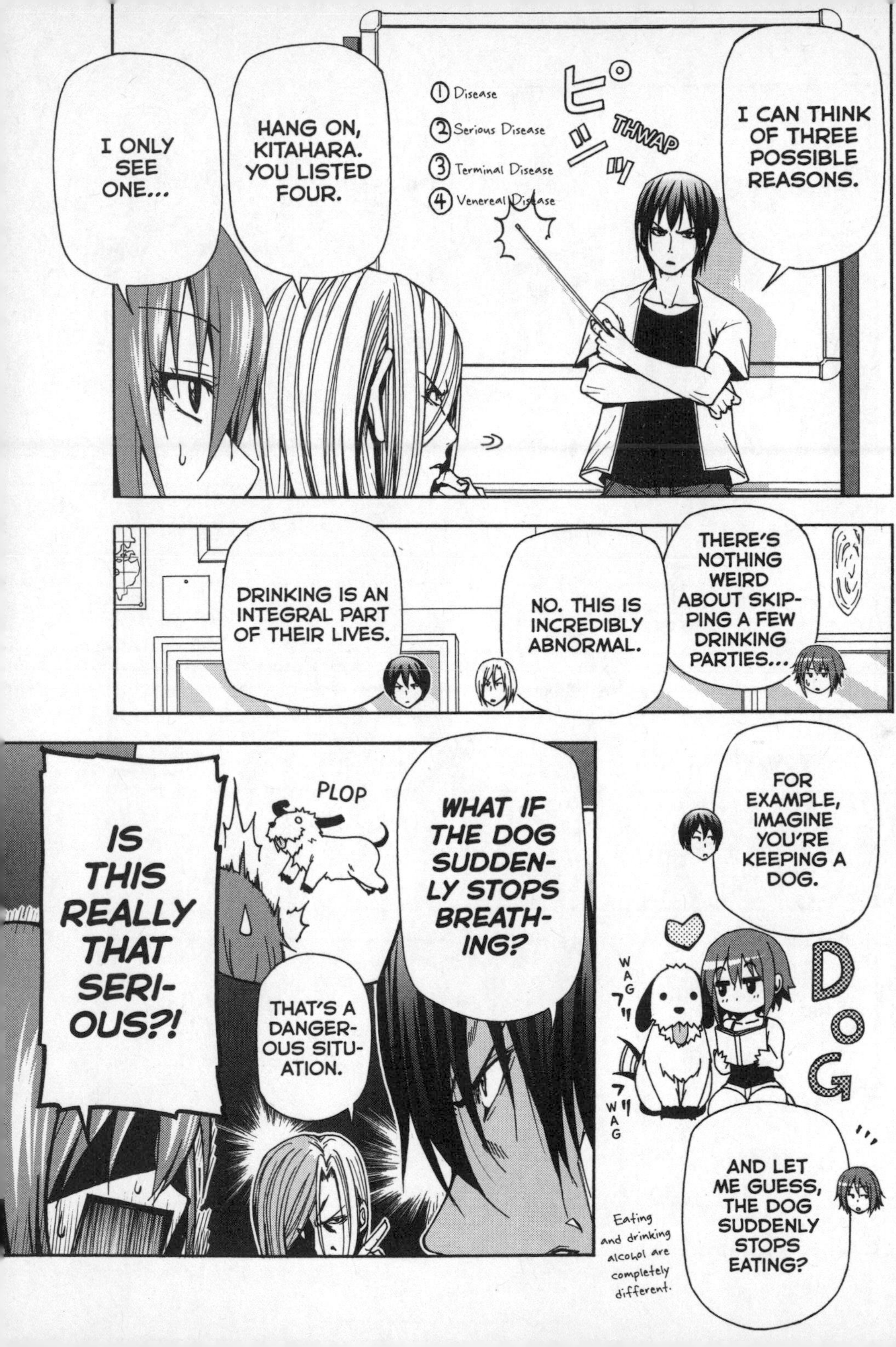
I CAN THINK OF THREE POSSIBLE REASONS.
THWAP
1 Disease
2 Serious Disease
3 Terminal Disease
4 Venereal Disease
HANG ON, KITAHARA. YOU LISTED FOUR.
I ONLY SEE ONE...
THERE'S NOTHING WEIRD ABOUT SKIP-PING A FEW DRINKING PARTIES...
NO. THIS IS INCREDIBLY ABNORMAL.
DRINKING IS AN INTEGRAL PART OF THEIR LIVES.
FOR EXAMPLE, IMAGINE YOU'RE KEEPING A DOG.
DOG
WAG
WAG
AND LET ME GUESS, THE DOG SUDDENLY STOPS EATING?
Eating and drinking alcohol are completely different.
WHAT IF THE DOG SUDDEN-LY STOPS BREATH-ING?
PLOP
THAT'S A DANGER-OUS SITU-ATION.
IS THIS REALLY THAT SERI-OUS?!

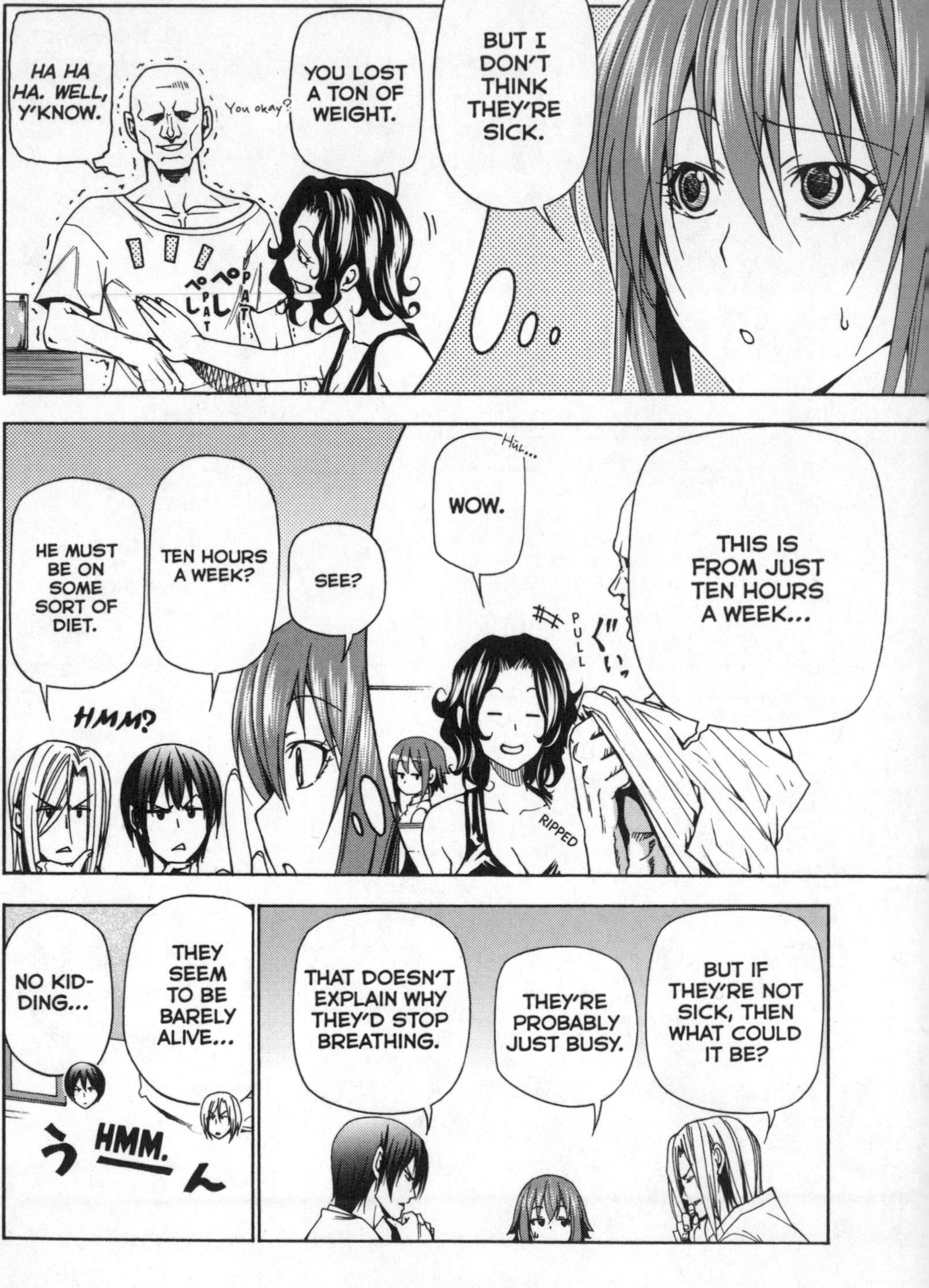
BUT I DON'T THINK THEY'RE SICK.
YOU LOST A TON OF WEIGHT.
You okay?
HA HA HA. WELL, Y'KNOW.
PAT PAT PAT
THIS IS FROM JUST TEN HOURS A WEEK...
Huh...
WOW.
PULL
SEE?
TEN HOURS A WEEK?
HE MUST BE ON SOME SORT OF DIET.
HMM?
RIPPED
BUT IF THEY'RE NOT SICK, THEN WHAT COULD IT BE?
THEY'RE PROBABLY JUST BUSY.
THAT DOESN'T EXPLAIN WHY THEY'D STOP BREATHING.
THEY SEEM TO BE BARELY ALIVE...
NO KID-DING...
HMM.

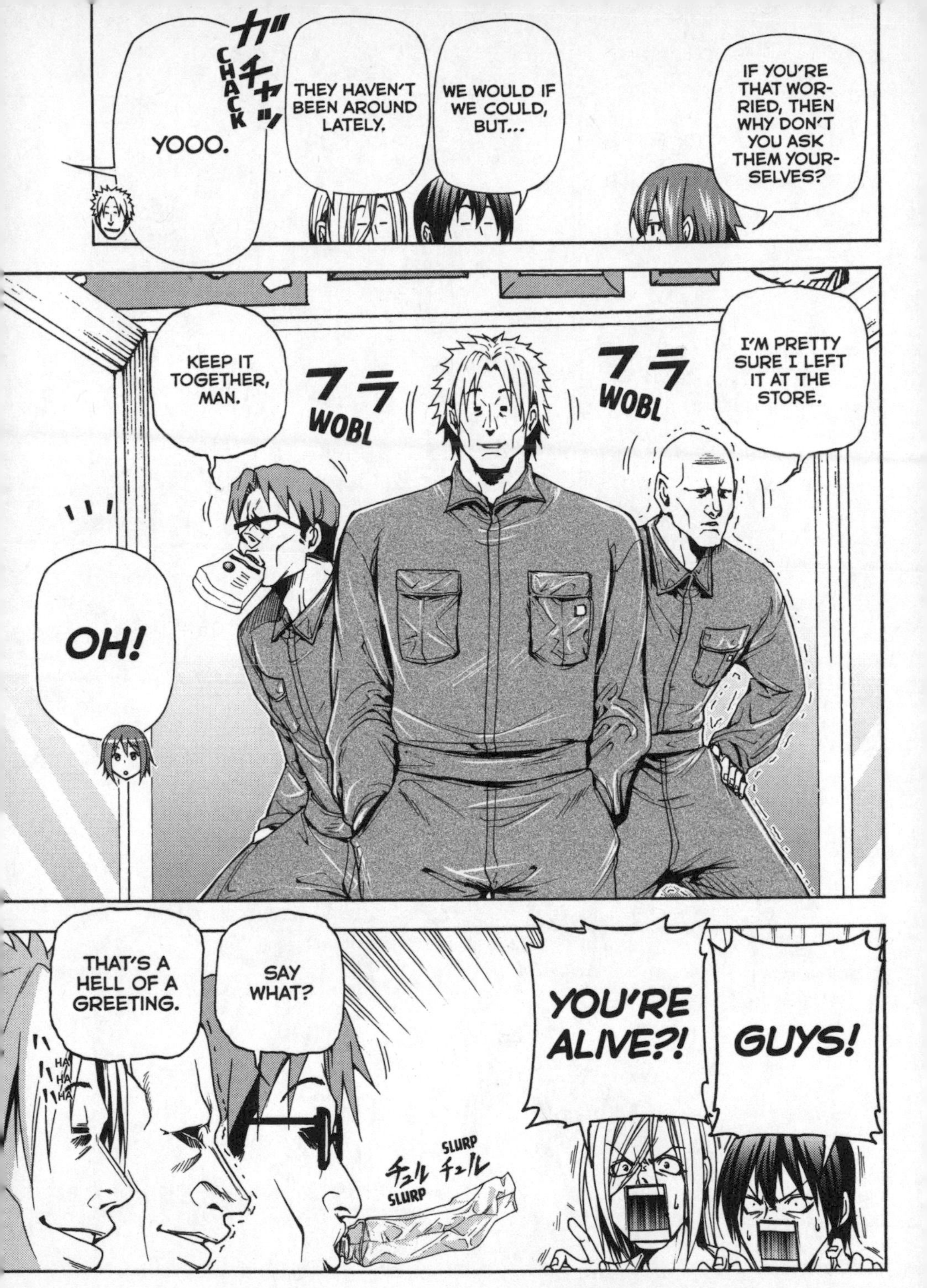
IF YOU'RE THAT WOR-RIED, THEN WHY DON'T YOU ASK THEM YOUR-SELVES?
WE WOULD IF WE COULD, BUT...
THEY HAVEN'T BEEN AROUND LATELY.
ガチャッ CHACK
YOOO.
I'M PRETTY SURE I LEFT IT AT THE STORE.
フラ WOBL
フラ WOBL
KEEP IT TOGETHER, MAN.
OH!
GUYS!
YOU'RE ALIVE?!
SAY WHAT?
THAT'S A HELL OF A GREETING.
チュルチュル SLURP SLURP
HA HA HA

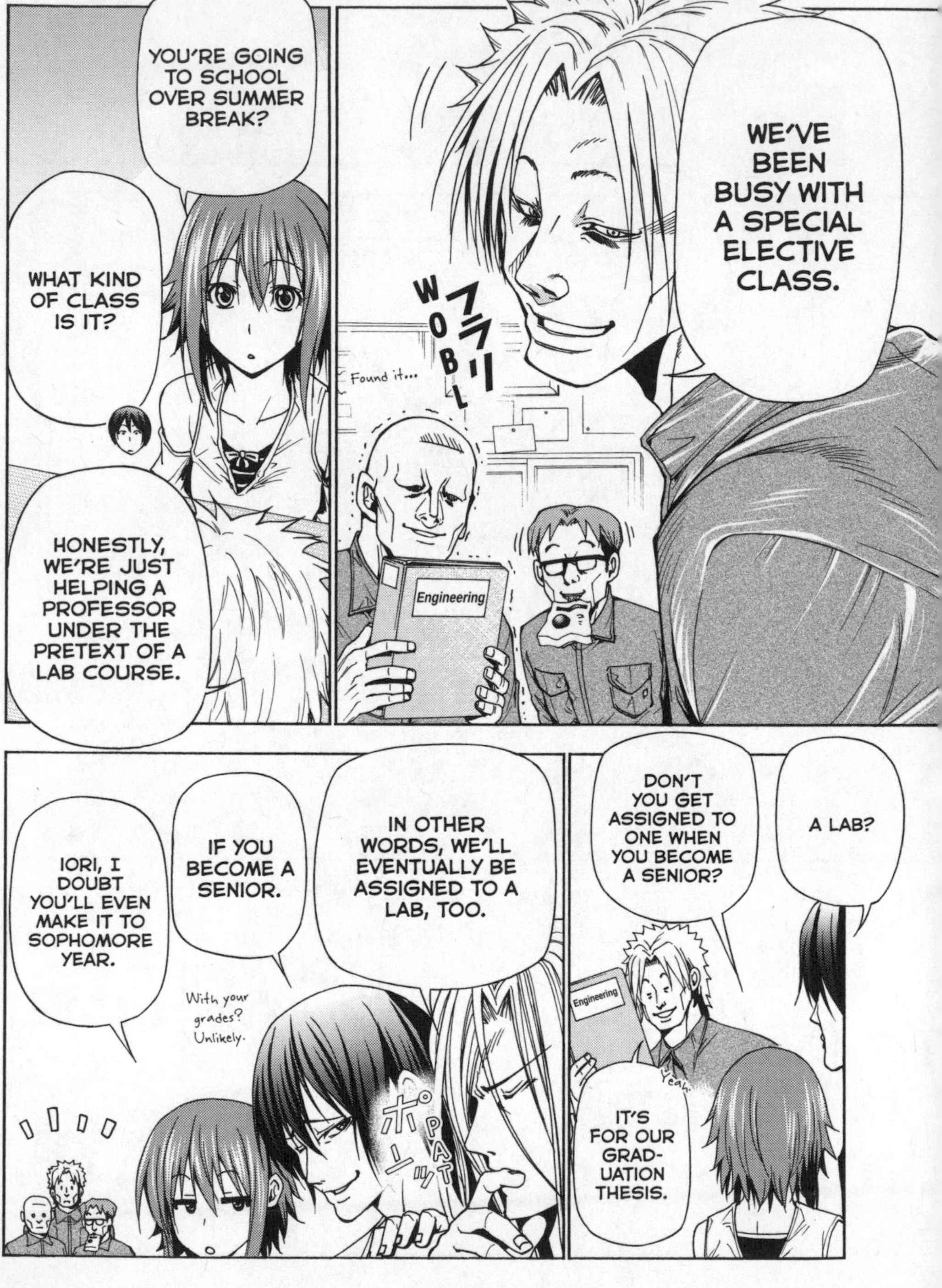
WE'VE BEEN BUSY WITH A SPECIAL ELECTIVE CLASS.
WOBBL
フラリ
Found it...
Engineering
YOU'RE GOING TO SCHOOL OVER SUMMER BREAK?
WHAT KIND OF CLASS IS IT?
HONESTLY, WE'RE JUST HELPING A PROFESSOR UNDER THE PRETEXT OF A LAB COURSE.
A LAB?
DON'T YOU GET ASSIGNED TO ONE WHEN YOU BECOME A SENIOR?
Engineering
Yeah.
IT'S FOR OUR GRAD-UATION THESIS.
IN OTHER WORDS, WE'LL EVENTUALLY BE ASSIGNED TO A LAB, TOO.
IF YOU BECOME A SENIOR.
IORI, I DOUBT YOU'LL EVEN MAKE IT TO SOPHOMORE YEAR.
With your grades? Unlikely.
ポンッ
PAT

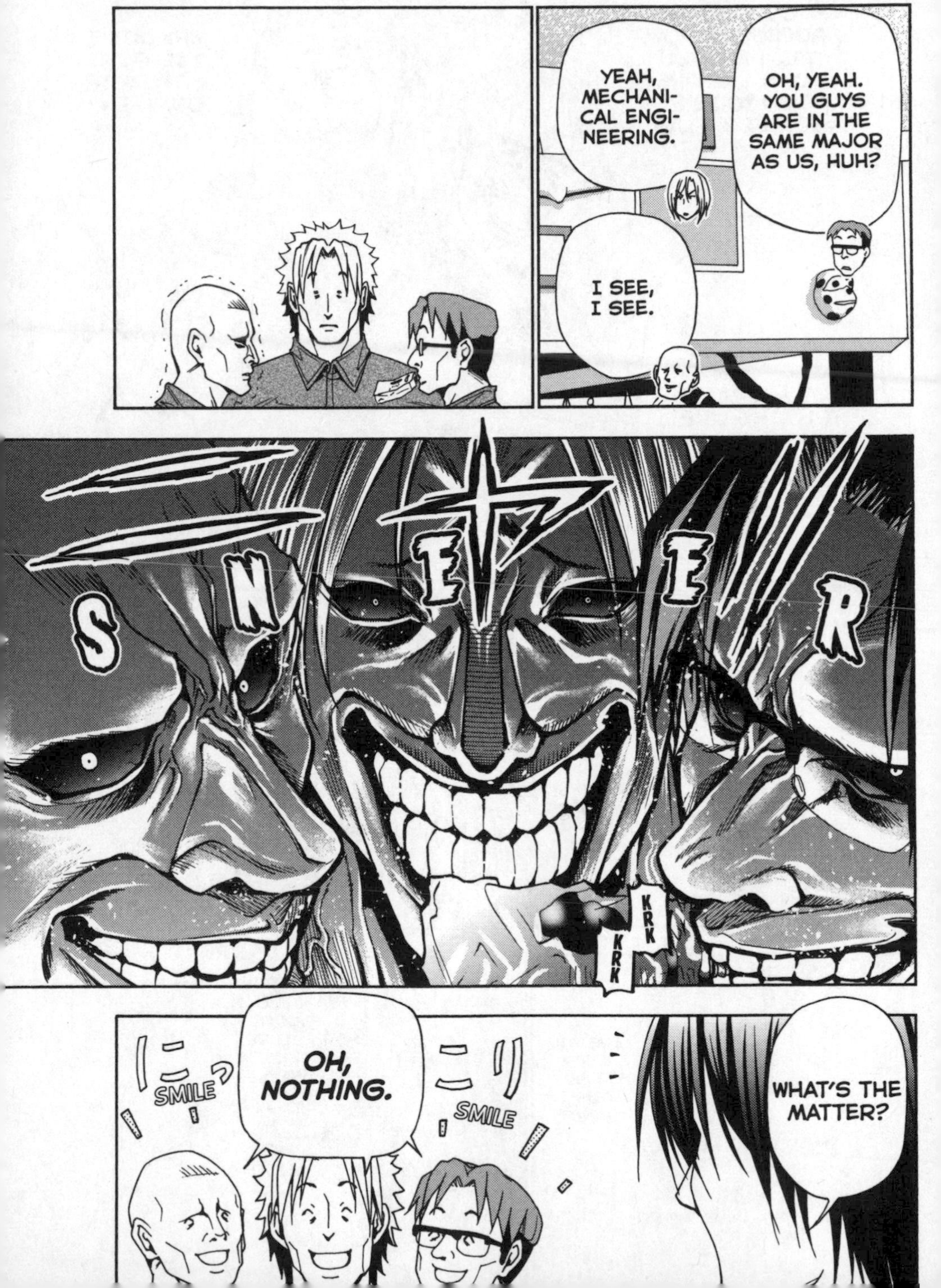
OH, YEAH. YOU GUYS ARE IN THE SAME MAJOR AS US, HUH?
YEAH, MECHANICAL ENGINEERING.
I SEE, I SEE.
SNEER
KRK KRK
WHAT'S THE MATTER?
SMILE
OH, NOTHING.
SMILE

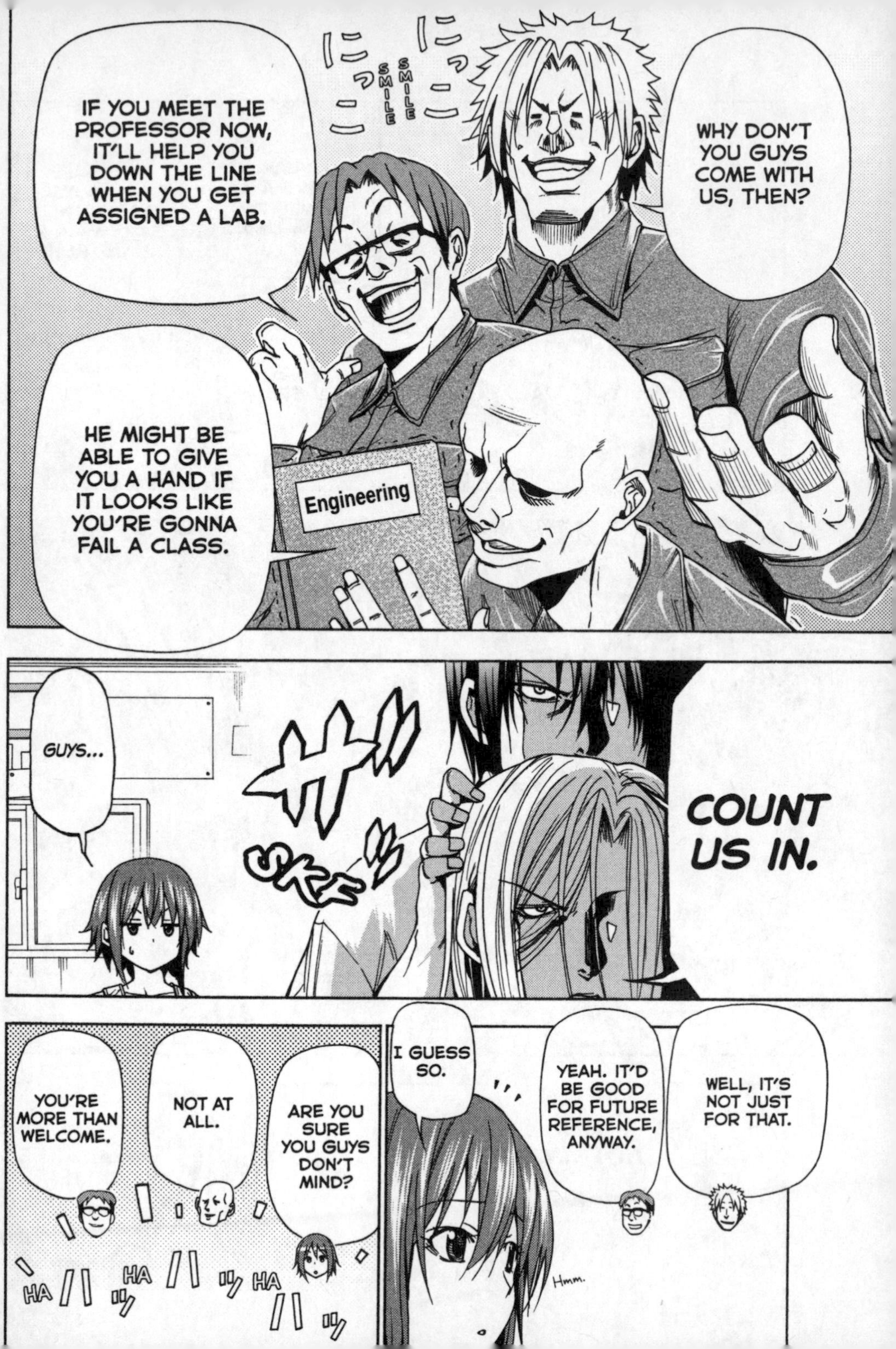
WHY DON'T YOU GUYS COME WITH US, THEN?
SMILE SMILE
IF YOU MEET THE PROFESSOR NOW, IT'LL HELP YOU DOWN THE LINE WHEN YOU GET ASSIGNED A LAB.
Engineering
HE MIGHT BE ABLE TO GIVE YOU A HAND IF IT LOOKS LIKE YOU'RE GONNA FAIL A CLASS.
COUNT US IN.
SKF
GUYS...
WELL, IT'S NOT JUST FOR THAT.
YEAH. IT'D BE GOOD FOR FUTURE REFERENCE, ANYWAY.
I GUESS SO.
Hmm.
ARE YOU SURE YOU GUYS DON'T MIND?
NOT AT ALL.
YOU'RE MORE THAN WELCOME.
HA HA HA

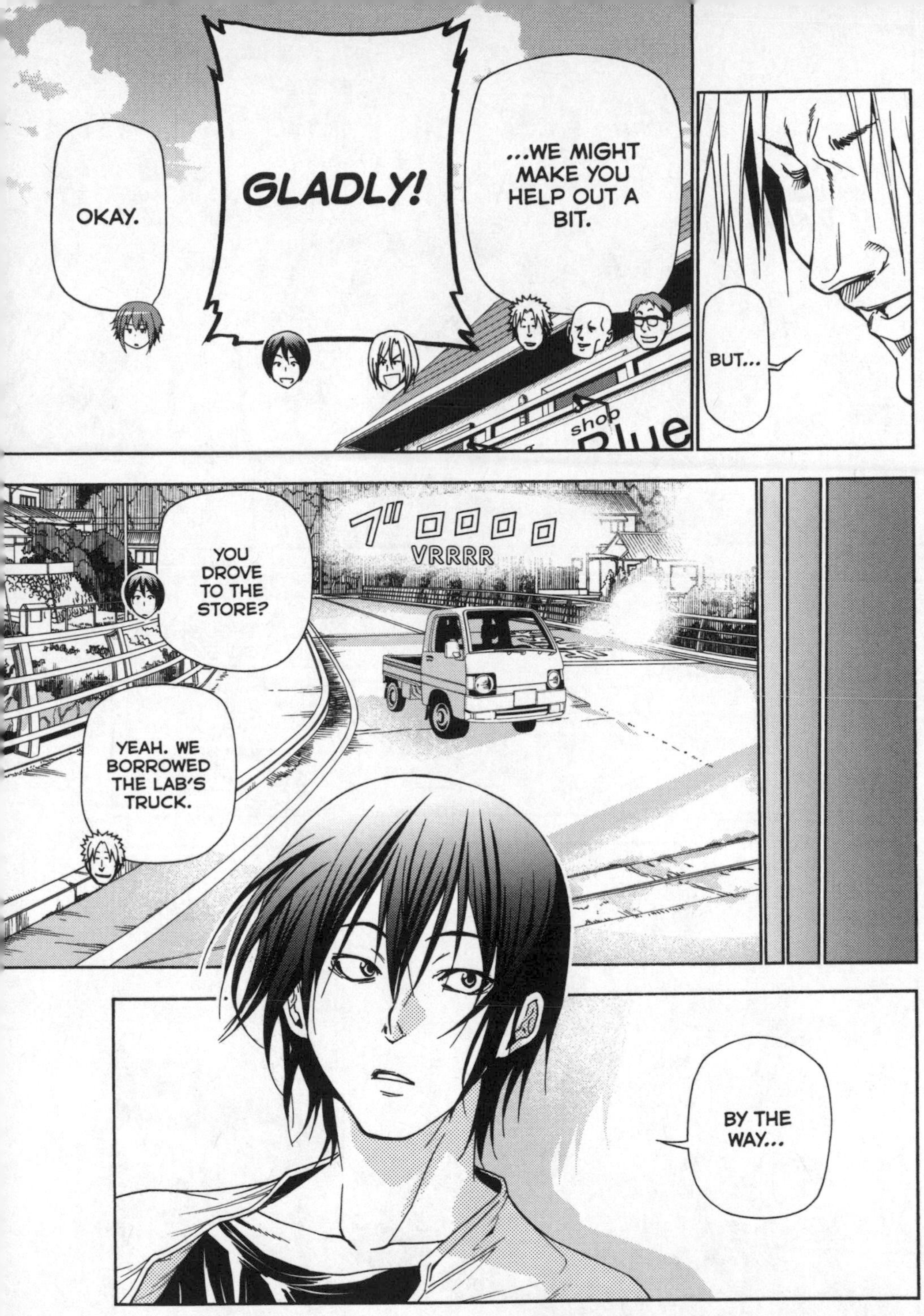
BUT...
...WE MIGHT MAKE YOU HELP OUT A BIT.
GLADLY!
OKAY.
shop
ブロロロロ
VRRRR
YOU DROVE TO THE STORE?
YEAH. WE BORROWED THE LAB'S TRUCK.
BY THE WAY...

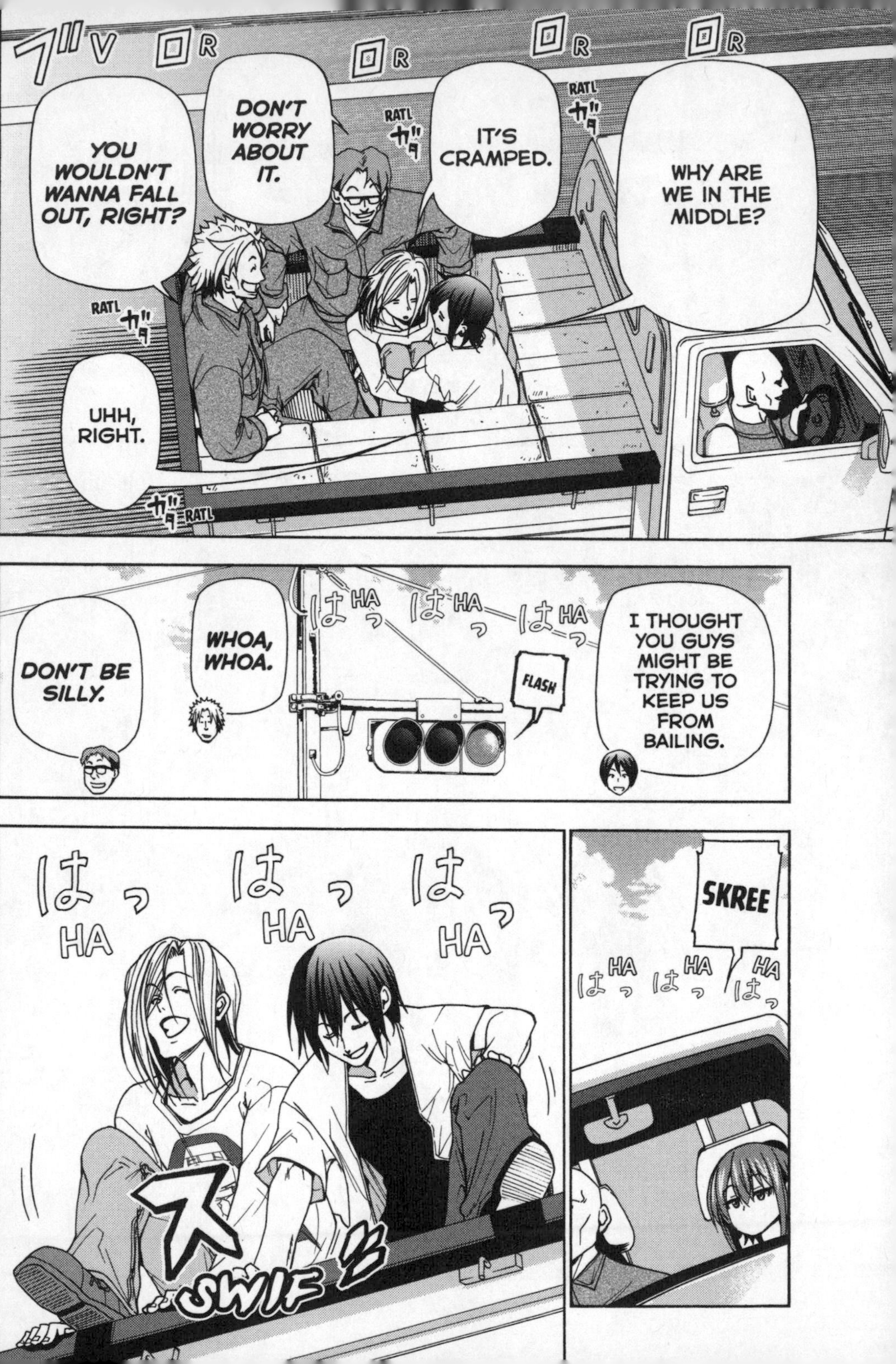

V R R R R
WHY ARE WE IN THE MIDDLE?
RATL
IT'S CRAMPED.
RATL
DON'T WORRY ABOUT IT.
YOU WOULDN'T WANNA FALL OUT, RIGHT?
RATL
UHH, RIGHT.
RATL
I THOUGHT YOU GUYS MIGHT BE TRYING TO KEEP US FROM BAILING.
FLASH
HA HA HA
WHOA, WHOA.
DON'T BE SILLY.
SKREE
HA HA HA
HA HA HA
SWIF

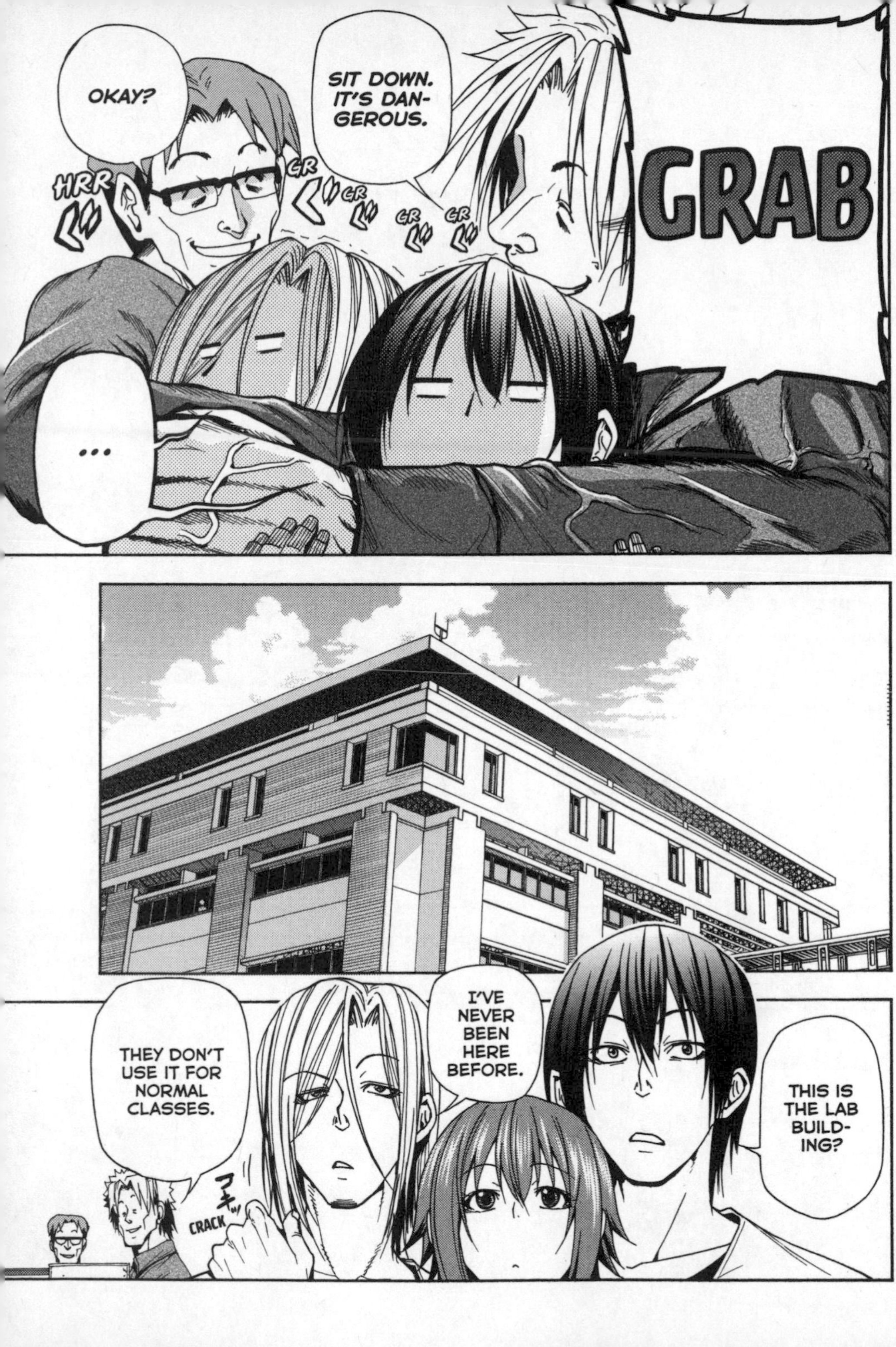
GRAB
SIT DOWN. IT'S DANGEROUS.
GR GR GR GR
OKAY?
HRR
...
THIS IS THE LAB BUILDING?
I'VE NEVER BEEN HERE BEFORE.
THEY DON'T USE IT FOR NORMAL CLASSES.
コキッ
CRACK

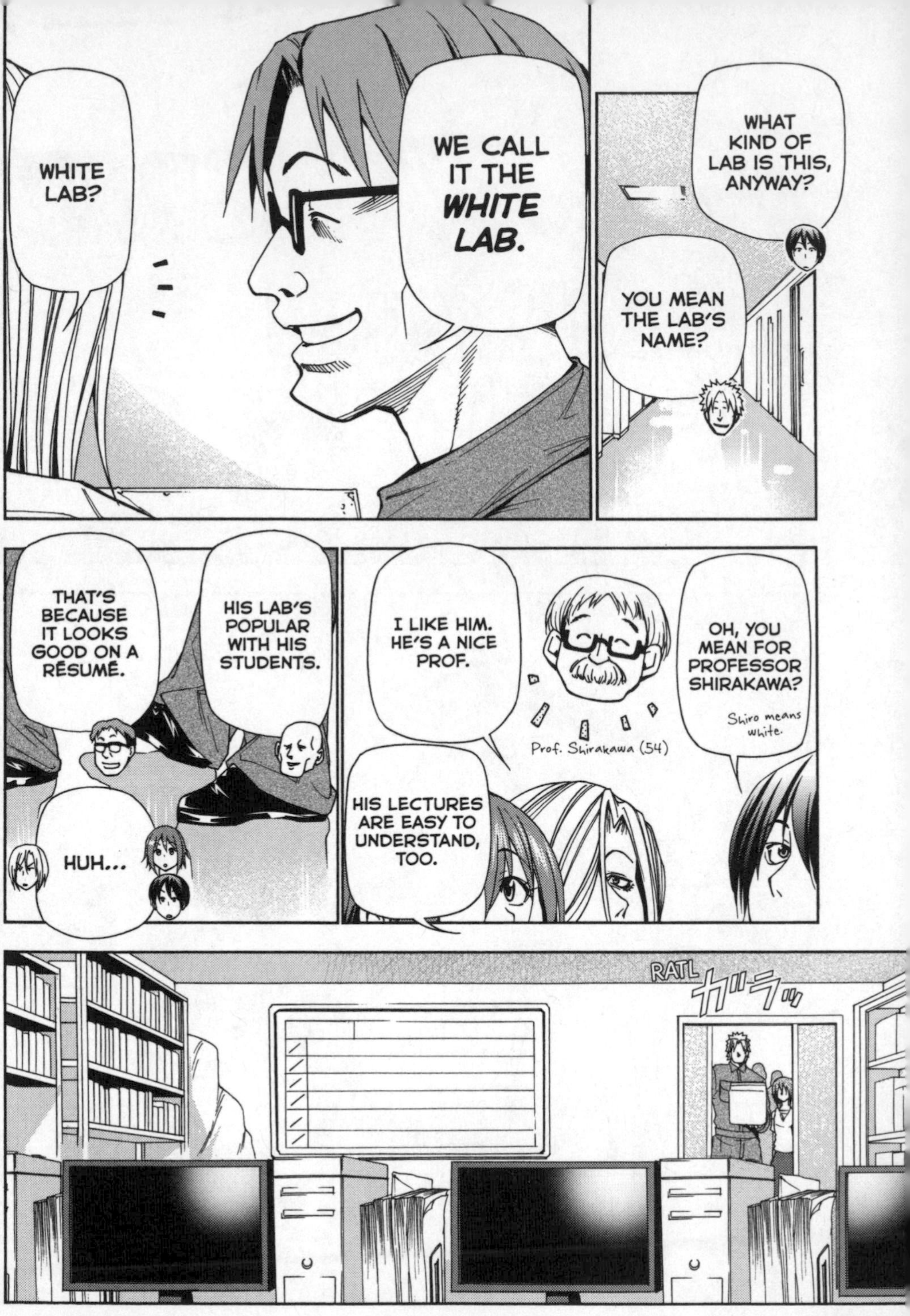
WHAT KIND OF LAB IS THIS, ANYWAY?
YOU MEAN THE LAB'S NAME?
WE CALL IT THE *WHITE LAB.*
WHITE LAB?
OH, YOU MEAN FOR PROFESSOR SHIRAKAWA?
Shiro means white.
I LIKE HIM. HE'S A NICE PROF.
Prof. Shirakawa (54)
HIS LECTURES ARE EASY TO UNDERSTAND, TOO.
HIS LAB'S POPULAR WITH HIS STUDENTS.
THAT'S BECAUSE IT LOOKS GOOD ON A RÉSUMÉ.
HUH...
RATL
ガラッ

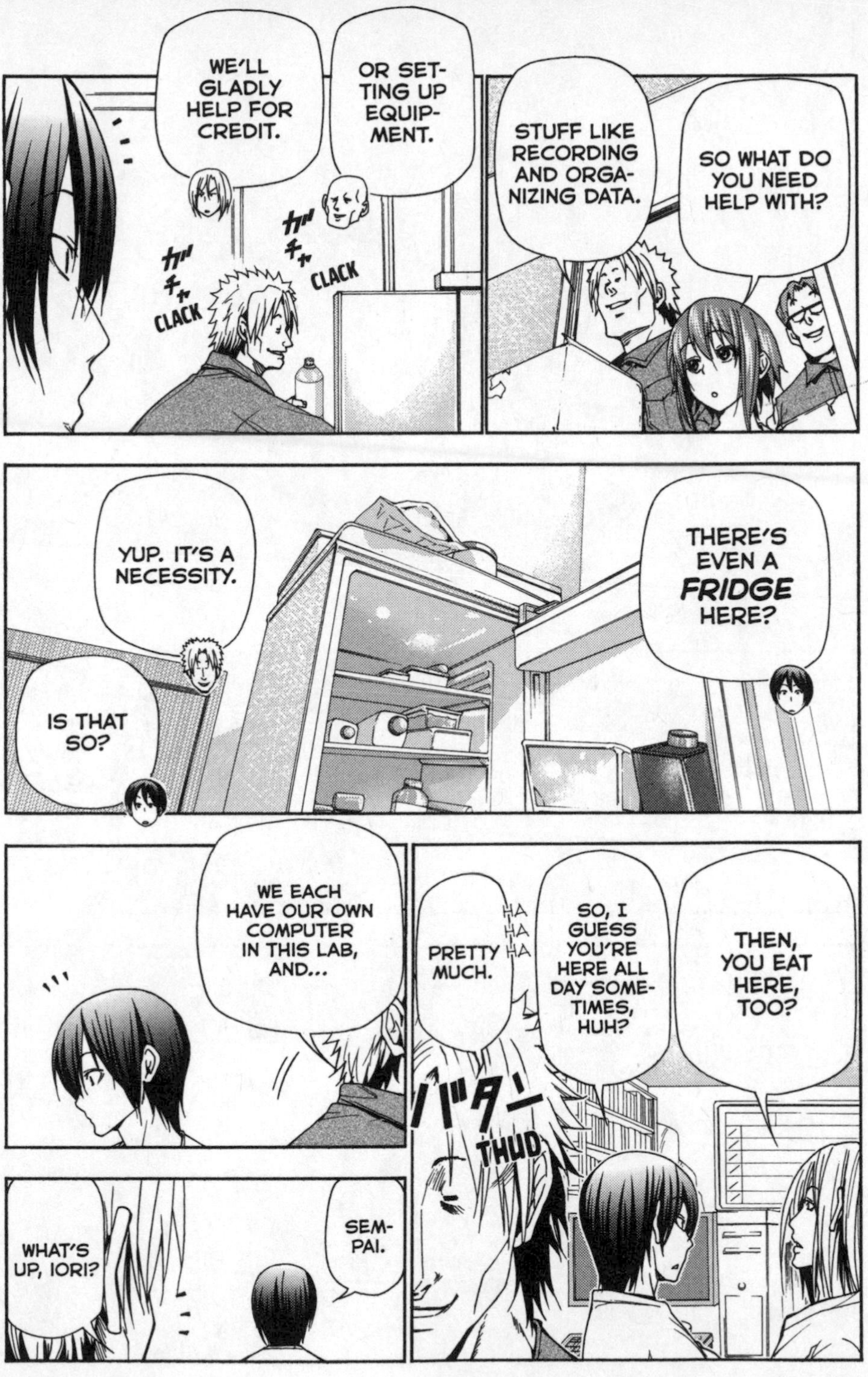
SO WHAT DO YOU NEED HELP WITH?
STUFF LIKE RECORDING AND ORGANIZING DATA.
OR SETTING UP EQUIPMENT.
WE'LL GLADLY HELP FOR CREDIT.
ガチャ CLACK
ガチャ CLACK
THERE'S EVEN A FRIDGE HERE?
YUP. IT'S A NECESSITY.
IS THAT SO?
THEN, YOU EAT HERE, TOO?
SO, I GUESS YOU'RE HERE ALL DAY SOMETIMES, HUH?
HA HA HA
PRETTY MUCH.
バタン THUD
WE EACH HAVE OUR OWN COMPUTER IN THIS LAB, AND...
SEMPAI.
WHAT'S UP, IORI?

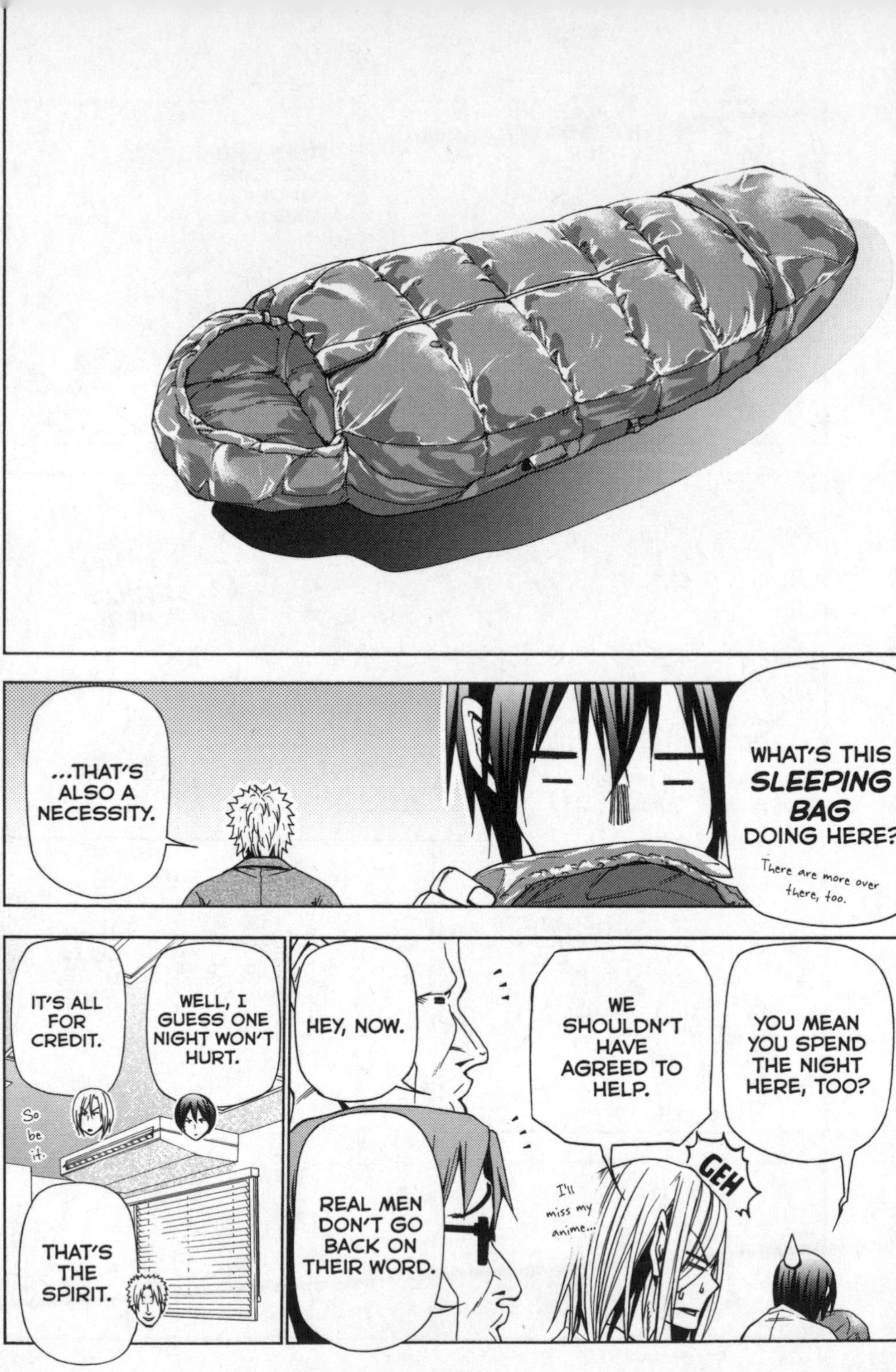
WHAT'S THIS SLEEPING BAG DOING HERE?
There are more over there, too.
...THAT'S ALSO A NECESSITY.
YOU MEAN YOU SPEND THE NIGHT HERE, TOO?
WE SHOULDN'T HAVE AGREED TO HELP.
GEH
I'll miss my anime...
HEY, NOW.
REAL MEN DON'T GO BACK ON THEIR WORD.
WELL, I GUESS ONE NIGHT WON'T HURT.
IT'S ALL FOR CREDIT.
So be it.
THAT'S THE SPIRIT.

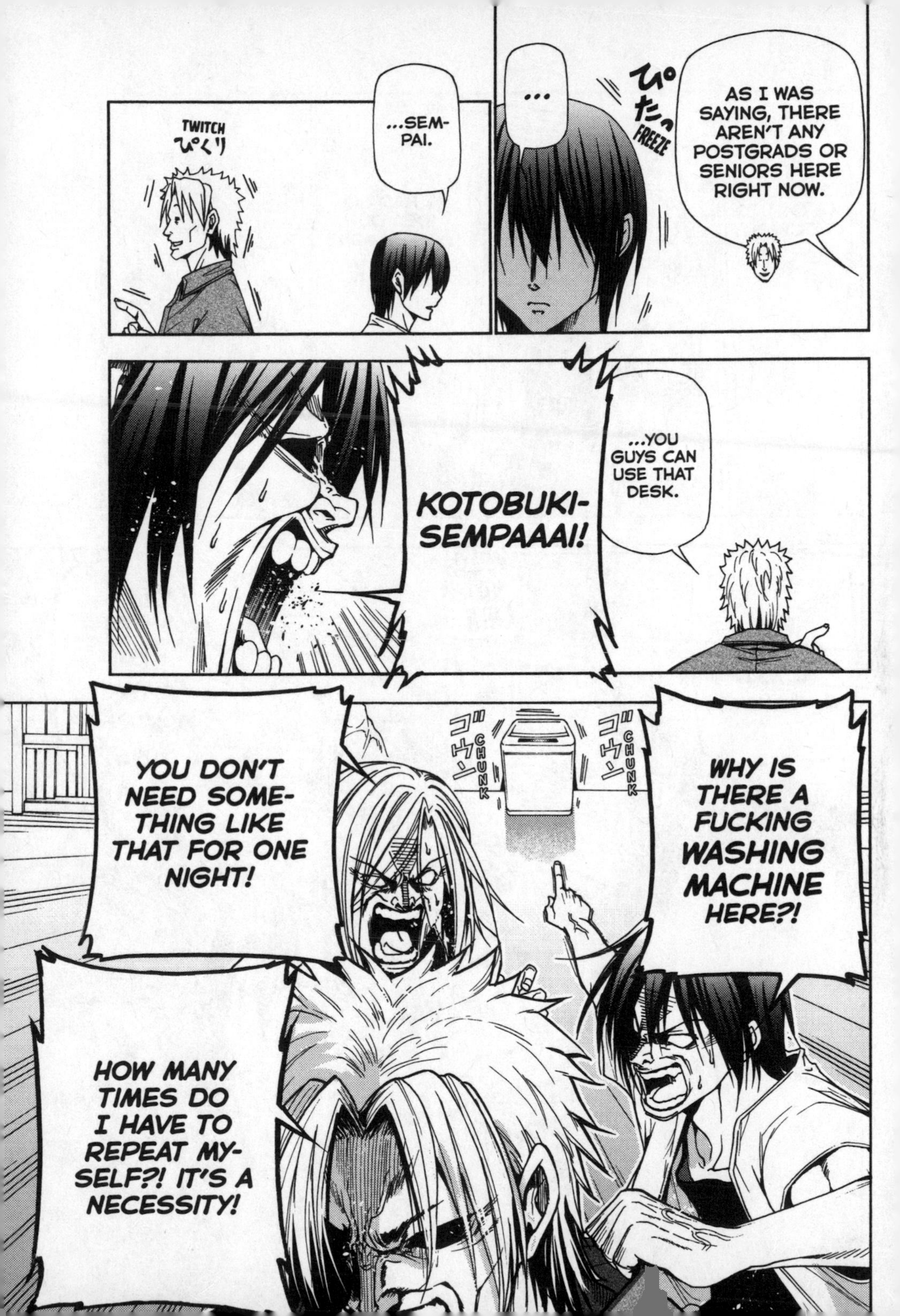
AS I WAS SAYING, THERE AREN'T ANY POSTGRADS OR SENIORS HERE RIGHT NOW.
ぴたっ
FREEZE
...
...SEM-PAI.
TWITCH
ぴくり
...YOU GUYS CAN USE THAT DESK.
KOTOBUKI-SEMPAAAI!
WHY IS THERE A FUCKING WASHING MACHINE HERE?!
ゴウン
CHUNK
ゴウン
CHUNK
YOU DON'T NEED SOME-THING LIKE THAT FOR ONE NIGHT!
HOW MANY TIMES DO I HAVE TO REPEAT MY-SELF?! IT'S A NECESSITY!

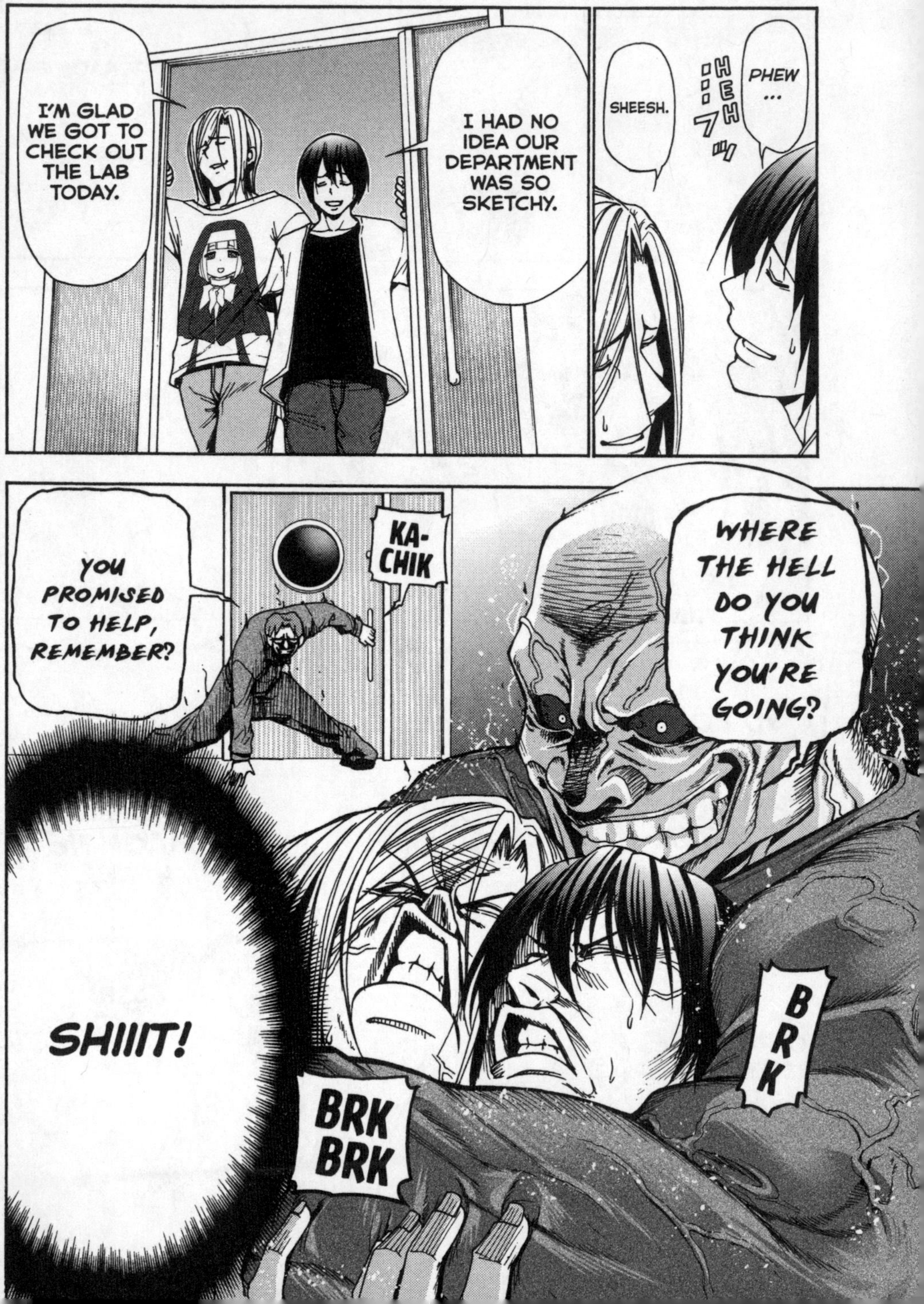
PHEW ...
HEH HEH
SHEESH.
I HAD NO IDEA OUR DEPARTMENT WAS SO SKETCHY.
I'M GLAD WE GOT TO CHECK OUT THE LAB TODAY.
WHERE THE HELL DO YOU THINK YOU'RE GOING?
KA-CHIK
YOU PROMISED TO HELP, REMEMBER?
BRK
BRK BRK
SHIIIT!

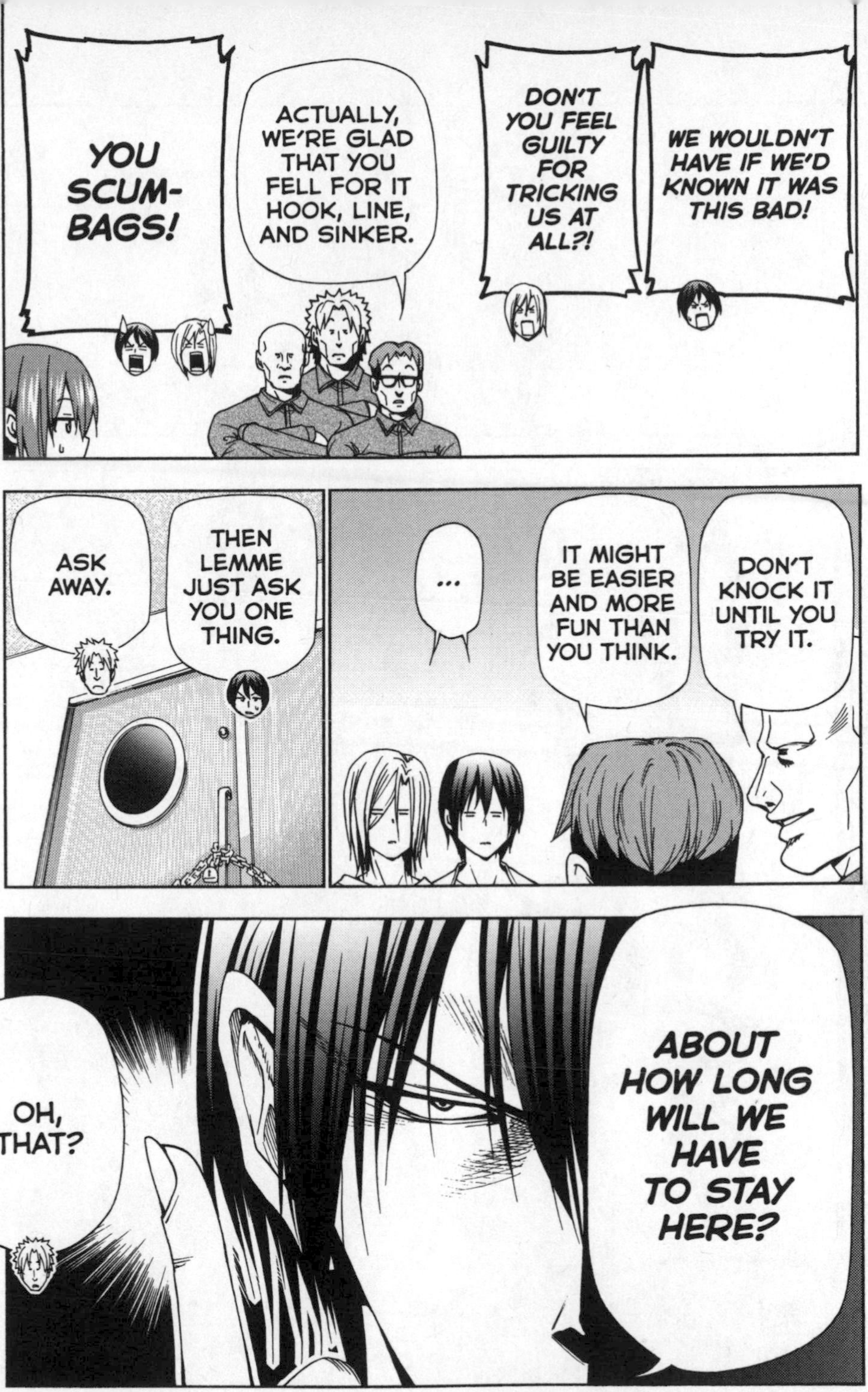
WE WOULDN'T HAVE IF WE'D KNOWN IT WAS THIS BAD!
DON'T YOU FEEL GUILTY FOR TRICKING US AT ALL?!
ACTUALLY, WE'RE GLAD THAT YOU FELL FOR IT HOOK, LINE, AND SINKER.
YOU SCUM-BAGS!
DON'T KNOCK IT UNTIL YOU TRY IT.
IT MIGHT BE EASIER AND MORE FUN THAN YOU THINK.
...
THEN LEMME JUST ASK YOU ONE THING.
ASK AWAY.
ABOUT HOW LONG WILL WE HAVE TO STAY HERE?
OH, THAT?

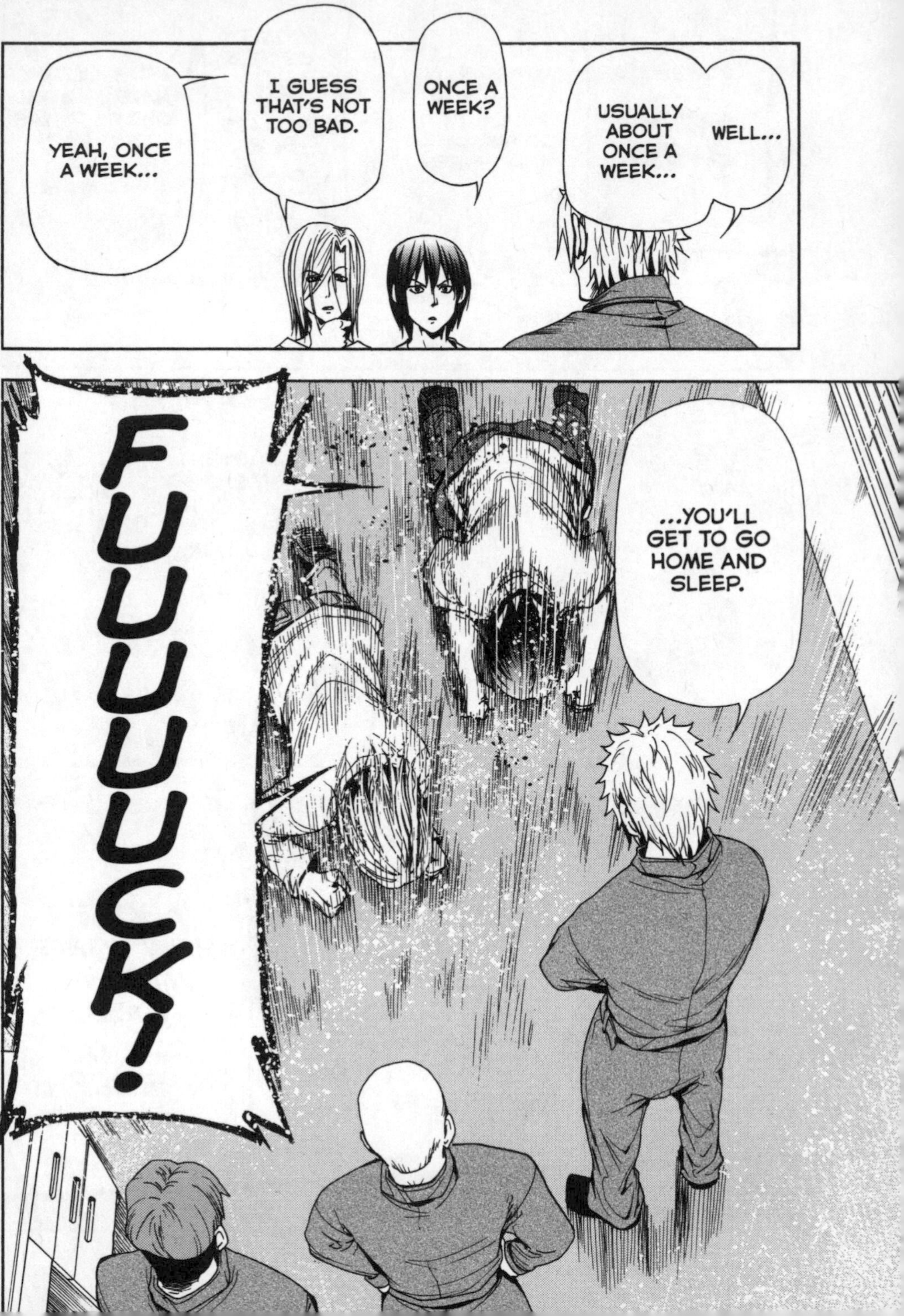
WELL...
USUALLY ABOUT ONCE A WEEK...
ONCE A WEEK?
I GUESS THAT'S NOT TOO BAD.
YEAH, ONCE A WEEK...
...YOU'LL GET TO GO HOME AND SLEEP.
FUUUUUCK!

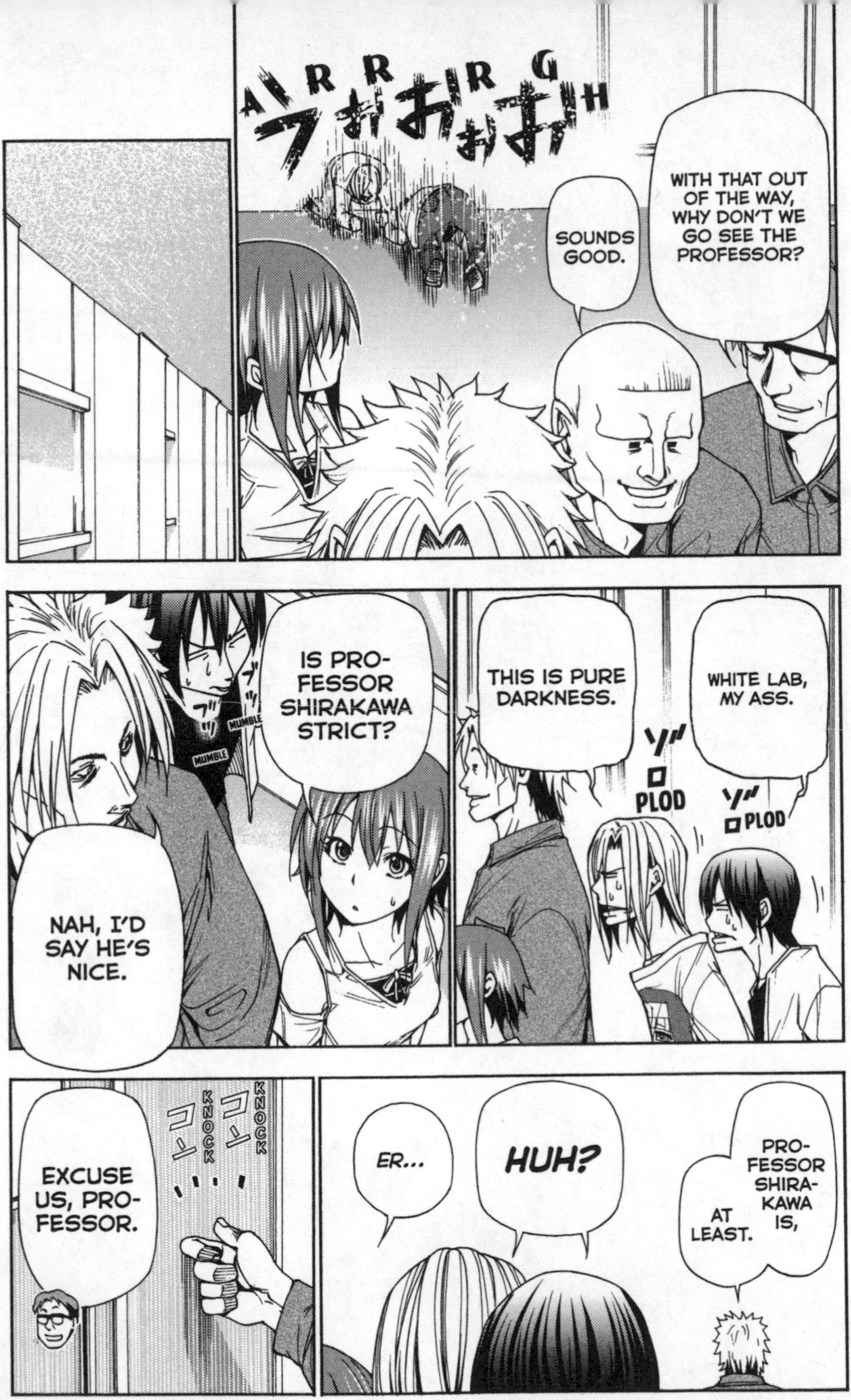
ARRRGH
WITH THAT OUT OF THE WAY, WHY DON'T WE GO SEE THE PROFESSOR?
SOUNDS GOOD.
WHITE LAB, MY ASS.
THIS IS PURE DARKNESS.
PLOD
PLOD
MUMBLE
MUMBLE
IS PRO-FESSOR SHIRAKAWA STRICT?
NAH, I'D SAY HE'S NICE.
PRO-FESSOR SHIRA-KAWA IS,
AT LEAST.
HUH?
ER...
KNOCK
KNOCK
EXCUSE US, PRO-FESSOR.

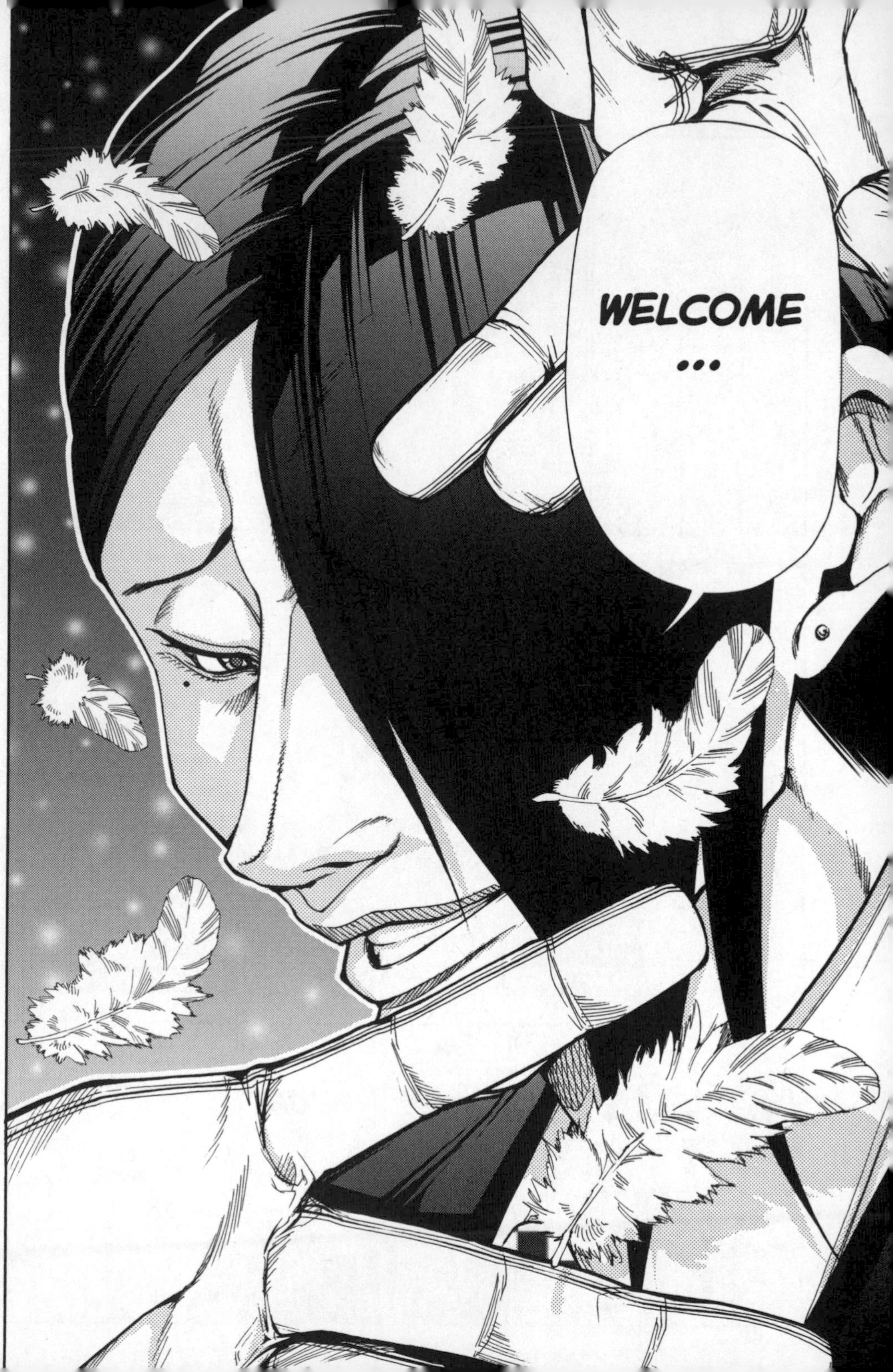
WELCOME
...

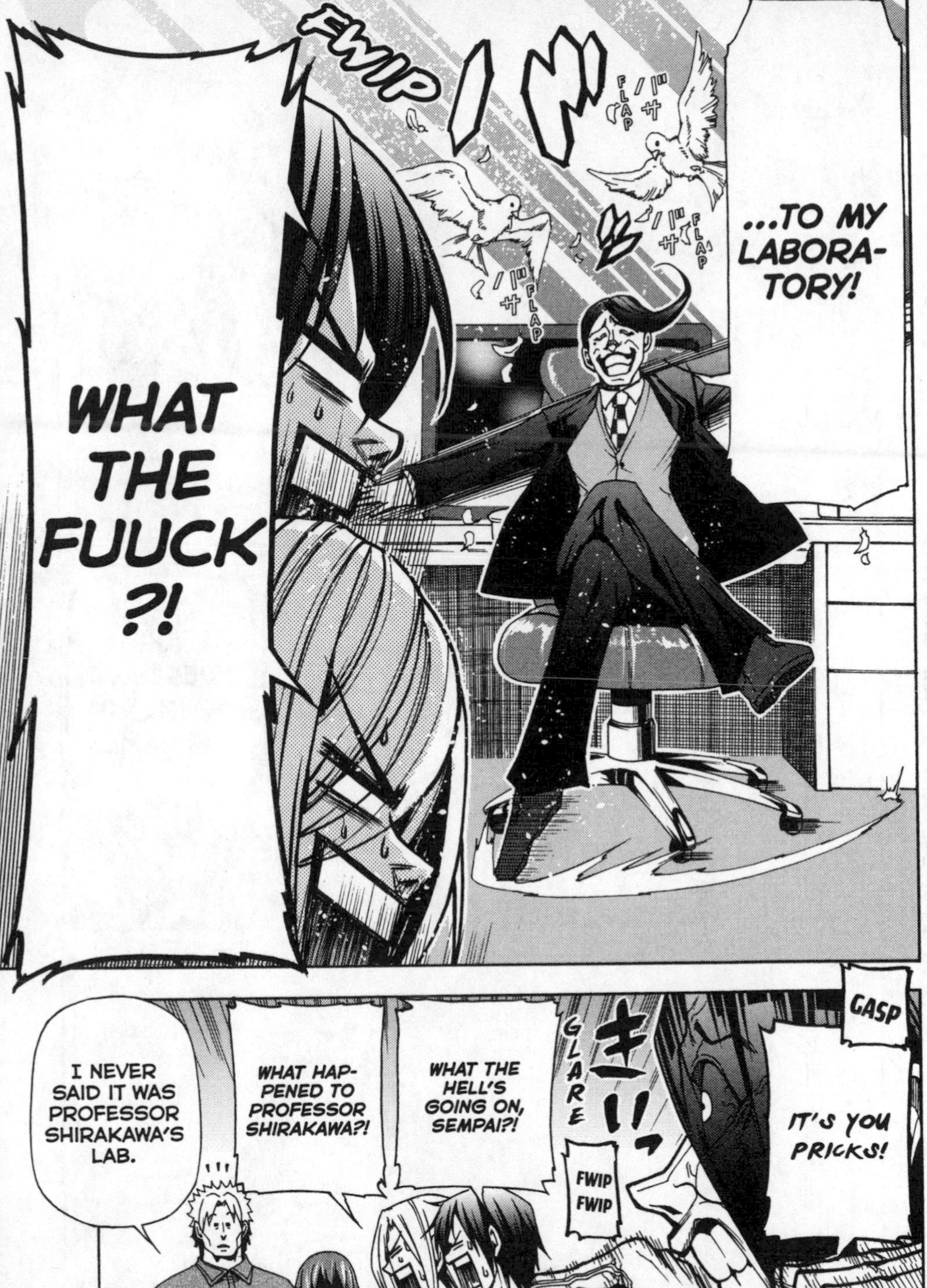
...TO MY LABORA-TORY!
FWIP
FLAP
FLAP
FLAP
WHAT THE FUUCK ?!
GASP
IT'S YOU PRICKS!
GLARE
FWIP FWIP
WHAT THE HELL'S GOING ON, SEMPAI?!
WHAT HAP-PENED TO PROFESSOR SHIRAKAWA?!
I NEVER SAID IT WAS PROFESSOR SHIRAKAWA'S LAB.

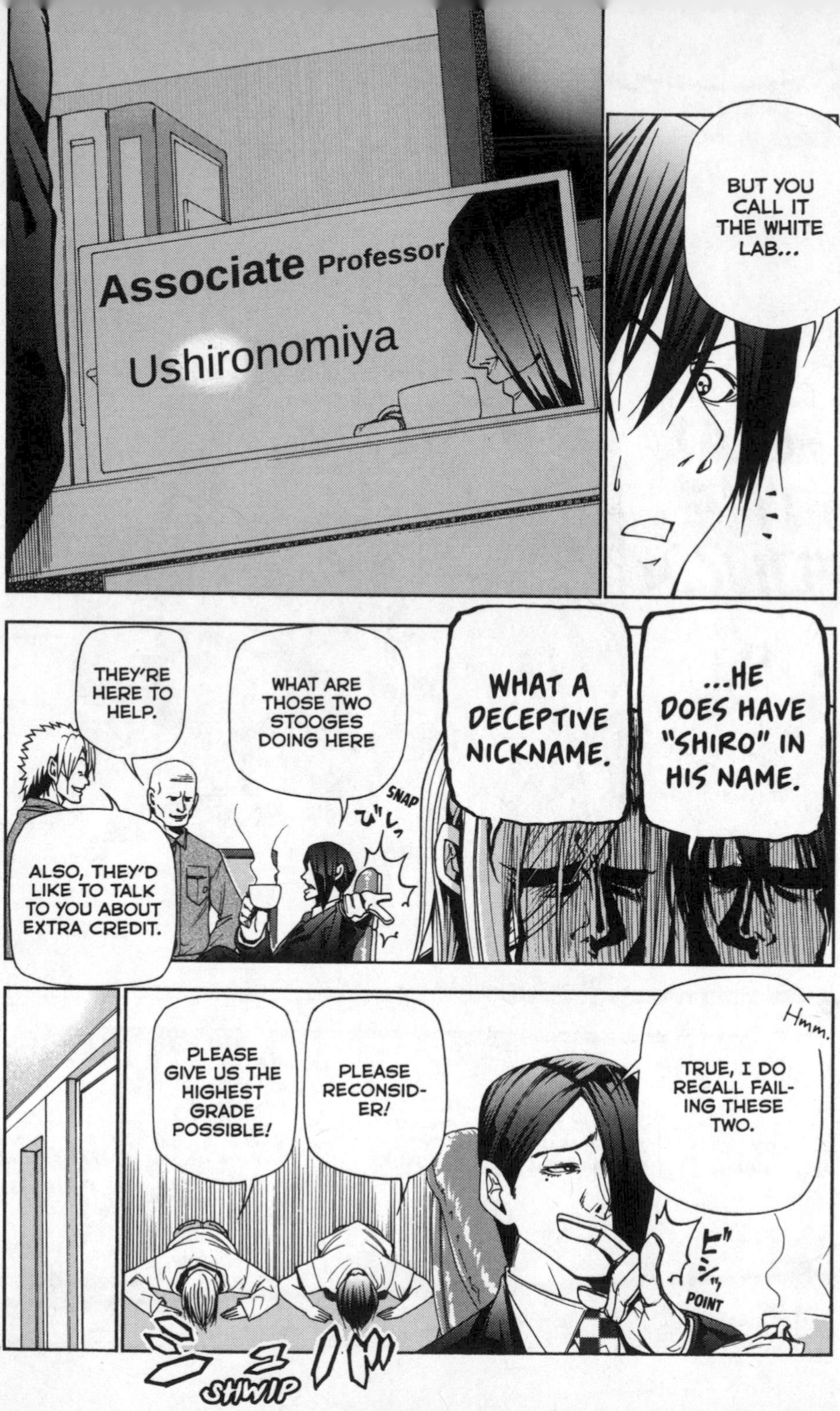
BUT YOU CALL IT THE WHITE LAB...
Associate Professor
Ushironomiya
...HE DOES HAVE "SHIRO" IN HIS NAME.
WHAT A DECEPTIVE NICKNAME.
WHAT ARE THOSE TWO STOOGES DOING HERE
SNAP
THEY'RE HERE TO HELP.
ALSO, THEY'D LIKE TO TALK TO YOU ABOUT EXTRA CREDIT.
Hmm.
TRUE, I DO RECALL FAIL-ING THESE TWO.
POINT
PLEASE RECONSID-ER!
PLEASE GIVE US THE HIGHEST GRADE POSSIBLE!
SHWIP

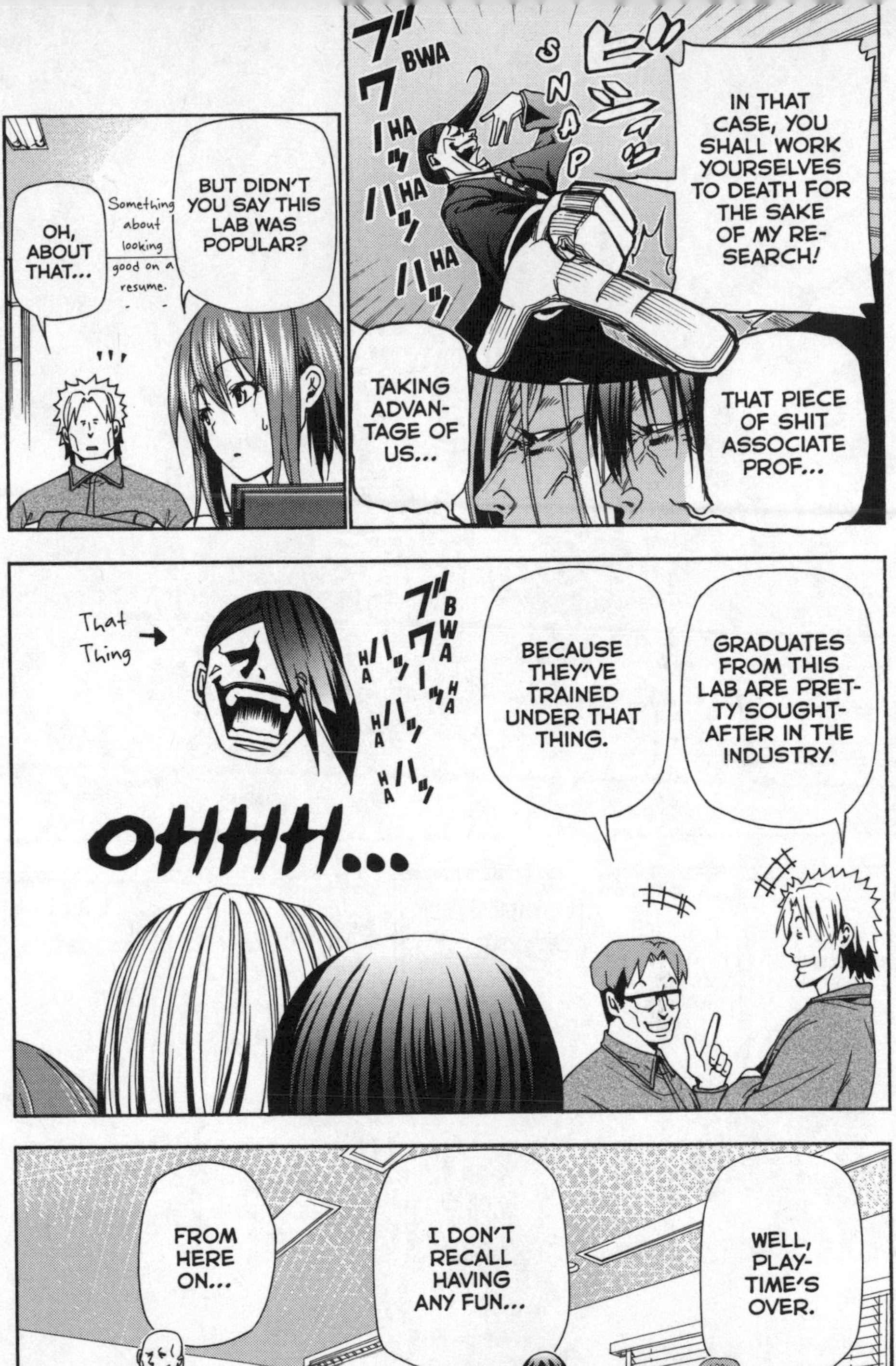

IN THAT CASE, YOU SHALL WORK YOURSELVES TO DEATH FOR THE SAKE OF MY RESEARCH!
SNAP
BWA HA HA HA
THAT PIECE OF SHIT ASSOCIATE PROF...
TAKING ADVANTAGE OF US...
BUT DIDN'T YOU SAY THIS LAB WAS POPULAR?
Something about looking good on a resume.
OH, ABOUT THAT...
GRADUATES FROM THIS LAB ARE PRETTY SOUGHT-AFTER IN THE INDUSTRY.
BECAUSE THEY'VE TRAINED UNDER THAT THING.
BWA HA HA HA HA
That Thing
OHHH...
WELL, PLAYTIME'S OVER.
I DON'T RECALL HAVING ANY FUN...
FROM HERE ON...

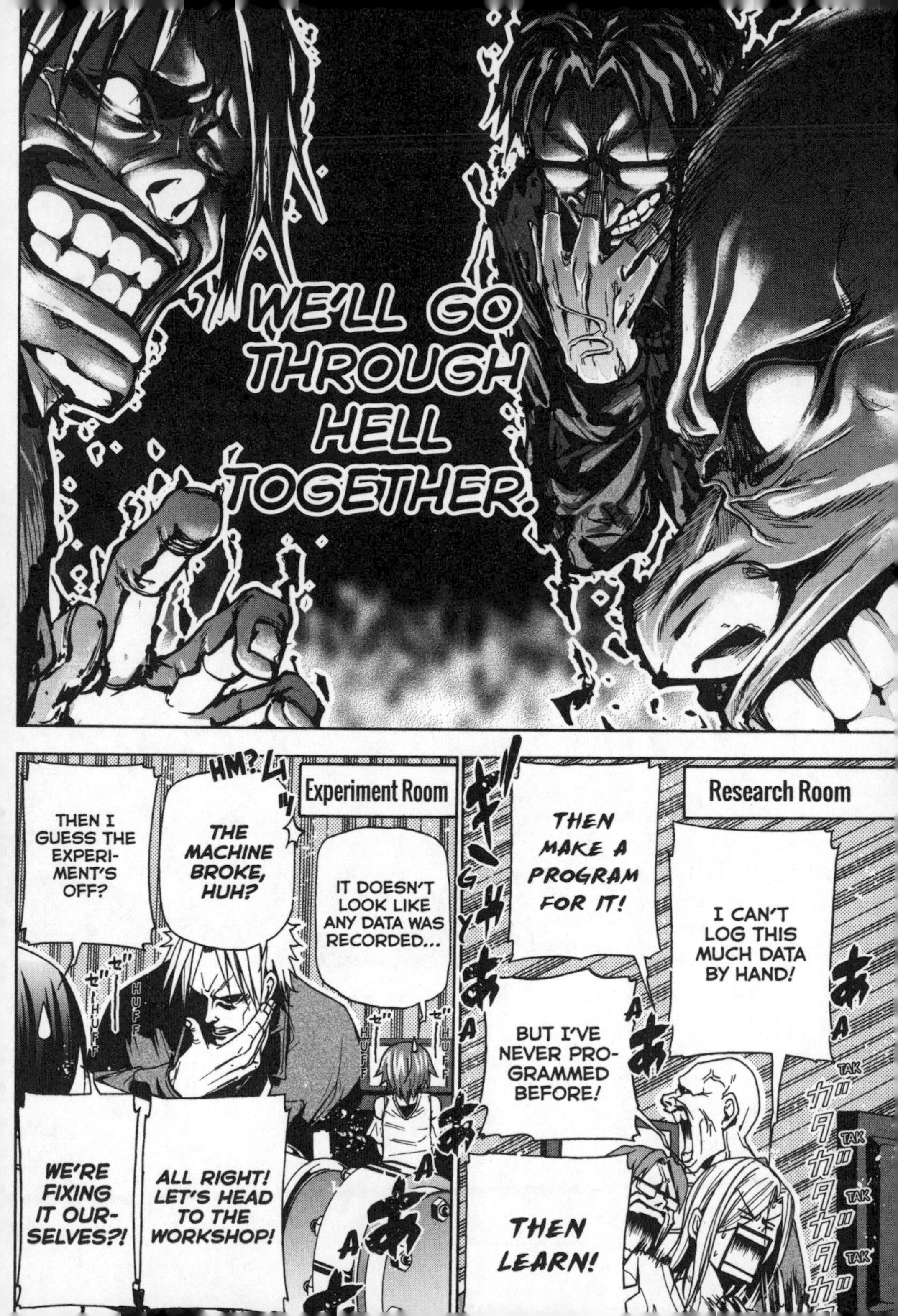
WE'LL GO THROUGH HELL TOGETHER.
Research Room
I CAN'T LOG THIS MUCH DATA BY HAND!
THEN MAKE A PROGRAM FOR IT!
A
BUT I'VE NEVER PROGRAMMED BEFORE!
THEN LEARN!
TAK
TAK
TAK
TAK
GYA
A
A
A
Experiment Room
IT DOESN'T LOOK LIKE ANY DATA WAS RECORDED...
HUFF
THE MACHINE BROKE, HUH?
HM?
THEN I GUESS THE EXPERIMENT'S OFF?
HUFF
ALL RIGHT! LET'S HEAD TO THE WORKSHOP!
WE'RE FIXING IT OURSELVES?!

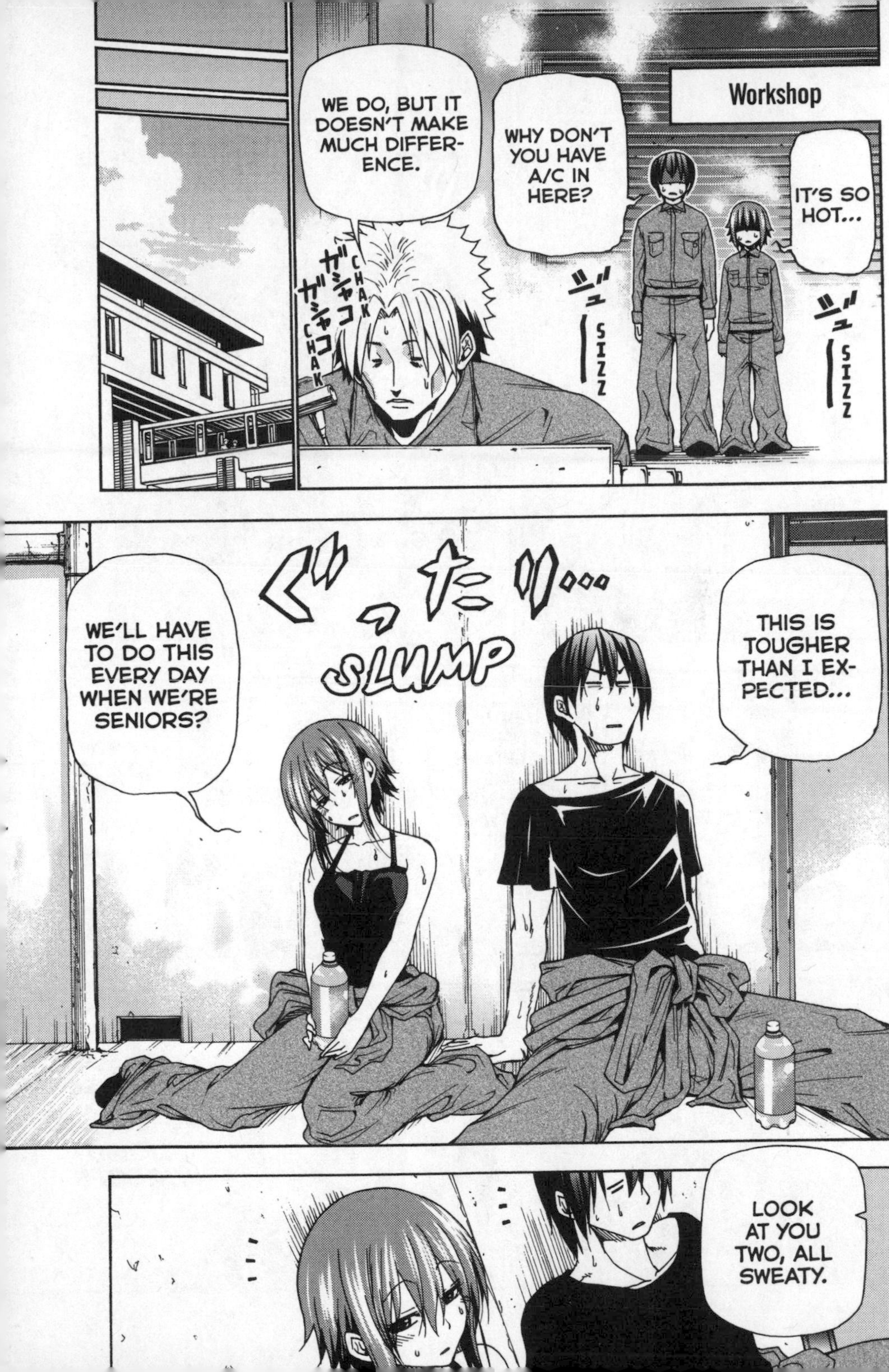
Workshop
IT'S SO HOT...
ジュー SIZZ
ジュー SIZZ
WHY DON'T YOU HAVE A/C IN HERE?
WE DO, BUT IT DOESN'T MAKE MUCH DIFFERENCE.
ガシャコ ガシャコ CHAK CHAK
THIS IS TOUGHER THAN I EXPECTED...
ぐったり... SLUMP
WE'LL HAVE TO DO THIS EVERY DAY WHEN WE'RE SENIORS?
LOOK AT YOU TWO, ALL SWEATY.

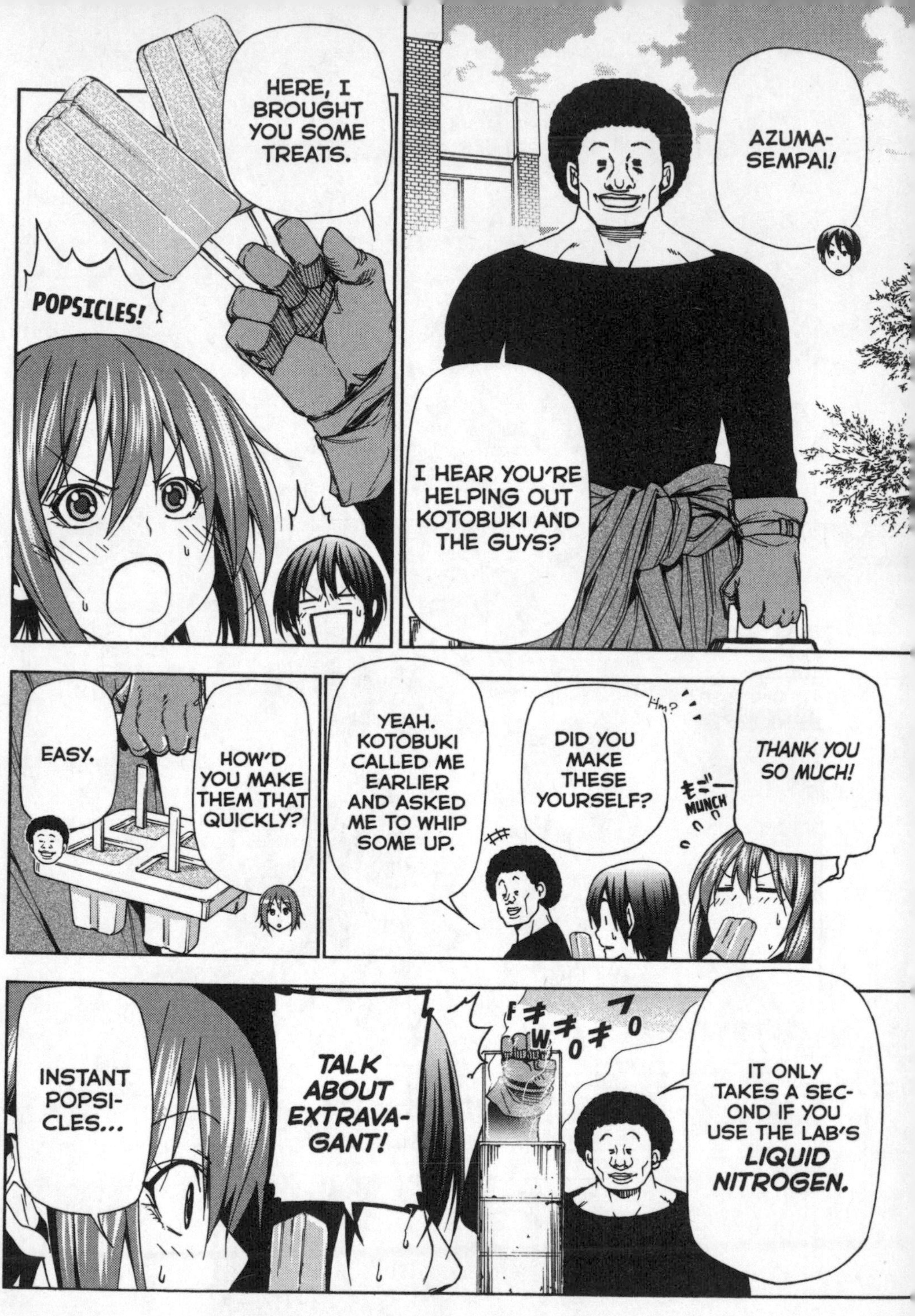
AZUMA-SEMPAI!
I HEAR YOU'RE HELPING OUT KOTOBUKI AND THE GUYS?
HERE, I BROUGHT YOU SOME TREATS.
POPSICLES!
THANK YOU SO MUCH!
MUNCH
Hm?
DID YOU MAKE THESE YOURSELF?
YEAH. KOTOBUKI CALLED ME EARLIER AND ASKED ME TO WHIP SOME UP.
HOW'D YOU MAKE THEM THAT QUICKLY?
EASY.
IT ONLY TAKES A SEC-OND IF YOU USE THE LAB'S LIQUID NITROGEN.
TALK ABOUT EXTRAVA-GANT!
INSTANT POPSI-CLES...

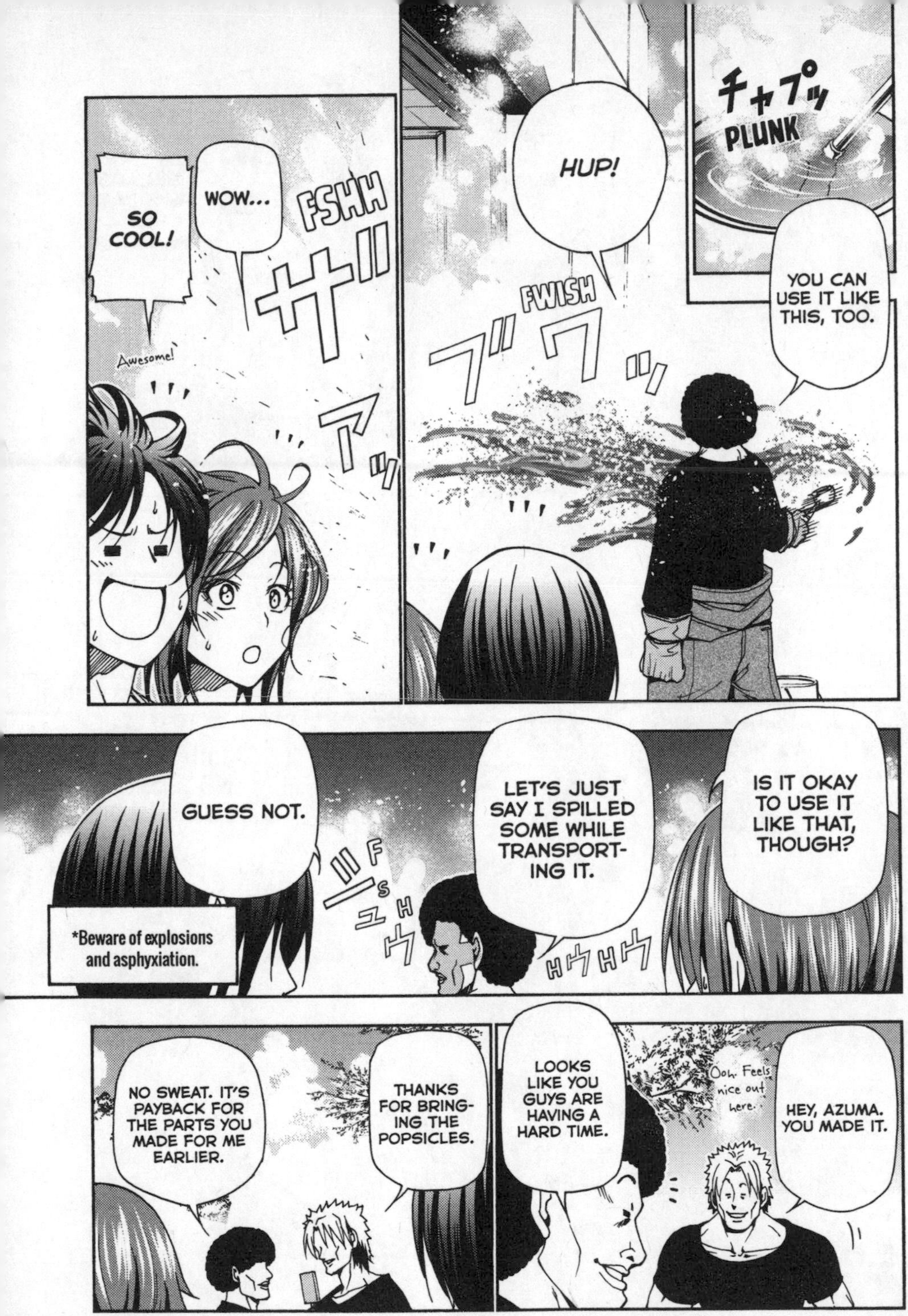
チャプッ
PLUNK
YOU CAN USE IT LIKE THIS, TOO.
HUP!
FWISH
WOW...
FSHH
SO COOL!
Awesome!
IS IT OKAY TO USE IT LIKE THAT, THOUGH?
HUH HUH
LET'S JUST SAY I SPILLED SOME WHILE TRANSPORT-ING IT.
FSHH
GUESS NOT.
*Beware of explosions and asphyxiation.
HEY, AZUMA. YOU MADE IT.
Ooh. Feels nice out here.
LOOKS LIKE YOU GUYS ARE HAVING A HARD TIME.
THANKS FOR BRING-ING THE POPSICLES.
NO SWEAT. IT'S PAYBACK FOR THE PARTS YOU MADE FOR ME EARLIER.

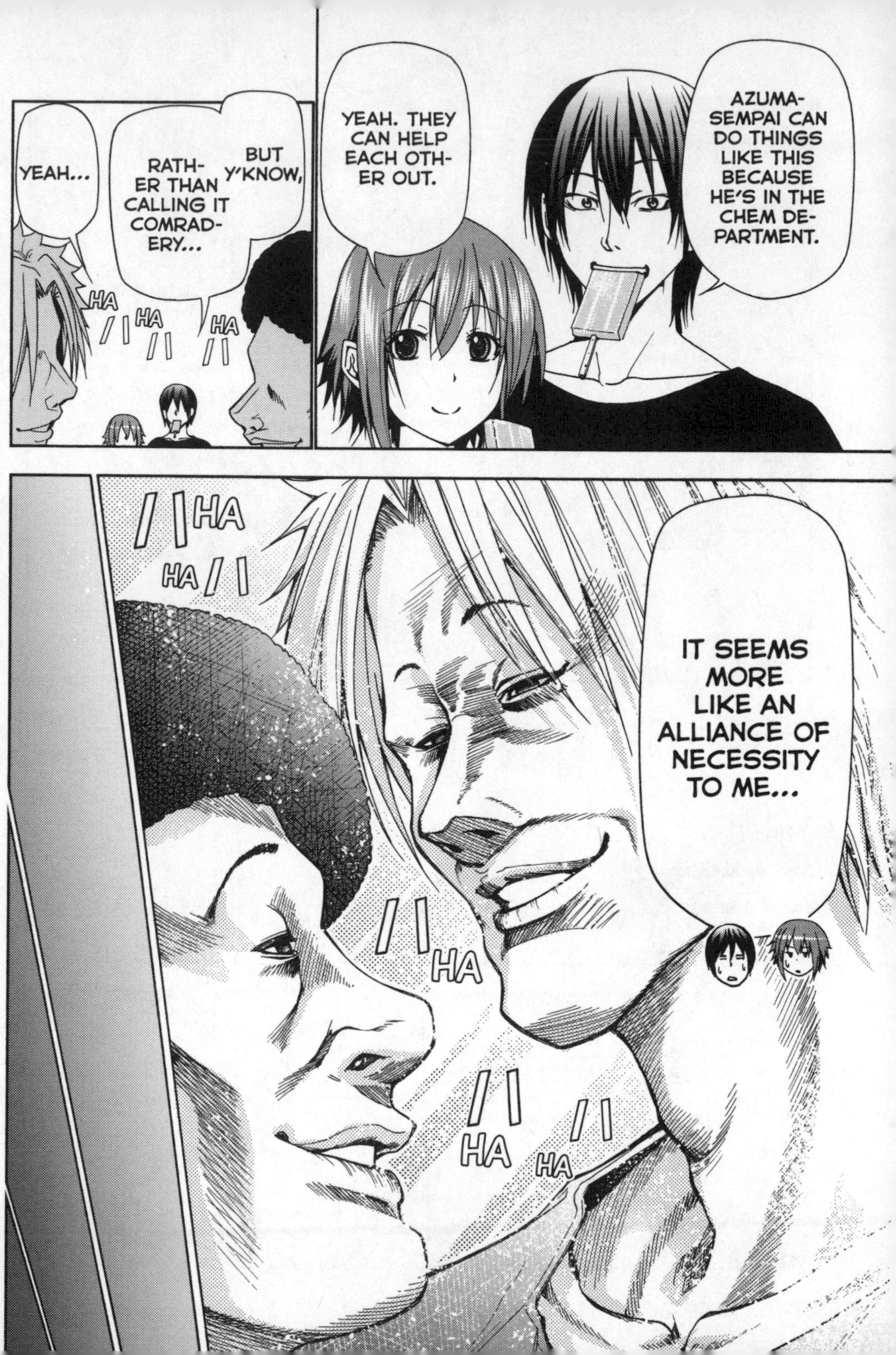
AZUMA-SEMPAI CAN DO THINGS LIKE THIS BECAUSE HE'S IN THE CHEM DEPARTMENT.
YEAH. THEY CAN HELP EACH OTHER OUT.
BUT Y'KNOW, RATHER THAN CALLING IT COMRADERY...
YEAH...
HA HA HA
IT SEEMS MORE LIKE AN ALLIANCE OF NECESSITY TO ME...
HA HA
HA
HA HA

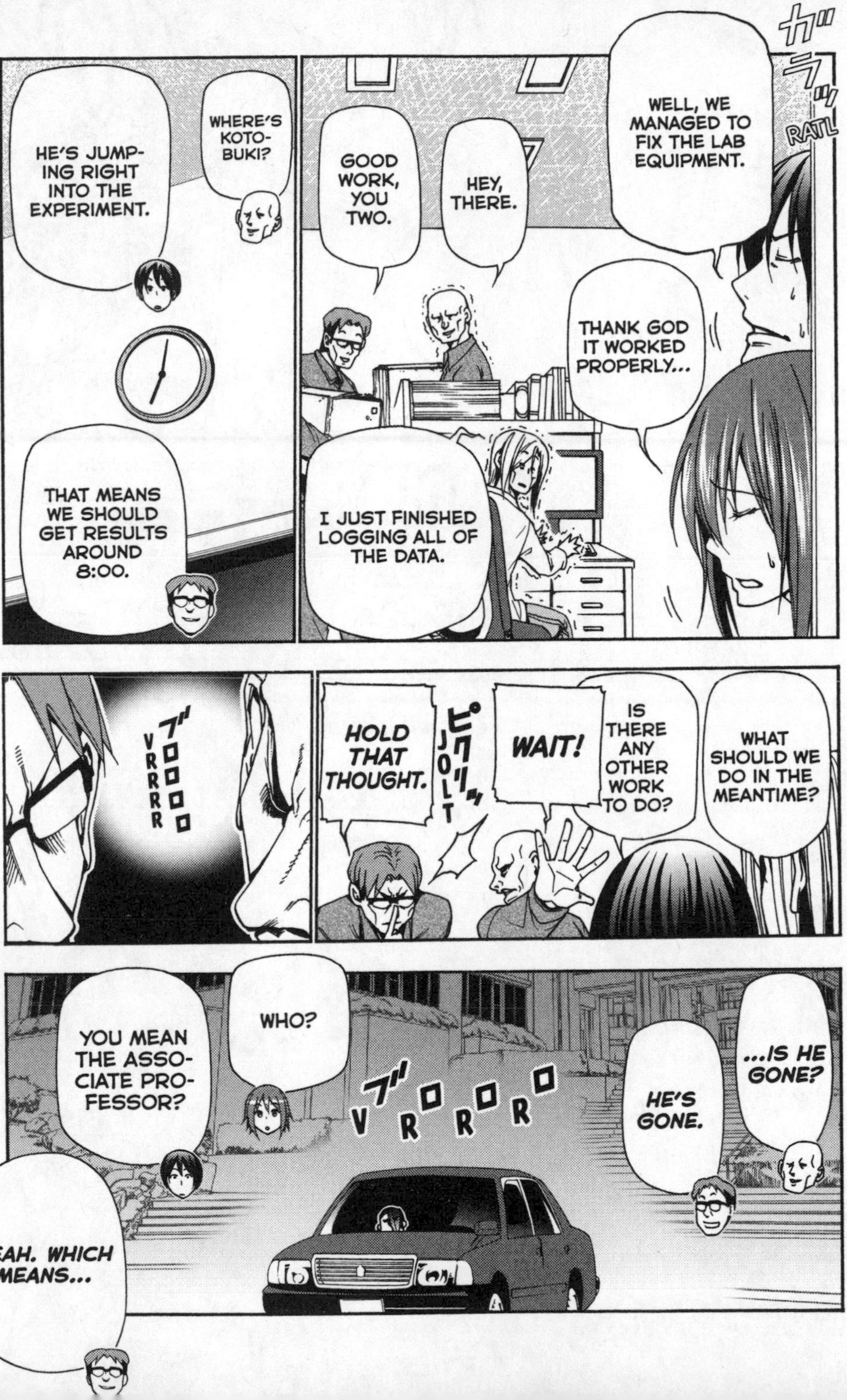
RATL
WELL, WE MANAGED TO FIX THE LAB EQUIPMENT.
HEY, THERE.
GOOD WORK, YOU TWO.
THANK GOD IT WORKED PROPERLY...
I JUST FINISHED LOGGING ALL OF THE DATA.
WHERE'S KOTOBUKI?
HE'S JUMPING RIGHT INTO THE EXPERIMENT.
THAT MEANS WE SHOULD GET RESULTS AROUND 8:00.
WHAT SHOULD WE DO IN THE MEANTIME?
IS THERE ANY OTHER WORK TO DO?
WAIT!
JOLT
HOLD THAT THOUGHT.
VRRRR
...IS HE GONE?
HE'S GONE.
VRRORRO
WHO?
YOU MEAN THE ASSOCIATE PROFESSOR?
YEAH. WHICH MEANS...

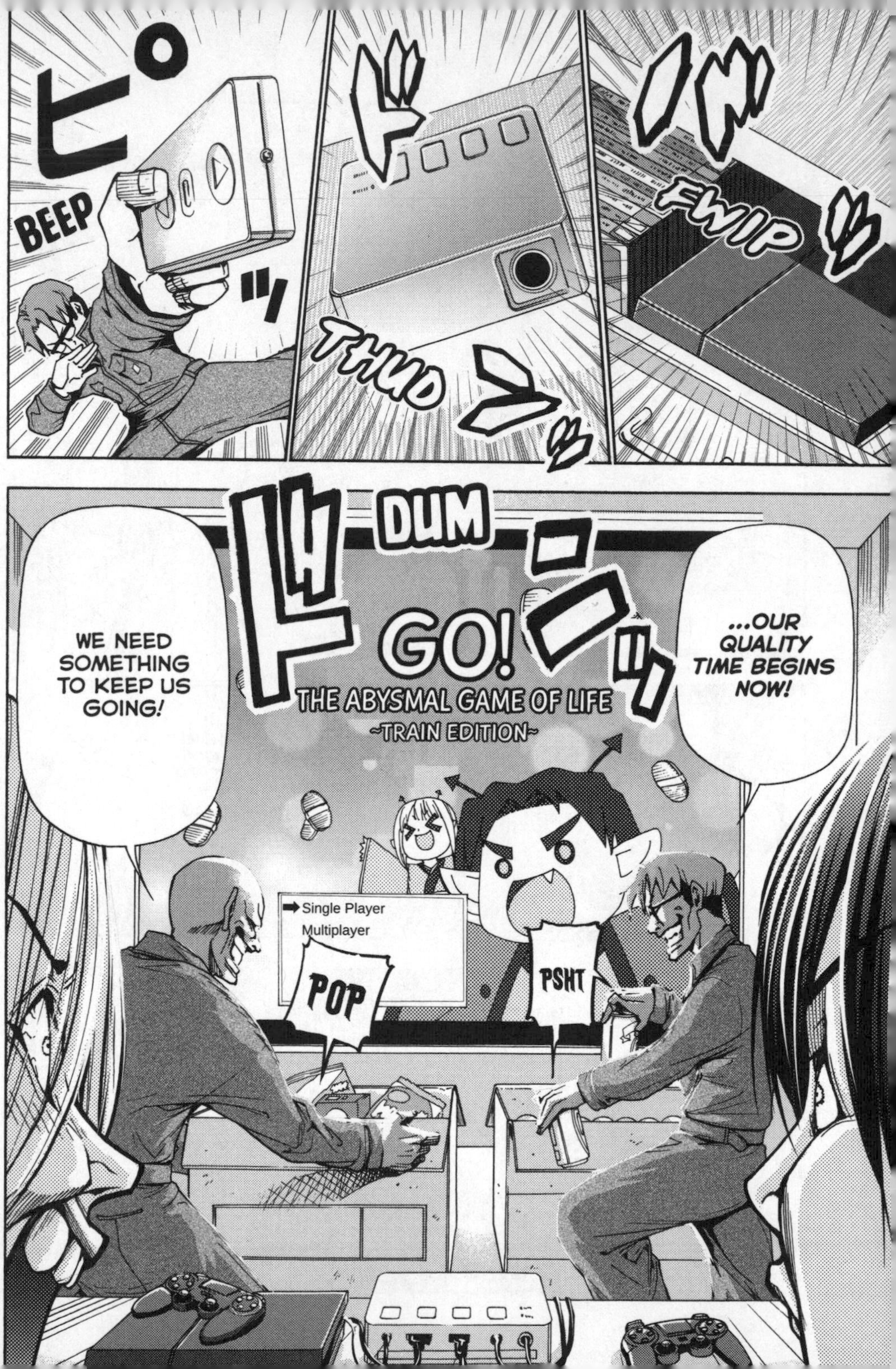
FWIP
THUD
BEEP
DUM
GO!
THE ABYSMAL GAME OF LIFE
~TRAIN EDITION~
...OUR QUALITY TIME BEGINS NOW!
WE NEED SOMETHING TO KEEP US GOING!
Single Player
Multiplayer
PSHT
POP

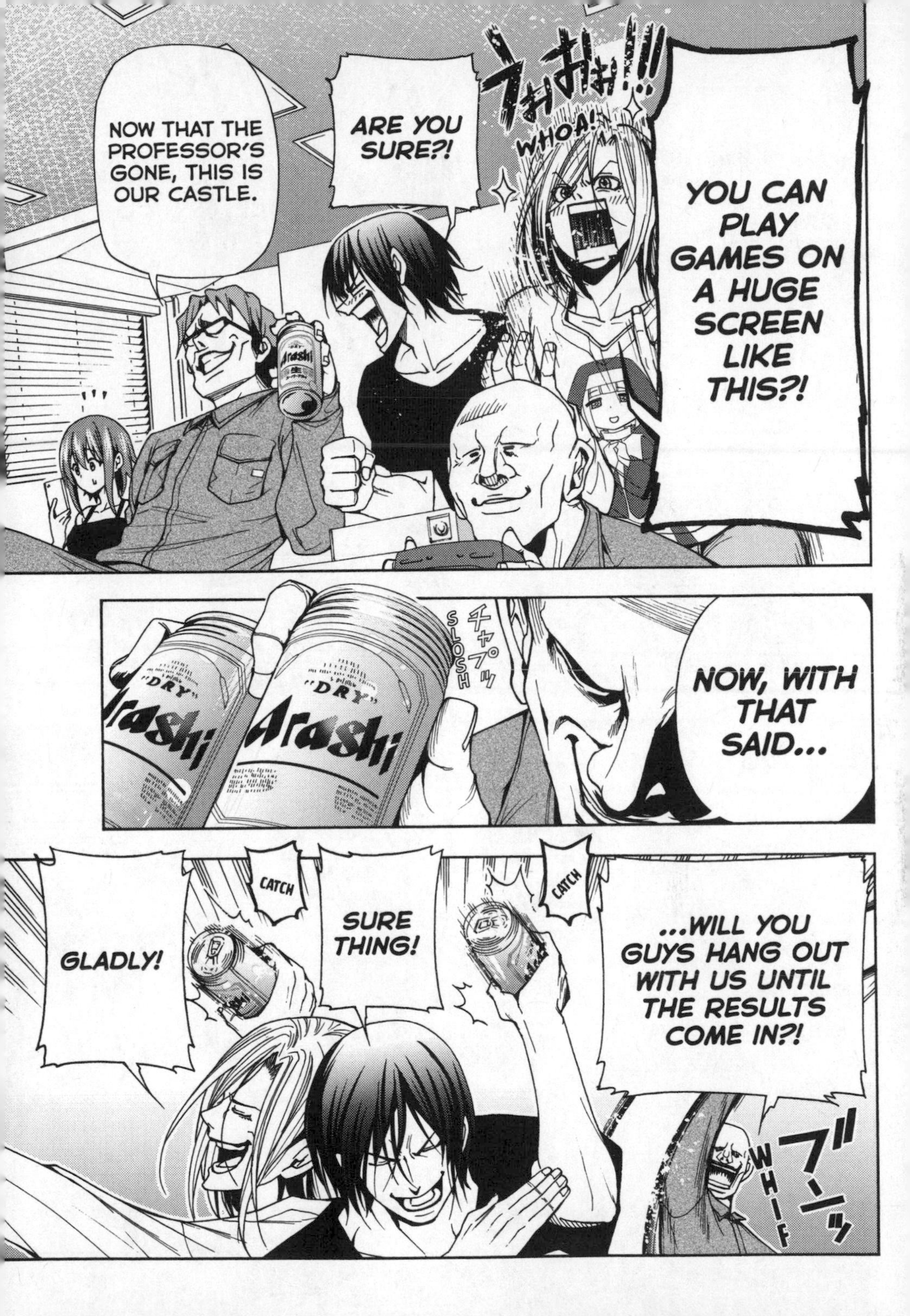
うぉおぉ!!!
WHOA!
YOU CAN PLAY GAMES ON A HUGE SCREEN LIKE THIS?!
ARE YOU SURE?!
NOW THAT THE PROFESSOR'S GONE, THIS IS OUR CASTLE.
NOW, WITH THAT SAID...
チャプッ
SLOSH
...WILL YOU GUYS HANG OUT WITH US UNTIL THE RESULTS COME IN?!
CATCH
SURE THING!
CATCH
GLADLY!
ブーッ
WHIFF

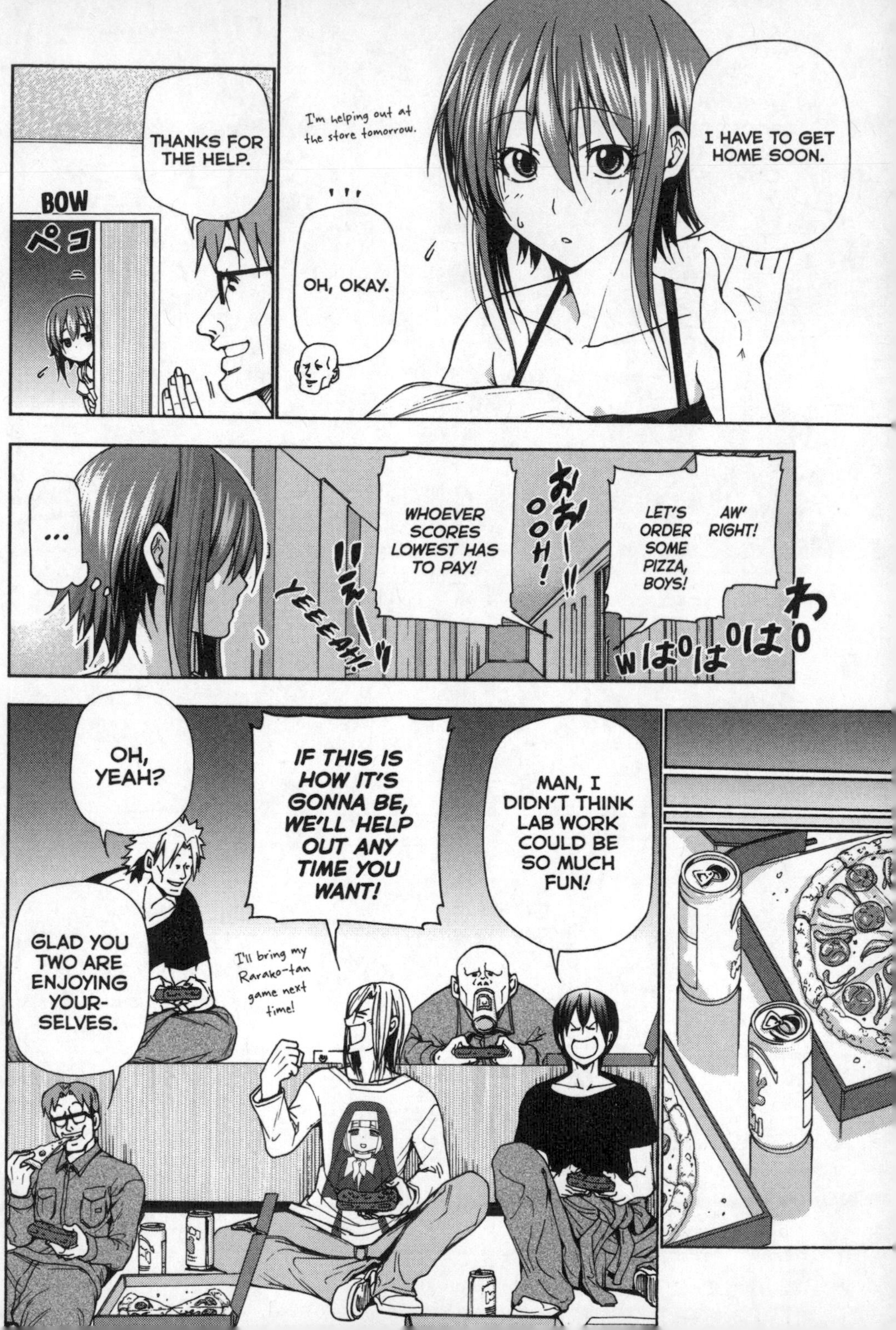
I HAVE TO GET HOME SOON.
I'm helping out at the store tomorrow.
OH, OKAY.
THANKS FOR THE HELP.
BOW
ペコ
わははは
LET'S ORDER SOME PIZZA, BOYS!
AW' RIGHT!
おおー!!
OOOH!
WHOEVER SCORES LOWEST HAS TO PAY!
イェーーッ
YEEEAH!
...
MAN, I DIDN'T THINK LAB WORK COULD BE SO MUCH FUN!
IF THIS IS HOW IT'S GONNA BE, WE'LL HELP OUT ANY TIME YOU WANT!
I'll bring my Rarako-tan game next time!
OH, YEAH?
GLAD YOU TWO ARE ENJOYING YOUR-SELVES.

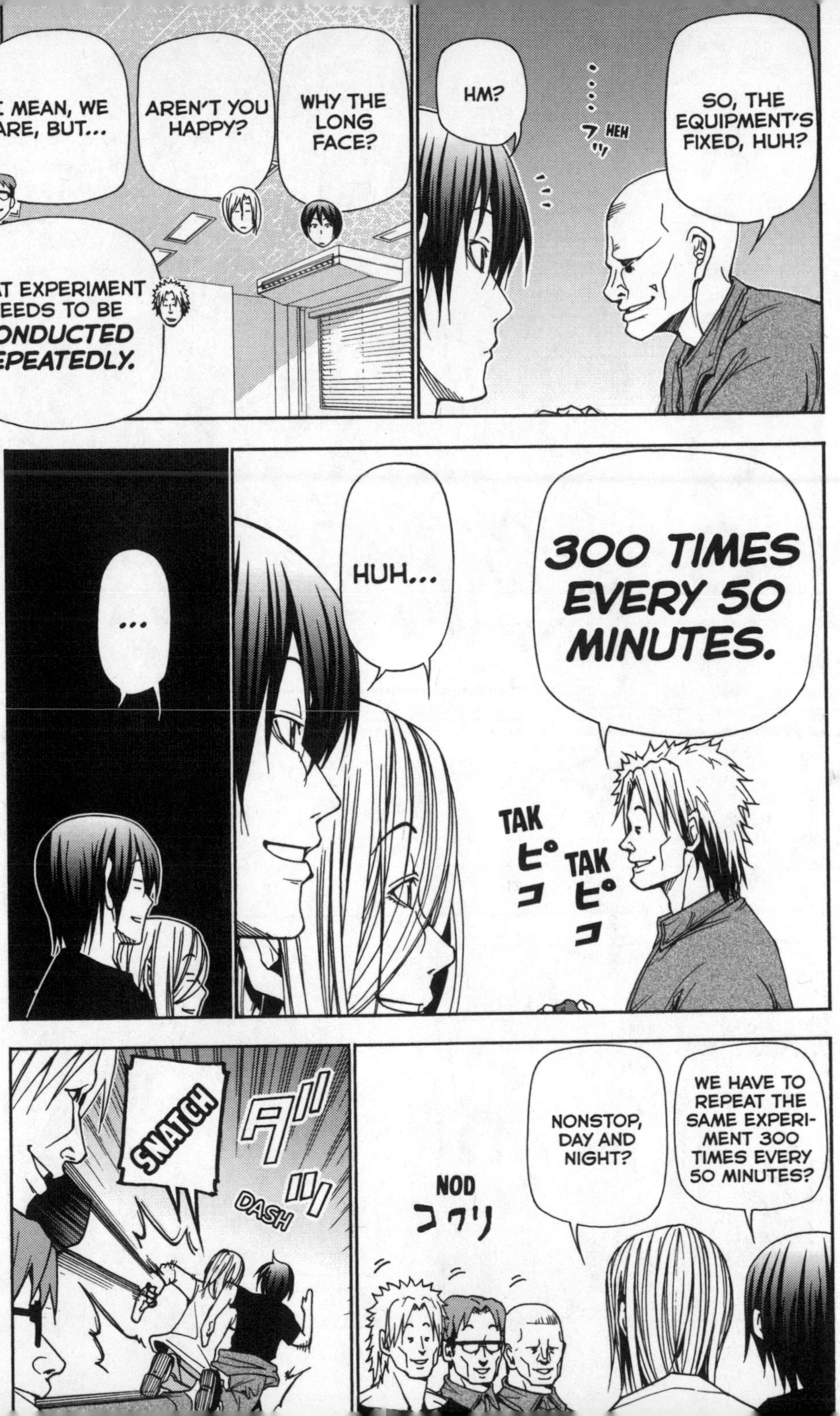
SO, THE EQUIPMENT'S FIXED, HUH?
...
HEH
フッ
HM?
WHY THE LONG FACE?
AREN'T YOU HAPPY?
I MEAN, WE ARE, BUT...
THAT EXPERIMENT NEEDS TO BE CONDUCTED REPEATEDLY.
300 TIMES EVERY 50 MINUTES.
TAK
ピコ
TAK
ピコ
HUH...
...
WE HAVE TO REPEAT THE SAME EXPERIMENT 300 TIMES EVERY 50 MINUTES?
NONSTOP, DAY AND NIGHT?
NOD
コクリ
SNATCH
DASH
ダッ

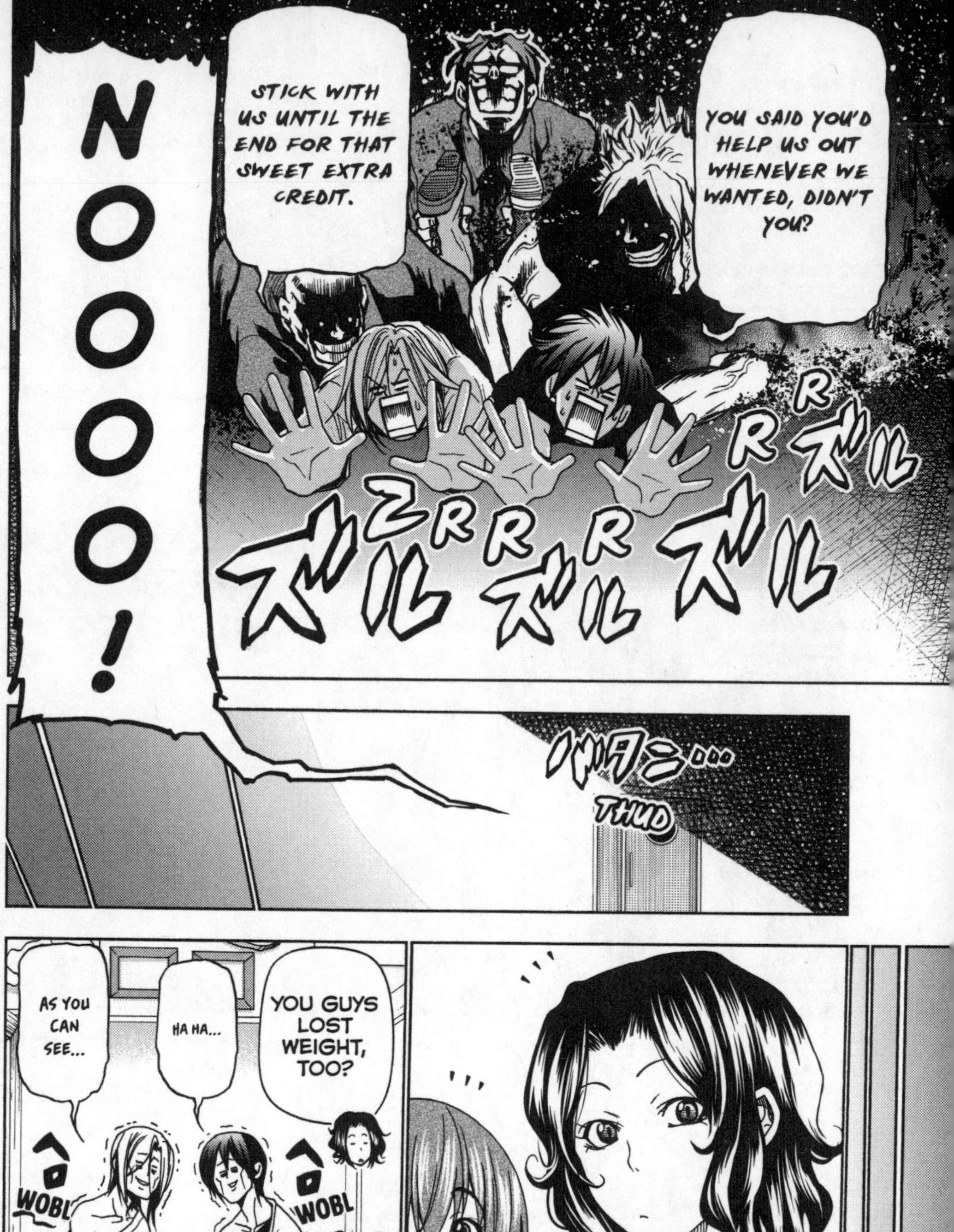
YOU SAID YOU'D HELP US OUT WHENEVER WE WANTED, DIDN'T YOU?
STICK WITH US UNTIL THE END FOR THAT SWEET EXTRA CREDIT.
NOOOOO!
ズルズル ズルズル ZRRRRR
バタン...
THUD
YOU GUYS LOST WEIGHT, TOO?
HA HA...
AS YOU CAN SEE...
WOBL
WOBL

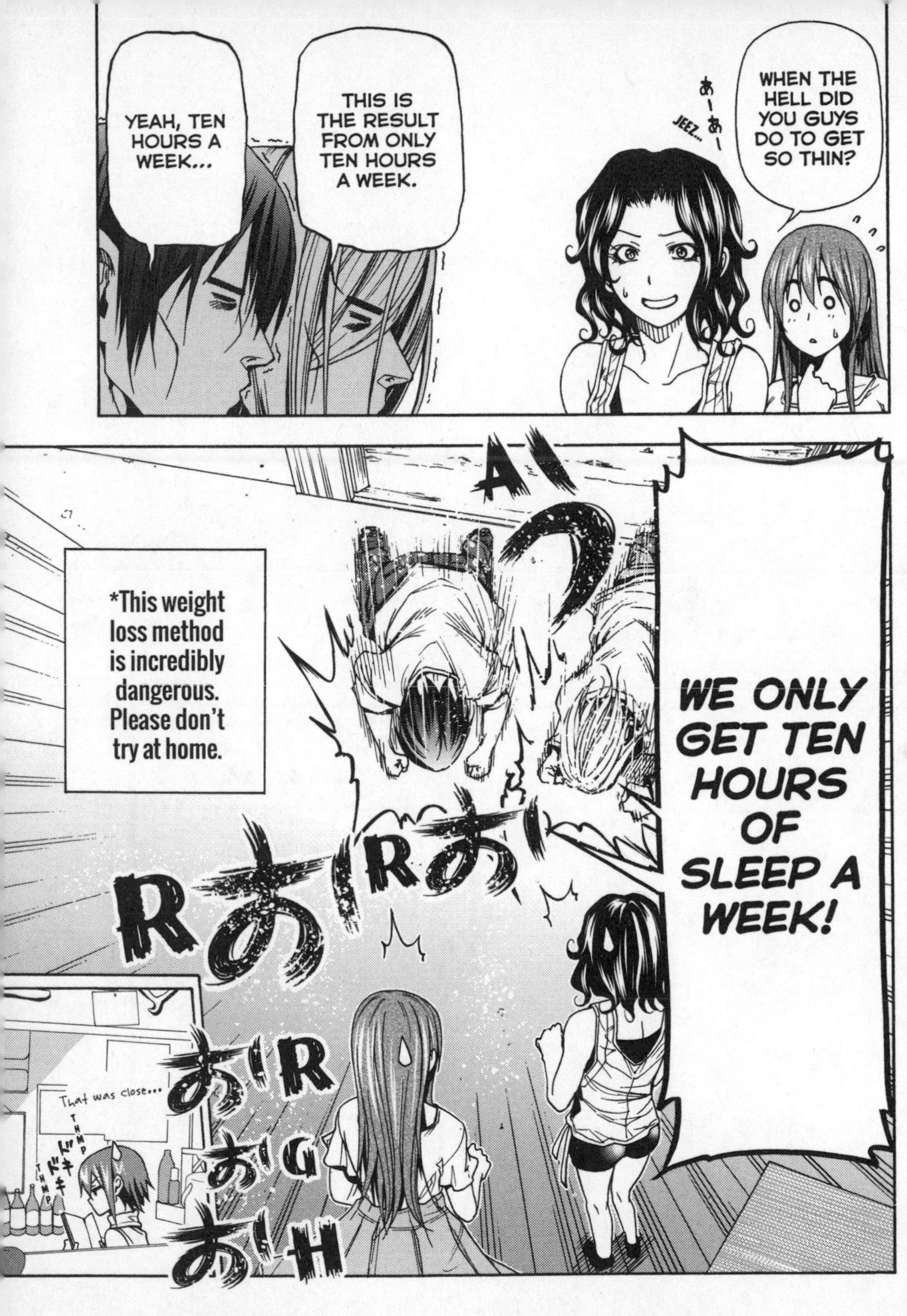
WHEN THE HELL DID YOU GUYS DO TO GET SO THIN?
あ～あ～
JEEZ...
THIS IS THE RESULT FROM ONLY TEN HOURS A WEEK.
YEAH, TEN HOURS A WEEK...
WE ONLY GET TEN HOURS OF SLEEP A WEEK!
*This weight loss method is incredibly dangerous. Please don't try at home.
That was close...
ドキドキ
THMP THMP

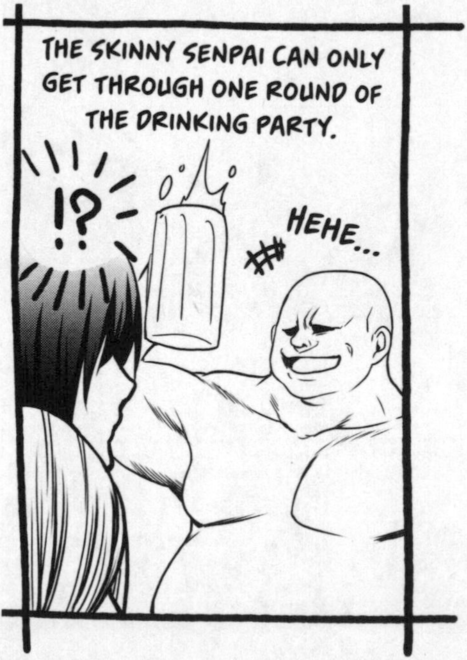
THE SKINNY SENPAI CAN ONLY GET THROUGH ONE ROUND OF THE DRINKING PARTY.
!?
HEHE...

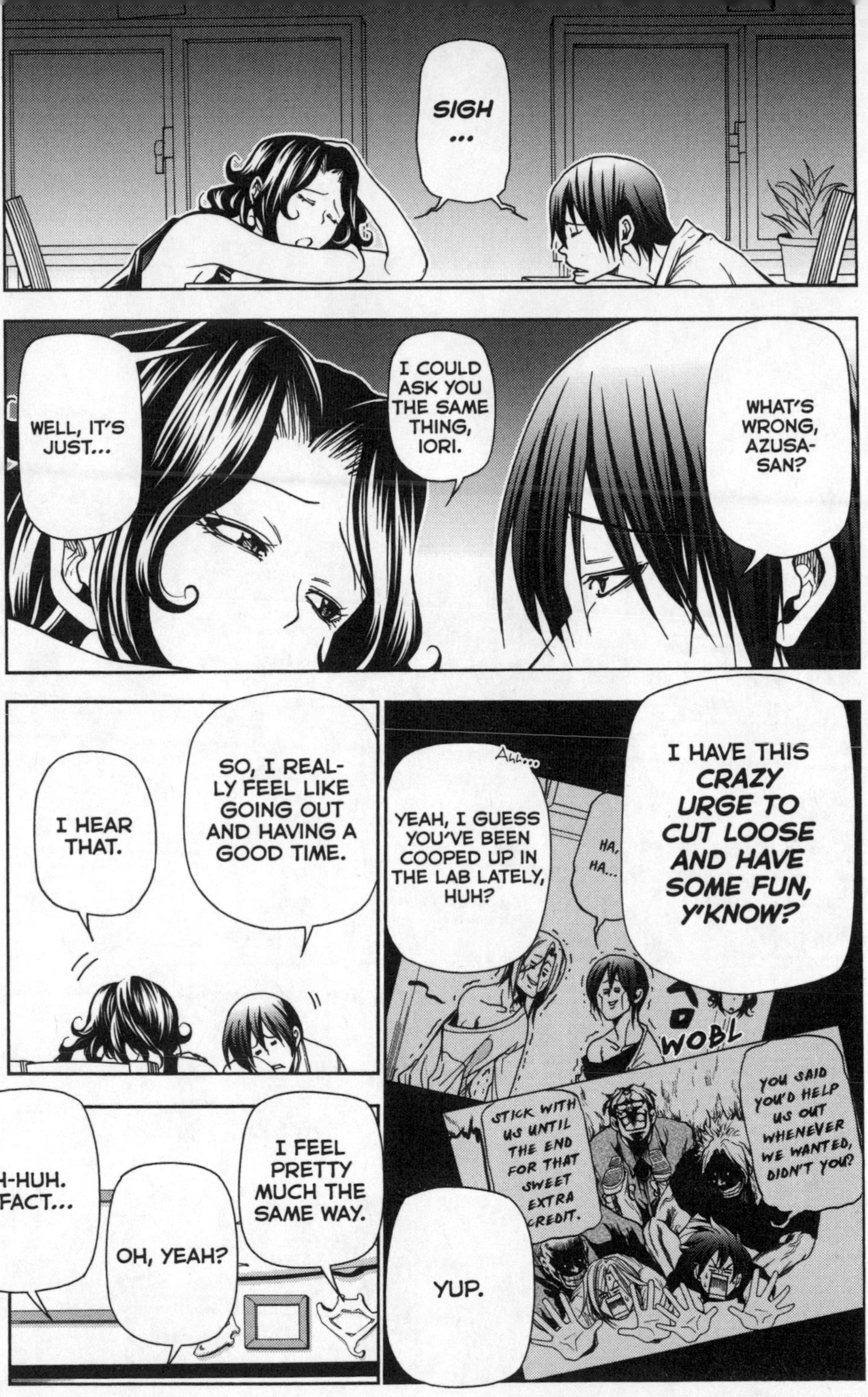
SIGH...
WHAT'S WRONG, AZUSA-SAN?
I COULD ASK YOU THE SAME THING, IORI.
WELL, IT'S JUST...
SO, I REALLY FEEL LIKE GOING OUT AND HAVING A GOOD TIME.
I HEAR THAT.
I FEEL PRETTY MUCH THE SAME WAY.
OH, YEAH?
UH-HUH. IN FACT...
I HAVE THIS CRAZY URGE TO CUT LOOSE AND HAVE SOME FUN, Y'KNOW?
Ahhooo
HA, HA...
YEAH, I GUESS YOU'VE BEEN COOPED UP IN THE LAB LATELY, HUH?
WOBL
YOU SAID YOU'D HELP US OUT WHENEVER WE WANTED, DIDN'T YOU?
STICK WITH US UNTIL THE END FOR THAT SWEET EXTRA CREDIT.
YUP.

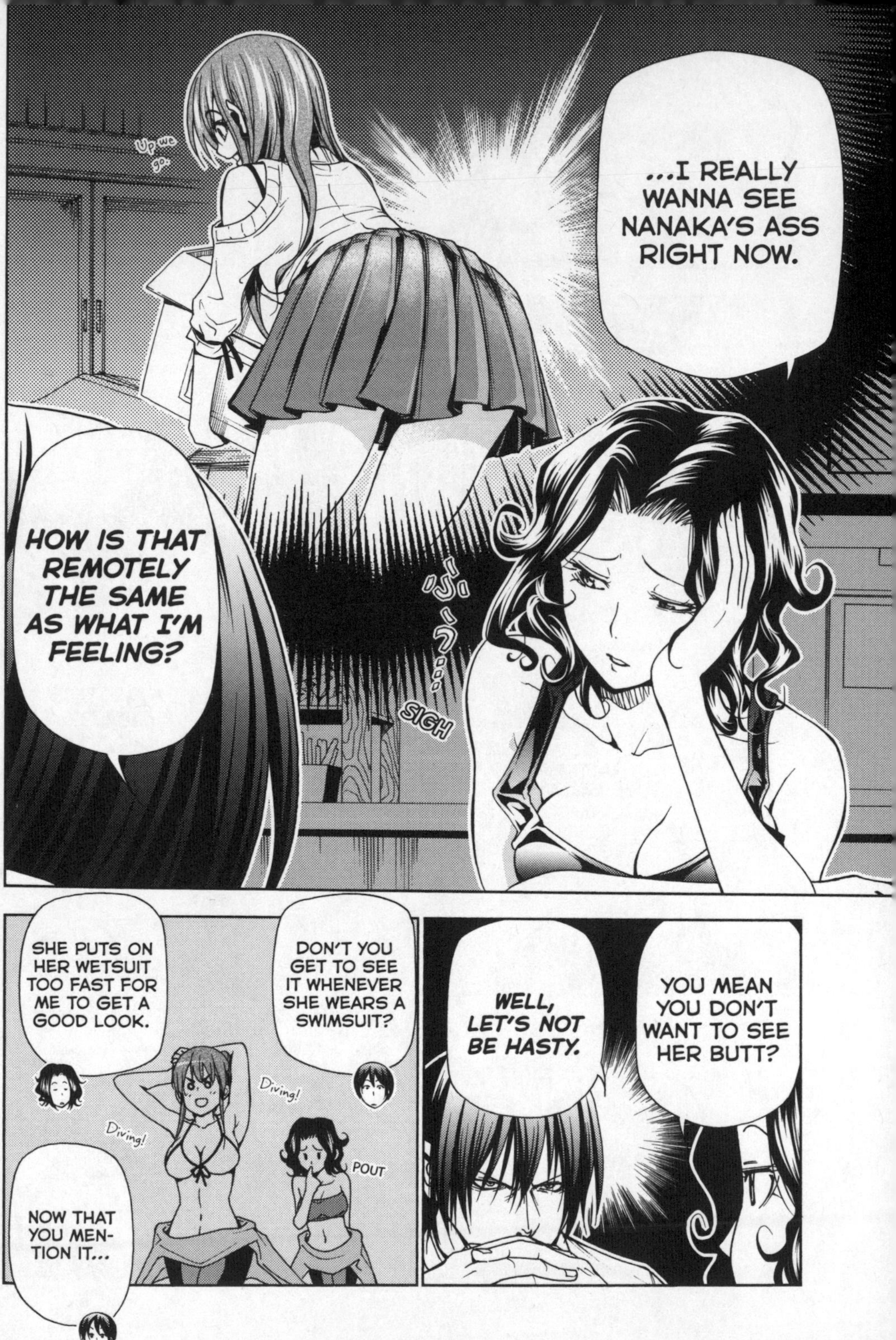
...I REALLY WANNA SEE NANAKA'S ASS RIGHT NOW.
Up we go.
SIGH
HOW IS THAT REMOTELY THE SAME AS WHAT I'M FEELING?
YOU MEAN YOU DON'T WANT TO SEE HER BUTT?
WELL, LET'S NOT BE HASTY.
DON'T YOU GET TO SEE IT WHENEVER SHE WEARS A SWIMSUIT?
SHE PUTS ON HER WETSUIT TOO FAST FOR ME TO GET A GOOD LOOK.
Diving!
Diving!
POUT
NOW THAT YOU MEN-TION IT...

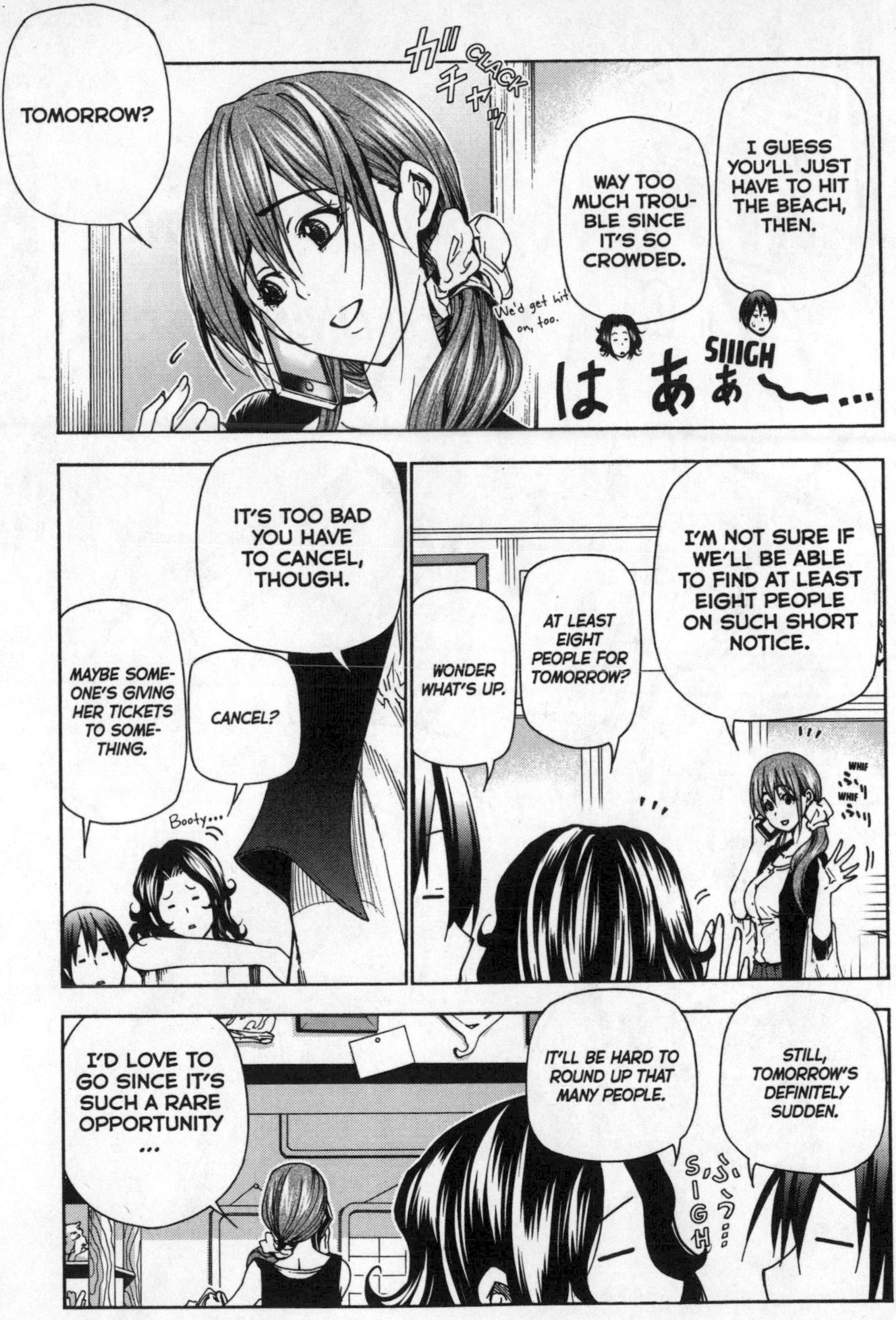
TOMORROW?
CLACK
ガチャッ
I GUESS YOU'LL JUST HAVE TO HIT THE BEACH, THEN.
WAY TOO MUCH TROUBLE SINCE IT'S SO CROWDED.
We'd get hit on, too.
SIIIGH
はぁぁ〜〜...
I'M NOT SURE IF WE'LL BE ABLE TO FIND AT LEAST EIGHT PEOPLE ON SUCH SHORT NOTICE.
WHIF
ふり
WHIF
ふり
AT LEAST EIGHT PEOPLE FOR TOMORROW?
WONDER WHAT'S UP.
IT'S TOO BAD YOU HAVE TO CANCEL, THOUGH.
CANCEL?
MAYBE SOME-ONE'S GIVING HER TICKETS TO SOME-THING.
Booty...
STILL, TOMORROW'S DEFINITELY SUDDEN.
SIGH
ふぅ...
IT'LL BE HARD TO ROUND UP THAT MANY PEOPLE.
I'D LOVE TO GO SINCE IT'S SUCH A RARE OPPORTUNITY ...

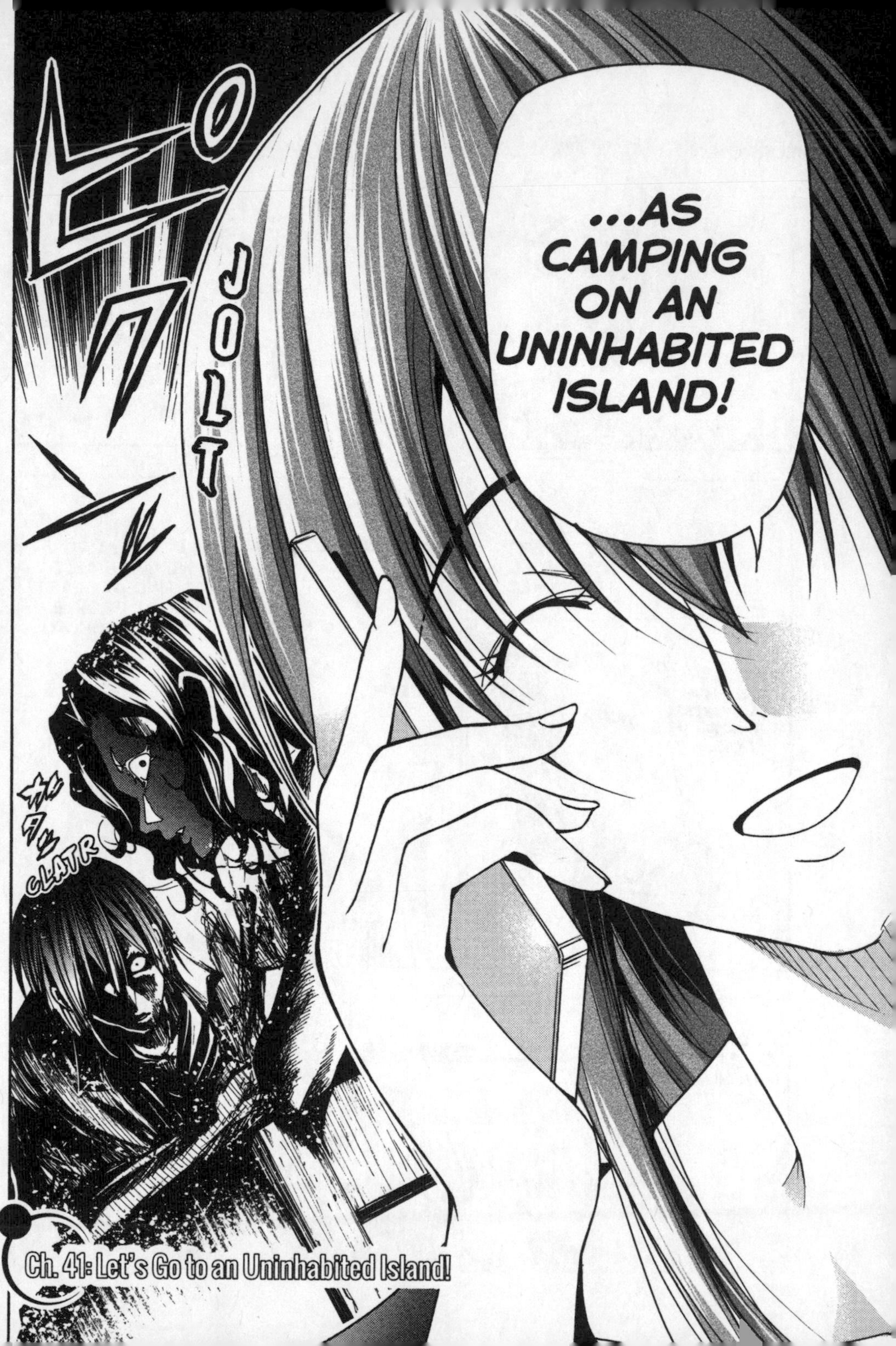
...AS CAMPING ON AN UNINHABITED ISLAND!
JOLT
CLATR
Ch. 41: Let's Go to an Uninhabited Island!

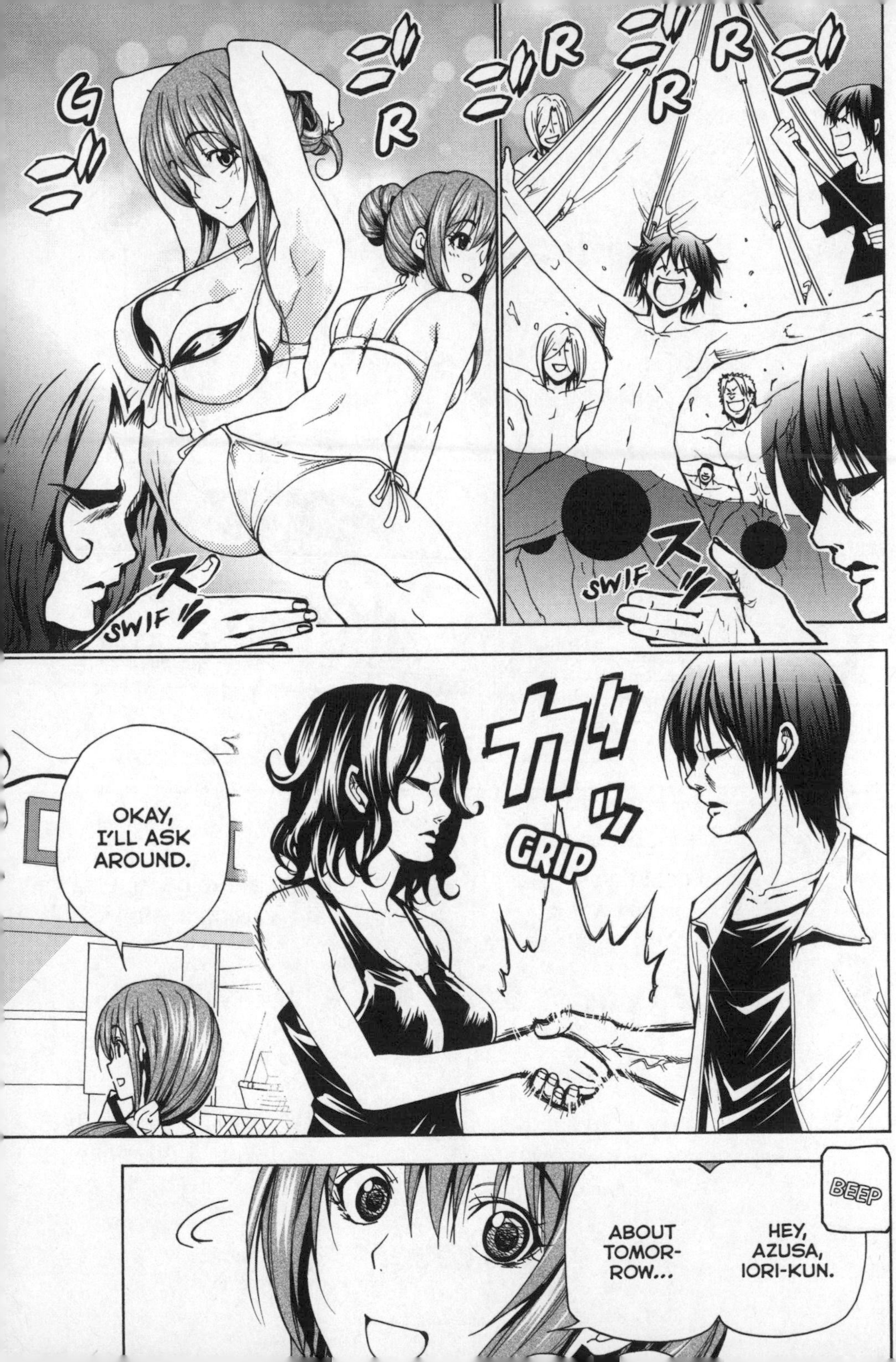
R
R
SWIF
G
R
SWIF
GRIP
OKAY, I'LL ASK AROUND.
BEEP
HEY, AZUSA, IORI-KUN.
ABOUT TOMOR-ROW...

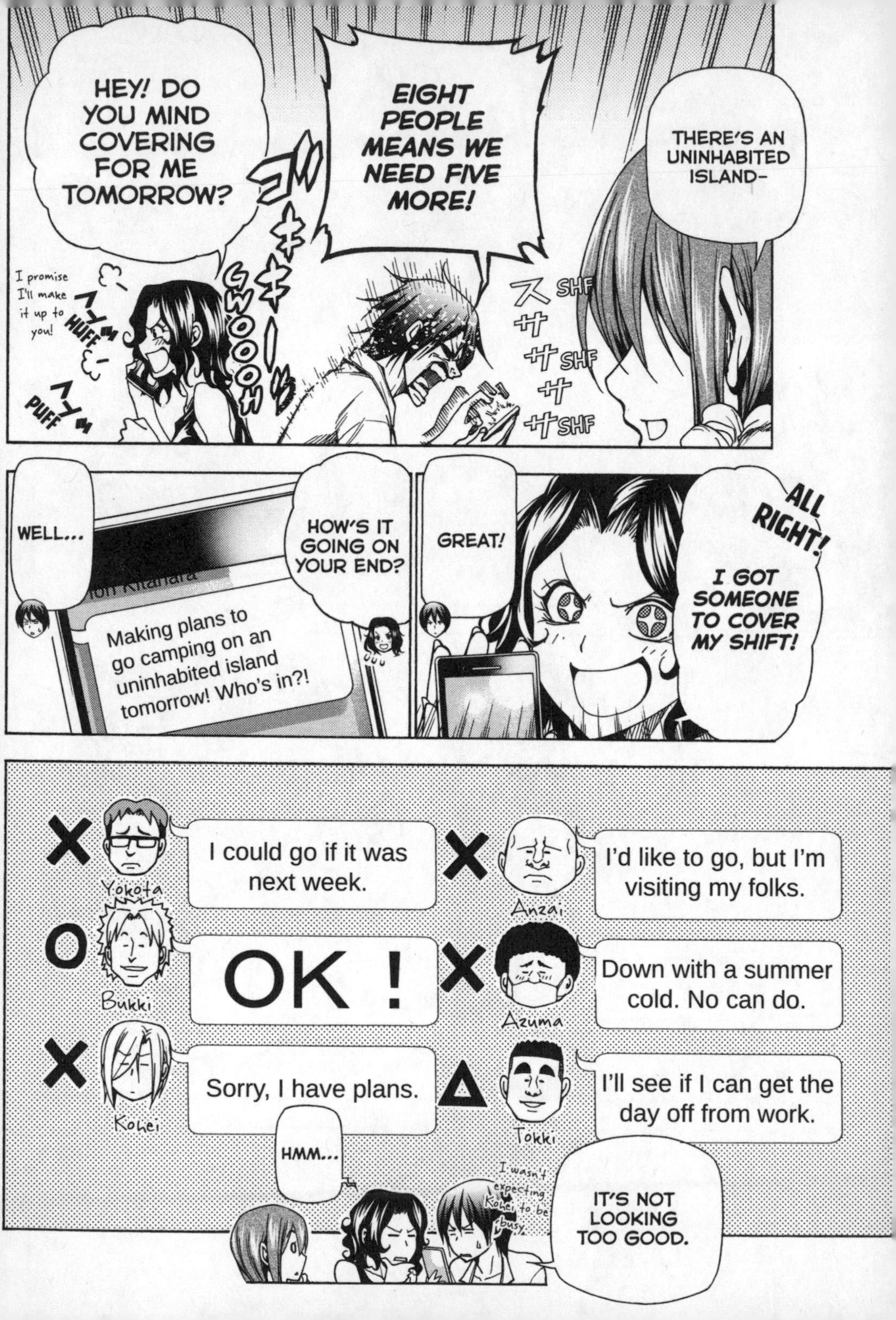
THERE'S AN UNINHABITED ISLAND–
SHF
SHF
SHF
EIGHT PEOPLE MEANS WE NEED FIVE MORE!
GWOOOOH
HEY! DO YOU MIND COVERING FOR ME TOMORROW?
I promise I'll make it up to you!
HUFF
PUFF
ALL RIGHT!
I GOT SOMEONE TO COVER MY SHIFT!
GREAT!
HOW'S IT GOING ON YOUR END?
WELL...
Making plans to go camping on an uninhabited island tomorrow! Who's in?!
Anzai
I'd like to go, but I'm visiting my folks.
Yokota
I could go if it was next week.
Azuma
Down with a summer cold. No can do.
Bukki
OK !
Tokki
I'll see if I can get the day off from work.
Kohei
Sorry, I have plans.
HMM...
I wasn't expecting Kohei to be busy.
IT'S NOT LOOKING TOO GOOD.

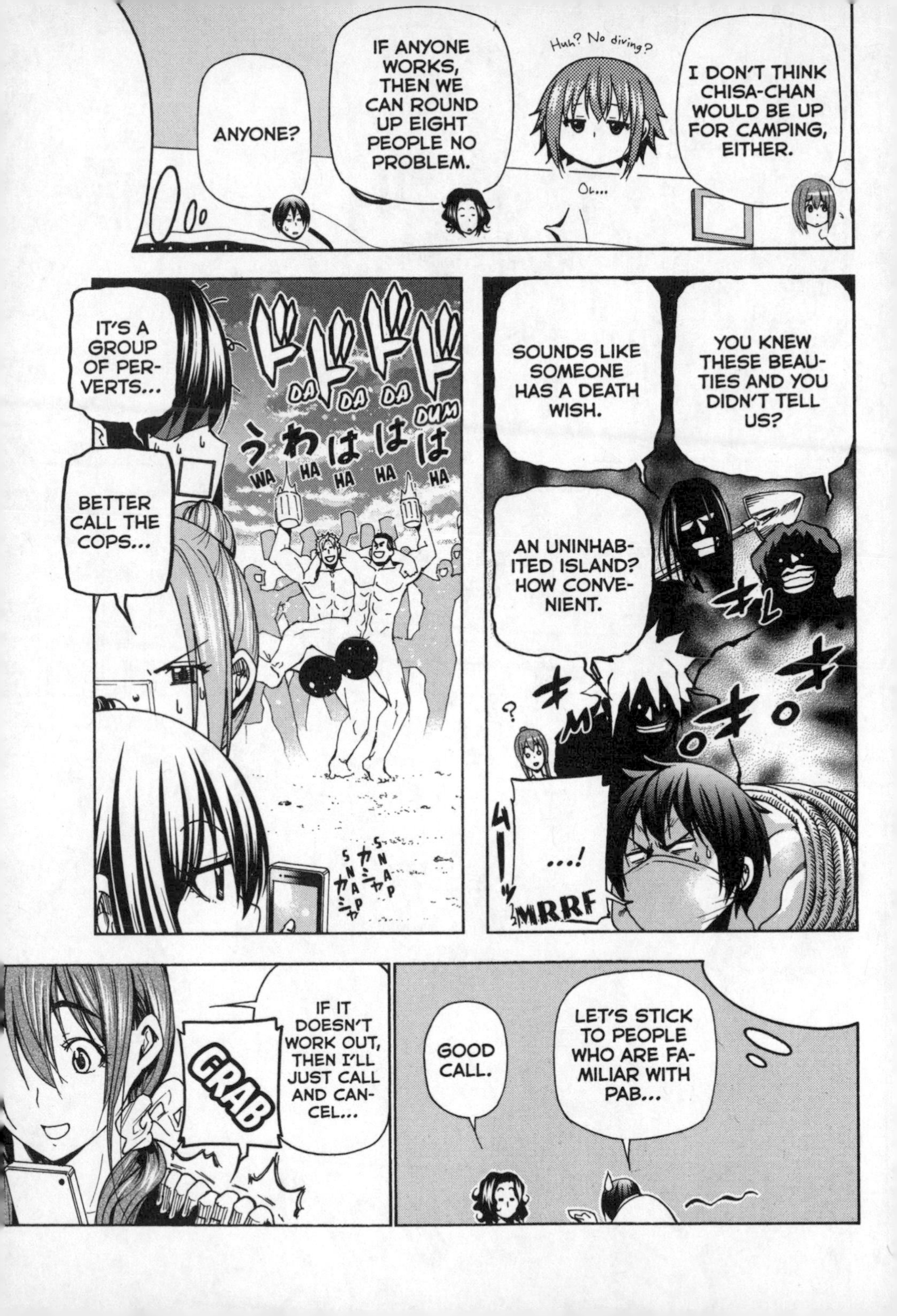
I DON'T THINK CHISA-CHAN WOULD BE UP FOR CAMPING, EITHER.
Huh? No diving?
Oh...
IF ANYONE WORKS, THEN WE CAN ROUND UP EIGHT PEOPLE NO PROBLEM.
ANYONE?
YOU KNEW THESE BEAUTIES AND YOU DIDN'T TELL US?
SOUNDS LIKE SOMEONE HAS A DEATH WISH.
AN UNINHABITED ISLAND? HOW CONVENIENT.
...!
MRRF
ドドドド
DA DA DA DUM
うわははは
WA HA HA HA HA
IT'S A GROUP OF PERVERTS...
BETTER CALL THE COPS...
カシャ カシャ
SNAP SNAP
LET'S STICK TO PEOPLE WHO ARE FAMILIAR WITH PAB...
GOOD CALL.
IF IT DOESN'T WORK OUT, THEN I'LL JUST CALL AND CANCEL...
GRAB

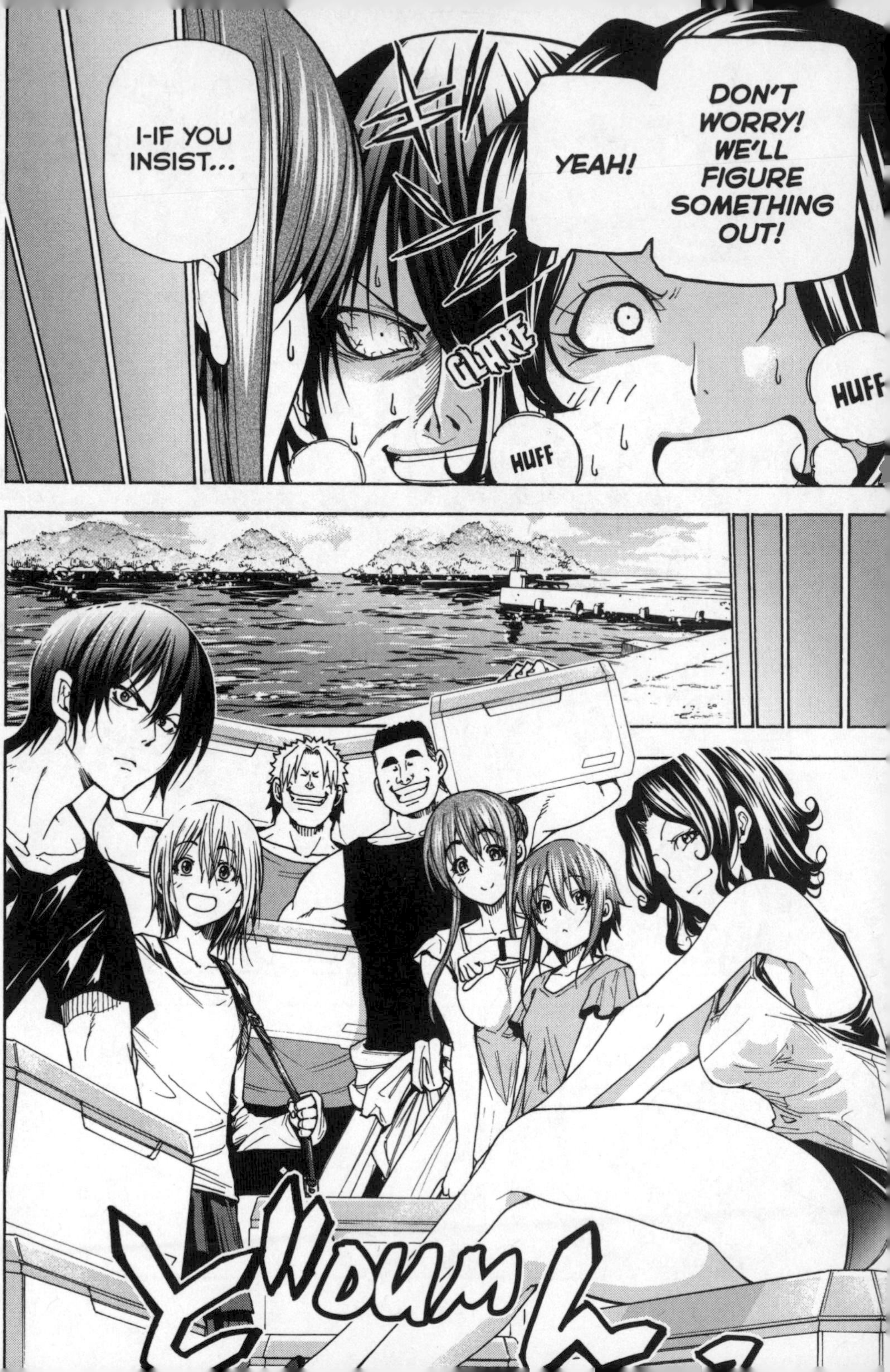
DON'T WORRY! WE'LL FIGURE SOMETHING OUT!
YEAH!
I-IF YOU INSIST...
HUFF
GLARE
HUFF

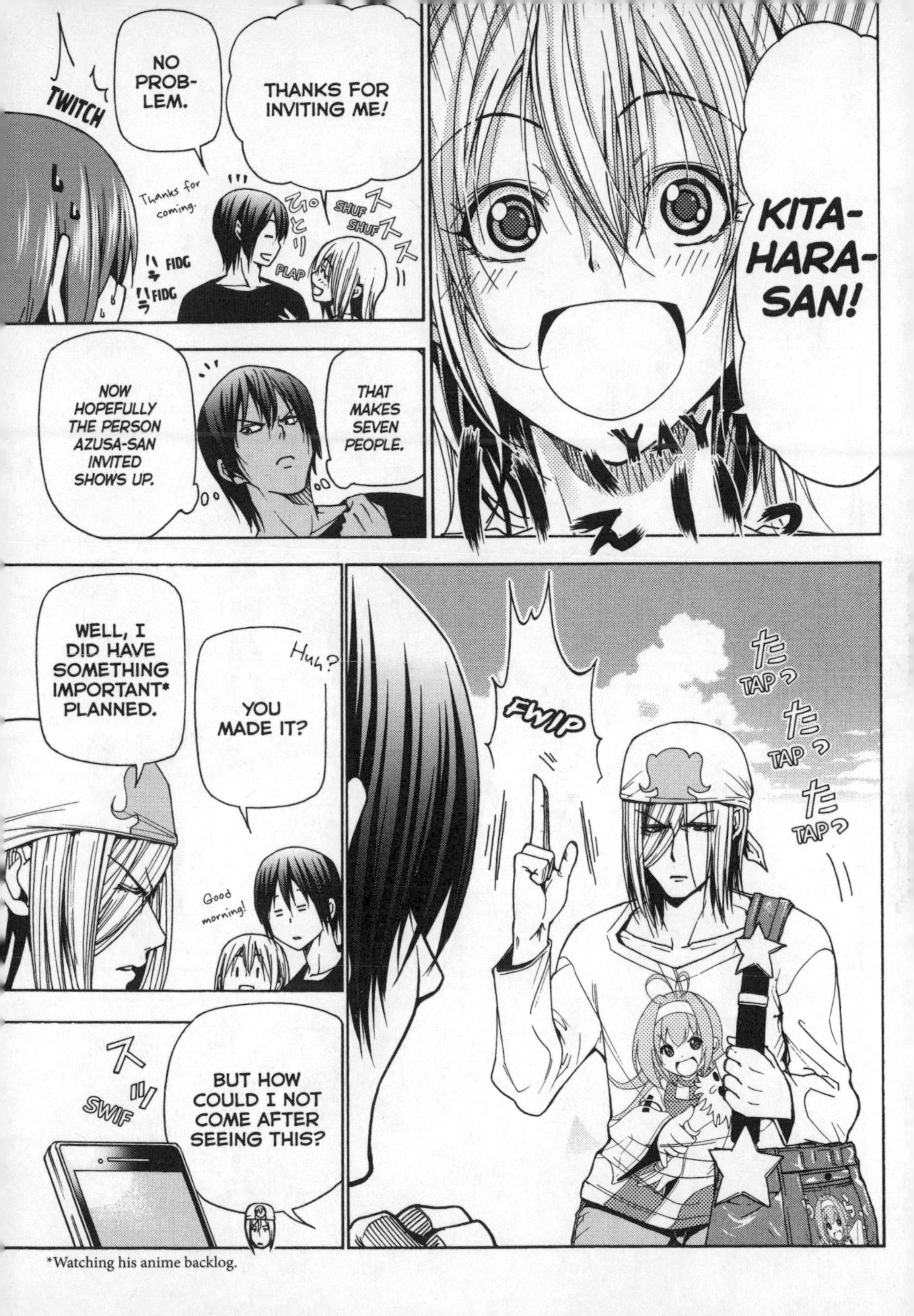
KITA-HARA-SAN!
YAY
THANKS FOR INVITING ME!
NO PROB-LEM.
Thanks for coming.
SHUF
SHUF
PLAP
TWITCH
FIDG
FIDG
THAT MAKES SEVEN PEOPLE.
NOW HOPEFULLY THE PERSON AZUSA-SAN INVITED SHOWS UP.
FWIP
TAP
TAP
TAP
Huh?
YOU MADE IT?
WELL, I DID HAVE SOMETHING IMPORTANT* PLANNED.
Good morning!
BUT HOW COULD I NOT COME AFTER SEEING THIS?
SWIF

*Watching his anime backlog.

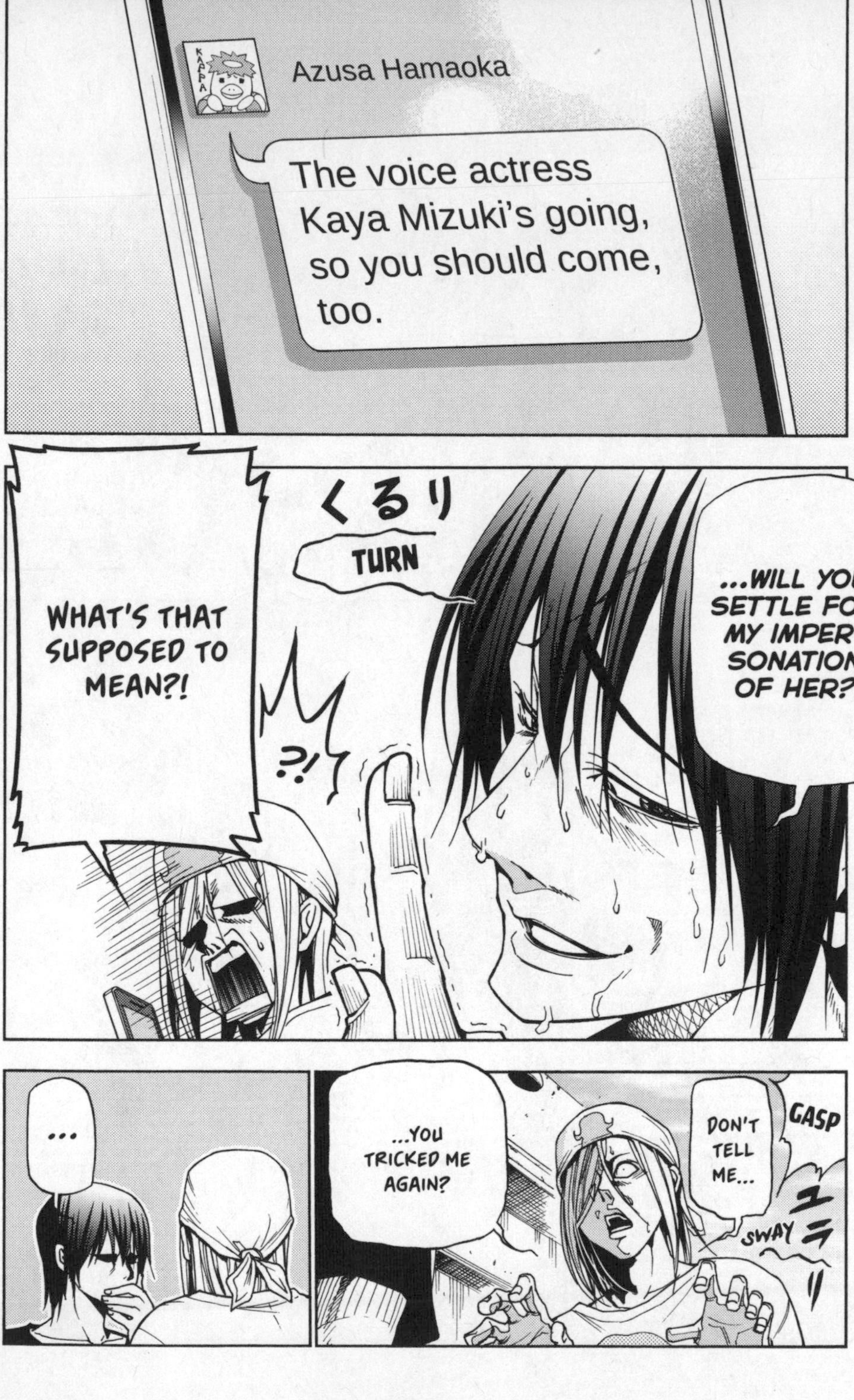

Azusa Hamaoka
KAPPA
The voice actress Kaya Mizuki's going, so you should come, too.
...WILL YOU SETTLE FOR MY IMPERSONATION OF HER?
くるり
TURN
?!
WHAT'S THAT SUPPOSED TO MEAN?!
GASP
DON'T TELL ME...
...YOU TRICKED ME AGAIN?
ユラ
SWAY
...

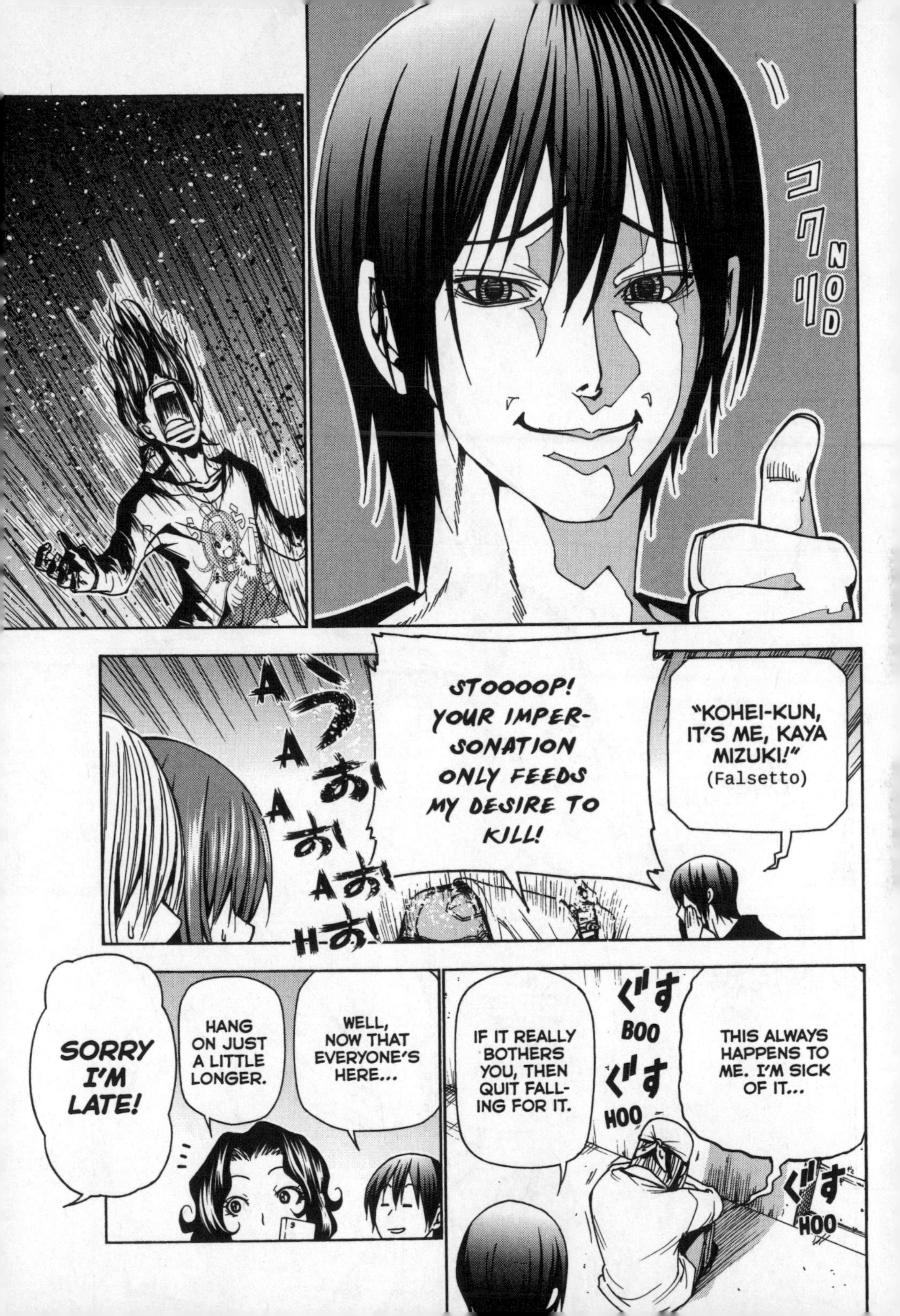
コクッ
NOD
"KOHEI-KUN, IT'S ME, KAYA MIZUKI!" (Falsetto)
STOOOOP! YOUR IMPERSONATION ONLY FEEDS MY DESIRE TO KILL!
AAAAAH-
THIS ALWAYS HAPPENS TO ME. I'M SICK OF IT...
ぐす BOO ぐす HOO ぐす HOO
IF IT REALLY BOTHERS YOU, THEN QUIT FALLING FOR IT.
WELL, NOW THAT EVERYONE'S HERE...
HANG ON JUST A LITTLE LONGER.
SORRY I'M LATE!

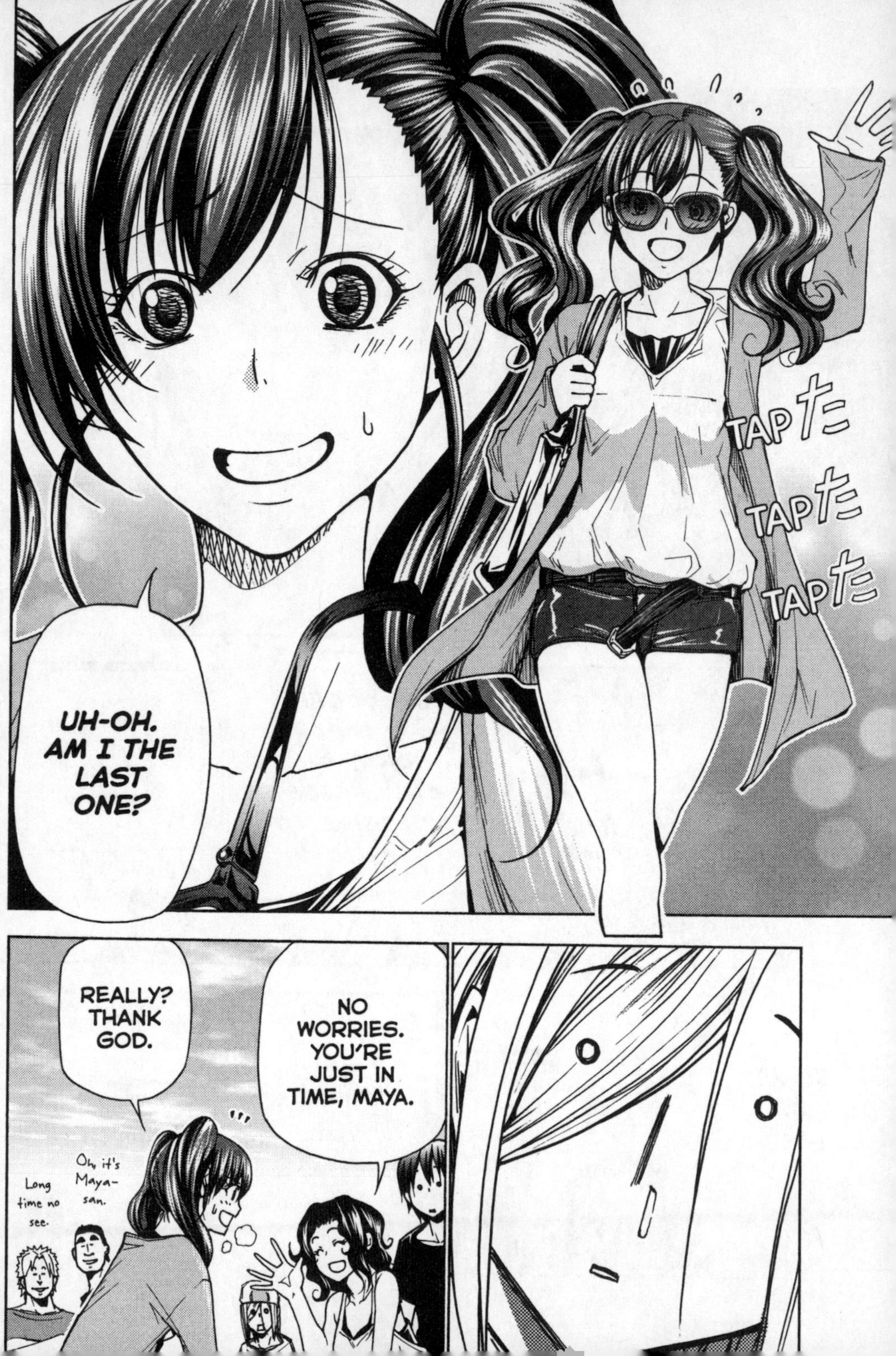
TAP た
TAP た
TAP た
UH-OH. AM I THE LAST ONE?
NO WORRIES. YOU'RE JUST IN TIME, MAYA.
REALLY? THANK GOD.
Oh, it's Maya-san.
Long time no see.

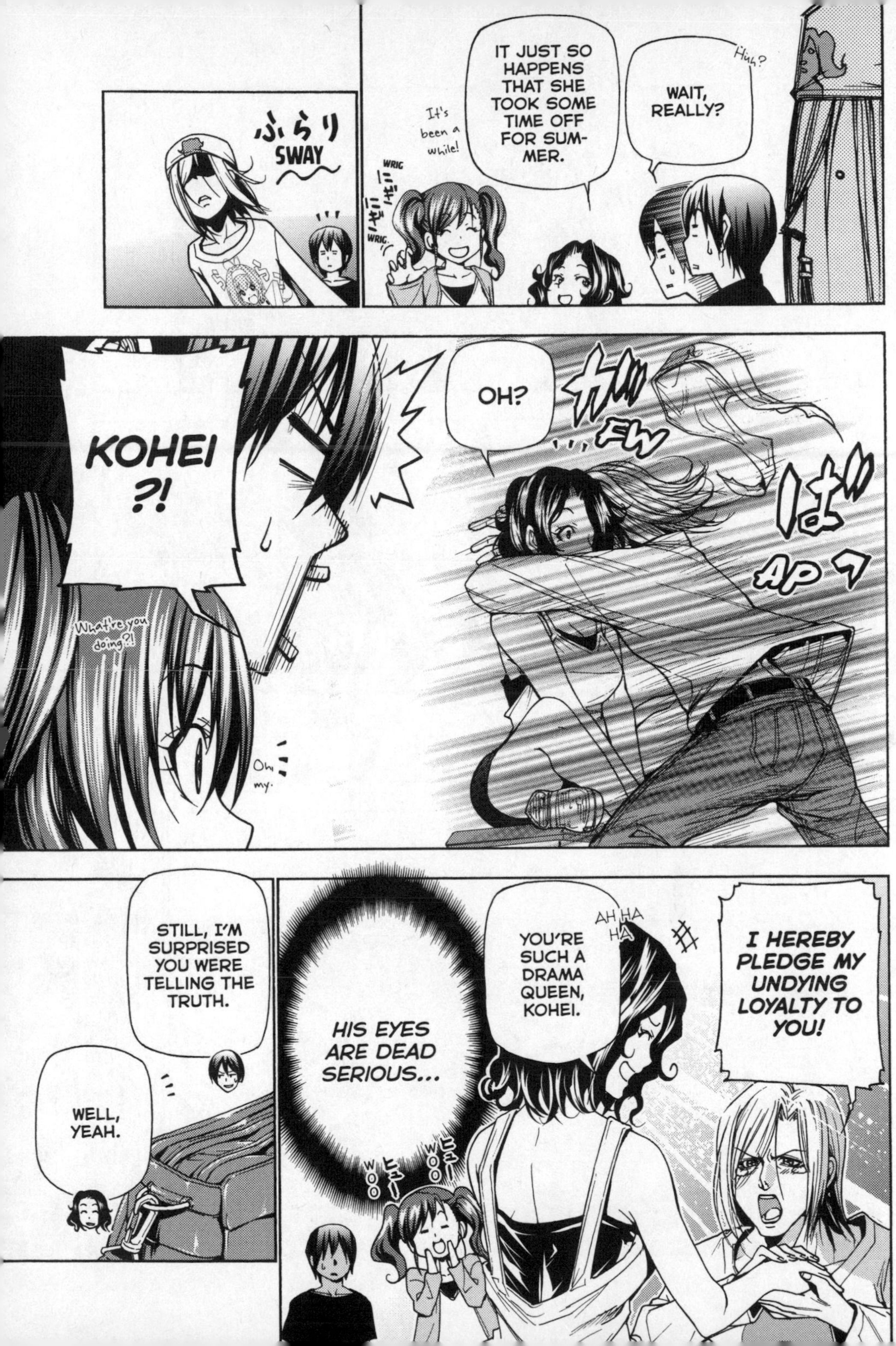
Huh?
WAIT, REALLY?
IT JUST SO HAPPENS THAT SHE TOOK SOME TIME OFF FOR SUM-MER.
It's been a while!
WRIG WRIG
ふらり
SWAY
FW
AP
OH?
KOHEI ?!
What're you doing?!
Oh my.
I HEREBY PLEDGE MY UNDYING LOYALTY TO YOU!
AH HA HA
YOU'RE SUCH A DRAMA QUEEN, KOHEI.
HIS EYES ARE DEAD SERIOUS...
WOO WOO
STILL, I'M SURPRISED YOU WERE TELLING THE TRUTH.
WELL, YEAH.

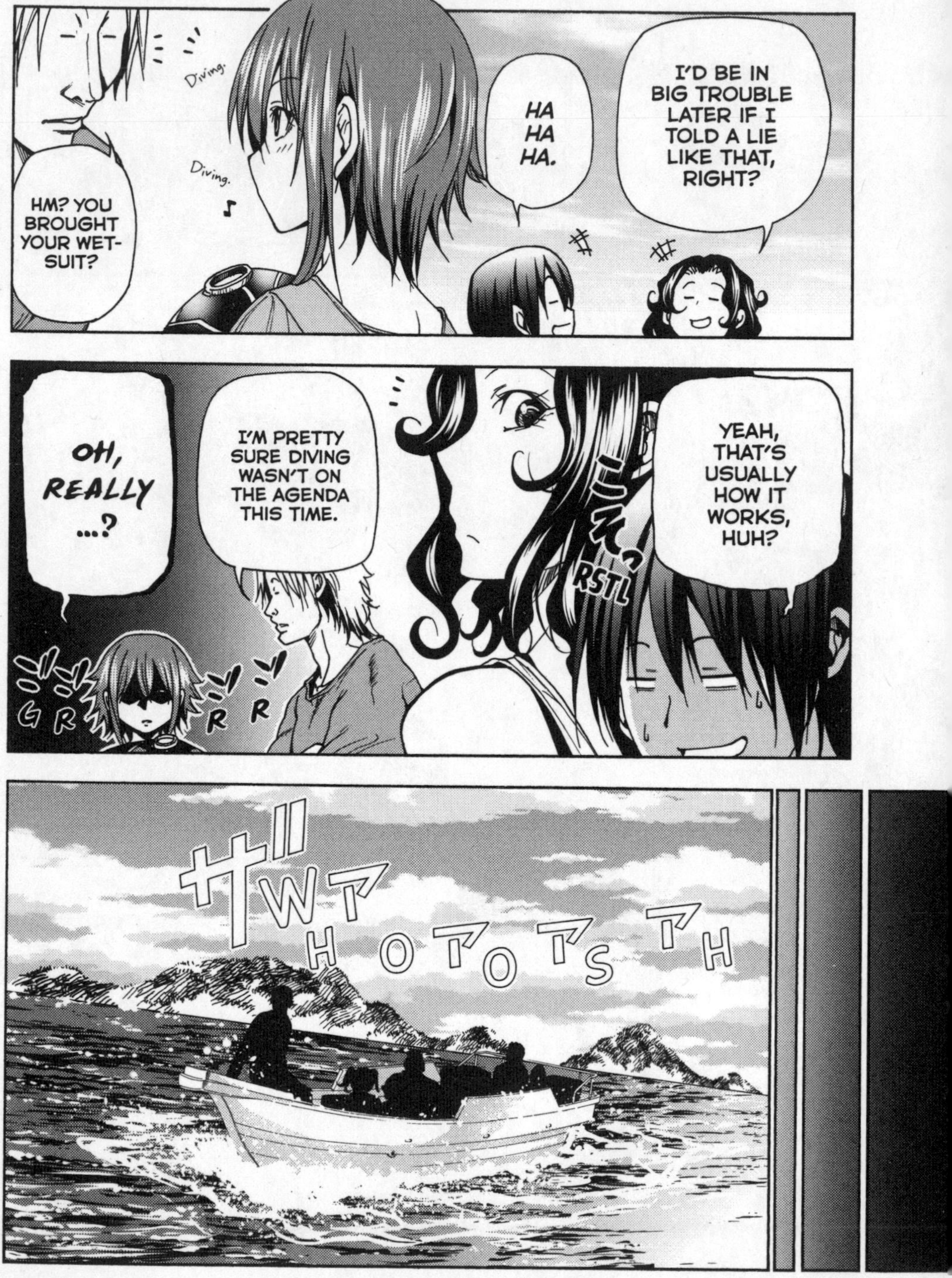
I'D BE IN BIG TROUBLE LATER IF I TOLD A LIE LIKE THAT, RIGHT?
HA HA HA.
Diving.
Diving.
HM? YOU BROUGHT YOUR WET-SUIT?
YEAH, THAT'S USUALLY HOW IT WORKS, HUH?
RSTL
I'M PRETTY SURE DIVING WASN'T ON THE AGENDA THIS TIME.
OH, REALLY ...?
R R
G R
WHOOSH

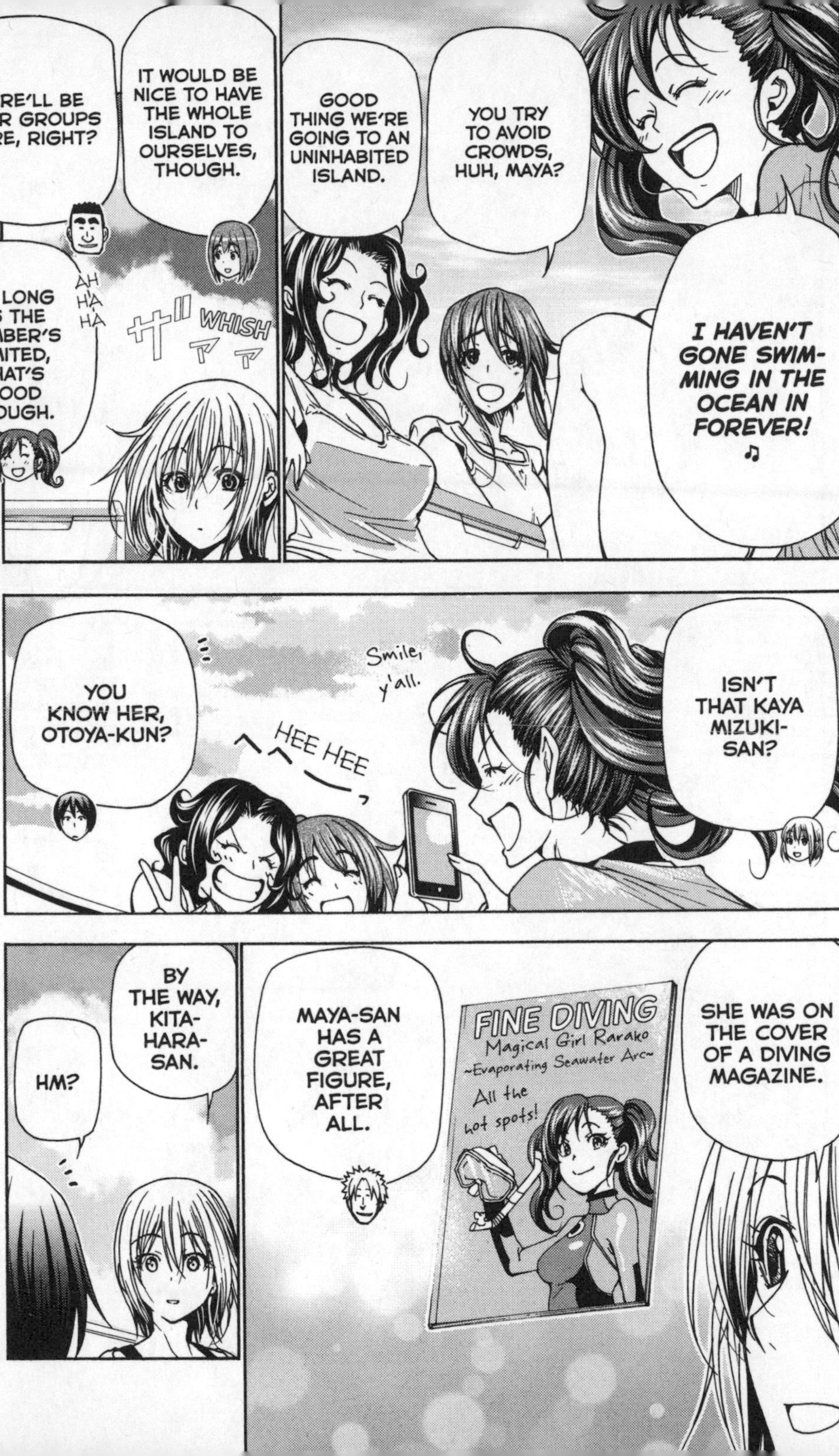
I HAVEN'T GONE SWIMMING IN THE OCEAN IN FOREVER! ♫
YOU TRY TO AVOID CROWDS, HUH, MAYA?
GOOD THING WE'RE GOING TO AN UNINHABITED ISLAND.
IT WOULD BE NICE TO HAVE THE WHOLE ISLAND TO OURSELVES, THOUGH.
THERE'LL BE OTHER GROUPS THERE, RIGHT?
AH HA HA
WHISH
AS LONG AS THE NUMBER'S LIMITED, THAT'S GOOD ENOUGH.
ISN'T THAT KAYA MIZUKI-SAN?
Smile, y'all.
HEE HEE
YOU KNOW HER, OTOYA-KUN?
SHE WAS ON THE COVER OF A DIVING MAGAZINE.
FINE DIVING
Magical Girl Rarako
~Evaporating Seawater Arc~
All the hot spots!
MAYA-SAN HAS A GREAT FIGURE, AFTER ALL.
BY THE WAY, KITAHARA-SAN.
HM?

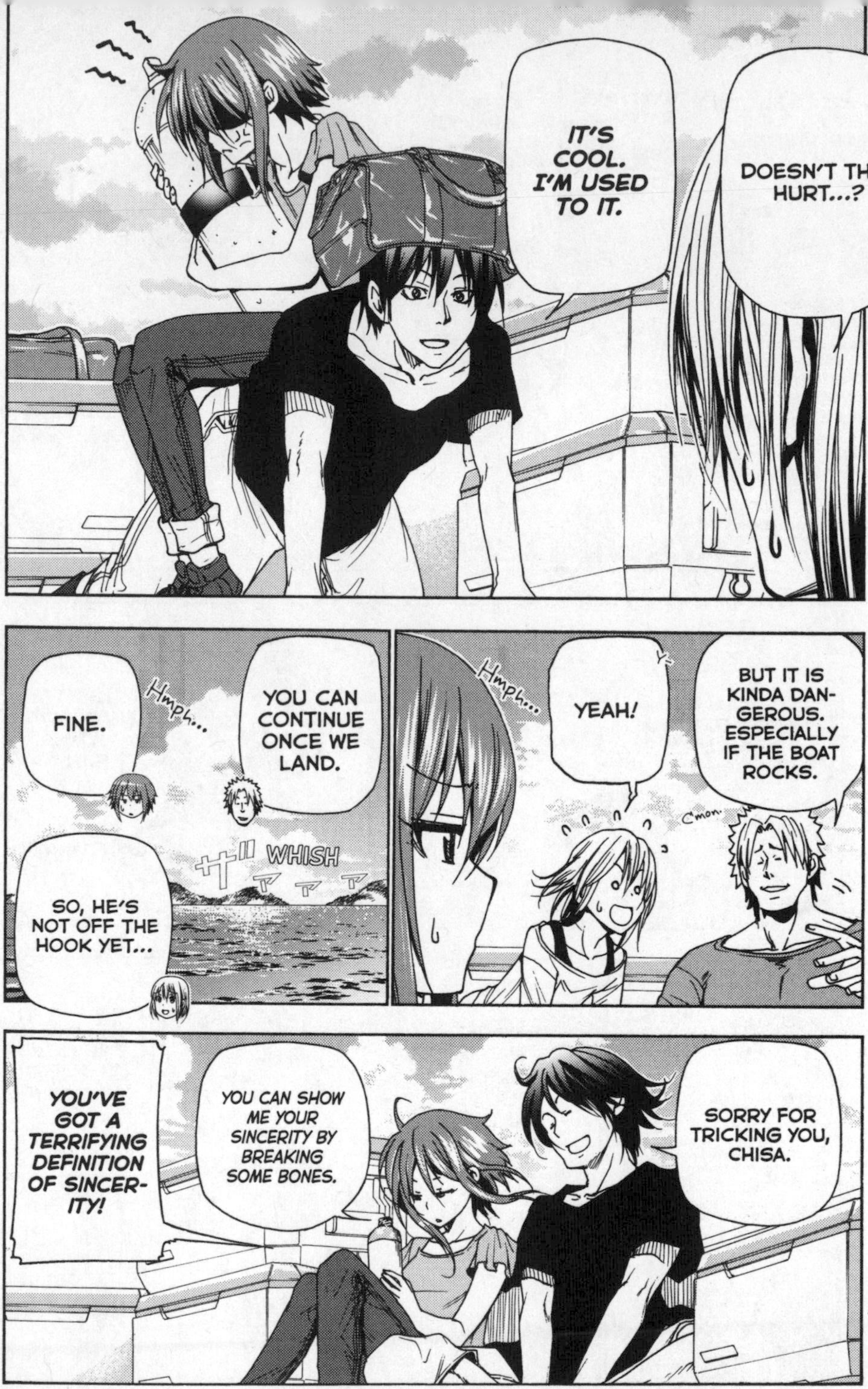
DOESN'T THAT HURT...?
IT'S COOL. I'M USED TO IT.
BUT IT IS KINDA DANGEROUS. ESPECIALLY IF THE BOAT ROCKS.
C'mon.
Y-YEAH!
Hmph...
YOU CAN CONTINUE ONCE WE LAND.
Hmph...
FINE.
WHISH
SO, HE'S NOT OFF THE HOOK YET...
SORRY FOR TRICKING YOU, CHISA.
YOU CAN SHOW ME YOUR SINCERITY BY BREAKING SOME BONES.
YOU'VE GOT A TERRIFYING DEFINITION OF SINCERITY!

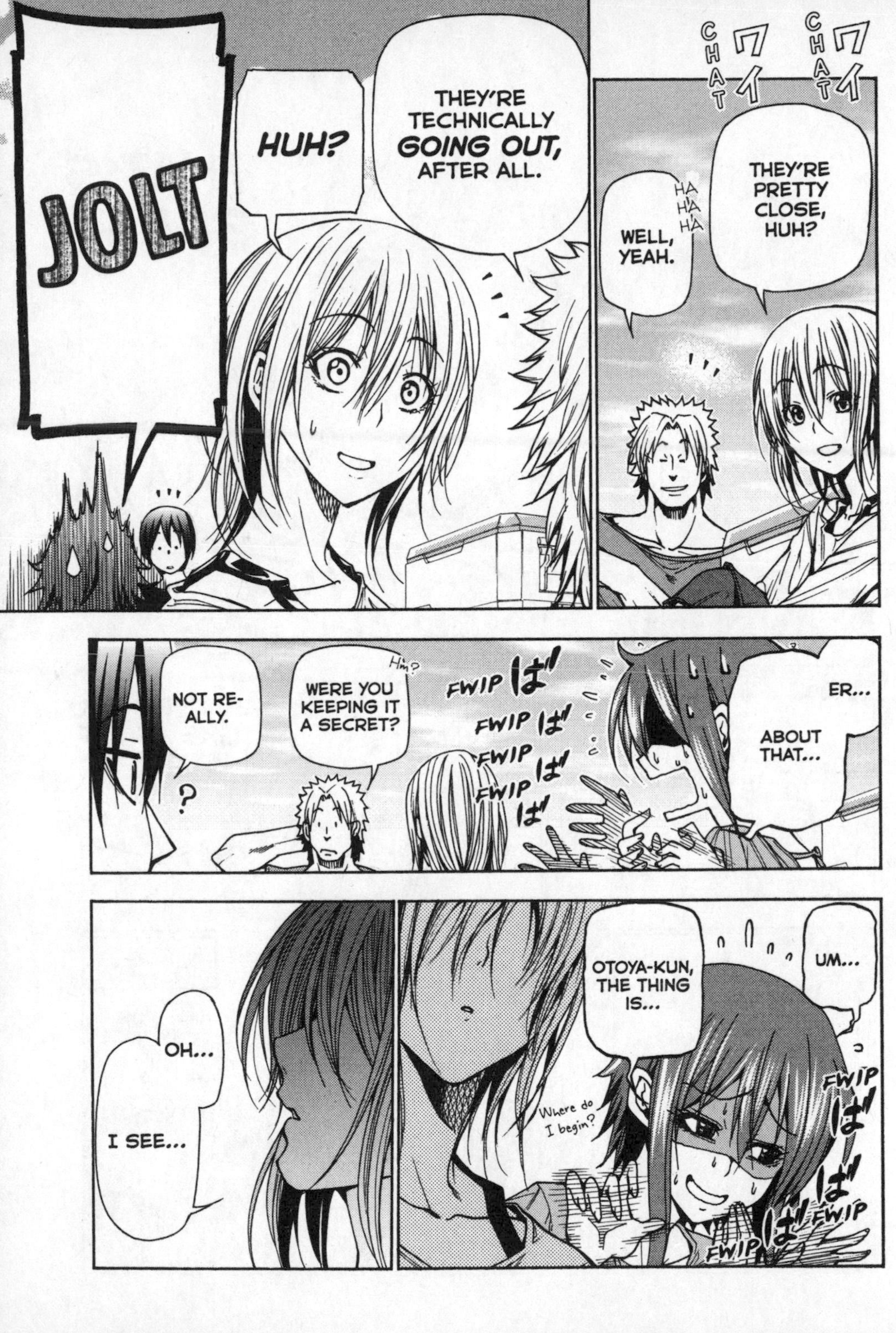
CHAT ワイ
CHAT ワイ
THEY'RE PRETTY CLOSE, HUH?
HA HA HA
WELL, YEAH.
THEY'RE TECHNICALLY GOING OUT, AFTER ALL.
HUH?
JOLT
ER...
ABOUT THAT...
FWIP ば
FWIP ば
FWIP ば
FWIP ば
Hm?
WERE YOU KEEPING IT A SECRET?
NOT RE-ALLY.
?
UM...
OTOYA-KUN, THE THING IS...
Where do I begin?
FWIP ば
FWIP ば
FWIP ば
OH...
I SEE...

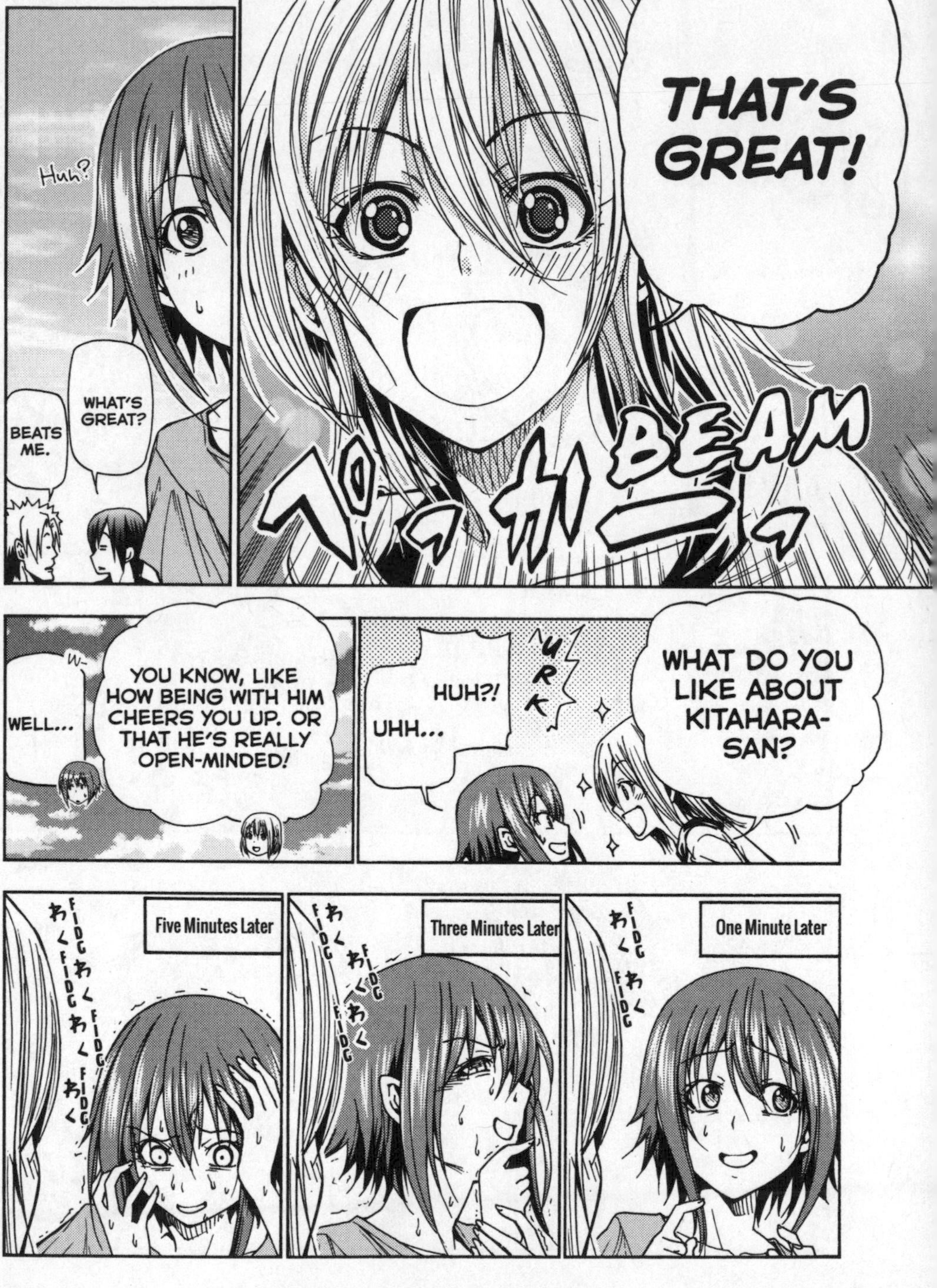
THAT'S GREAT!
BEAM
Huh?
WHAT'S GREAT?
BEATS ME.
WHAT DO YOU LIKE ABOUT KITAHARA-SAN?
URK
HUH?! UHH...
YOU KNOW, LIKE HOW BEING WITH HIM CHEERS YOU UP. OR THAT HE'S REALLY OPEN-MINDED!
W- WELL...
One Minute Later
わく FIDG わく FIDG
Three Minutes Later
わく FIDG わく FIDG わく FIDG
Five Minutes Later
わく FIDG わく FIDG わく FIDG わく FIDG

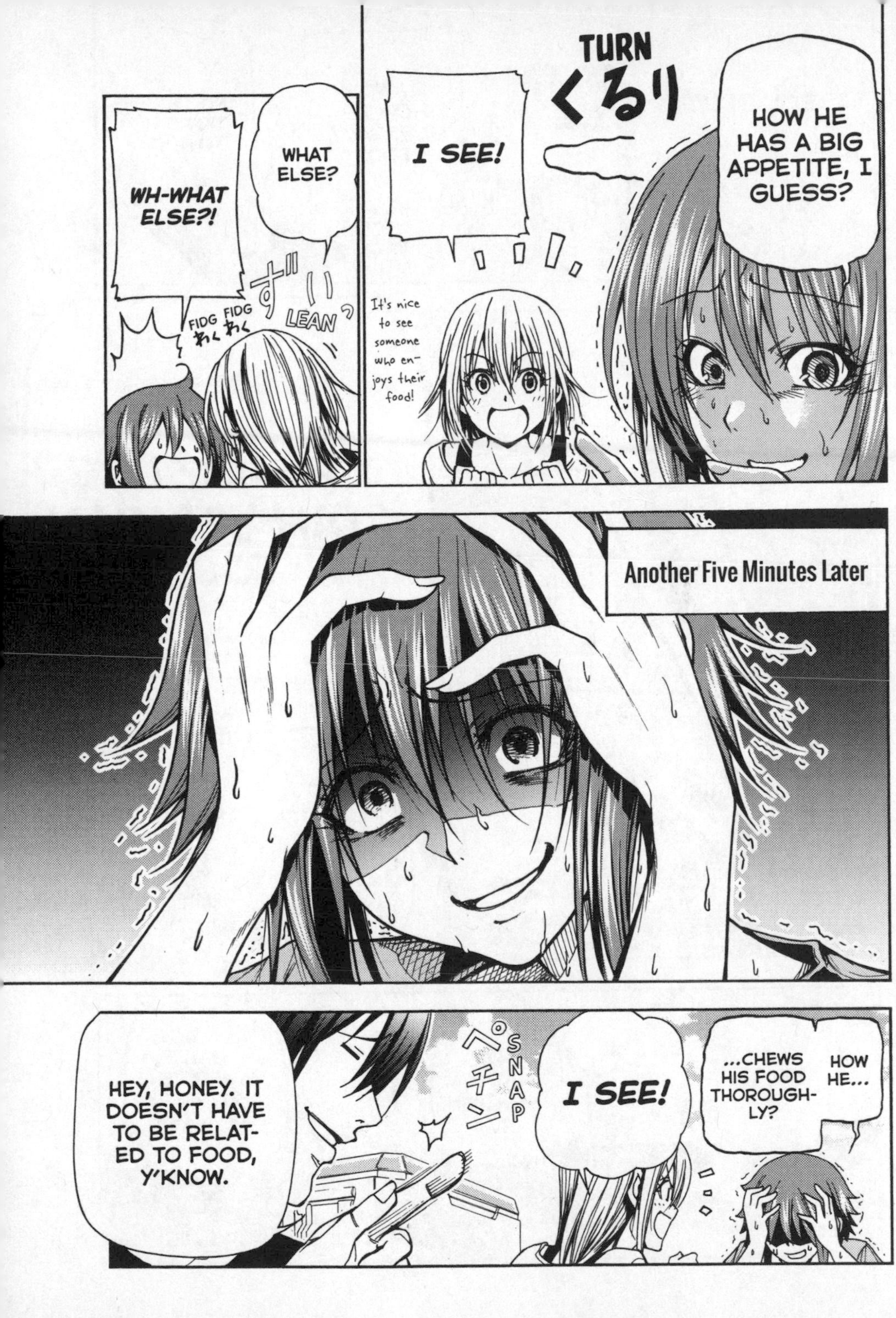
HOW HE HAS A BIG APPETITE, I GUESS?
TURN
くるり
I SEE!
It's nice to see someone who enjoys their food!
WHAT ELSE?
WH-WHAT ELSE?!
ずい
LEAN
FIDG FIDG
わくわく
Another Five Minutes Later
HOW HE...
...CHEWS HIS FOOD THOROUGHLY?
I SEE!
SNAP
ペチン
HEY, HONEY. IT DOESN'T HAVE TO BE RELATED TO FOOD, Y'KNOW.

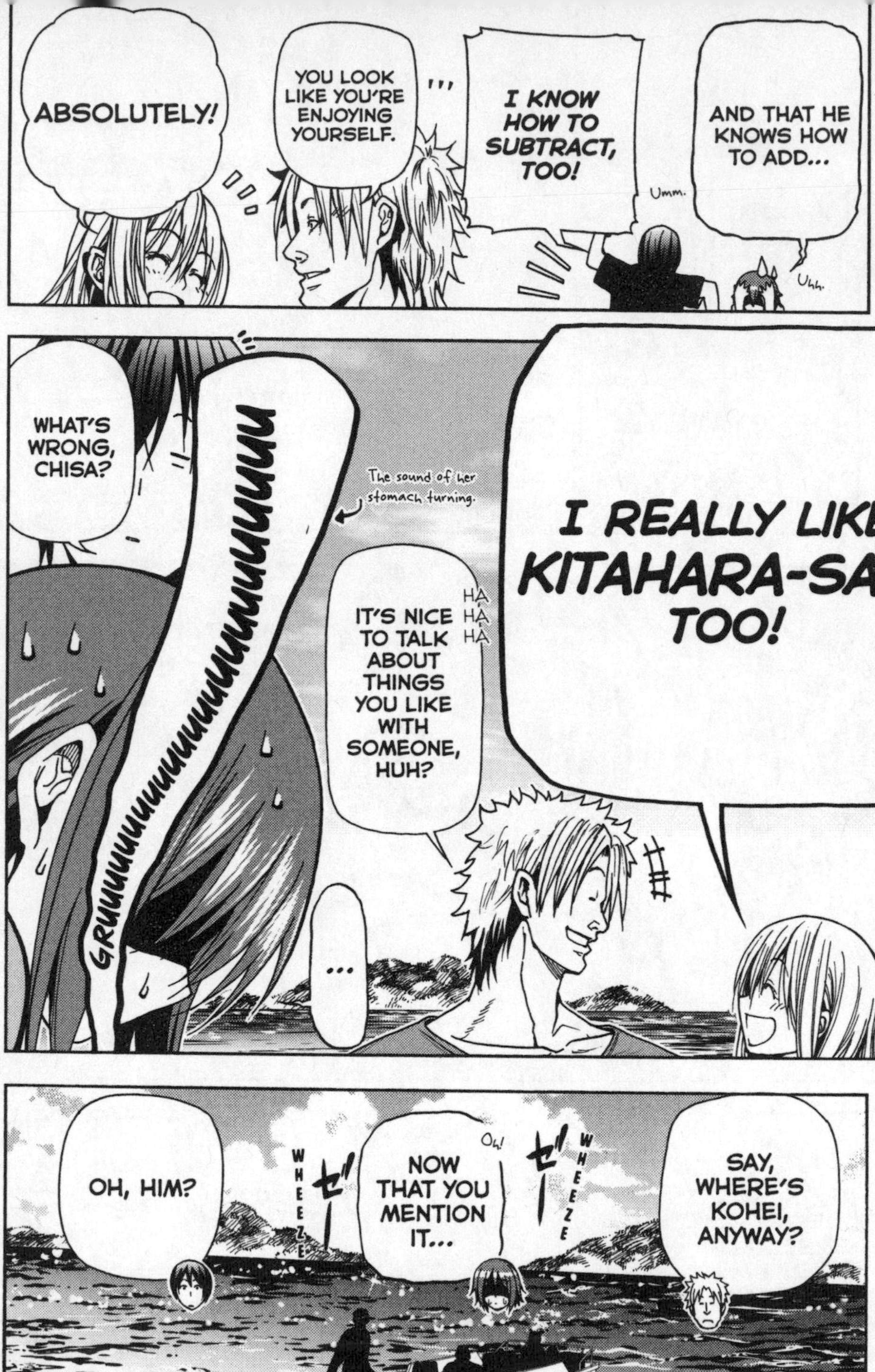
AND THAT HE KNOWS HOW TO ADD...
Umm.
Uhh.
I KNOW HOW TO SUBTRACT, TOO!
YOU LOOK LIKE YOU'RE ENJOYING YOURSELF.
ABSOLUTELY!
I REALLY LIKE KITAHARA-SAN, TOO!
IT'S NICE TO TALK ABOUT THINGS YOU LIKE WITH SOMEONE, HUH?
HA HA HA
...
The sound of her stomach turning.
GRUUUUUUUUUUUUUUUUUUUUUUUU
WHAT'S WRONG, CHISA?
SAY, WHERE'S KOHEI, ANYWAY?
WHEEZE
Oh!
NOW THAT YOU MENTION IT...
WHEEZE
OH, HIM?

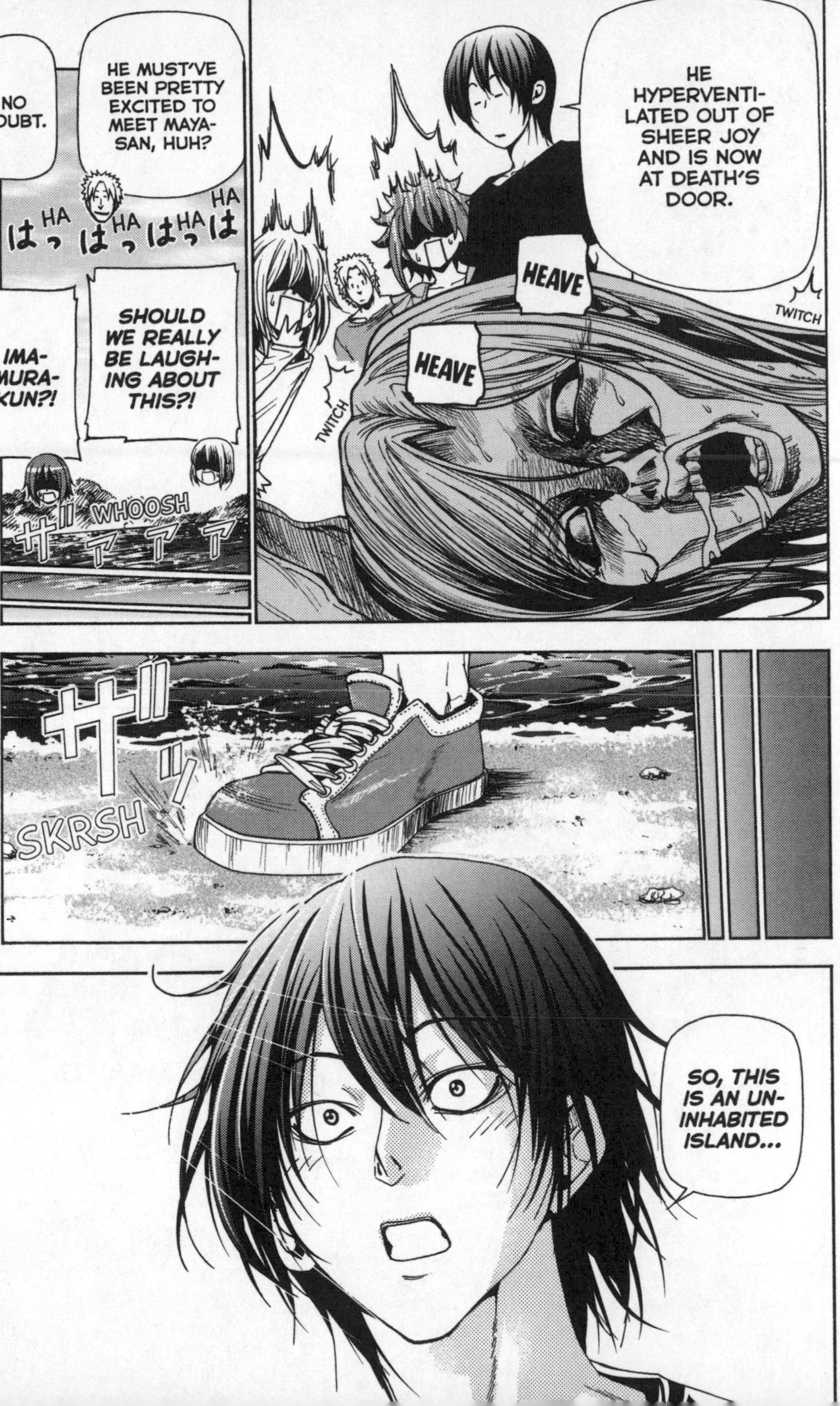
HE HYPERVENTI-LATED OUT OF SHEER JOY AND IS NOW AT DEATH'S DOOR.
TWITCH
HEAVE
HEAVE
TWITCH
HE MUST'VE BEEN PRETTY EXCITED TO MEET MAYA-SAN, HUH?
NO DOUBT.
HA HA HA HA
SHOULD WE REALLY BE LAUGHING ABOUT THIS?!
IMA-MURA-KUN?!
WHOOSH
SKRSH
SO, THIS IS AN UN-INHABITED ISLAND...

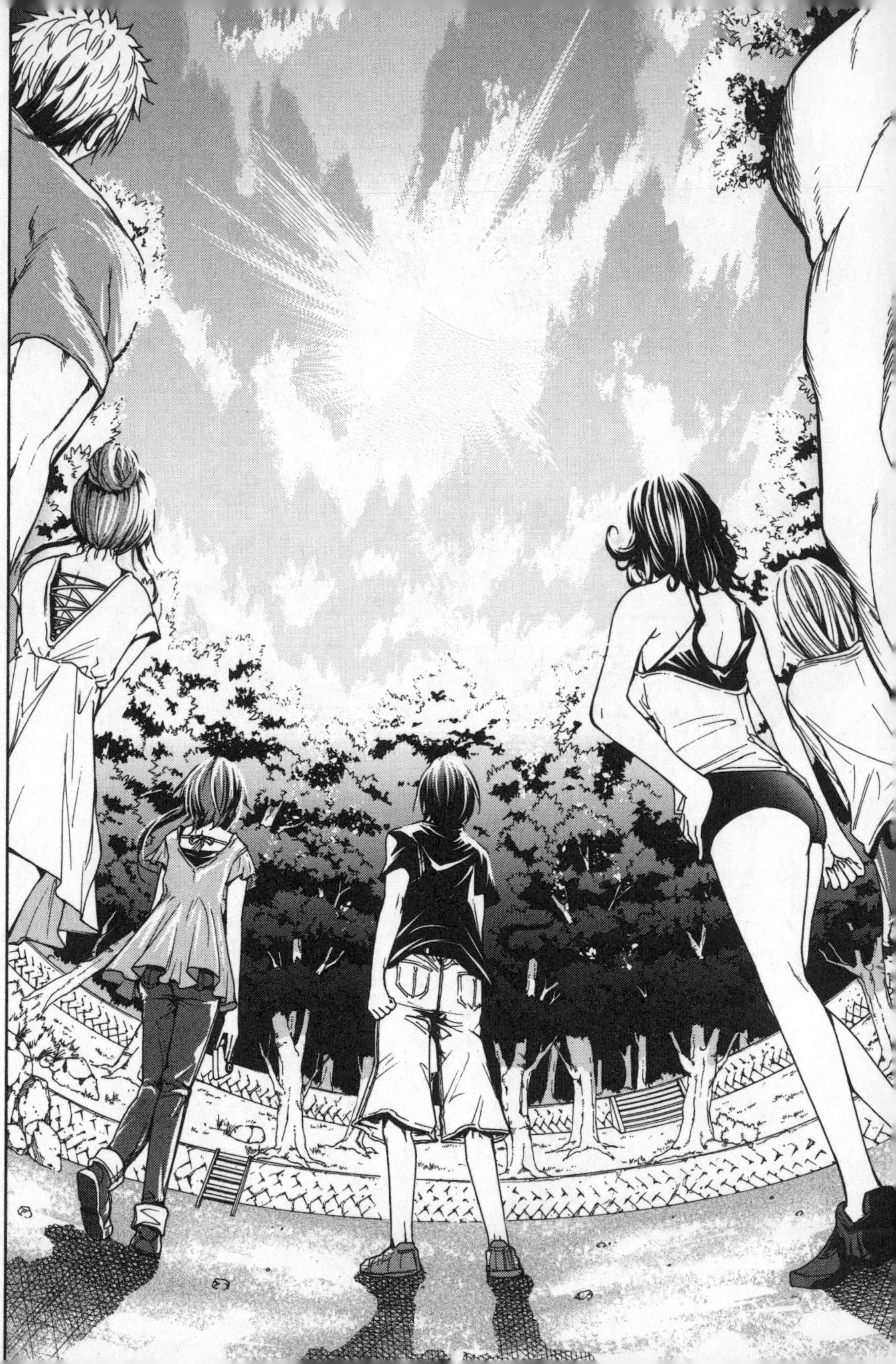

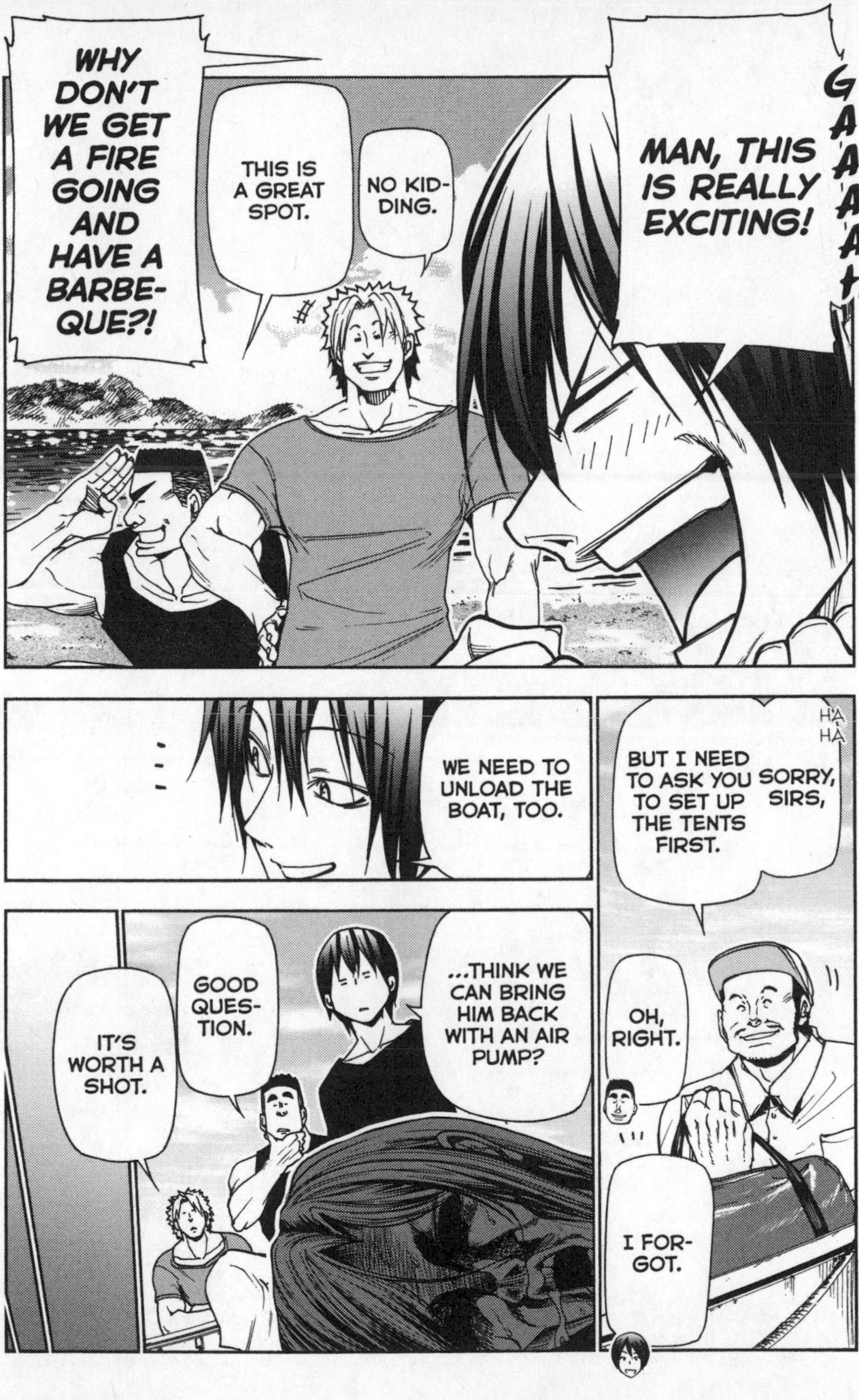
GAAAAAH
MAN, THIS IS REALLY EXCITING!
NO KID-DING.
THIS IS A GREAT SPOT.
WHY DON'T WE GET A FIRE GOING AND HAVE A BARBE-QUE?!
HA HA
SORRY, SIRS,
BUT I NEED TO ASK YOU TO SET UP THE TENTS FIRST.
OH, RIGHT.
I FOR-GOT.
...
WE NEED TO UNLOAD THE BOAT, TOO.
...THINK WE CAN BRING HIM BACK WITH AN AIR PUMP?
GOOD QUES-TION.
IT'S WORTH A SHOT.

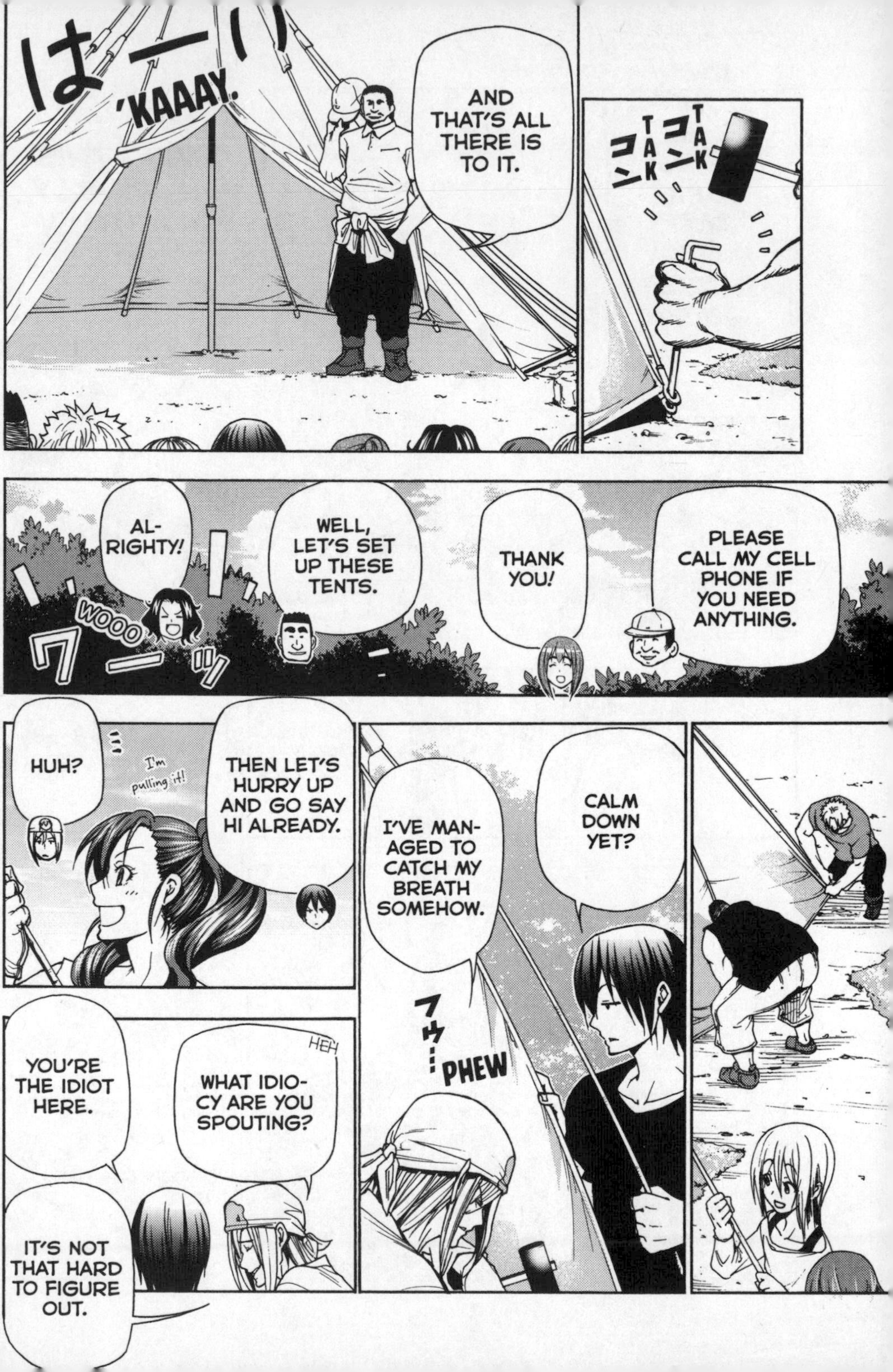
コンコン
TAK TAK
AND THAT'S ALL THERE IS TO IT.
はーい
'KAAAY.
PLEASE CALL MY CELL PHONE IF YOU NEED ANYTHING.
THANK YOU!
WELL, LET'S SET UP THESE TENTS.
AL-RIGHTY!
ワーッ
WOOO
CALM DOWN YET?
I'VE MAN-AGED TO CATCH MY BREATH SOMEHOW.
フゥ
PHEW
THEN LET'S HURRY UP AND GO SAY HI ALREADY.
I'm pulling it!
HUH?
HEH
WHAT IDIO-CY ARE YOU SPOUTING?
YOU'RE THE IDIOT HERE.
IT'S NOT THAT HARD TO FIGURE OUT.

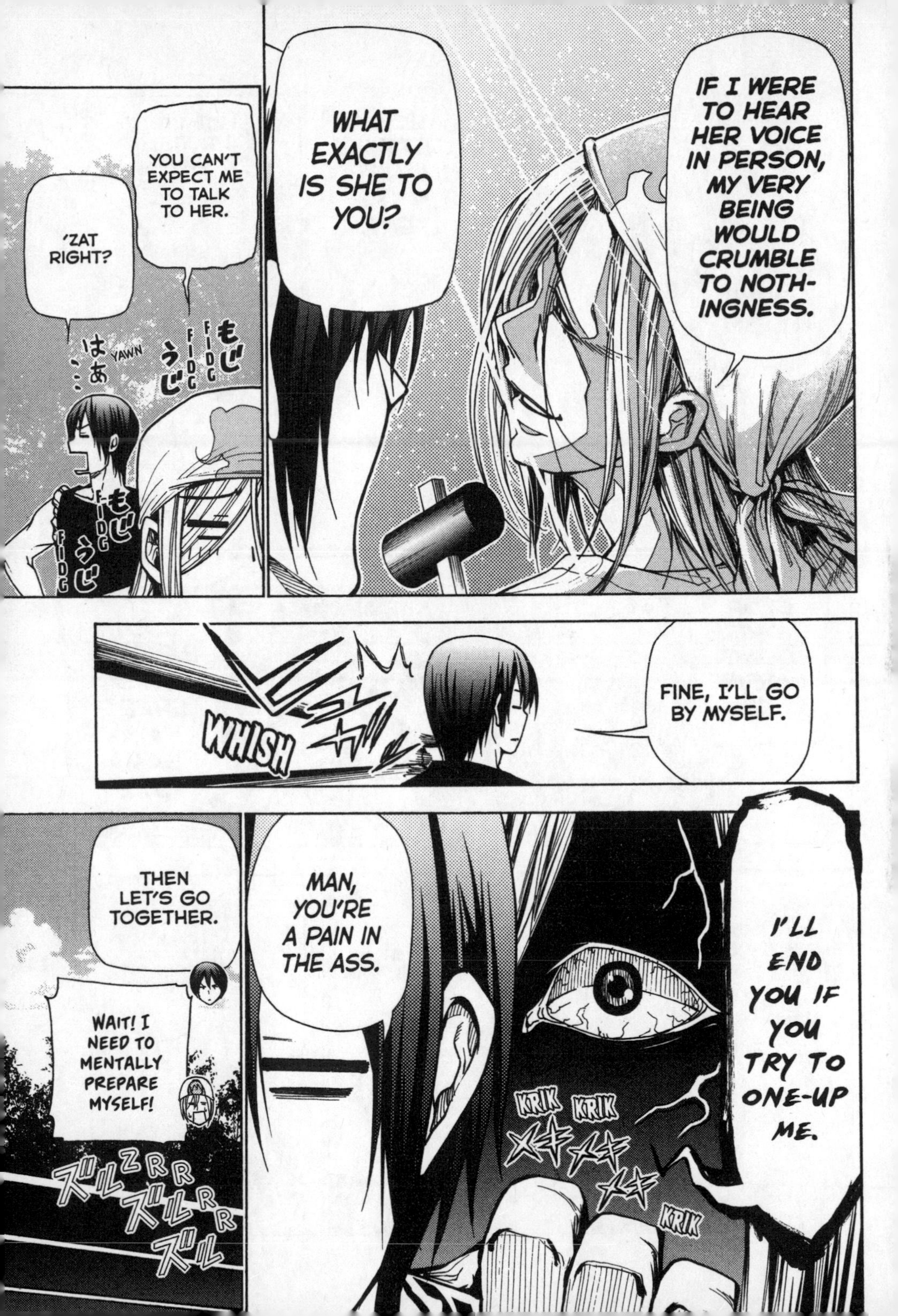
IF I WERE TO HEAR HER VOICE IN PERSON, MY VERY BEING WOULD CRUMBLE TO NOTH-INGNESS.
WHAT EXACTLY IS SHE TO YOU?
YOU CAN'T EXPECT ME TO TALK TO HER.
もじ FIDG うじ FIDG
'ZAT RIGHT?
はぁ YAWN
もじ FIDG うじ FIDG
FINE, I'LL GO BY MYSELF.
WHISH
I'LL END YOU IF YOU TRY TO ONE-UP ME.
KRIK KRIK メキメキメキ KRIK
MAN, YOU'RE A PAIN IN THE ASS.
THEN LET'S GO TOGETHER.
WAIT! I NEED TO MENTALLY PREPARE MYSELF!
ズル ZRRR ズル RRR ズル

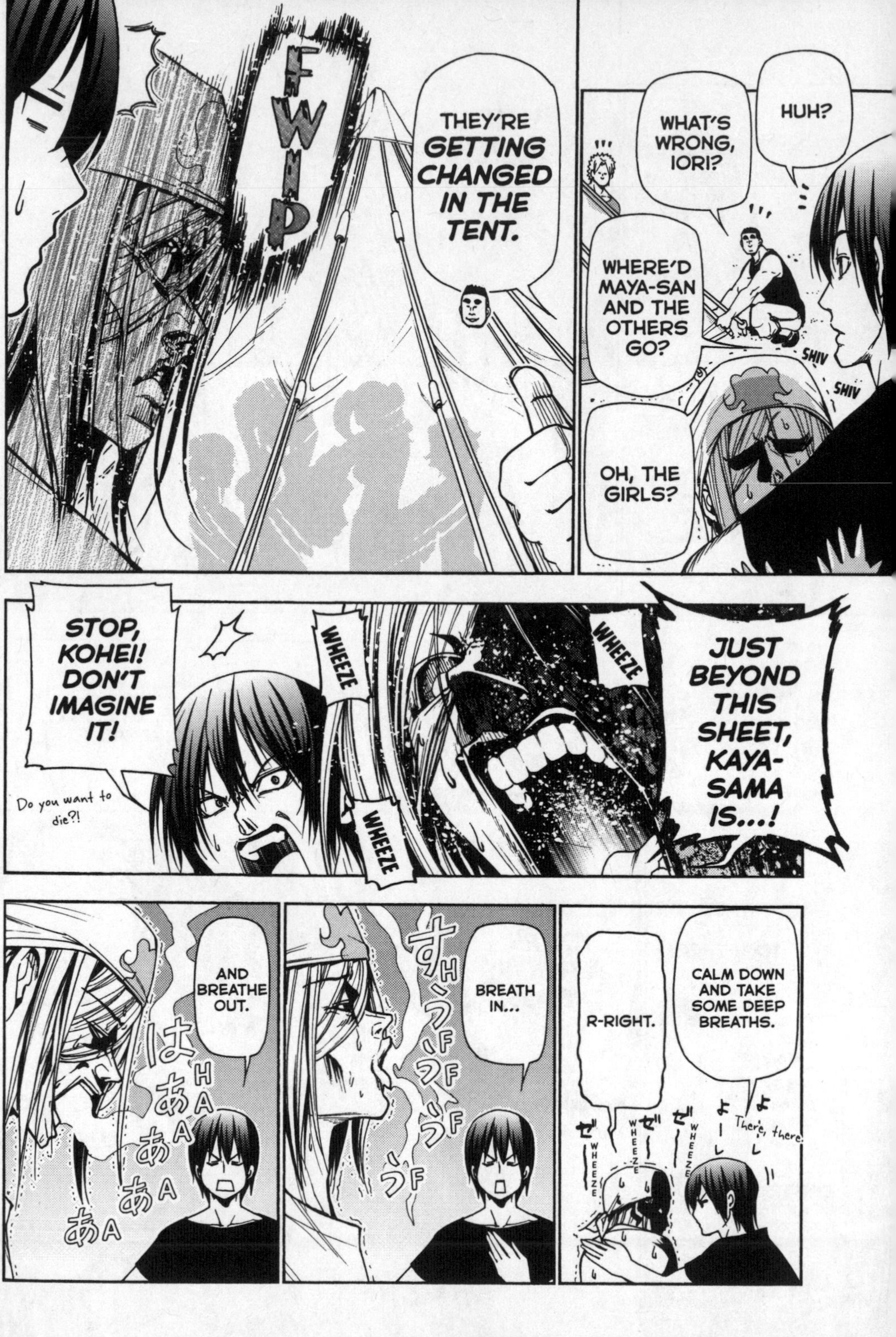
HUH?
WHAT'S WRONG, IORI?
WHERE'D MAYA-SAN AND THE OTHERS GO?
SHIV
SHIV
OH, THE GIRLS?
THEY'RE GETTING CHANGED IN THE TENT.
FWIP
JUST BEYOND THIS SHEET, KAYA-SAMA IS...!
WHEEZE
WHEEZE
WHEEZE
STOP, KOHEI! DON'T IMAGINE IT!
Do you want to die?!
CALM DOWN AND TAKE SOME DEEP BREATHS.
R-RIGHT.
よーしよーし
There, there.
ぜーぜーぜー
WHEEZE
WHEEZE
WHEEZE
BREATH IN...
すーうっうっうっうっ
H F F F F
AND BREATHE OUT.
はあああああ
H A A A A

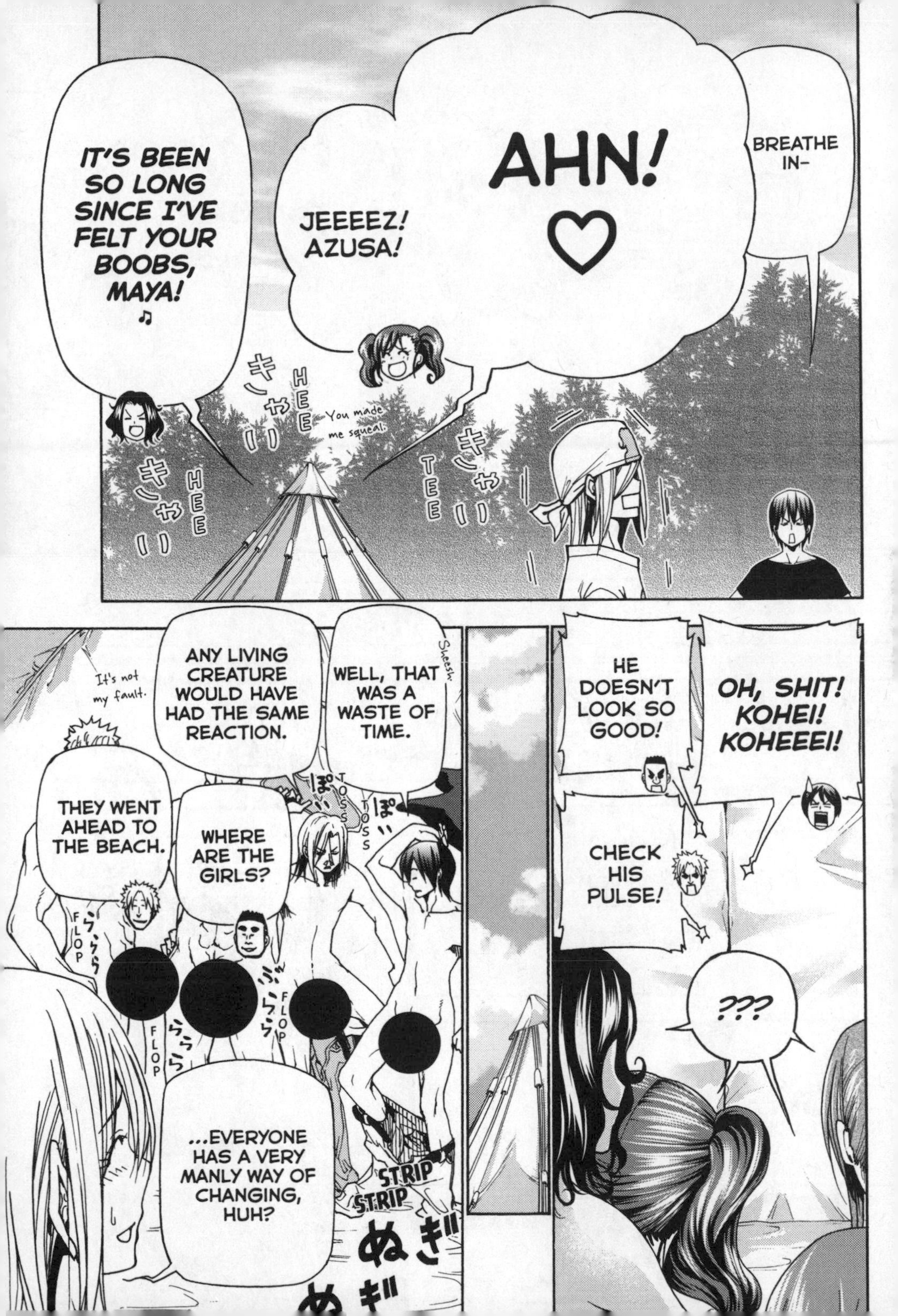
BREATHE IN–
AHN! ♥
JEEEEZ! AZUSA!
IT'S BEEN SO LONG SINCE I'VE FELT YOUR BOOBS, MAYA! ♫
TEE
You made me squeal.
HEE
HEE
OH, SHIT! KOHEI! KOHEEEI!
HE DOESN'T LOOK SO GOOD!
CHECK HIS PULSE!
???
WELL, THAT WAS A WASTE OF TIME.
Sheesh
ANY LIVING CREATURE WOULD HAVE HAD THE SAME REACTION.
It's not my fault.
TOSS
TOSS
WHERE ARE THE GIRLS?
THEY WENT AHEAD TO THE BEACH.
FLOP
FLOP
FLOP
...EVERYONE HAS A VERY MANLY WAY OF CHANGING, HUH?
STRIP
STRIP
ぬぎ
ぬぎ

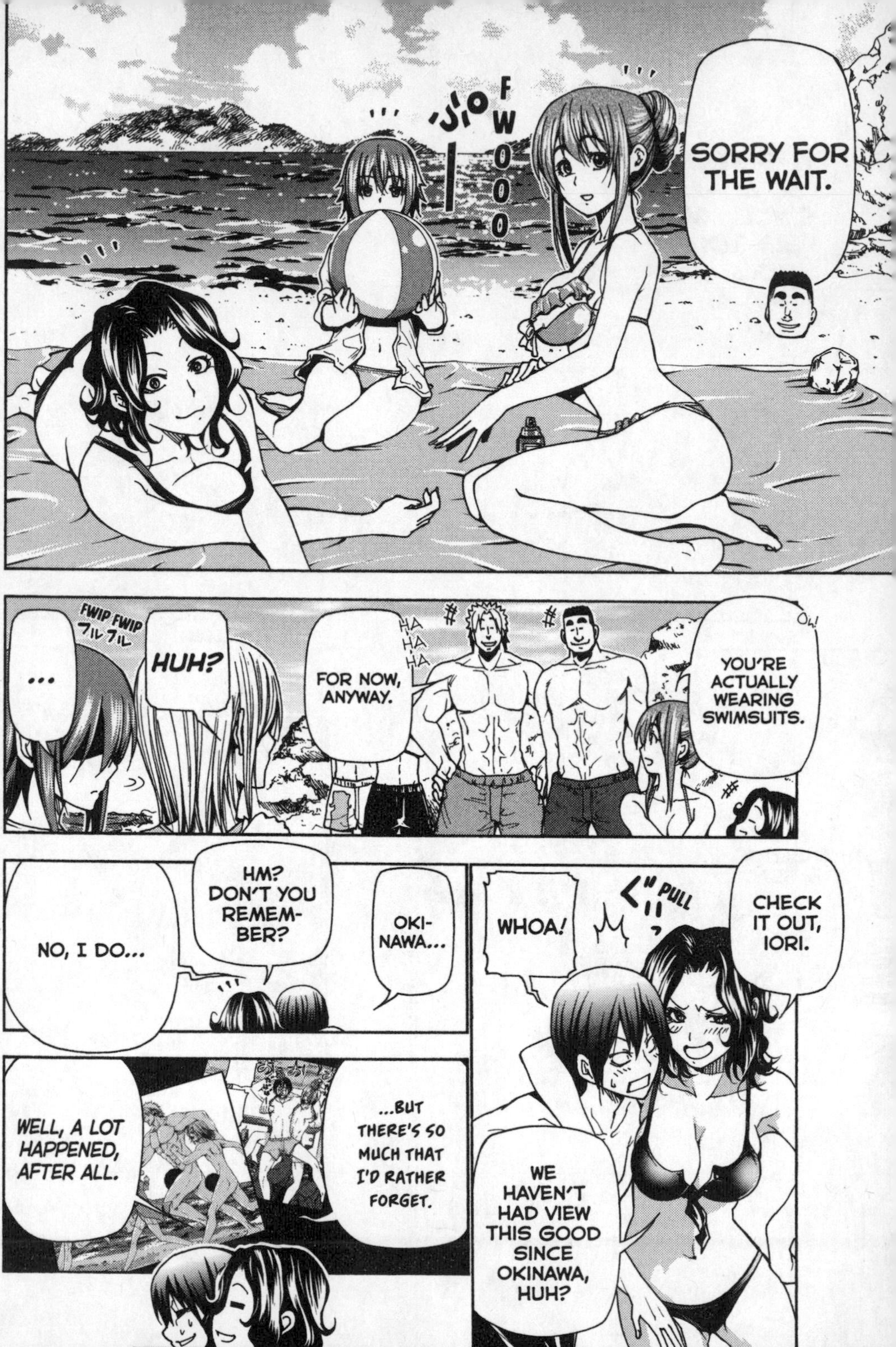
SORRY FOR THE WAIT.
FWOOO
Oh!
YOU'RE ACTUALLY WEARING SWIMSUITS.
HA HA HA
FOR NOW, ANYWAY.
HUH?
FWIP FWIP フルフル
...
CHECK IT OUT, IORI.
PULL
WHOA!
WE HAVEN'T HAD VIEW THIS GOOD SINCE OKINAWA, HUH?
OKI-NAWA...
HM? DON'T YOU REMEM-BER?
NO, I DO...
...BUT THERE'S SO MUCH THAT I'D RATHER FORGET.
WELL, A LOT HAPPENED, AFTER ALL.

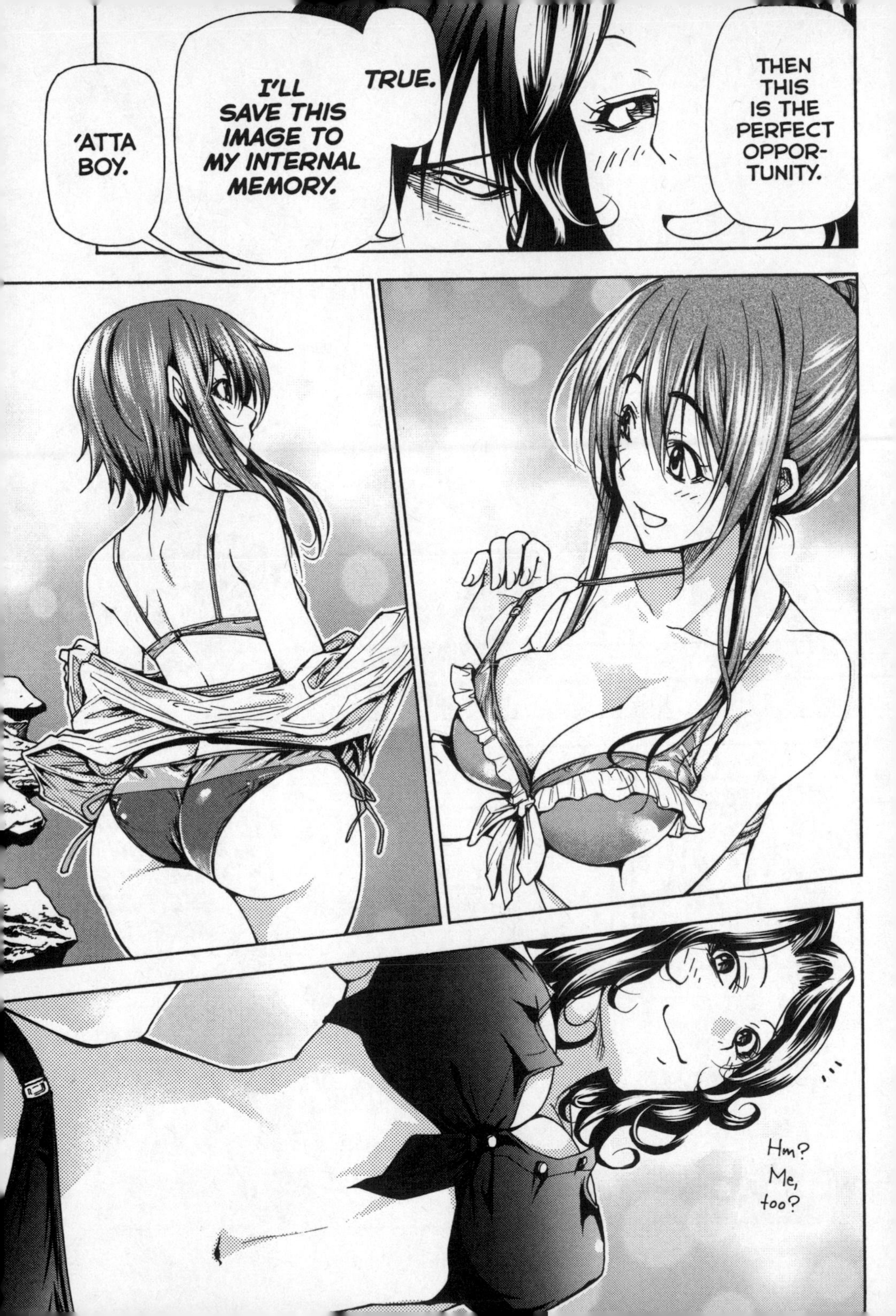
THEN THIS IS THE PERFECT OPPOR-TUNITY.
TRUE.
I'LL SAVE THIS IMAGE TO MY INTERNAL MEMORY.
'ATTA BOY.
...
Hm? Me, too?

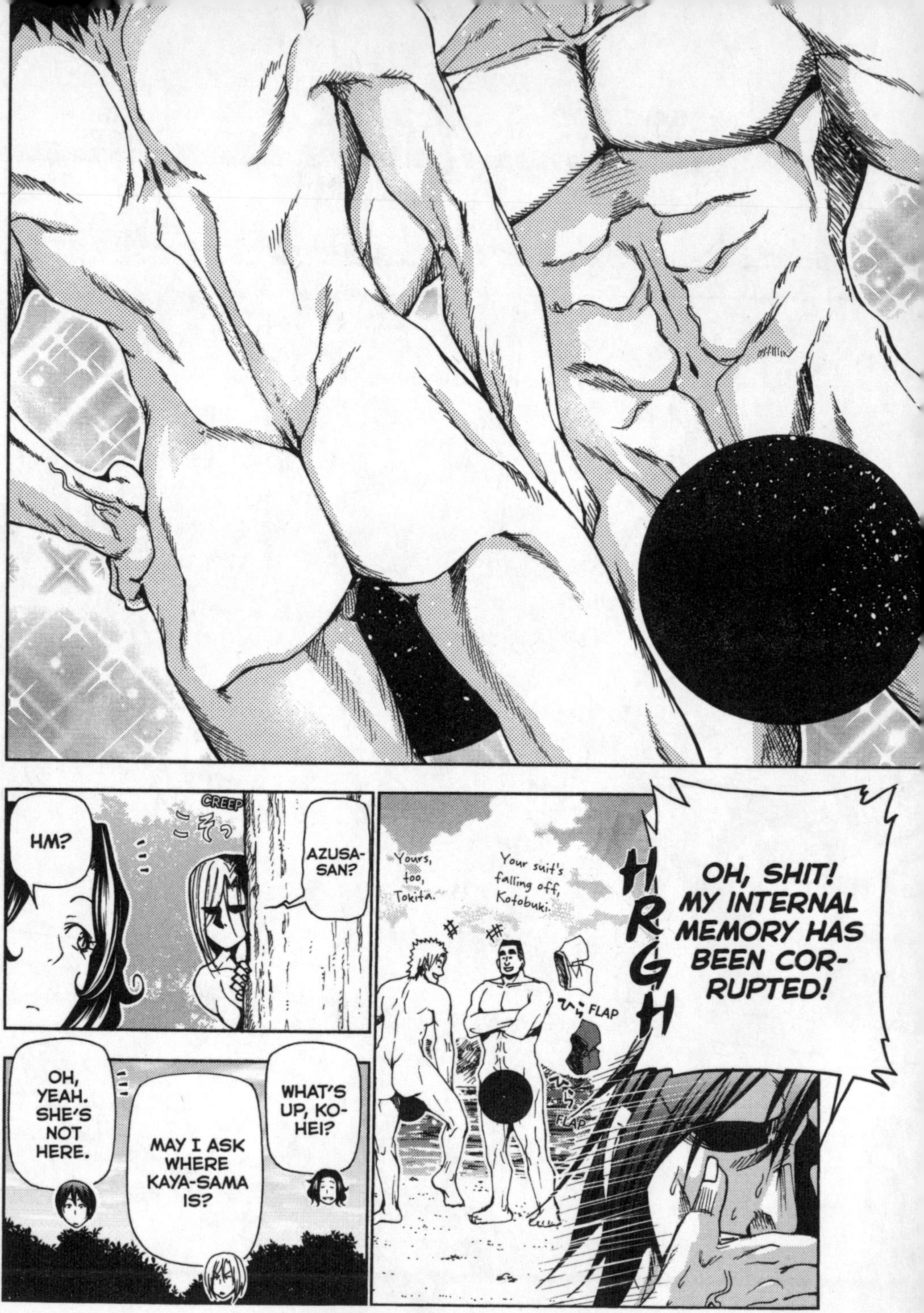
HRGH
OH, SHIT! MY INTERNAL MEMORY HAS BEEN COR-RUPTED!
Your suit's falling off, Kotobuki.
Yours, too, Tokita.
FLAP
FLAP
AZUSA-SAN?
CREEP
HM?
WHAT'S UP, KO-HEI?
MAY I ASK WHERE KAYA-SAMA IS?
OH, YEAH. SHE'S NOT HERE.

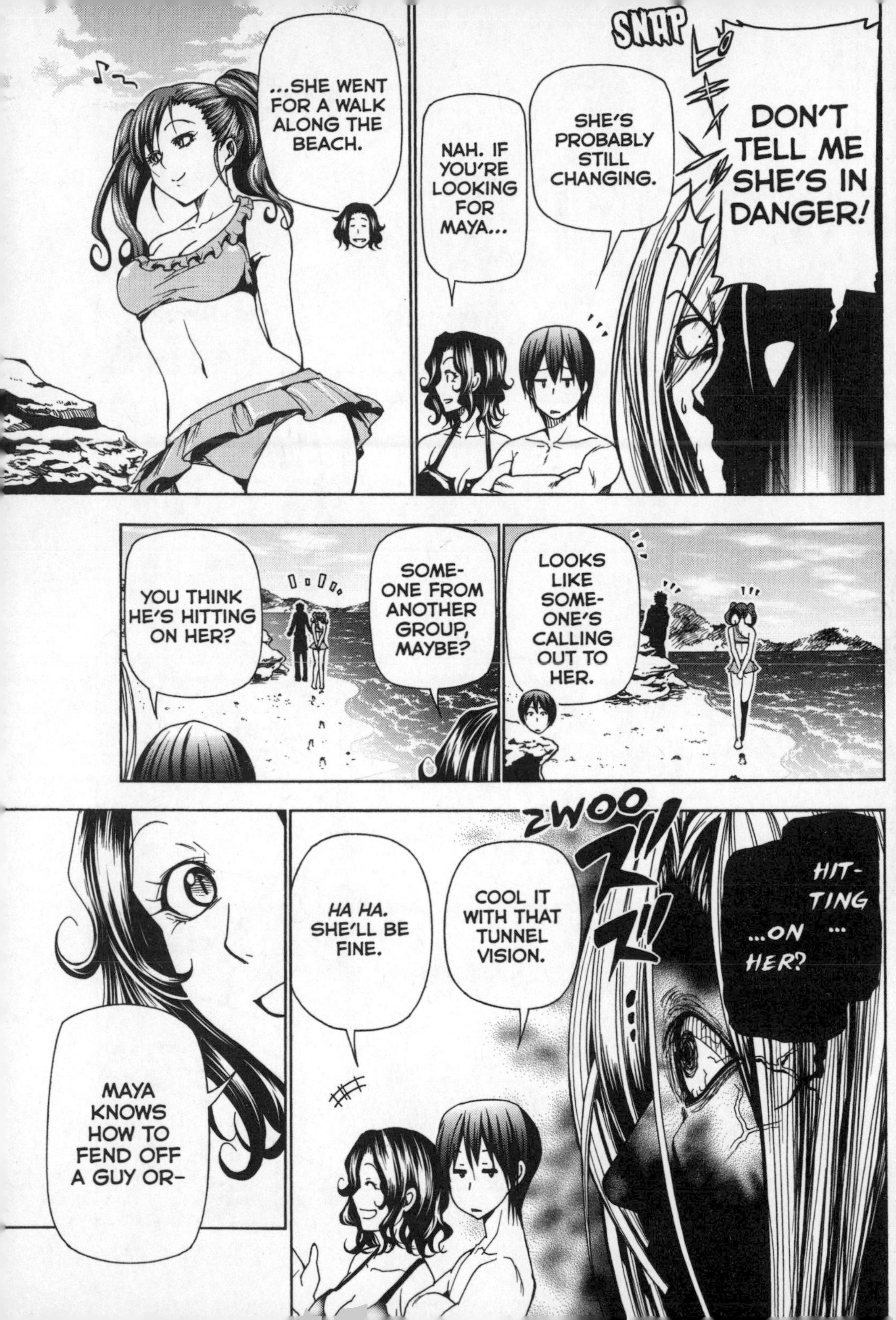
SNAP
DON'T TELL ME SHE'S IN DANGER!
SHE'S PROBABLY STILL CHANGING.
NAH. IF YOU'RE LOOKING FOR MAYA...
...SHE WENT FOR A WALK ALONG THE BEACH.
LOOKS LIKE SOME-ONE'S CALLING OUT TO HER.
SOME-ONE FROM ANOTHER GROUP, MAYBE?
YOU THINK HE'S HITTING ON HER?
ZWOO
HIT-TING ... ...ON HER?
COOL IT WITH THAT TUNNEL VISION.
HA HA. SHE'LL BE FINE.
MAYA KNOWS HOW TO FEND OFF A GUY OR-

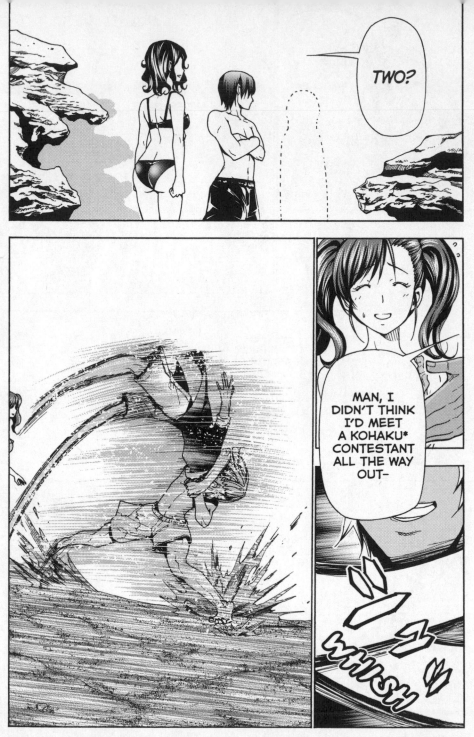

TWO?

MAN, I DIDN'T THINK I'D MEET A KOHAKU* CONTESTANT ALL THE WAY OUT—

WHISH

*Kohaku Uta Gassen, officially translated as "Year-end Song Festival", is an annual Japanese music show produced and broadcast on New Year's Eve by NHK. The show features popular musical artists competing in all-male and all-female teams.

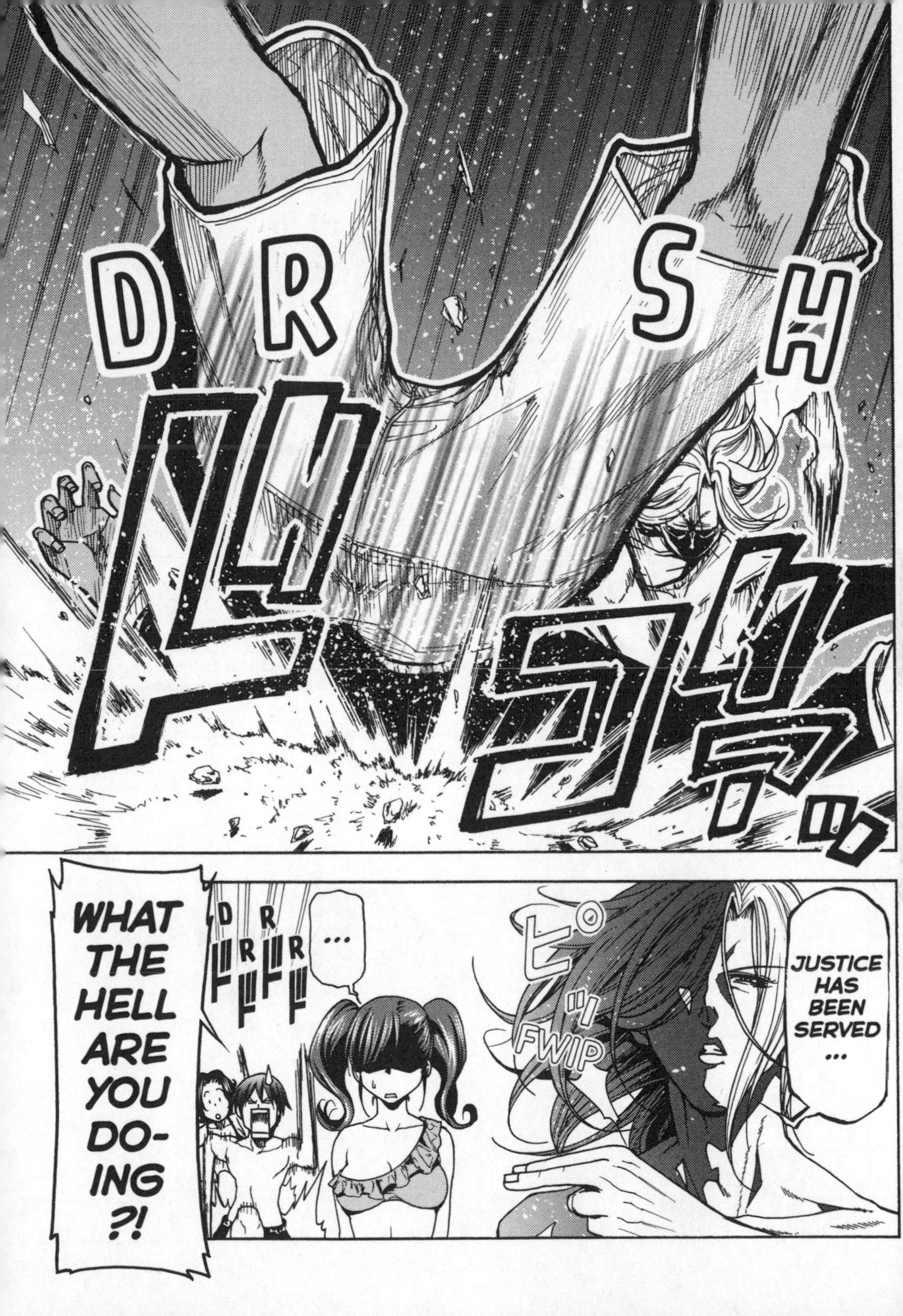
DRSH
JUSTICE HAS BEEN SERVED...
FWIP
...
DRRR
WHAT THE HELL ARE YOU DOING?!

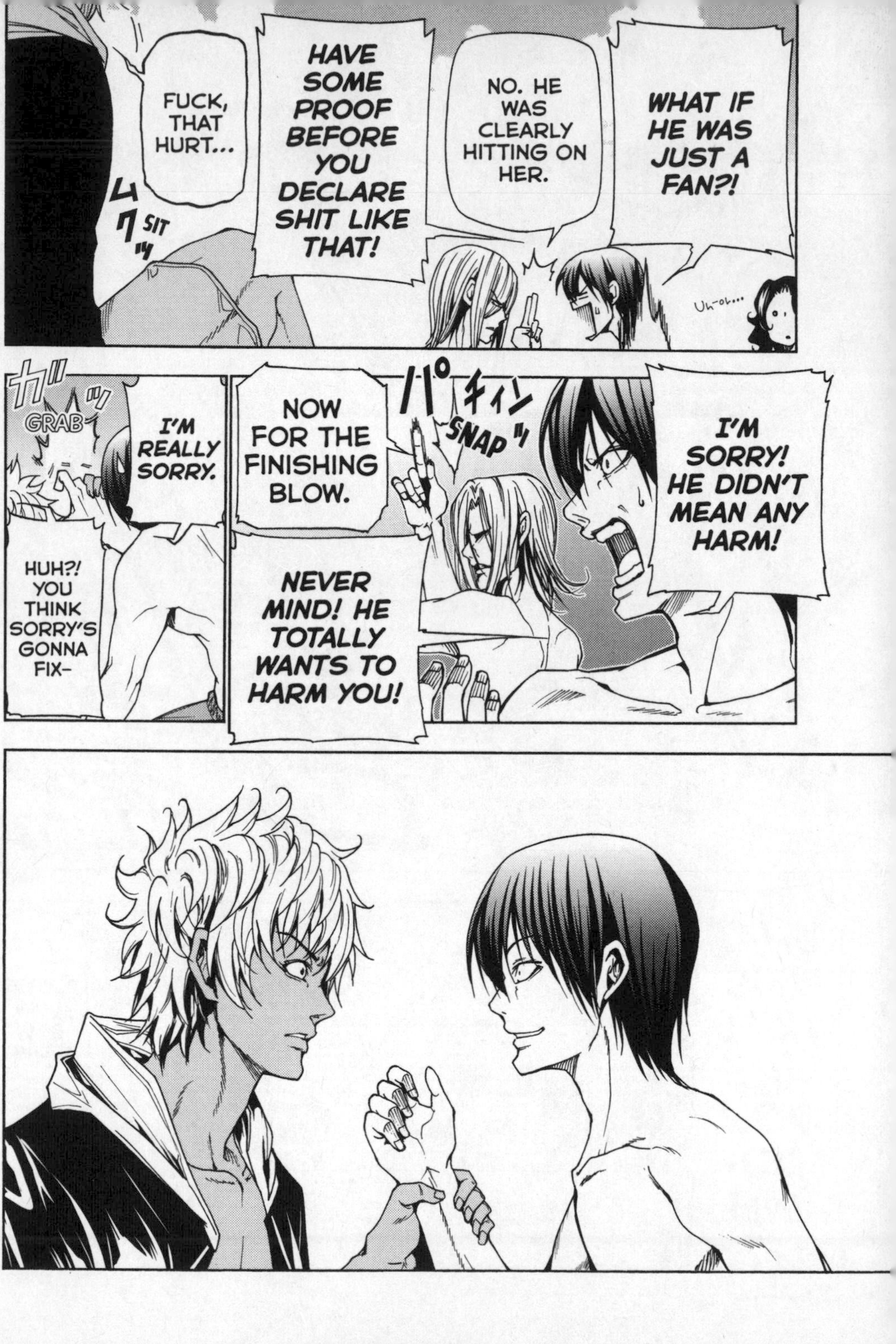
WHAT IF HE WAS JUST A FAN?!
NO. HE WAS CLEARLY HITTING ON HER.
HAVE SOME PROOF BEFORE YOU DECLARE SHIT LIKE THAT!
SIT
FUCK, THAT HURT...
Uh-oh...
I'M SORRY! HE DIDN'T MEAN ANY HARM!
SNAP
NOW FOR THE FINISHING BLOW.
NEVER MIND! HE TOTALLY WANTS TO HARM YOU!
GRAB
I'M REALLY SORRY.
HUH?! YOU THINK SORRY'S GONNA FIX-

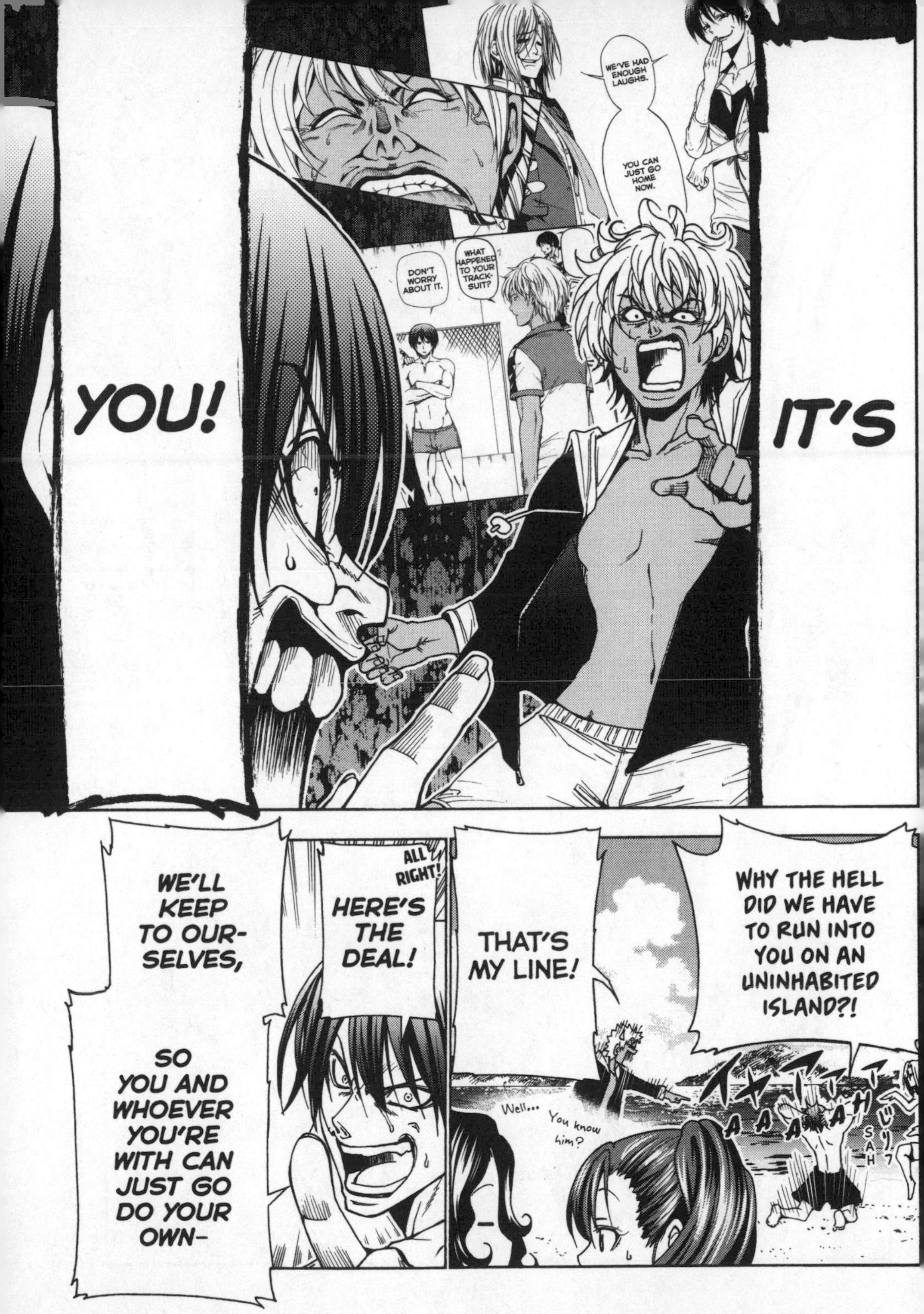
WE'VE HAD ENOUGH LAUGHS.
YOU CAN JUST GO HOME NOW.
WHAT HAPPENED TO YOUR TRACK-SUIT?
DON'T WORRY ABOUT IT.
IT'S
YOU!
WHY THE HELL DID WE HAVE TO RUN INTO YOU ON AN UNINHABITED ISLAND?!
AAAAAH
SAH
You know him?
Well...
THAT'S MY LINE!
ALL RIGHT!
HERE'S THE DEAL!
WE'LL KEEP TO OUR-SELVES,
SO YOU AND WHOEVER YOU'RE WITH CAN JUST GO DO YOUR OWN–

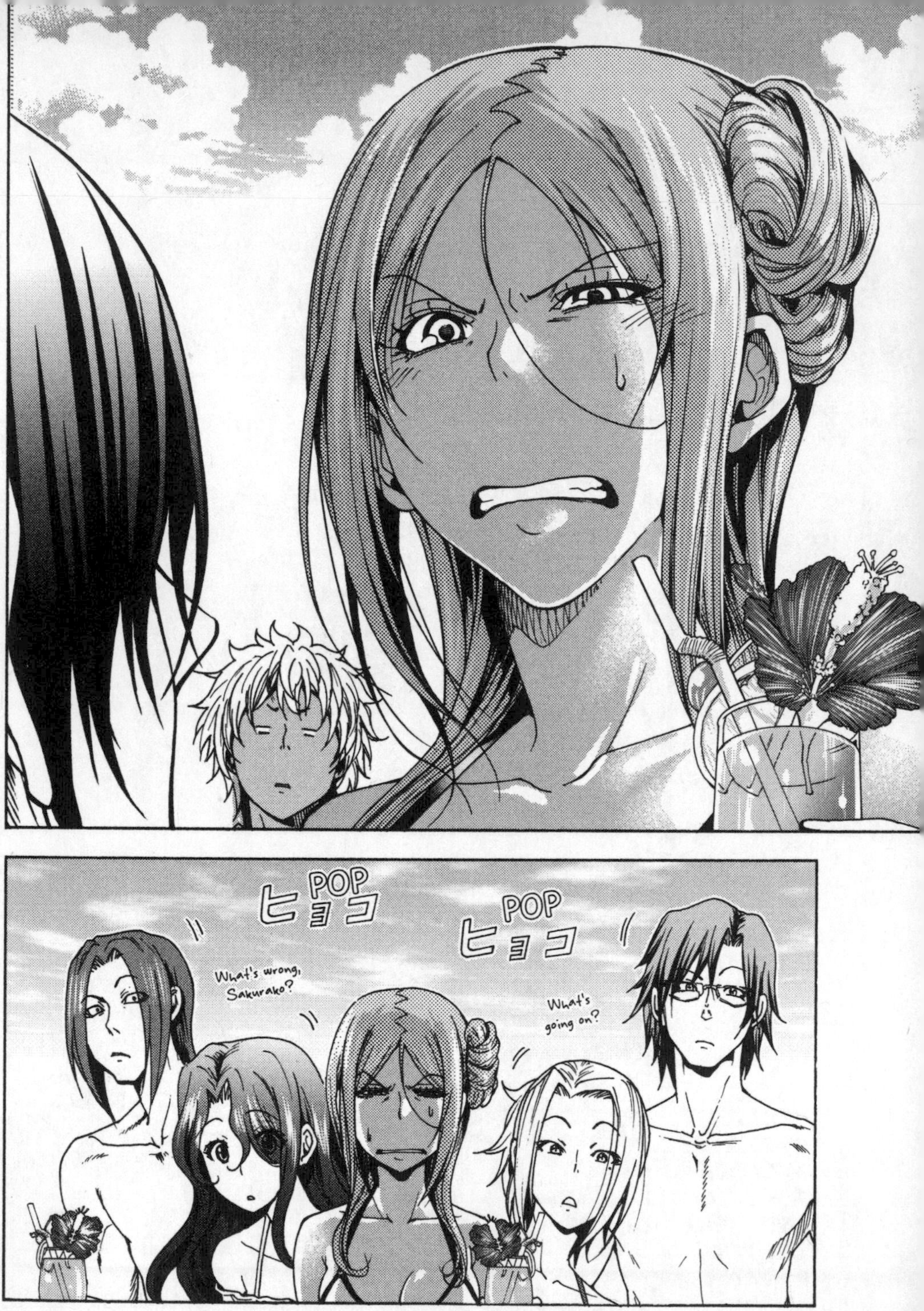
POP ヒョコ
POP ヒョコ
What's going on?
What's wrong, Sakurako?

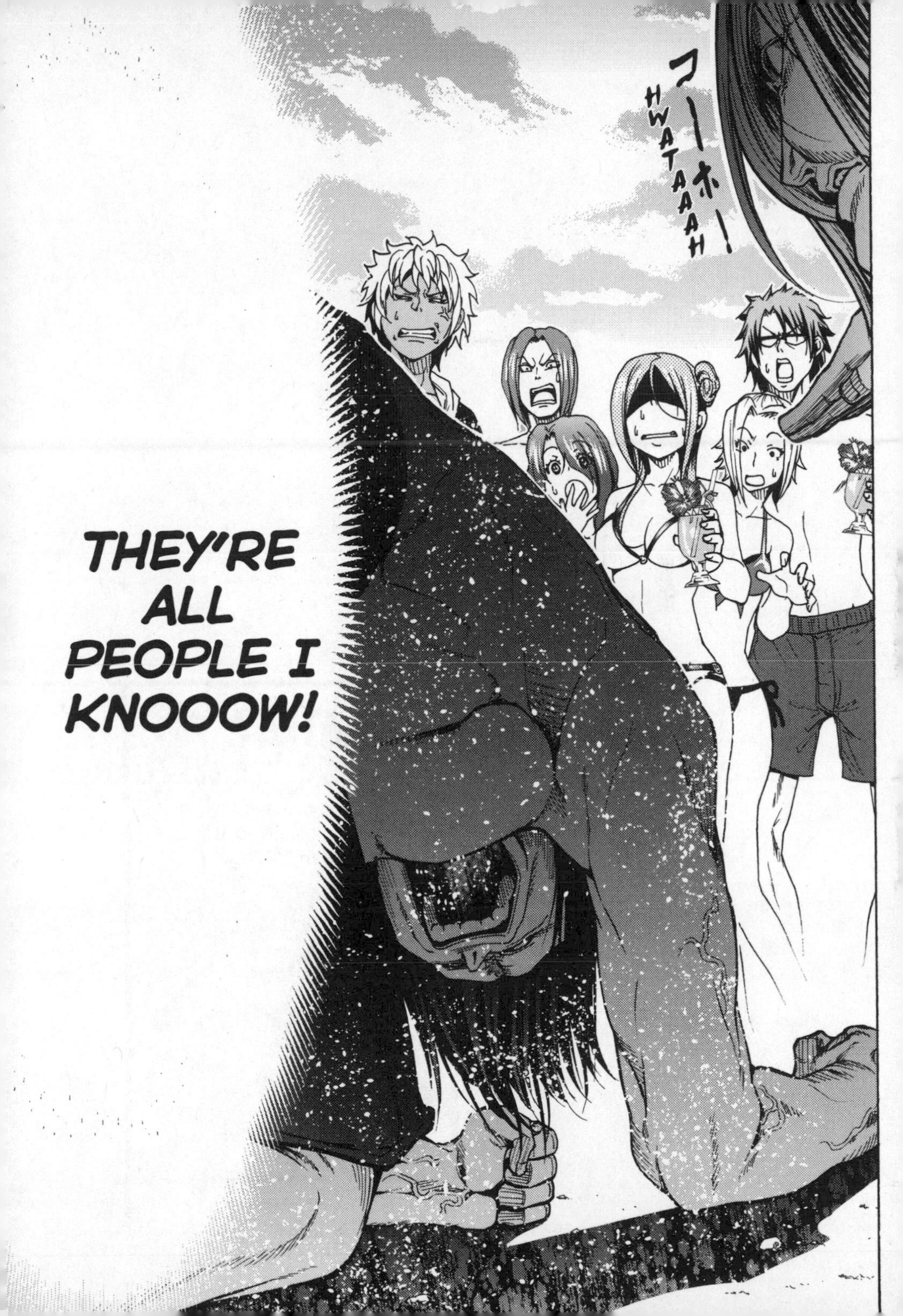
コーホー!!
HWATAAAH
THEY'RE ALL PEOPLE I KNOOOW!

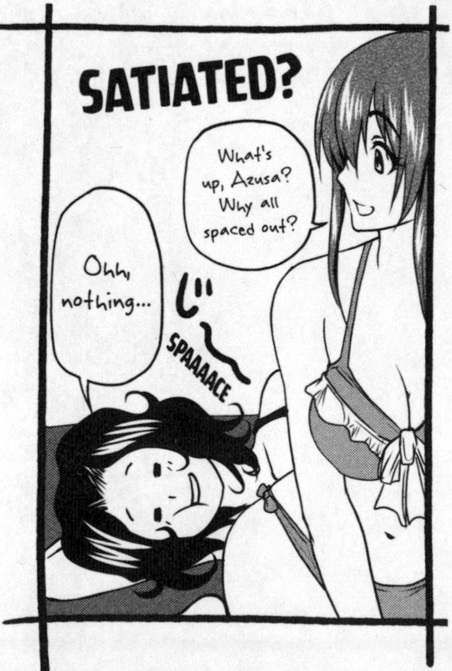
SATIATED?
What's up, Azusa? Why all spaced out?
じ~
SPAAAACE
Ohh, nothing...

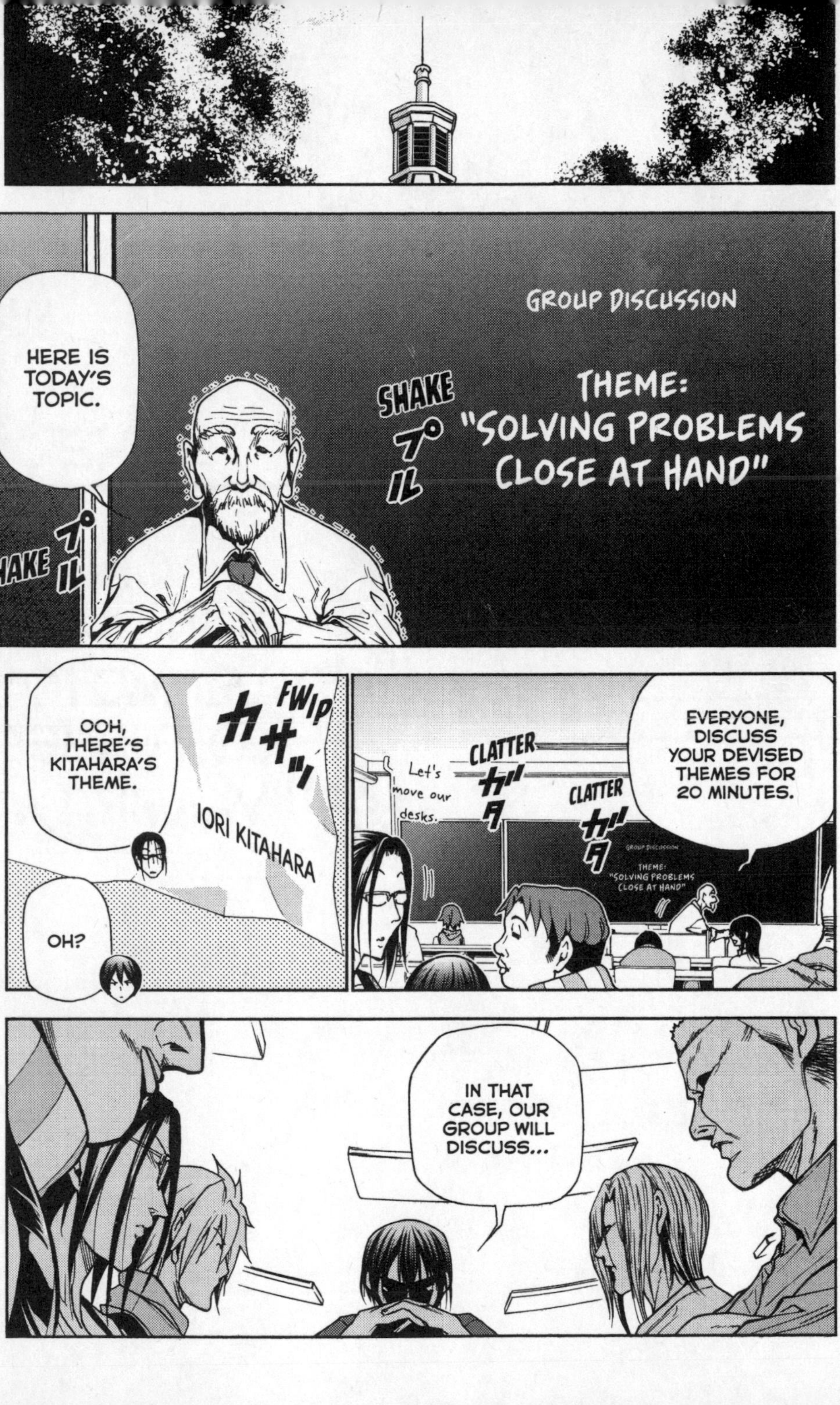
GROUP DISCUSSION
THEME: "SOLVING PROBLEMS CLOSE AT HAND"
SHAKE
プル
HERE IS TODAY'S TOPIC.
SHAKE
プル
EVERYONE, DISCUSS YOUR DEVISED THEMES FOR 20 MINUTES.
CLATTER
ガタ
CLATTER
ガタ
Let's move our desks.
GROUP DISCUSSION
THEME: "SOLVING PROBLEMS CLOSE AT HAND"
FWIP
カサッ
OOH, THERE'S KITAHARA'S THEME.
IORI KITAHARA
OH?
IN THAT CASE, OUR GROUP WILL DISCUSS...

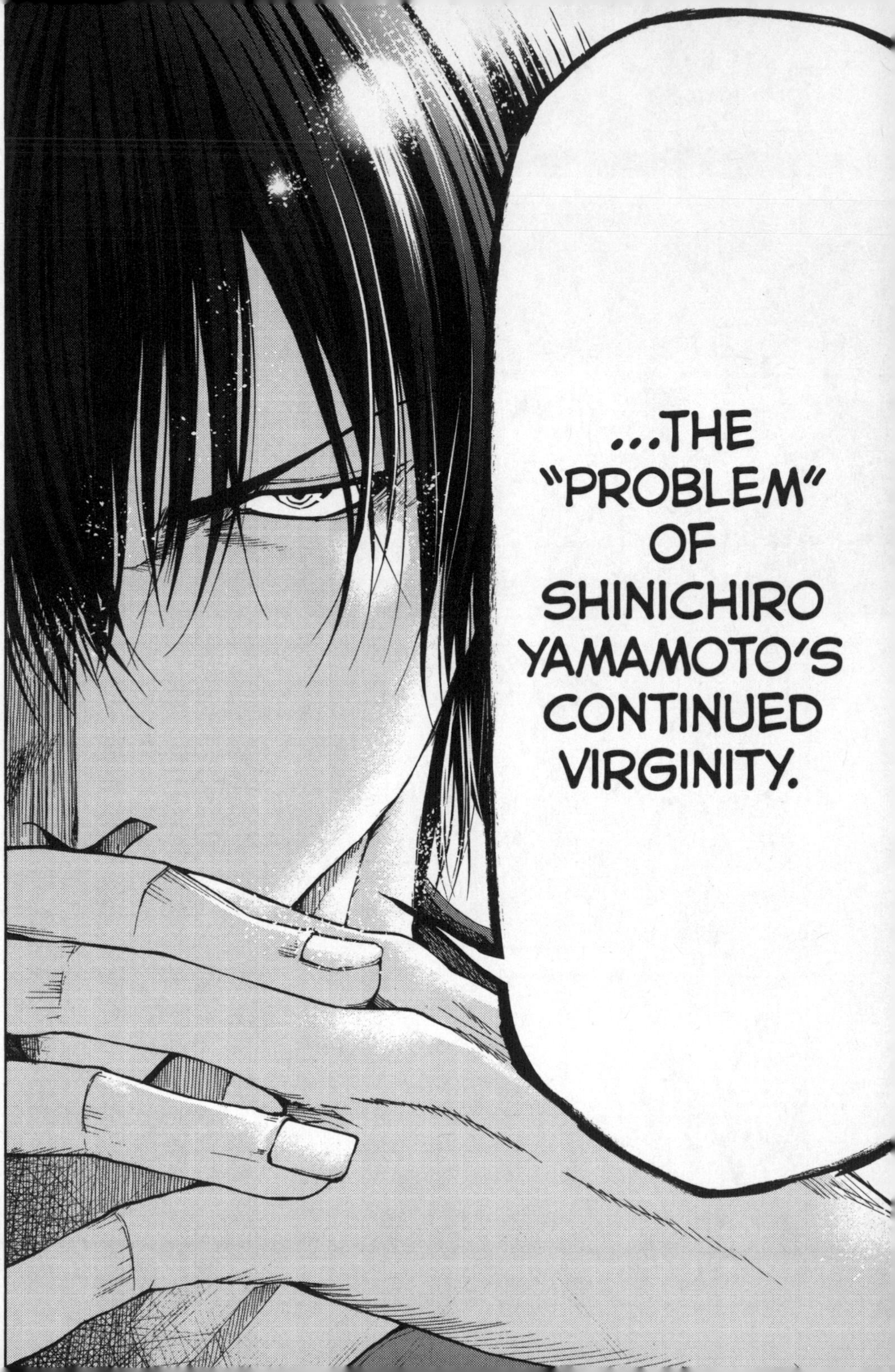
...THE "PROBLEM" OF SHINICHIRO YAMAMOTO'S CONTINUED VIRGINITY.

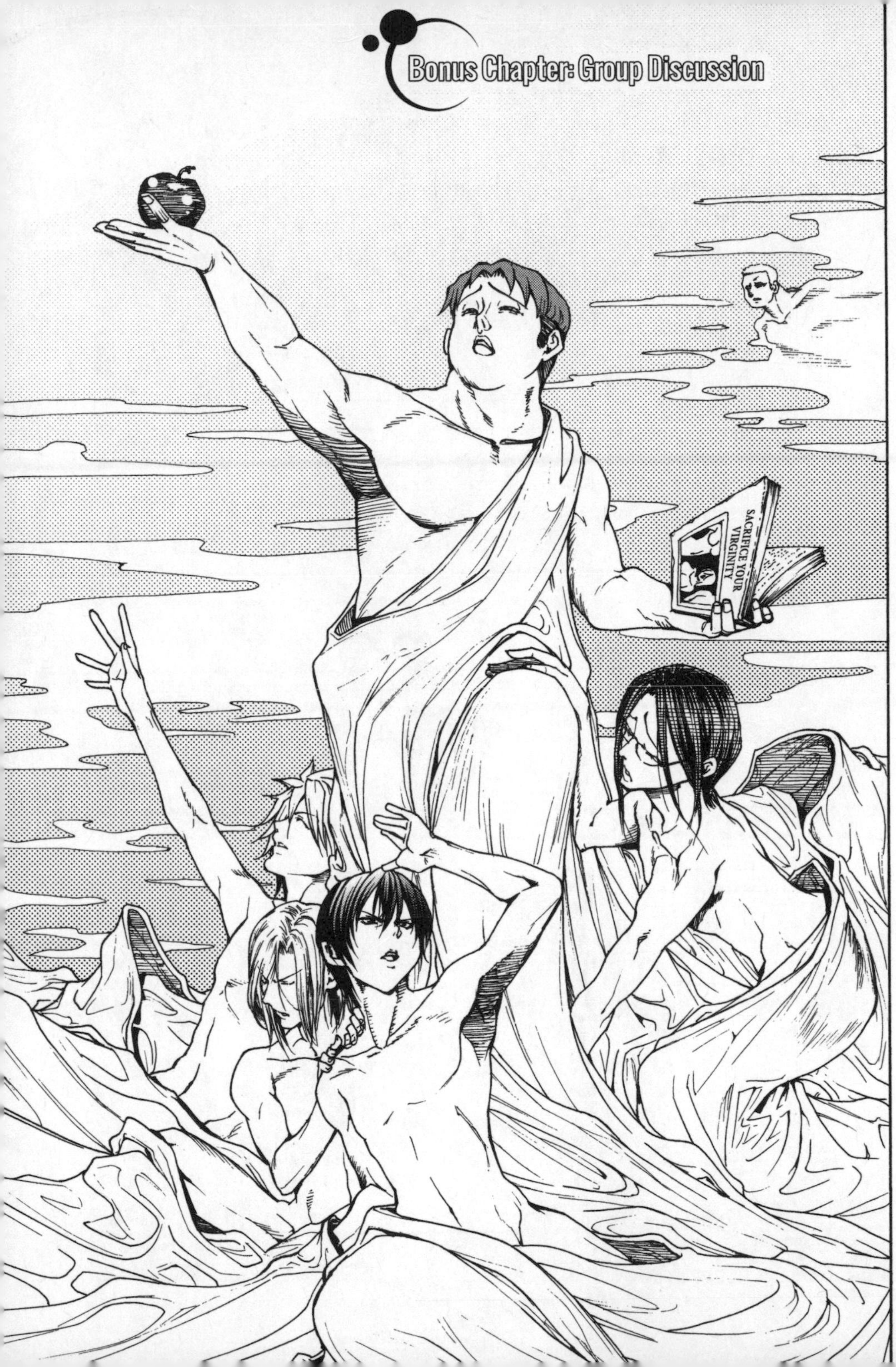
Bonus Chapter: Group Discussion
SACRIFICE YOUR VIRGINITY

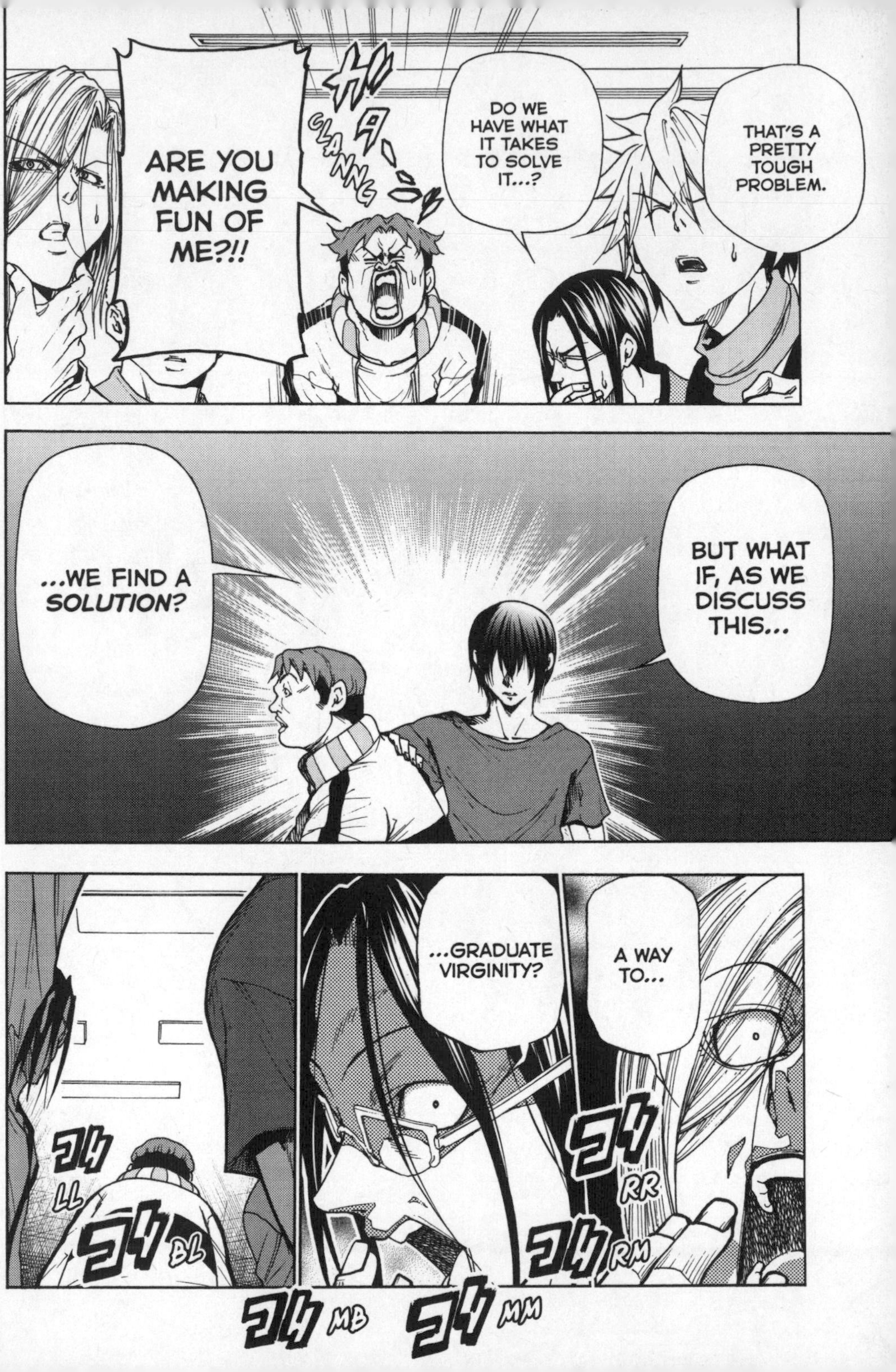
THAT'S A PRETTY TOUGH PROBLEM.
DO WE HAVE WHAT IT TAKES TO SOLVE IT...?
CLANNG
ARE YOU MAKING FUN OF ME?!!
BUT WHAT IF, AS WE DISCUSS THIS...
...WE FIND A *SOLUTION*?
A WAY TO...
...GRADUATE VIRGINITY?
RR
RM
LL
BL
MM
MB

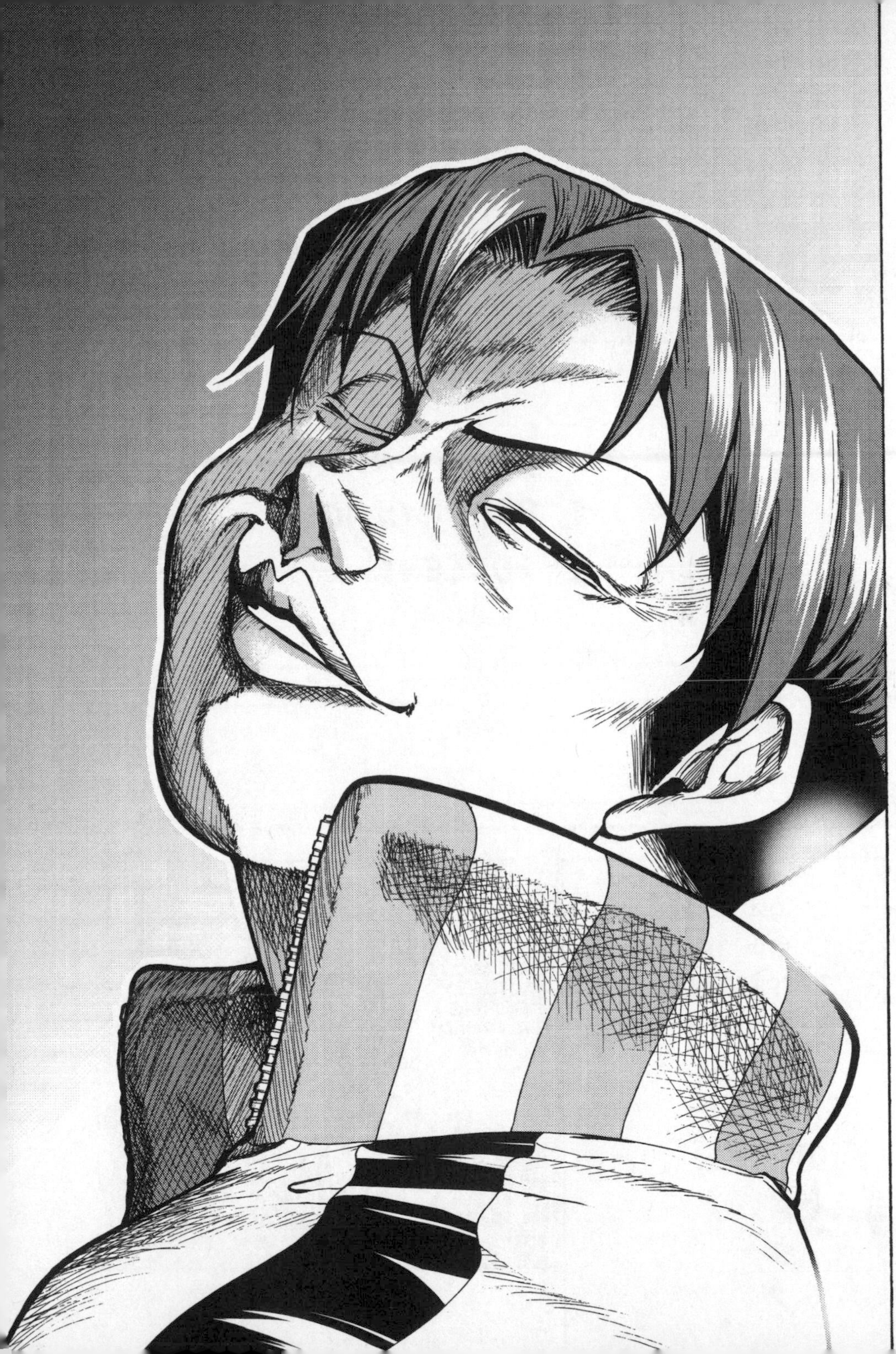

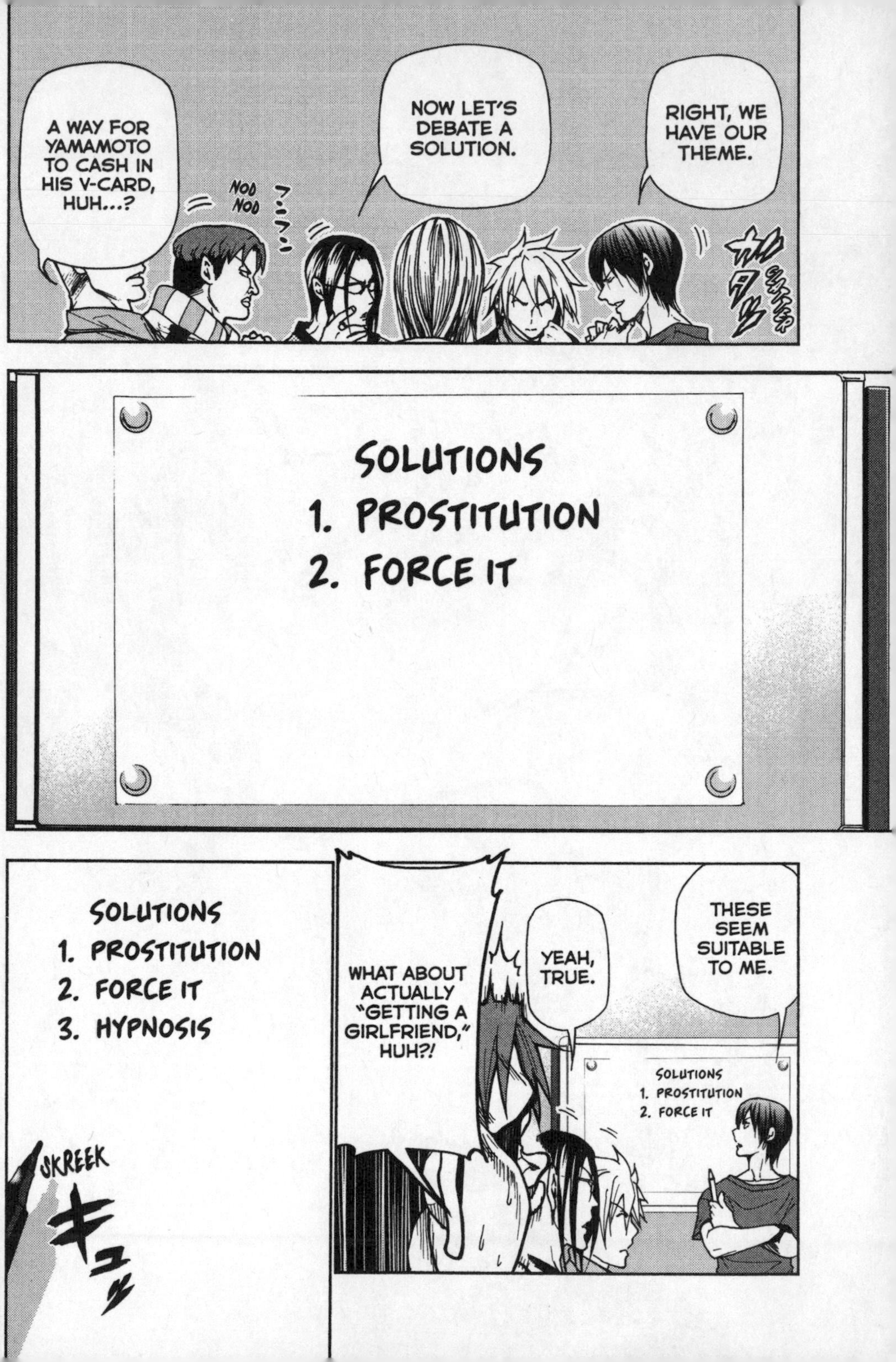
RIGHT, WE HAVE OUR THEME.
GLITTER
NOW LET'S DEBATE A SOLUTION.
NOD NOD
A WAY FOR YAMAMOTO TO CASH IN HIS V-CARD, HUH...?
SOLUTIONS
1. PROSTITUTION
2. FORCE IT
THESE SEEM SUITABLE TO ME.
YEAH, TRUE.
WHAT ABOUT ACTUALLY "GETTING A GIRLFRIEND," HUH?!
SOLUTIONS
1. PROSTITUTION
2. FORCE IT
SOLUTIONS
1. PROSTITUTION
2. FORCE IT
3. HYPNOSIS
SKREEK

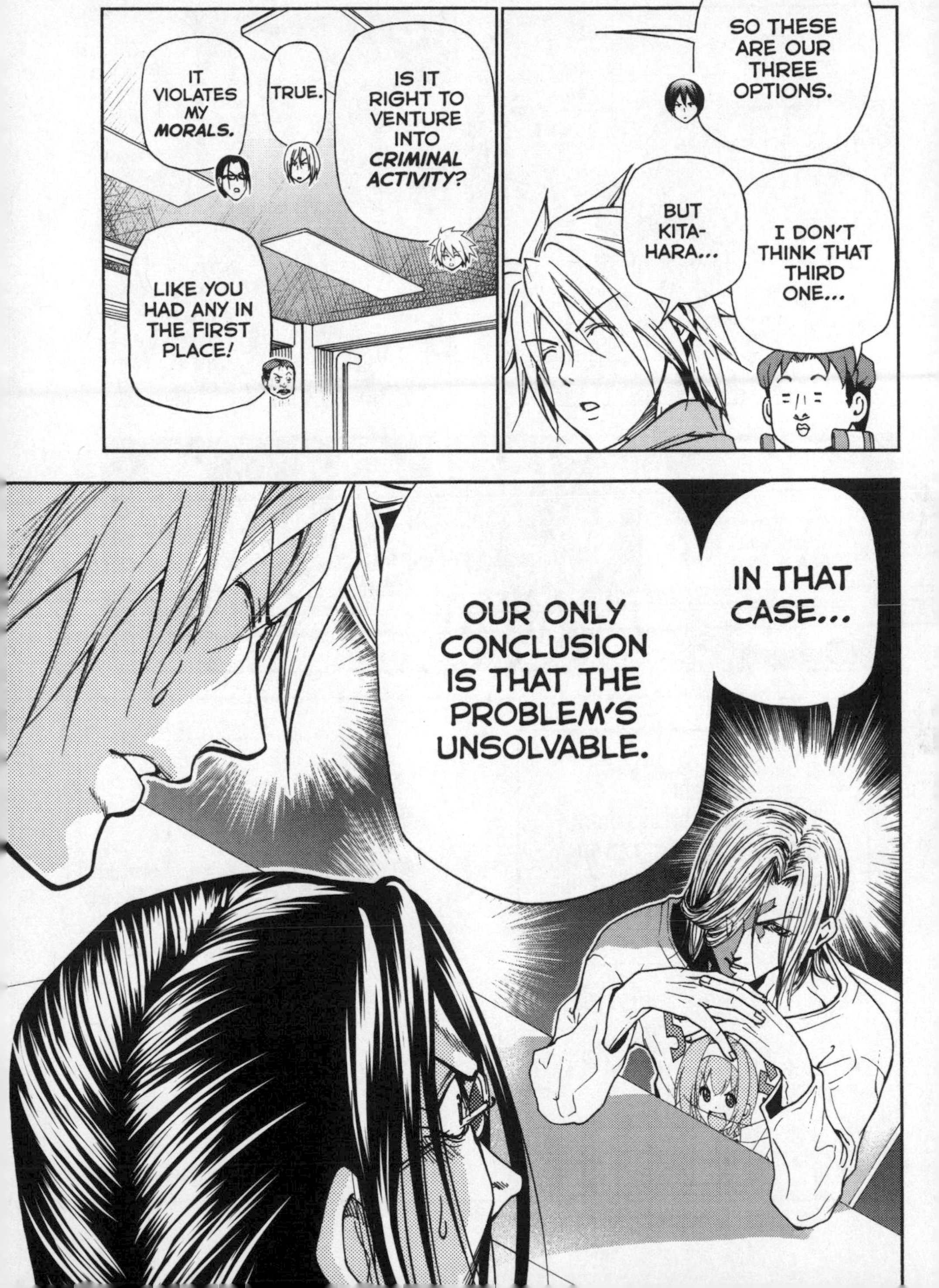
SO THESE ARE OUR THREE OPTIONS.
I DON'T THINK THAT THIRD ONE...
BUT KITA-HARA...
IS IT RIGHT TO VENTURE INTO *CRIMINAL ACTIVITY*?
TRUE.
IT VIOLATES MY *MORALS*.
LIKE YOU HAD ANY IN THE FIRST PLACE!
IN THAT CASE...
OUR ONLY CONCLUSION IS THAT THE PROBLEM'S UNSOLVABLE.

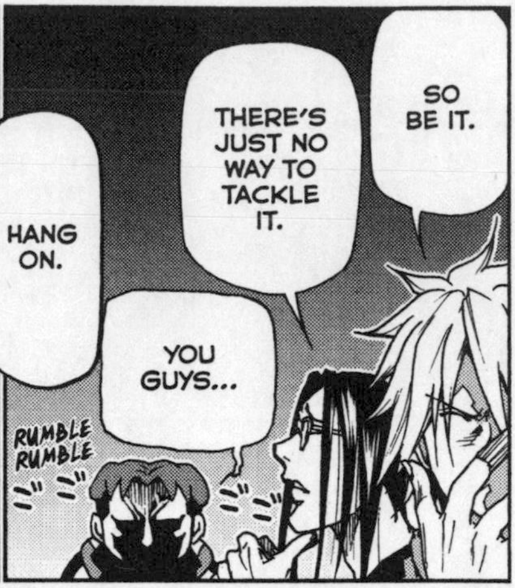
SO BE IT.
THERE'S JUST NO WAY TO TACKLE IT.
HANG ON.
YOU GUYS...
RUMBLE RUMBLE
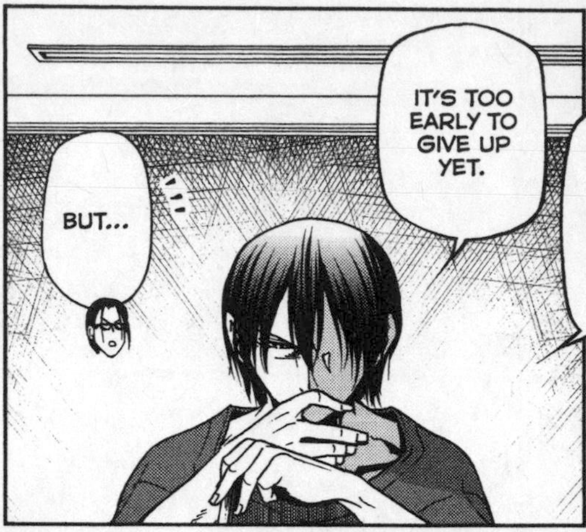
IT'S TOO EARLY TO GIVE UP YET.
BUT...
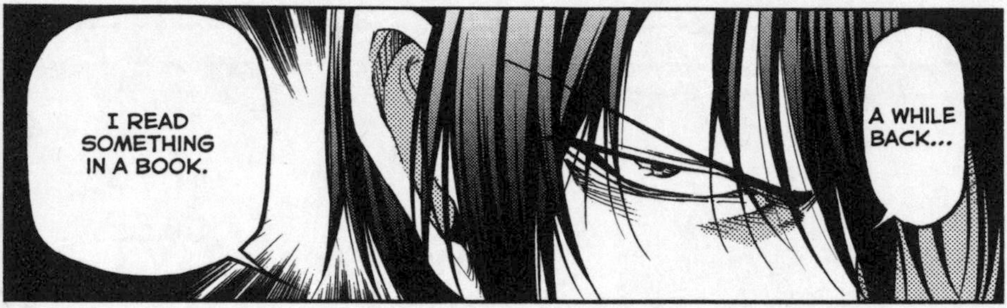
A WHILE BACK...
I READ SOMETHING IN A BOOK.

Methods to Solving Problems

IF YOU CANNOT DIRECTLY ADDRESS A PROBLEM THAT OCCURS, TRY TO CHANGE YOUR APPROACH TO REACHING YOUR GOALS.

Example:
If your bicycle breaks down and repairing it isn't an option, reconsider whether you need to use the bike at all.

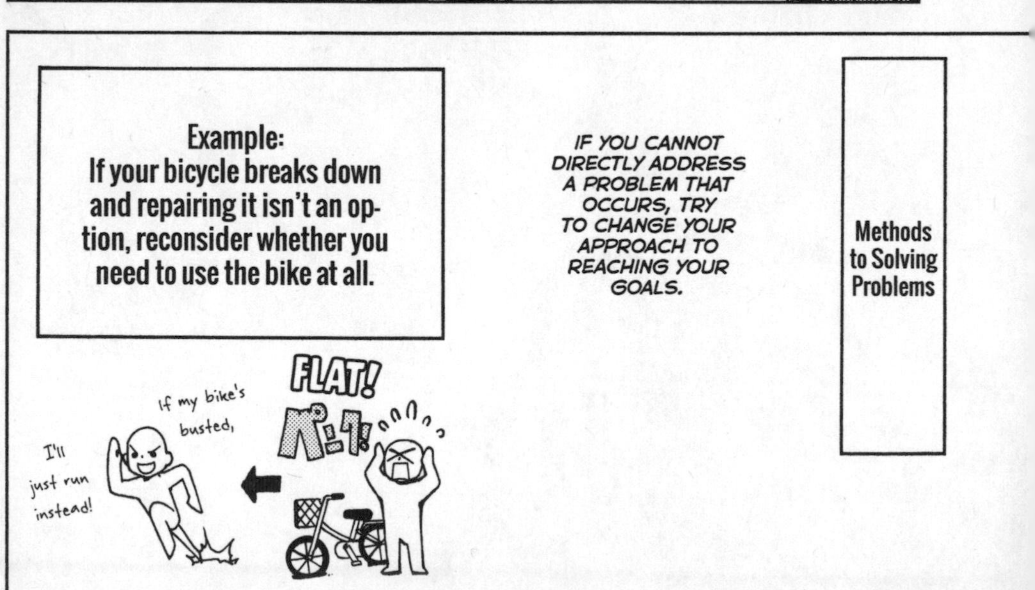
FLAT!
If my bike's busted,
I'll just run instead!

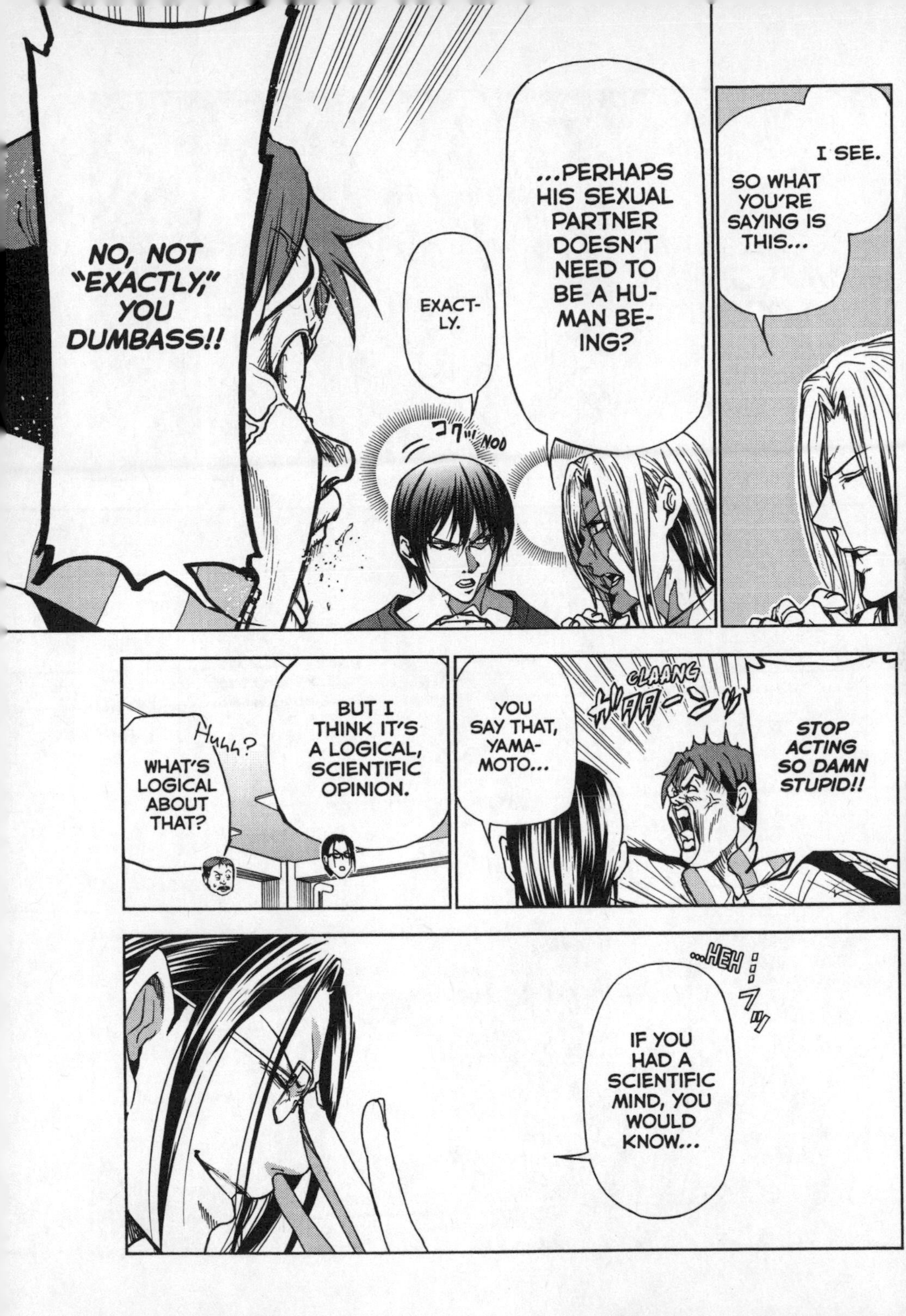
I SEE.
SO WHAT YOU'RE SAYING IS THIS...
...PERHAPS HIS SEXUAL PARTNER DOESN'T NEED TO BE A HUMAN BEING?
EXACTLY.
NOD
NO, NOT "EXACTLY," YOU DUMBASS!!
CLAANG
STOP ACTING SO DAMN STUPID!!
YOU SAY THAT, YAMAMOTO...
BUT I THINK IT'S A LOGICAL, SCIENTIFIC OPINION.
Huhh?
WHAT'S LOGICAL ABOUT THAT?
...HEH
IF YOU HAD A SCIENTIFIC MIND, YOU WOULD KNOW...

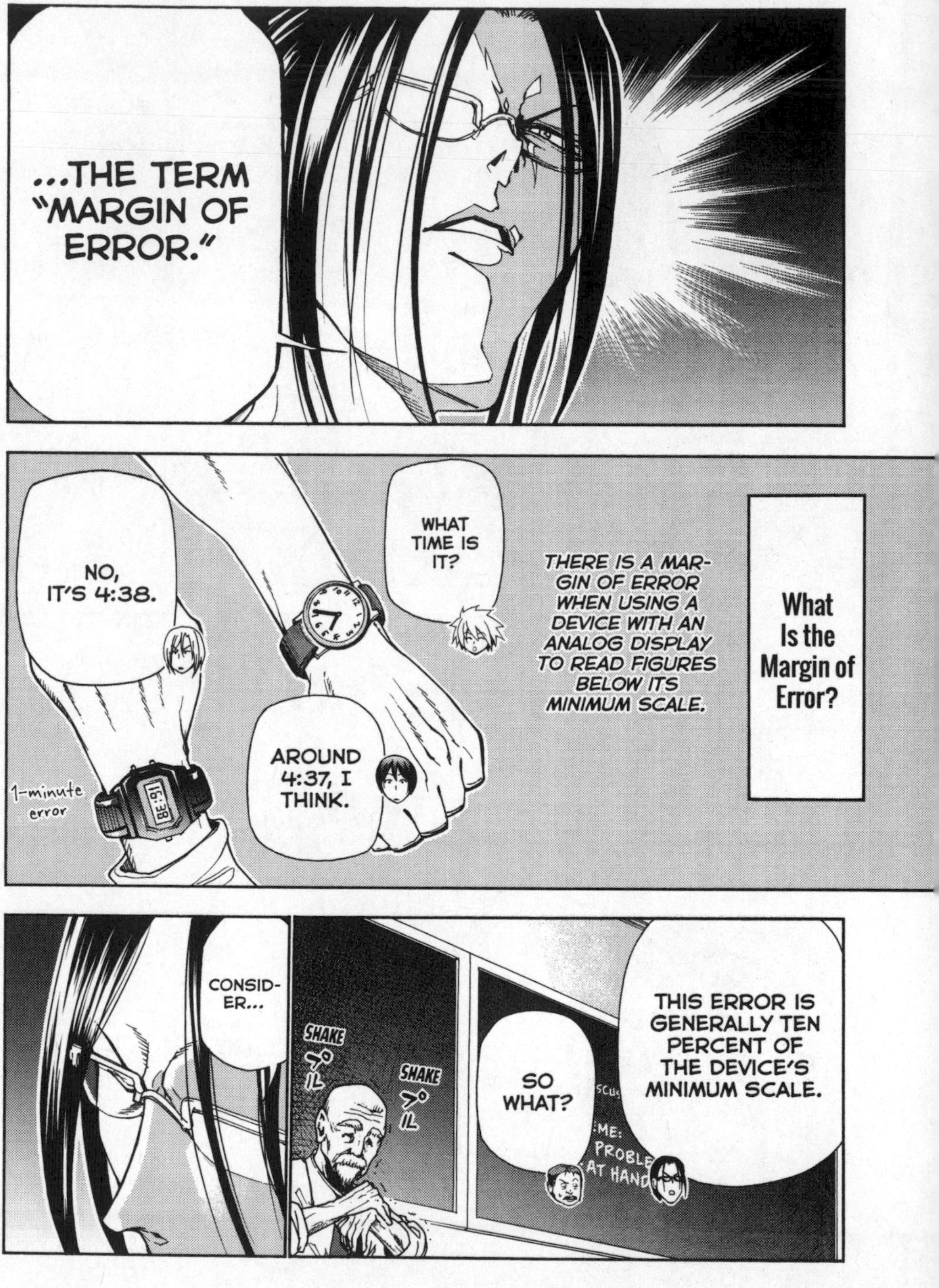
...THE TERM "MARGIN OF ERROR."
What Is the Margin of Error?
THERE IS A MARGIN OF ERROR WHEN USING A DEVICE WITH AN ANALOG DISPLAY TO READ FIGURES BELOW ITS MINIMUM SCALE.
WHAT TIME IS IT?
AROUND 4:37, I THINK.
NO, IT'S 4:38.
1-minute error
THIS ERROR IS GENERALLY TEN PERCENT OF THE DEVICE'S MINIMUM SCALE.
SO WHAT?
SHAKE
プル
SHAKE
プル
CONSIDER...

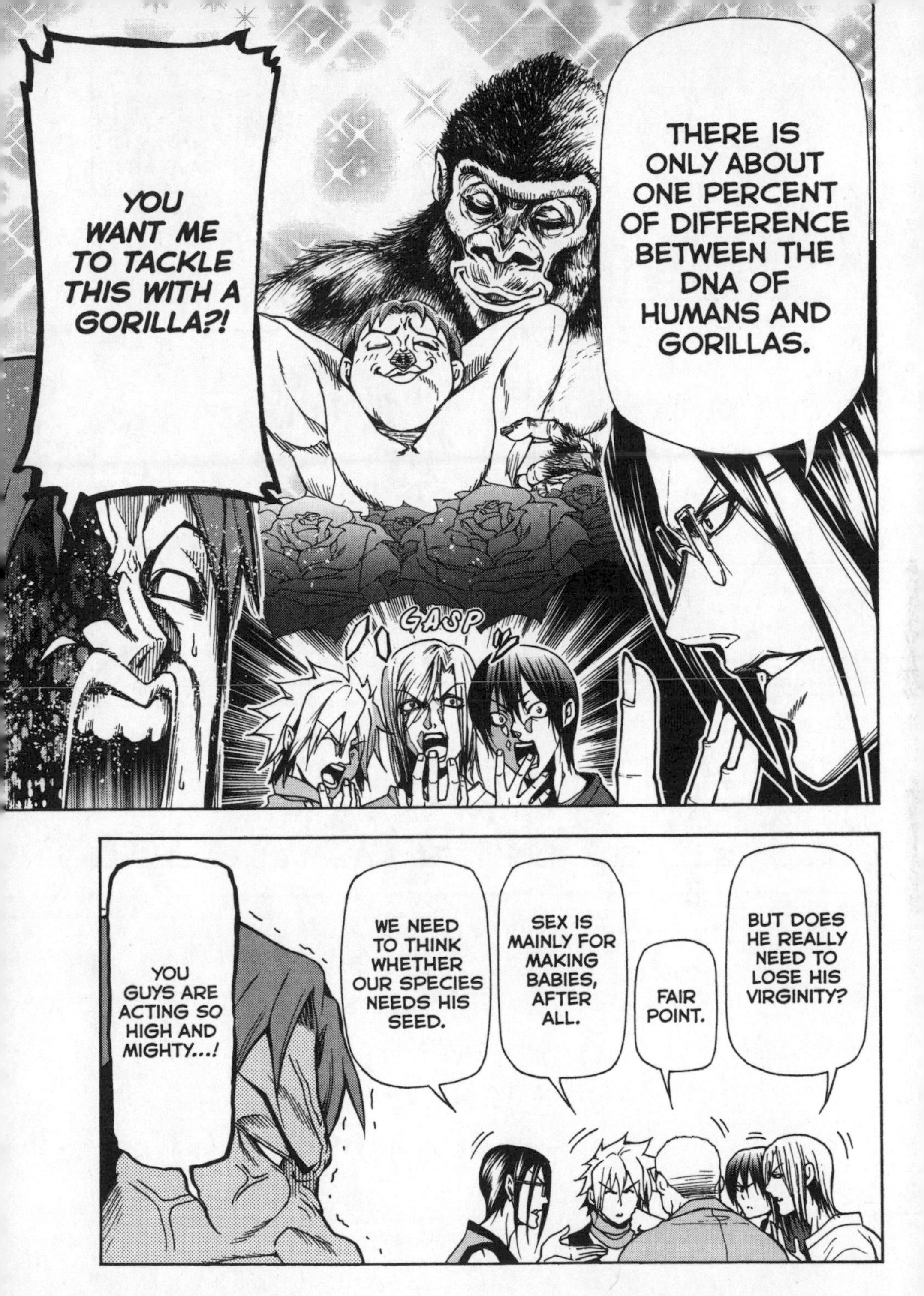
THERE IS ONLY ABOUT ONE PERCENT OF DIFFERENCE BETWEEN THE DNA OF HUMANS AND GORILLAS.
YOU WANT ME TO TACKLE THIS WITH A GORILLA?!
GASP
BUT DOES HE REALLY NEED TO LOSE HIS VIRGINITY?
FAIR POINT.
SEX IS MAINLY FOR MAKING BABIES, AFTER ALL.
WE NEED TO THINK WHETHER OUR SPECIES NEEDS HIS SEED.
YOU GUYS ARE ACTING SO HIGH AND MIGHTY...!

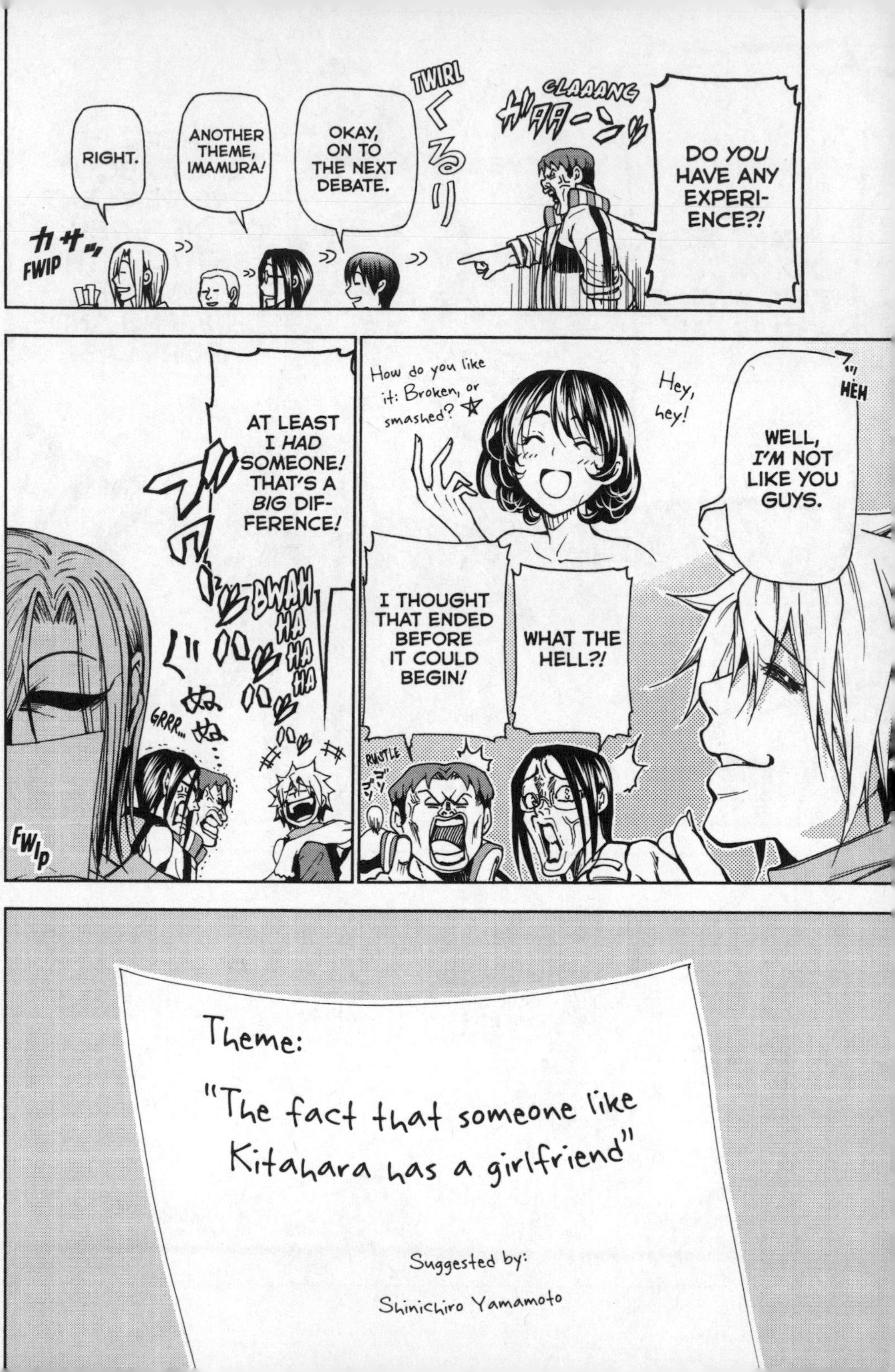
DO *YOU* HAVE ANY EXPERI-ENCE?!
CLAAANG
TWIRL
OKAY, ON TO THE NEXT DEBATE.
ANOTHER THEME, IMAMURA!
RIGHT.
FWIP
HEH
WELL, *I'M* NOT LIKE YOU GUYS.
Hey, hey!
How do you like it: Broken, or smashed? ☆
WHAT THE HELL?!
I THOUGHT THAT ENDED BEFORE IT COULD BEGIN!
RUSTLE
AT LEAST I *HAD* SOMEONE! THAT'S A *BIG* DIF-FERENCE!
BWAH HA HA HA
GRRR...
FWIP
Theme:
"The fact that someone like Kitahara has a girlfriend"
Suggested by:
Shinichiro Yamamoto

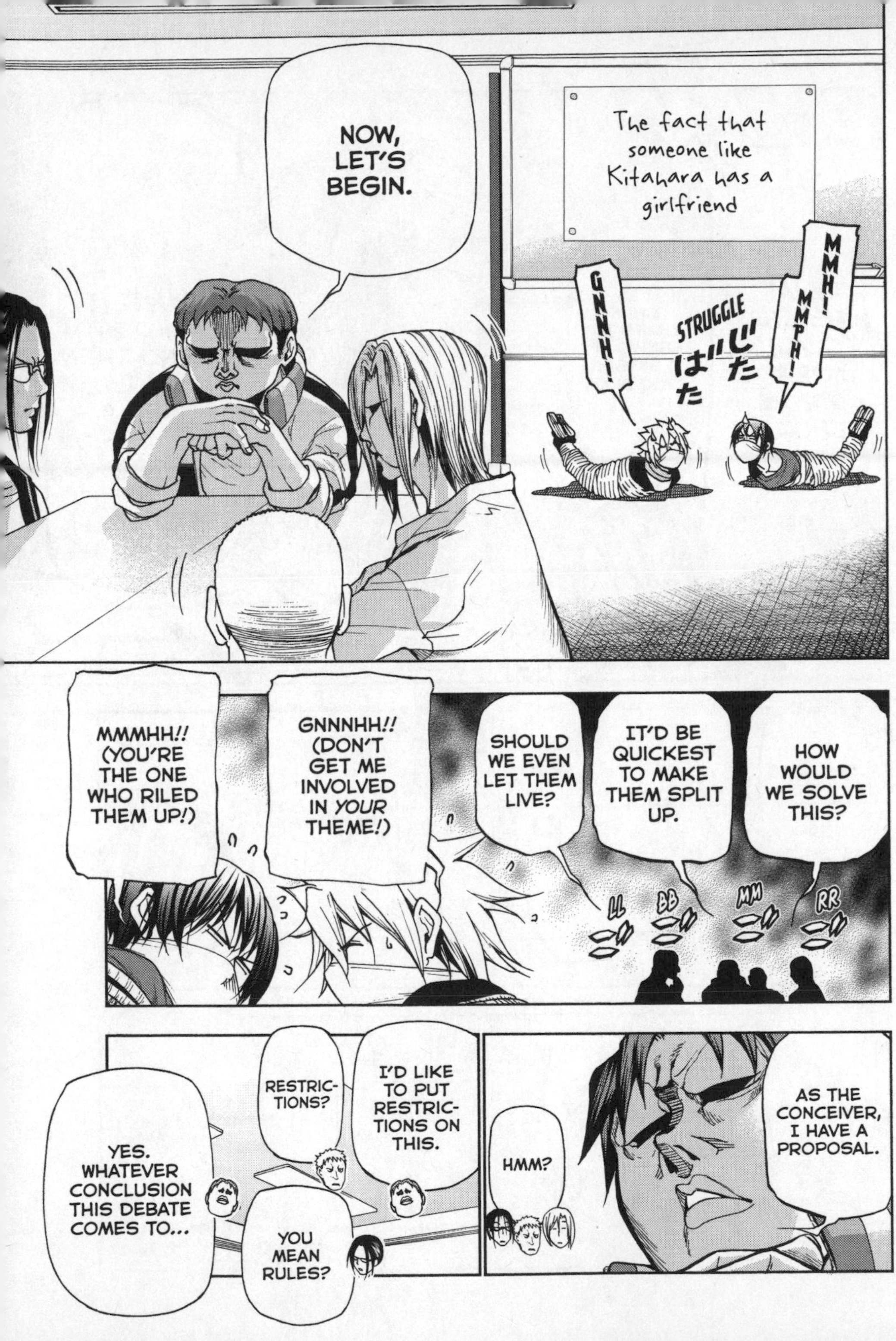
The fact that someone like Kitahara has a girlfriend
MMH! MMPH!
STRUGGLE
ばた
じた
GNNH!
NOW, LET'S BEGIN.
HOW WOULD WE SOLVE THIS?
RR
IT'D BE QUICKEST TO MAKE THEM SPLIT UP.
MM
BB
SHOULD WE EVEN LET THEM LIVE?
LL
GNNNHH!! (DON'T GET ME INVOLVED IN YOUR THEME!)
MMMHH!! (YOU'RE THE ONE WHO RILED THEM UP!)
AS THE CONCEIVER, I HAVE A PROPOSAL.
HMM?
I'D LIKE TO PUT RESTRICTIONS ON THIS.
RESTRICTIONS?
YES. WHATEVER CONCLUSION THIS DEBATE COMES TO...
YOU MEAN RULES?

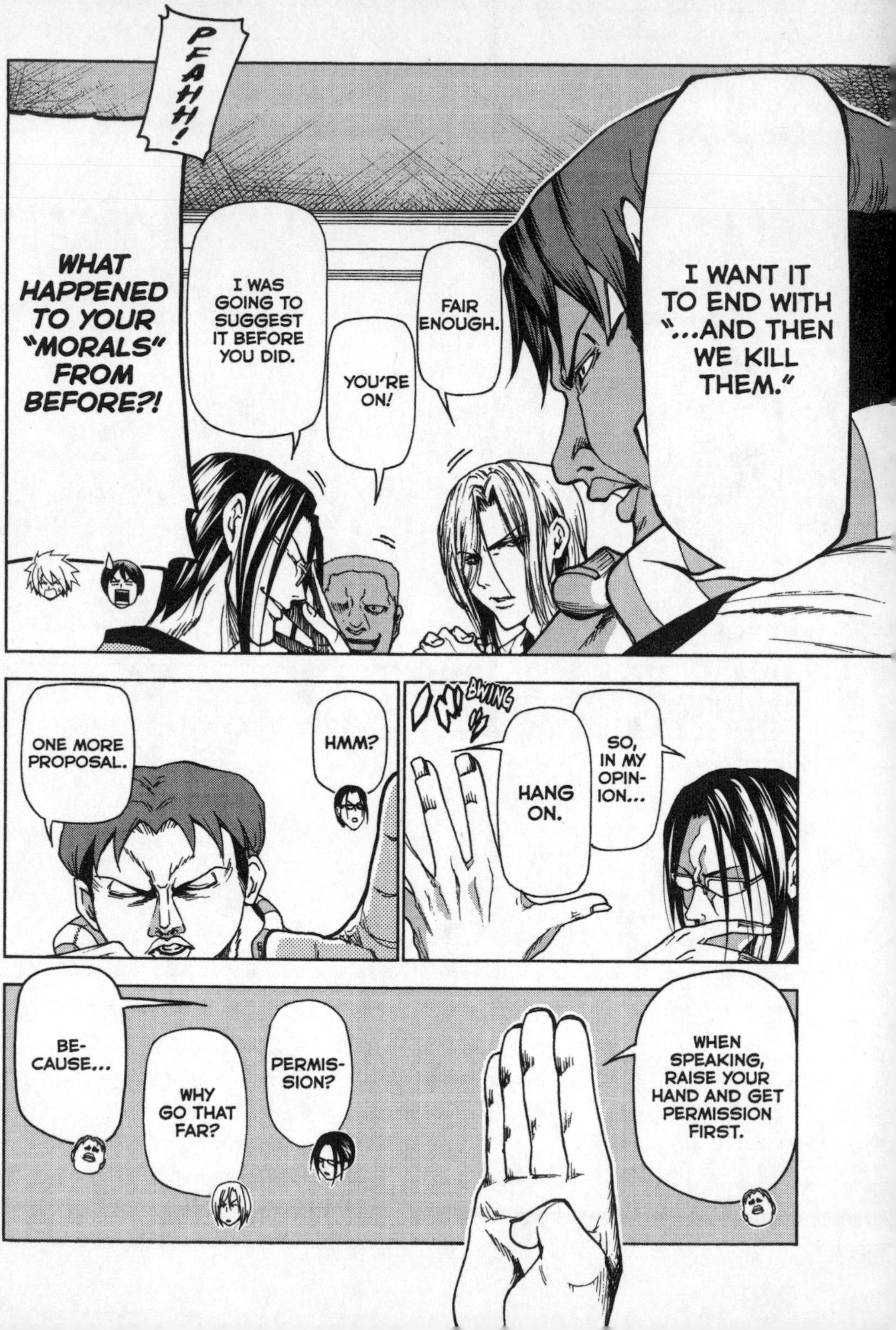
I WANT IT TO END WITH "...AND THEN WE KILL THEM."
FAIR ENOUGH.
YOU'RE ON!
I WAS GOING TO SUGGEST IT BEFORE YOU DID.
WHAT HAPPENED TO YOUR "MORALS" FROM BEFORE?!
PFAHH!
SO, IN MY OPIN-ION...
HANG ON.
BWING
HMM?
ONE MORE PROPOSAL.
WHEN SPEAKING, RAISE YOUR HAND AND GET PERMISSION FIRST.
PERMIS-SION?
WHY GO THAT FAR?
BE-CAUSE...

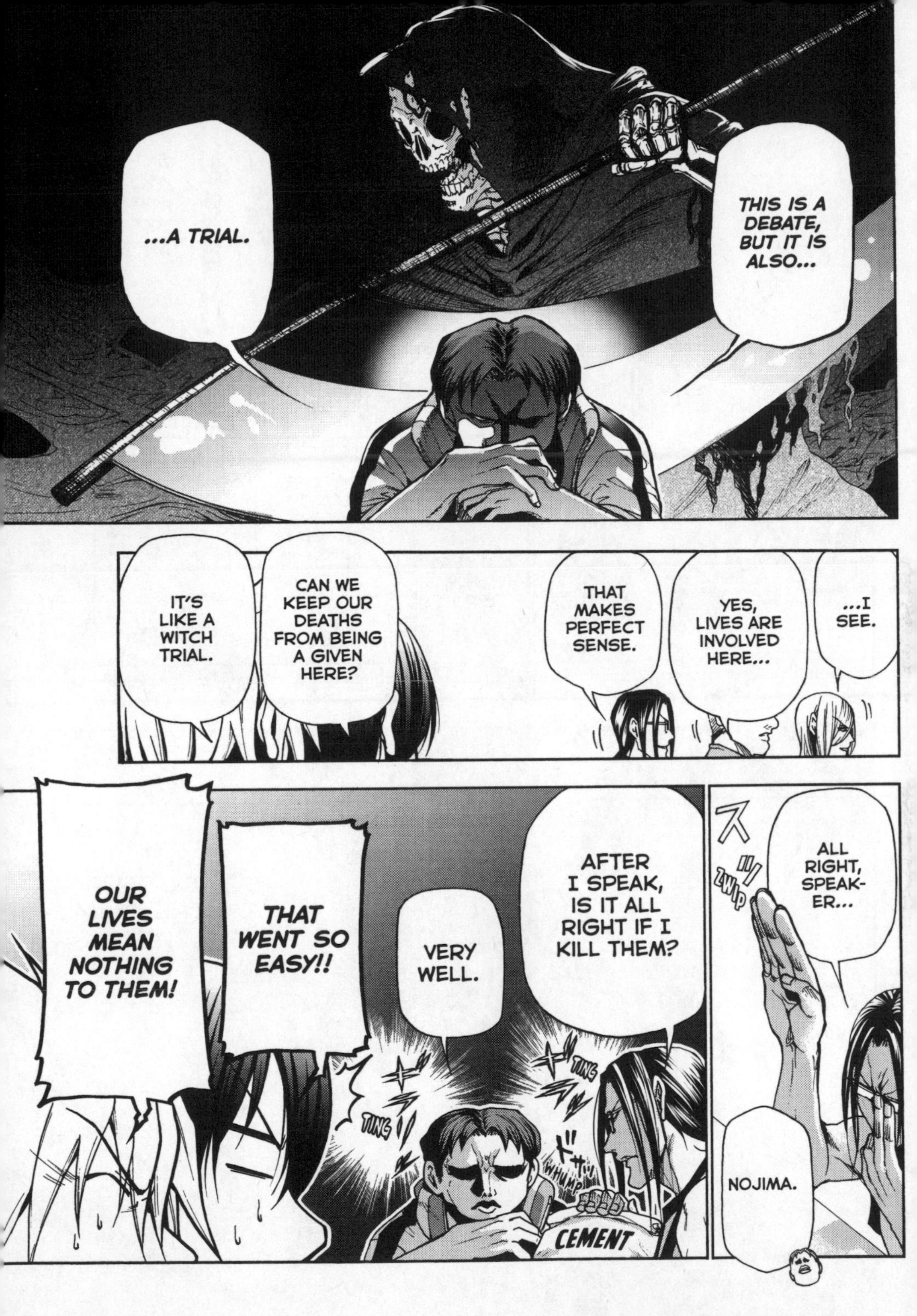
THIS IS A DEBATE, BUT IT IS ALSO...
...A TRIAL.
...I SEE.
YES, LIVES ARE INVOLVED HERE...
THAT MAKES PERFECT SENSE.
CAN WE KEEP OUR DEATHS FROM BEING A GIVEN HERE?
IT'S LIKE A WITCH TRIAL.
ス
ZWIP
ALL RIGHT, SPEAKER...
NOJIMA.
AFTER I SPEAK, IS IT ALL RIGHT IF I KILL THEM?
VERY WELL.
TING
TING
WHUMP
CEMENT
THAT WENT SO EASY!!
OUR LIVES MEAN NOTHING TO THEM!

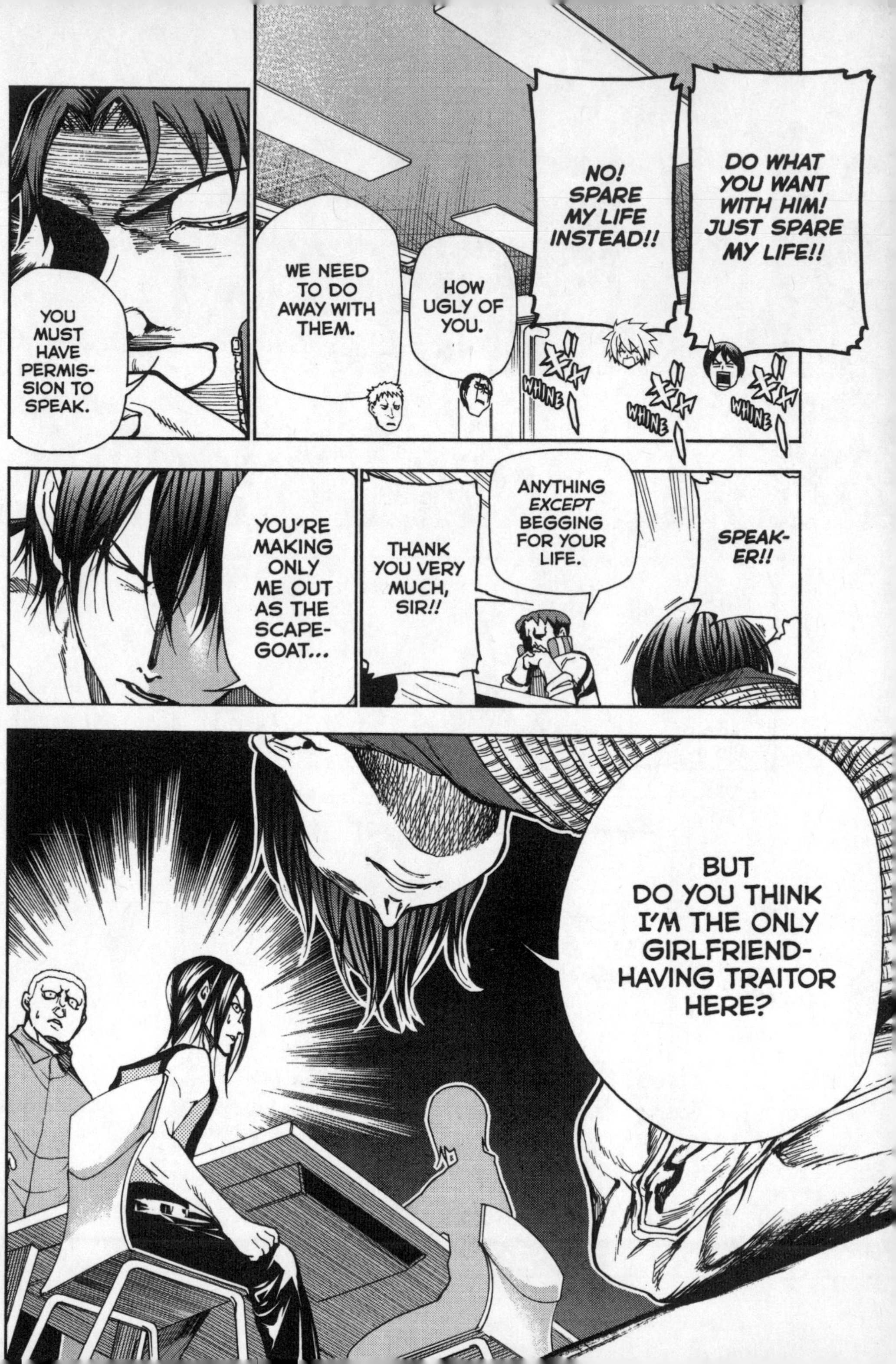
DO WHAT YOU WANT WITH HIM! JUST SPARE MY LIFE!!
NO! SPARE MY LIFE INSTEAD!!
WHINE
WHINE
WHINE
HOW UGLY OF YOU.
WE NEED TO DO AWAY WITH THEM.
YOU MUST HAVE PERMISSION TO SPEAK.
SPEAKER!!
ANYTHING *EXCEPT* BEGGING FOR YOUR LIFE.
THANK YOU VERY MUCH, SIR!!
YOU'RE MAKING ONLY ME OUT AS THE SCAPEGOAT...
BUT DO YOU THINK I'M THE ONLY GIRLFRIEND-HAVING TRAITOR HERE?

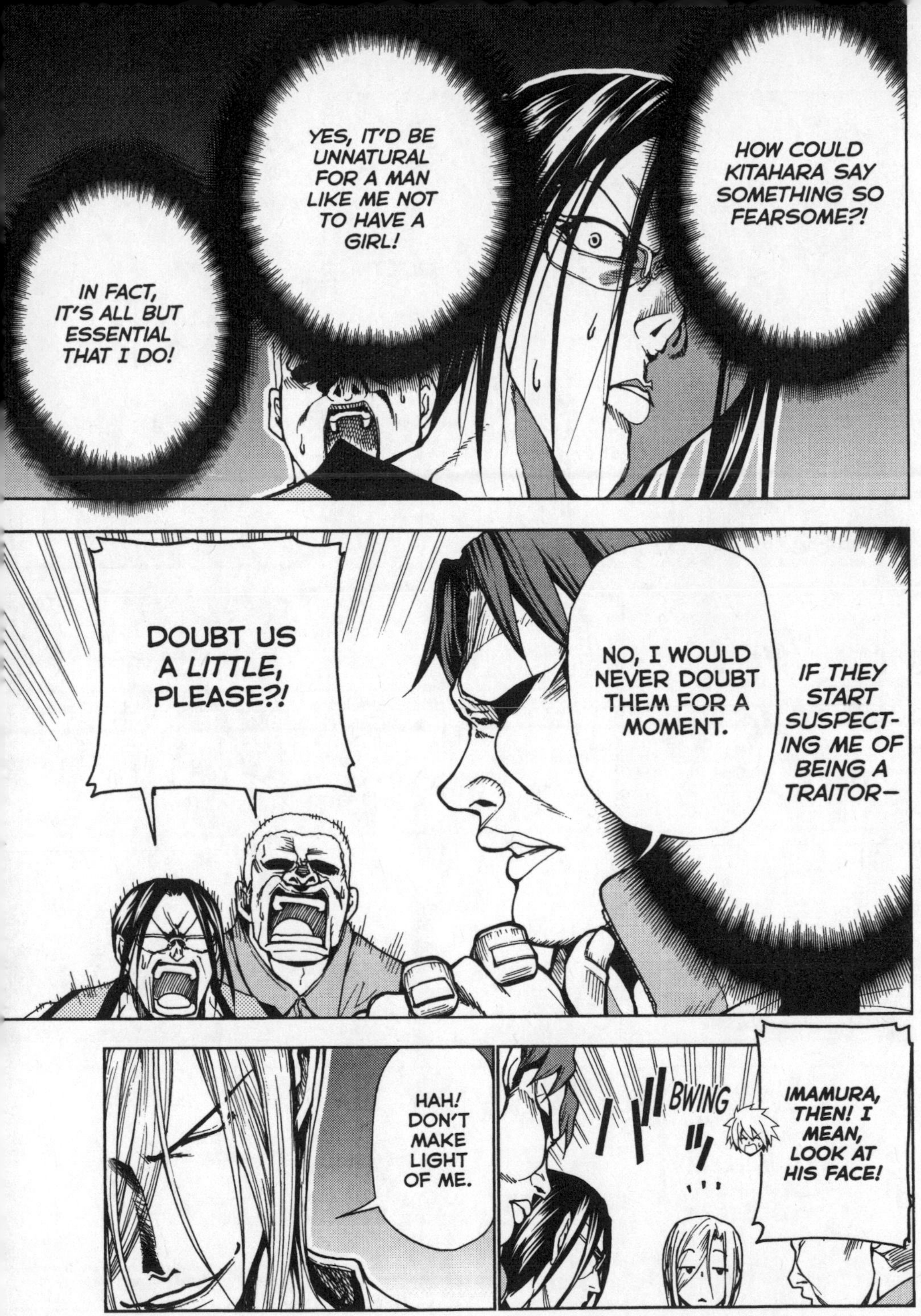
HOW COULD KITAHARA SAY SOMETHING SO FEARSOME?!
YES, IT'D BE UNNATURAL FOR A MAN LIKE ME NOT TO HAVE A GIRL!
IN FACT, IT'S ALL BUT ESSENTIAL THAT I DO!
IF THEY START SUSPECT-ING ME OF BEING A TRAITOR—
NO, I WOULD NEVER DOUBT THEM FOR A MOMENT.
DOUBT US A *LITTLE*, PLEASE?!
IMAMURA, THEN! I MEAN, LOOK AT HIS FACE!
BWING
HAH! DON'T MAKE LIGHT OF ME.

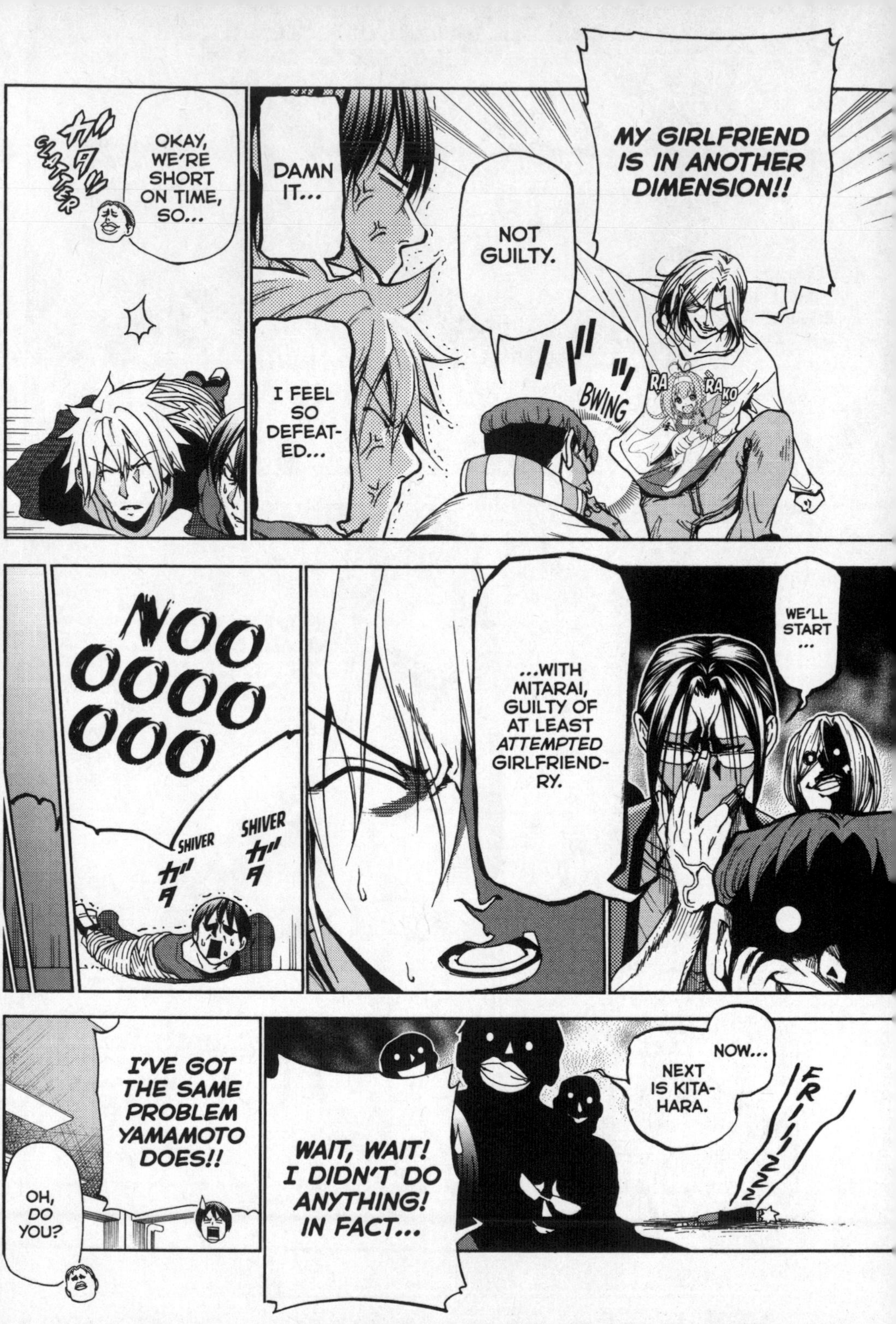
MY GIRLFRIEND IS IN ANOTHER DIMENSION!!
NOT GUILTY.
BWING
DAMN IT...
I FEEL SO DEFEATED...
OKAY, WE'RE SHORT ON TIME, SO...
CLATTER
WE'LL START...
...WITH MITARAI, GUILTY OF AT LEAST ATTEMPTED GIRLFRIENDRY.
NOOOOOOOOOOOO
SHIVER
SHIVER
NOW...
NEXT IS KITAHARA.
FRIIIZZZ
WAIT, WAIT! I DIDN'T DO ANYTHING! IN FACT...
I'VE GOT THE SAME PROBLEM YAMAMOTO DOES!!
OH, DO YOU?

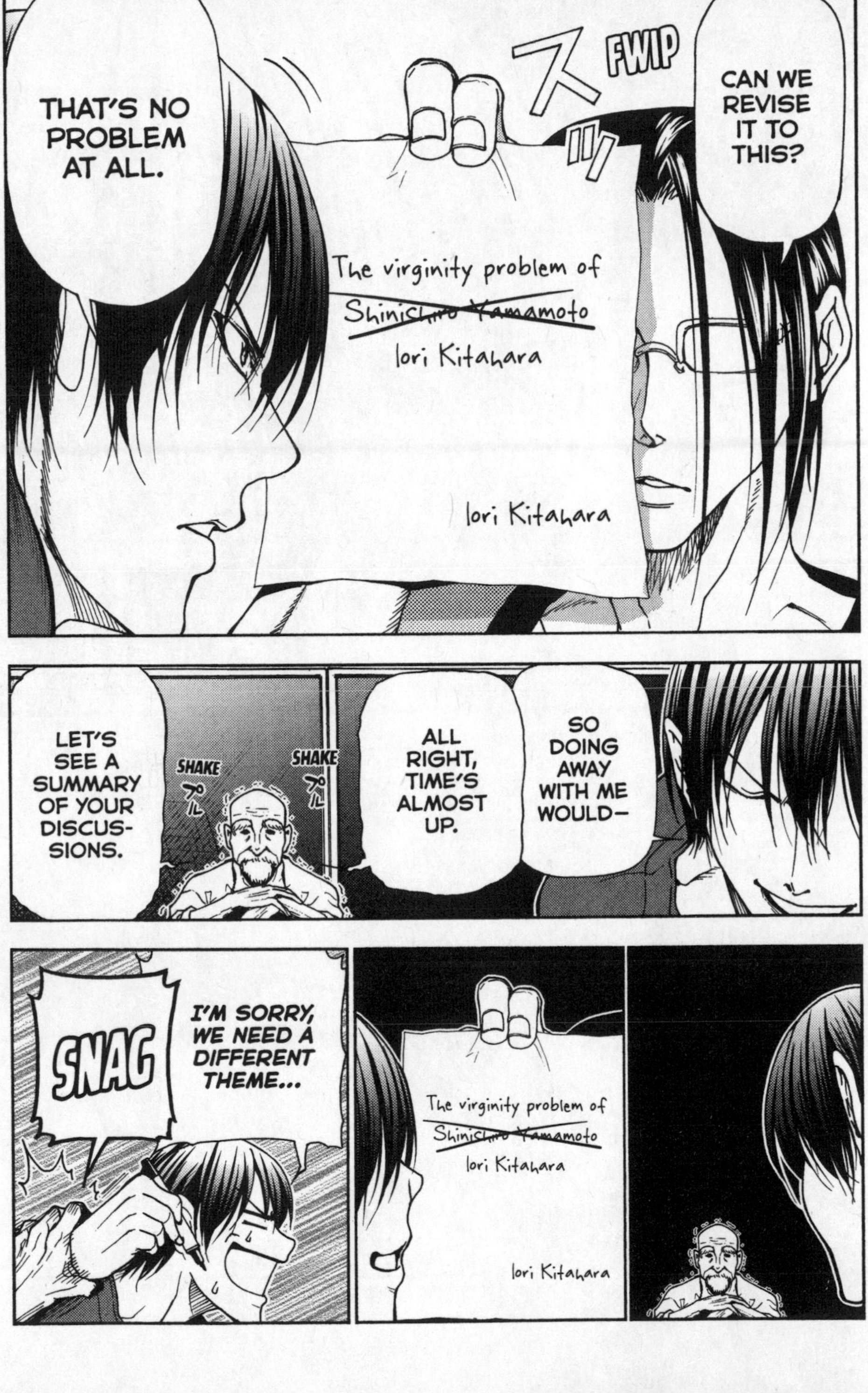
CAN WE REVISE IT TO THIS?
FWIP
THAT'S NO PROBLEM AT ALL.
The virginity problem of
~~Shinichiro Yamamoto~~
Iori Kitahara
Iori Kitahara
SO DOING AWAY WITH ME WOULD—
ALL RIGHT, TIME'S ALMOST UP.
SHAKE
SHAKE
LET'S SEE A SUMMARY OF YOUR DISCUSSIONS.
The virginity problem of
~~Shinichiro Yamamoto~~
Iori Kitahara
Iori Kitahara
SNAG
I'M SORRY, WE NEED A DIFFERENT THEME...

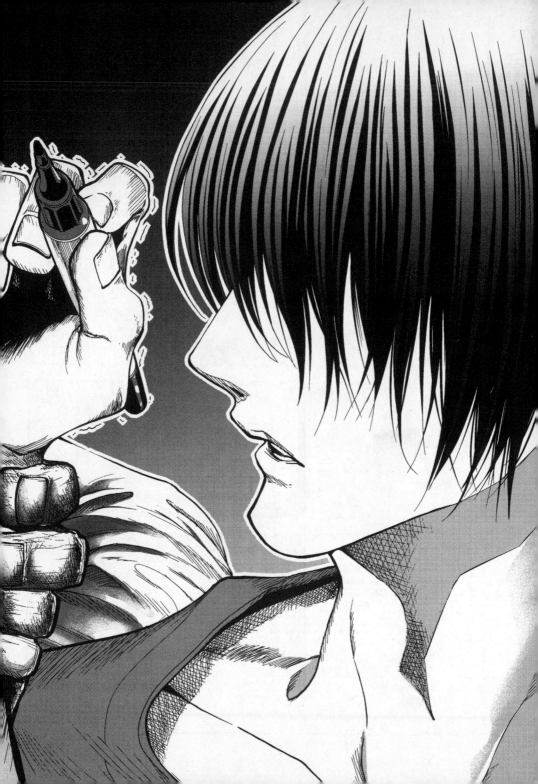

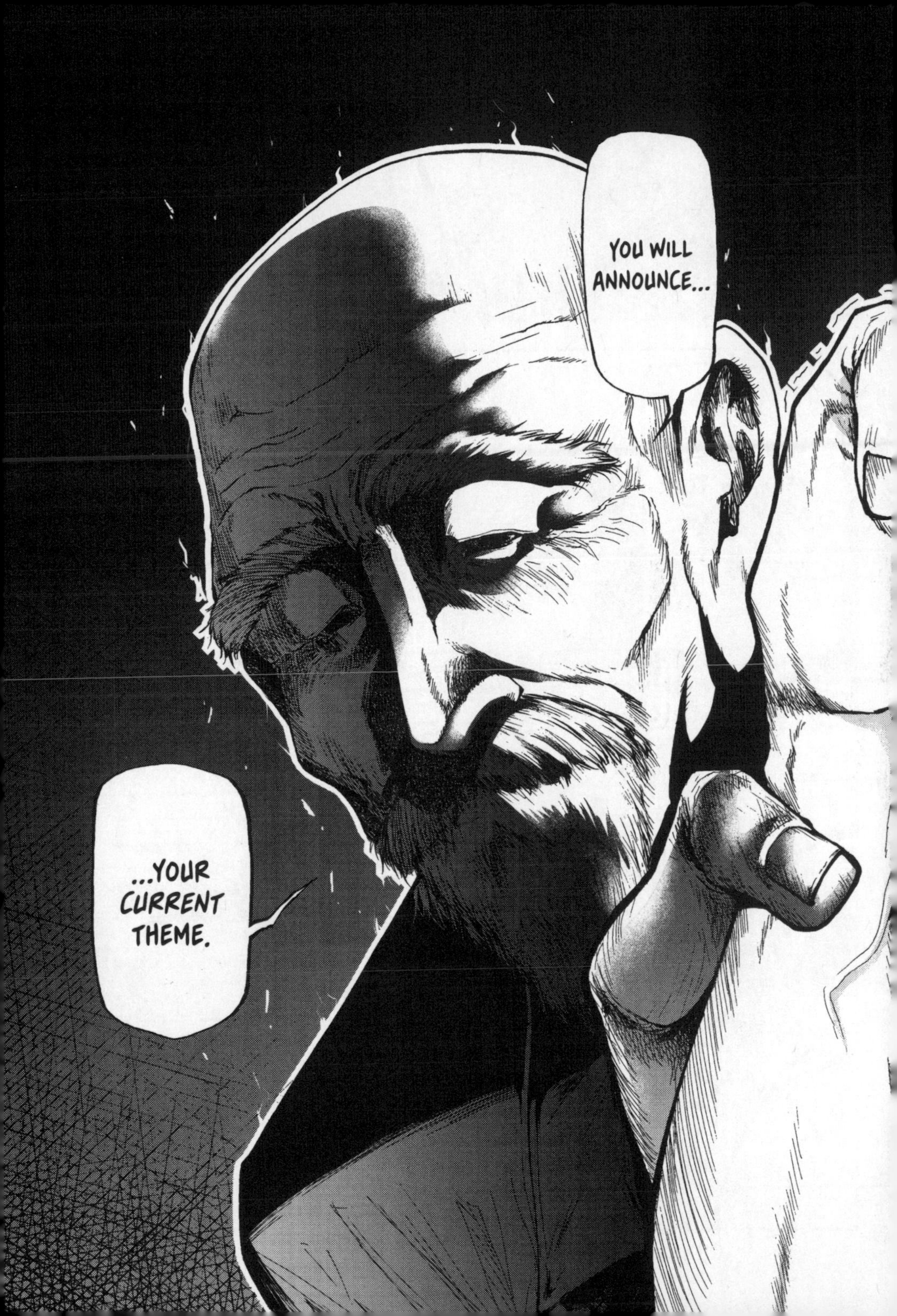
YOU WILL ANNOUNCE...
...YOUR CURRENT THEME.

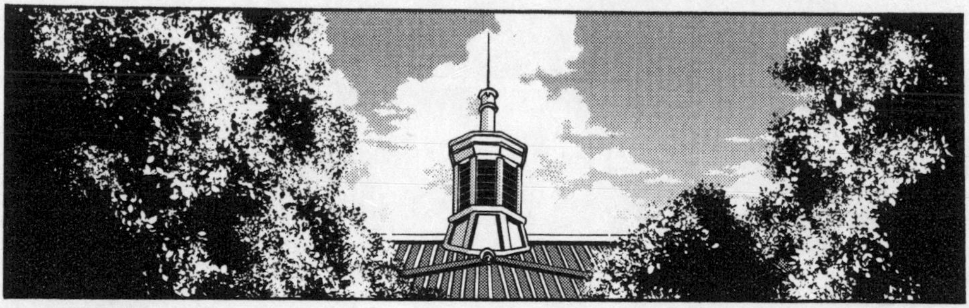

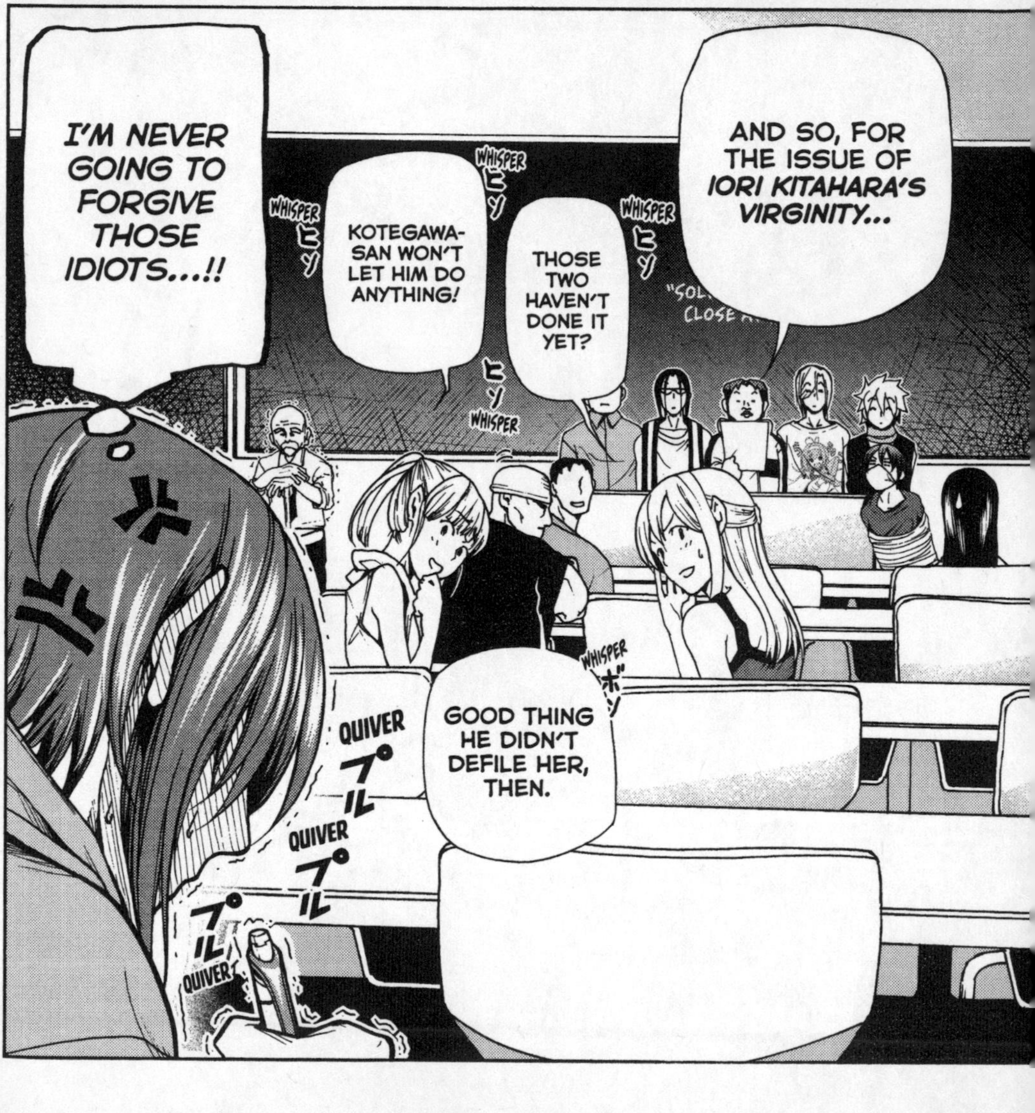
AND SO, FOR THE ISSUE OF IORI KITAHARA'S VIRGINITY...
WHISPER ヒソ
THOSE TWO HAVEN'T DONE IT YET?
WHISPER ヒソ
WHISPER ヒソ
KOTEGAWA-SAN WON'T LET HIM DO ANYTHING!
WHISPER ヒソ
I'M NEVER GOING TO FORGIVE THOSE IDIOTS...!!
WHISPER ボソ
GOOD THING HE DIDN'T DEFILE HER, THEN.
QUIVER プル
QUIVER プル
QUIVER プル

HOW'D HE GET
SUCH A GOOD GRADE?

Iori Kitahara's Virginity

A+

A Kodansha Comics Trade Paperback Original
Grand Blue Dreaming 10 copyright © 2018 Kenji Inoue/Kimitake Yoshioka
English translation copyright © 2020 Kenji Inoue/Kimitake Yoshioka

All rights reserved.

Published in the United States by Kodansha Comics, an imprint of Kodansha USA Publishing, LLC, New York.

Publication rights for this English edition arranged through Kodansha Ltd., Tokyo.

First published in Japan in 2018 by Kodansha Ltd., Tokyo.

ISBN 978-1-63236-910-9

Original cover design by YUKI YOSHIDA (futaba)

Printed in the United States of America.

www.kodanshacomics.com

9 8 7 6 5 4 3 2
Translation: Adam Hirsch
Lettering: Jan Lan Ivan Concepcion
Editing: Sarah Tilson
Additional Layout: Sara Linsley
Editorial Assistance: YKS Services LLC/SKY Japan, INC.
Kodansha Comics edition cover design by Phil Balsman

Publisher: Kiichiro Sugawara
Managing editor: Maya Rosewood
Vice president of marketing & publicity: Naho Yamada

Director of publishing services: Ben Applegate
Associate director of operations: Stephen Pakula
Publishing services managing editor: Noelle Webster
Assistant production manager: Emi Lotto, Angela Zurlo